The School Counselor's Study Guide for Credentialing Exams

The School Counselor's Study Guide for Credentialing Exams

Rita Schellenberg

Routledge
Taylor & Francis Group
New York   London

Routledge
Taylor & Francis Group
711 Third Avenue
New York, NY 10017

Routledge
Taylor & Francis Group
27 Church Road
Hove, East Sussex BN3 2FA

© 2012 by Taylor & Francis Group, LLC
Routledge is an imprint of Taylor & Francis Group, an Informa business

Printed in the United States of America on acid-free paper
Version Date: 20120126

International Standard Book Number: 978-0-415-88875-2 (Paperback)

Visit the Taylor & Francis Web site at
http://www.taylorandfrancis.com

and the Routledge Web site at
http://www.routledgementalhealth.com

This book is dedicated to all professional school counselors, school counselor educators and supervisors, and school-counselors-in-training. May I express my gratitude and applaud your tireless efforts toward positively impacting the lives of millions of children, adolescents, and parents. You have quieted restless minds, calmed distressed souls, and taught forgiveness, acceptance, and an appreciation for all people. Your drive for excellence is shaping our practices and securing a rock-solid future for our profession. You are at the helm of one of the greatest professions in the fleet. Together as shipmates, we are cutting through the sometimes rough seas on what is the voyage of our life—what a great time to be a professional school counselor!

John, I find myself at a loss for words to express my gratitude for the years of dedication, rations of solitude, and emotional support that you have shown me just as naturally as breathing. Your love transcends the vows of marriage.

Mom and Dad, thank you for the abundance of unconditional love. Rogerians rejoice in the knowledge of the power of nurturing and encouragement—'cause we sure didn't have money! More precious than doe—Mom, you gave me your strength and compassionate nature, and Dad, you gave me your sense of humor and determination—I love you.

Kenny, Teresa, Ronnie, Donna, and Kelly, oh, the journey we've had—the joyous laughter and the heartrending tears (mostly mine because of your relentless teasing—not you Kelly!). I wouldn't trade those years for a lifetime supply of Razzles and Mountain Dew.

Above all else, I thank my Lord, God, and Heavenly Father for all and everything.

Stopped @ p 22

Contents

Section E: Early Intervention 73
Section F: Early Intervention 74
Chapter 1: Guided Reflection 76

upto

2 Counseling, Prevention, and Intervention 81
Comprehensive School Counseling Programs 82
Personal–Social Development 86
Transitioning 89
Crisis Management 90
Dropout 93
School Violence and Bullying 94
Internet Safety and Cyberbullying 96
Substance Use, Abuse, Addiction 98
Divorce 100
Parenting Style 101
Career Development .... 102 *
Influences on Career Decision Making 103
Career Development Theory and Career Counseling 104
Career and College Transitions 109
Assessment Instruments and Career Information Delivery Systems 112
Academic Development 114
Delivery 115
Classroom Guidance and Group Work 115
Individual Student Planning 119
Individual Student Counseling 119
Responsive Services 120
Systems Support 122
Theories and Techniques for the School Setting .... 122 *
Adlerian 126
Behavioral 127
Cognitive Behavioral 128
Gestalt 130
Person-Centered 131
Rational Emotive Behavior Therapy 131
Reality Counseling 133
Solution-Focused Brief Counseling 134
Strengths-Based Counseling 135

Foreword

Rita Schellenberg has successfully created a book that serves as a resource and guide for members of the counseling community. In this era of educational reform and accountability, educators are required to be highly skilled and trained. Professional school counselors currently practicing in the field and counselors-in-training recognize the need to demonstrate that they are highly qualified, well-trained professionals in the field of education and counseling. Obtaining national certification is an excellent way to enhance a professional school counselor's career and provide documentation of highly qualified status.

As with many aspects of her professional life, Dr. Schellenberg recognized a critical need and proceeded forward with a plan to effectively address the need. The creation of this valuable resource was truly a labor of love for Dr. Schellenberg. Her professional goals led her to seek national certification as a counselor. Dr. Schellenberg's enthusiasm for pursuing such a goal was met with the frustration of being unable to find the resources needed to assist her in preparing for the certification process. Before this study guide, a school counselor would have to perform the daunting task of compiling information from several different resources, which requires exhausting hours of research. With the numerous responsibilities and workloads of most practicing school counselors, this search for adequate resources becomes an extraordinary source of frustration and a major hindrance in the pursuit of certification. Dr. Schellenberg has eliminated this barrier, and this book has the potential to encourage more school counselors to pursue national credentials.

As a counselor educator, Dr. Schellenberg also noticed that counselors-in-training lacked a study guide for comprehensive examinations of graduate programs. By writing this book, Dr. Schellenberg provides counselors-in-training with an excellent resource to prepare them for their comprehensive examinations. The unique benefit of this book is that it provides counselors-in-training with a pathway from their comprehensive examination to national certification.

The School Counselor's Study Guide for Credentialing Exams bridges the gap between theoretical knowledge, practice, and certification. This book is a valuable resource to any practicing school counselor or counselor-in-training. Regardless of a school counselor's professional aspirations, this book will enhance the counselor's professional development. This comprehensive resource should be included in every professional library.

Sylinda Gilchrist-Banks, EdD
Norfolk State University
American School Counselor Association, President 2012–2013

Preface

Discovering "It"

The growing demand for accountability and enhanced mental health services for children and adolescents has further heightened the need for credentialing requirements. Engaging in continuous professional development and credentialing beyond minimal requirements is vital to continued competency.

Obtaining advanced voluntary school counselor credentials depicts school counselors' preparation and readiness to provide optimal mental health services in the school. This has become increasingly important when we consider that the school counselor is often the only counselor a troubled child or adolescent may ever see. Also, aligning our credentials with those of other mental health professionals is critical to the continued growth of the school counseling profession.

My own journey to align my credentials, nationally, with those of mental health counselors led me to the National Board for Certified Counselors (NBCC). The NBCC is the professional counseling board that monitors the certification system for general counseling and specialty areas of counseling. The NBCC maintains a national register of certified counselors. In addition to national credentialing, NBCC examinations are used by more than 48 states to credential professional counselors on a state level. NBCC was created by the American Counseling Association (ACA), and both organizations work closely to advance the profession of counseling and maintain high standards of excellence.

While exploring the NBCC website for information pertaining to the National Certified Counselor (NCC) credential, I stumbled upon *it*. I was tired and thought my eyes were playing tricks on me. I wiped my eyes, looked again and, still, there *it* was—the National Certified School Counselor (NCSC) credential. Who knew? My body and spirit were renewed!

Energized with fervor equivalent to that of Rob Pattinson's childhood mission to save the snails (enchants the heart), I read further to discover that I could pass one exam that would result in my earning both the NCC and the NCSC credentials—a twofer! At the height of glory, I began printing the application (while considering that I could use some counseling myself when something as innocuous as a credential could become the pinnacle of my existence at any moment in time) and searching for more information about *it*.

As I explored NCSC, I found that *it* is a specialty counseling credential and the product of a collaborative effort between key professional counseling organizations such as the Association for Counselor Education and Supervision (ACES) and supported by the Council for Accreditation of Counseling and Related Educational Programs (CACREP) and the American School Counselor Association (ASCA). Furthermore, the NCSC is the credential of choice recognized in many states for aligning school counselor with mental health counselor requirements. School counselors who hold the NCSC are recognized as having demonstrated (1) competence in areas specific to contemporary school counseling, (2) the ability to provide high-quality school counseling services, and (3) a professional commitment that goes beyond required state licensing. My decision to obtain this valued credential was further solidified when I discovered that a growing number of states provide supplements for the NCSC credential and allow *it* to be used in lieu of educational requirements, teaching licensure and/or Praxis exams, and to renew state certification/license. And, since the National Certified Counselor (NCC) credential is a prerequisite or corequisite for the NCSC, school counselors who hold the NCSC have established equivalency to graduation from a CACREP-accredited program and mastery of the high standards set by this major accrediting body—JACKPOT!

I was thrilled to find that I already possessed the education, training, and experience requirements for the NCSC. The only thing I needed was to pass the challenging National Certified School Counselor Exam (NCSCE). With the gravest confidence, I thought, no problem, with the right study guide *it* was in the bag.

Imagine my apprehension when I could not find a study guide for the NCSCE. Imagine my astonishment when I learned that NBCC does not offer a study guide for the NCSCE. I searched text after text for content close to that described for the NCSCE. I looked for a study guide for school counselor comprehensive exams—nothing. How was this possible? I could not fathom the nonexistence of a study guide for such an important exam.

As I searched and searched, I became frustrated. Yes, yes I did, I said frustrated—and that is exactly how I felt!

Tarot cards could not have seen this coming, but necessity being the "father of invention" or "mother of invention" (I wouldn't want to provoke any cross-gender discomfort), I created my own study guide for the NCSCE and passed the exam! The exam was updated in 2010 after I took it, allowing me to ethically author this textbook, which does not divulge actual NCSCE exam questions.

As time passed, I thought, why limit the study guide to the NCSCE? Why not create a text that can be used as a study guide for all school counseling exams? And, so, *The School Counselor's Study Guide for Credentialing Exams* was crafted.

Acknowledgments

I owe a debt of gratitude to countless and extraordinary colleagues, who, over the years and as a collective, have informed, encouraged, supported, challenged, and propelled me forward. This study guide is not the work of one, but of the many, as demonstrated by the exhaustive references section.

I am thrilled to acknowledge my students—past, present, and future. Bearing witness to your sincere yearning for knowledge has pushed me to continue learning so that I might continue to have something more to share. It is my hope that I might encourage you to be explorers of your own world while exploring the worlds of others and to live in the world, not just on it.

I would especially like to express my gratitude to Dr. Sylinda Gilchrist-Banks, president of the American School Counselor Association, for writing the Foreword in support of this text and my work related to professional school counseling. Sylinda, your history of laudable altruistic acts has not gone unnoticed. Your expertise has been recognized at the local, state, and national levels resulting in leadership positions such as School Counseling Program Specialist for the Virginia Department of Education, president of the Virginia School Counselor Association, and, now, ASCA's president. Your book, *Choice Theory: Using Choice Theory and Reality Therapy to Enhance Student Achievement and Responsibility* (2009), reminds us of the power and ability that lies within each of us, all of us, to make change and author our own lives. What strikes me most is the humility you carry in the midst of your importance and expertise. When esteemed, you reply that you are just "a country girl." May your professional stewardship and humble, inspirational leadership serve as a beacon to us all.

Special thanks is extended to Dana Bliss, senior editor; Christopher Tominich, senior editorial assistant; Fred Coppersmith, development editor;

Robert Sims, project editor; Megan Guiney, production coordinator; and Eleanor Reading, marketing coordinator at Routledge for their exceptional service during the production of this book. I would also like to thank Howard Rosenthal, EdD, author of the academic bestseller, *Encyclopedia of Counseling* (2007), for his review and helpful comments.

Rita Schellenberg, PhD

About the Author

**Dr. Rita Schellenberg** is professor and director of the school counseling program at Liberty University in Virginia. She also serves as the chair of the research committee on her state's school counseling association board. She received her training in school counseling from the College of William and Mary in Virginia. Dr. Schellenberg holds a PhD in counselor education and supervision and is a licensed professional counselor. She earned the credentials of National Certified Counselor, National Certified School Counselor, Approved Clinical Supervisor, and Distance Credentialed Counselor.

Dr. Schellenberg has authored many successful publications on professional school counseling and has presented at numerous conferences across the country on topics related to the contemporary practice of school counseling. Her recent book, *The New School Counselor: Strategies for Universal Achievement* (2008), includes software for developing interactive action plans and results reports.

Dr. Schellenberg has over a decade of experience as a school counselor at both the elementary and secondary levels. She has been recognized at the local and national levels for her contributions in education and counseling. In 2010, Dr. Schellenberg was named one of the top 15 school counselors in the nation by the American School Counselor Association.

Dr. Schellenberg was one of six children born to loving parents who, without high school educations, labored tirelessly to support the family. Dr. Schellenberg did not give up on the college dream. She worked full time while going to college at night to earn her degrees. Her humble beginnings are an inspiration to her students and to others who are overcoming obstacles to achieving the college dream.

You can learn more about Dr. Schellenberg's new vision for school counseling by visiting her professional website, Cultivating Performance, at www.thenewschoolcounselor.org.

Abbreviations

AACD	American Association for Counseling and Development
AACE	Association for Assessment in Counseling and Education
AASA	American Association of School Administrators
ACA	American Counseling Association
ACES	Association for Counselor Education and Supervision
ACSCI	Association of Computer-Based Systems for Career Information
ACT	American College Testing
ADHD	Attention-deficit/hyperactivity disorder
AMCD	Association for Multicultural Counseling and Development
AOD	Alcohol and other drugs
APGA	American Personnel and Guidance Association
ASCA	American School Counselor Association
ASGW	Association for Specialists in Group Work
ASVAB	Armed Services Vocational Aptitude Battery
AYP	Adequate Yearly Progress
BIP	Behavior intervention plan
CACGS	Computer-assisted career guidance systems
CACREP	Council for Accreditation of Counseling and Related Educational Programs
CAPTA	Child Abuse Prevention and Treatment Act
CBT	Cognitive Behavioral Theory/Therapy
CIDS	Career information delivery systems
CPCE	Counselor Preparation Comprehensive Examination
CPS	Child Protective Services
CSCORE	Center for School Counseling Outcome Research and Evaluation
ELL	English language learners
ESEA	Elementary and Secondary Education Act
ESL	English as a second language
FERPA	Family Educational Rights and Privacy Act

GATB	General Aptitude Test Battery
GED	General equivalency diploma
GPA	Grade Point Average
HIPAA	Health Insurance Portability and Accountability Act
IDEA	Individuals with Disabilities Education Act
IEP	Individualized education program/plan
KOIS	Kuder Occupational Interest Survey
LEP	Limited English proficient
MBTI	Myers-Briggs Type Indicator
MOS	Microsoft Office specialist
NBCC	National Board for Certified Counselors
NBPTS	National Board for Professional Teaching Standards
NCATE	National Council for Accreditation of Teacher Education
NCC	National Certified Counselor
NCDA	National Career Development Association
NCE	National Counselor Examination
NCLB	No Child Left Behind
NCSC	National Certified School Counselor
NCSCE	National Certified School Counselor Examination
NCTSC	National Center for Transforming School Counseling
NOCTI	National Occupational Competency Testing Institute
NRF	National Retail Federation
NSCTI	National School Counselor Training Initiative
NTE	National Teachers Examination
O*Net	Occupational Information Network
PIAT	Peabody Individual Achievement Test
PSAT	Preliminary Scholastic Aptitude Test
PSC	Professional school counselor
PTA	Parent–Teacher Association
PTSA	Parent–Teacher–Student Association
REBT	Rational emotive behavior therapy
SAT	Scholastic Aptitude Test
SCA	Student Council Association
SCALE	School Counseling Analysis, Leadership and Evaluation
SCOPE	School Counseling Operational Plan for Effectiveness
SCORE	School Counseling Operational Report of Effectiveness
SDS	Self-directed search
SES	Socioeconomic status

SII   Strong interest inventory
SOL   Standards of learning
TSCI Transforming School Counseling Initiative
WAIS Wechsler adult intelligence scale
WISC Wechsler intelligence scale for children

Introduction

The School Counselor's Study Guide for Credentialing Exams is the only school-counseling-specific study guide available for the National Certified School Counselor Examination (NCSCE) and all school counseling exams and the only one that covers essential information, concepts, theories, approaches, and techniques for developing professional school counselor competency as defined by

■ The 2009 Council for Accreditation of Counseling and Related Educational Programs (CACREP, 2009) Standards (www.cacrep.org)
■ The American School Counselor Association (ASCA, 2008) School Counselor Competencies (www.schoolcounselor.org)
■ The National Board for Professional Teaching Standards (NBPTS, 2002) for School Counseling (www.nbpts.org)
■ The Council for Accreditation of Teacher Education (NCATE, 2008) Standards (Knowledge, Skills, and Professional Dispositions for Other School Professionals, 1e-g) (www.ncate.org)

This manual is organized into eight chapters. Each chapter aligns with the eight CACREP content areas for the specialty of school counseling:

■ Chapter 1: The Foundations of School Counseling
■ Chapter 2: Counseling, Prevention, and Intervention
■ Chapter 3: Diversity and Advocacy
■ Chapter 4: Assessment
■ Chapter 5: Research and Evaluation
■ Chapter 6: Academic Development
■ Chapter 7: Collaboration and Consultation
■ Chapter 8: Leadership

Chapter 1 focuses on the foundation of school counseling and how we evolved into a specialty of the counseling profession. The chapter includes topics that promote the professional identity of school counselors, including a concise history of the profession, current trends, professional associations, accrediting bodies, voluntary credentials, roles of the school counselor, and the professional, ethical, and legal aspects of counseling in the schools. This chapter also includes the basic principles and theories of human development and learning essential to establishing a solid developmental foundation from which to practice. The following standards and school counselor competencies are addressed in Chapter 1:

- CACREP, School Counseling: A1-7
- NCATE, Other School Professionals: 1e-g
- ASCA, School Counselor Competencies: I-A1-3, A7-8; II-A1-8; III-A1, A6
- NBPTS, School Counseling Standards: III, X, XI

Chapter 2 is dedicated to traditional and emerging counseling perspectives, theories, and techniques most appropriate to pre-K–12 student populations. Working from a systems perspective is discussed, and the three developmental domains of a comprehensive school counseling program are examined. Methods of prevention and intervention service delivery for a variety of school-age problems and situations are described. The following standards and school counselor competencies are addressed in Chapter 2:

- CACREP, School Counseling: C1-6
- NCATE, Other School Professionals: 1e-g
- ASCA, School Counselor Competencies: I-A2-3, A5, A8-9; II-A1, A8; III-A1-5, A7-8
- NBPTS, School Counseling Standards: I, II, IV, VIII, XI

Chapter 3 emphasizes the critical roles of diversity and advocacy in school counseling. The importance of advocacy in relation to ensuring that all students have access to a rigorous academic curriculum and educational opportunities and programs is also discussed. Multicultural competence is defined and applied to the roles of the school counselor, and the role of *data analysis* in identifying access, attainment, and achievement gaps is examined. The following standards and school counselor competencies are addressed in Chapter 3:

- CACREP, School Counseling: E1-4
- NCATE, Other School Professionals: 1e-g
- ASCA, School Counselor Competencies: I-A1, A3, A5-6, A8; III-A6; IV-A2, A5
- NBPTS, School Counseling Standards: I, II, IV, V, VI, VIII, X, XI

Chapter 4 examines formal and informal approaches and instruments most often used in the educational setting for individual student assessment, or appraisal. The chapter also discusses the development and implementation of needs assessments and how information from needs assessments and existing data sources is used to make programming and service delivery decisions. The following standards and school counselor competencies are addressed in Chapter 4:

- CACREP, School Counseling: G1-3
- NCATE, Other School Professionals: 1e-g
- ASCA, School Counselor Competencies: III-A6; IV-A5; V-A3
- NBPTS, School Counseling Standards: VIII, IX, XI

Chapter 5 describes the roles of research, data, and evaluation in creating accountable and outcome-driven school counseling services and programs. Methods of program evaluation most often used in the school setting are described along with results reports for documenting and sharing outcomes with stakeholders. The following standards and school counselor competencies are addressed in Chapter 5:

- CACREP, School Counseling: I1-5
- NCATE, Other School Professionals: 1e-g
- ASCA, School Counselor Competencies: IV-A3-A5; V-A1-2, A4
- NBPTS, School Counseling Standards: VIII, IX, XI

Chapter 6 focuses on academic development—the domain that sets school counseling apart from other counseling specialties. Crosswalking and response-to-intervention approaches used by school counselors to aid in closing achievement gaps are described and illustrated along with instructional strategies, classroom management, curriculum development, and the development of action plans. Alternative education programs to meet the special needs of diverse student populations are introduced. The following standards and school counselor competencies are addressed in Chapter 6:

- CACREP, School Counseling: K1-3
- NCATE, Other School Professionals: 1e-g
- ASCA, School Counselor Competencies: I-A1, A3, A5; II-A1-2; III-A7
- NBPTS, School Counseling Standards: I, II, III, V, VIII, X, XI

Chapter 7 describes approaches used by school counselors to engage in collaboration and consultation with stakeholders in order to provide students with a comprehensive school counseling program. The following standards and school counselor competencies are addressed in Chapter 7:

- CACREP, School Counseling: M1-7
- NCATE, Other School Professionals: 1e-g
- ASCA, School Counselor Competencies: I-A1, A6; IV-A2
- NBPTS, School Counseling Standards: I, V, VI, VII, X

Chapter 8 focuses on the many aspects of effective leadership and its importance in establishing and maintaining a comprehensive school counseling program and fostering school administrator–school counselor alliances critical to the success of the school counseling program. The role of family and community involvement in promoting student learning and systemic change is discussed. The role of technology is also reviewed as it relates to student learning and professional advocacy. The following standards and school counselor competencies are addressed in Chapter 8:

- CACREP, School Counseling: O1-5
- NCATE, Other School Professionals: 1e-g
- ASCA, School Counselor Competencies: I-A1, A4, A6; II-A2; IV-A1-4, A6
- NBPTS, School Counseling Standards: I, V, VI, VII, VIII, X, XI

Conquer All Exams School Counseling

This study guide offers preparation for the NCSCE, the Praxis II School Counseling and Guidance Exam, the NBPTS School Counselor Assessment,

School Counselor Preparation Comprehensive Exams, and individual States' School Counseling Subject Exams—*all exams school counseling.* Recent changes to the CACREP Standards (2009) require counselor educators to systematically engage in the application of both formative and summative measures in order to assess student learning outcomes, making this text a valuable tool for school counselors in training throughout matriculation in the school counseling program.

The School Counselor's Study Guide for Credentialing Exams is designed to build knowledge and skills that are transferrable to any test format (e.g., multiple choice, short answer, essay, case simulation, recorded client–counselor interactions). Below is a brief overview of the major examinations in school counselor preparation and credentialing for which this manual will help to prepare you.

NBCC National Certified School Counselor Exam

The National Board for Certified Counselors (NBCC) designs and administers examinations for the general counseling practitioner credential and specialty counseling credentials governed by counselors and the counseling profession. The National Certified School Counselor (NCSC) is one of NBCC's national specialty credentials designed to promote the school counselor identity of counselor. The NCSC is grounded in the core propositions of what school counselors should know and be able to do as counselors in the school setting.

School counselors who do not currently hold the National Certified Counselor (NCC), a prerequisite or corequisite to the NCSC, are advised to use this study in combination with a study guide for the National Counselor Examination (NCE) because a portion (40 multiple choice questions) of the NCSCE assesses general knowledge, skills, and abilities viewed as essential to counseling. More information about the NCE and available study guides that cover the general counselor knowledge assessed by the NCE are available at www.nbcc.org/study.

A recent study shows that 2277 school counselors pursued the NCSC between 1994 and 2003, but only 1302 received the credential (Milsom & Akos, 2007). Since most who achieved the credential were from CACREP accredited schools and students from CACREP-accredited programs get better scores on the NCE (the exam used for the NCSC during that time period), it is critical that school counselors use a study guide such as this one whereby the content is developed from current CACREP Standards.

The NCSCE is a 4-hour, paper-and-pencil examination that consists of a broad range of competencies designed to assess the school counselor's knowledge, skills, and abilities related to student well-being, namely identifying, analyzing, and addressing student issues. The full-length exam consists of seven case simulations that are divided into five to eight sections and categorized as either information gathering (IG) or decision making (DM). Each simulation, or scenario, provides introductory information pertaining to the setting and case background.

Progression through the simulations is not necessarily sequential (e.g., page by page, alphabetical), but determined by your responses. Examinees use a latent image marker supplied by the testing center to uncover the response section, which provides you with information about your response and consequences of your response or directs you to the next section.

The NSCSE's case simulations, and the practice exams in this study guide, instruct school counselors to provide the *single best option* or *multiple options*. When instructed to provide multiple options, be careful to select ONLY the options appropriate at that given time in the case scenario or your score may be adversely affected. If you select responses that are deemed irrelevant, premature, and a waste of your and the student's time, you will not gain points and may lose points.

While striving for order in our world, we think in terms of alphabetical listings and sequential numbering. DANGER—progression through case simulations is not necessarily alphabetical or sequential! Follow the directions precisely regarding proceeding to the next section. Also, check the simulation name at the top of each page to be sure you are still working in the section indicated as you move through the case.

According to the NBCC, each case simulation item is assigned a weight ranging from +3 to −3, which is based on the level of appropriateness of the response. Weights are not assigned in this study guide. Instead, responses and response explanations are provided, which denote the relevance of your response for the specific scenario section and item.

Each exam item pertains to specific school counselor knowledge, eliciting information related to the following areas covered in the content and/or simulations in this study guide:

■ School counseling program delivery
  – Consult with teachers
  – Develop academic intervention plans

- – Adapt counseling for diverse populations
- – Facilitate conflict resolution among group members
- – Counsel the students(s) concerning divorce
- – Conduct violence prevention activities
- – Engage in ongoing evaluation of the school counseling program
- ■ Assessment and career development
  - – Evaluate students' social functioning
  - – Assess students' strengths and weaknesses
  - – Assist students in understanding test results
  - – Use test results for student decision making
  - – Use interest inventories
  - – Provide career counseling for student(s)
- ■ Program administration and professional development
  - – Obtain students' evaluations of counseling outcome(s)
  - – Manage the school counseling program
  - – Read relevant professional literature
  - – Use resources to apply relevant legal statutes and regulations
  - – Use technology for program data management
- ■ Counseling process, concepts, and applications
  - – Counsel student(s) concerning personal change
  - – Assess potential for students to harm self/others
  - – Evaluate students' progress toward counseling goals
  - – Assess students' psychological functioning
  - – Explain counselor and student roles
  - – Develop behavior management plans
  - – Assess need for student referral
- ■ Family–school involvement
  - – Consult with parents
  - – Counsel student(s) concerning lifestyle change
  - – Counsel student(s) concerning substance abuse
  - – Facilitate family conflict resolution strategies
  - – Educate student(s) regarding human growth and development

NBCC does not offer a study guide for the NCSCE. An information booklet that identifies the exam content areas and describes the exam process, structure, and registration information is made available by NBCC at http://nbcc.org.

School Counseling Certification Exam

The NBPTS school counseling credential is a national, voluntary certification governed by teachers and the teaching profession. The NBPTS school counseling credential promotes the school counselor identity of educator grounded in the core propositions of what school counselors should know and be able to do as educators/teachers.

School counselors are given 30 minutes to respond to each of six "exercises" or scenarios that pertain to specific school counselor knowledge related to the following areas and covered in the content and/or simulations in this study guide:

- Human growth and development
- School counseling programs
- Diverse populations
- Theories
- Data and change
- Collaboration

Responses to the scenarios are given in essay style, answering specific questions or "entries" related to each scenario. Essay responses are scored by teachers practicing in the school counseling specialty area using a four-level rubric to evaluate candidate responses. Levels three and four represent accomplished teaching practice. Levels one and two represent limited, little, or no evidence of accomplished teaching practice. School counselors do not need to score at a level of three or four on every scenario. A high score in one area can compensate for a lower score in another area.

Keep in mind that each entry for a given scenario is scored independently of one another, meaning that an assessor for one entry may not see other entries. For this reason, it is important that school counselors provide complete responses to each entry. Do not anticipate that the assessor will consider information presented on an earlier or subsequent entry. More information about the NBPTS school counseling certification exam can be found at www.pearsonvue.com/nbpts.

NTE/Praxis II School Counseling and Guidance Exam

The National Teachers Examination (NTE), also known as the Praxis, offers the Praxis II School Counseling and Guidance Exam. This exam is sometimes used by school counselor preparation programs to measure student learning outcomes and/or to satisfy licensure requirements as required by state policy. It may also be administered to school counselors by individual states and/or school divisions to make hiring and retention decisions.

The Praxis II school counseling specialty exam is comprised of 120 multiple choice questions, 40 of which include listening to and conceptualizing recorded client–counselor interactions. Test takers are allowed 2 hours to complete the exam.

The exam covers the following four content areas:

■ Professional issues (18 items)
■ Coordinating services (18 items)
■ Issues in consulting (18 items)
■ Guidance and counseling (66 items)

The professional issues portion of the exam covers legal and ethical concerns and professional development. The coordinating services section includes program organization, management, and assessment, as well as data collection and data dissemination. The consulting section of the exam explores school climate, curriculum, human development, interpersonal relationships, staff, family counseling, and assessing community agencies. The larger portion of the exam, which is guidance and counseling, covers classroom guidance, counseling individuals and groups, dyadic counseling, assessment, human development, multiculturalism, and diversity. For more information about the Praxis II School Counseling and Guidance exam, visit the Educational Testing Service at www.ets.org.

State School Counseling Exams

Some states have developed their own school counseling specialty exam, which is generally used to making hiring and retention decisions and also for licensure determination. While these exams vary in length and structure, the content of state school counseling exams is generally based on the ASCA National Model, ASCA *Ethical Standards for School Counselors*, and ASCA School Counselor Competencies; NCATE Standards and NBPTS Standards for School Counseling; and/or CACREP Standards for School Counseling Programs. To find out more about your state's requirements, visit the ASCA website at www.schoolcounseling.org or visit the state's department of education website.

School Counselor Preparation Comprehensive Exams

Counselor education programs are responsible for supplementing the Counselor Preparation Comprehensive Examination (CPCE) with specialty sections that reflect students' chosen specializations. At the present time, over 220 colleges and universities across the nation use the CPCE for program evaluation and exit examination. Counselor education programs encourage students to engage in ongoing study throughout the program to prepare for the CPCE and its specialty examination sections.

Comprehensive exam specialty sections vary in length and structure. Generally, school counseling specialty sections include case scenarios to assess the preservice school counselor's ability to effectively apply that which they have learned in the classroom to the practice setting. Talk to your program advisor to find out more about the comprehensive exam requirements for your counselor education program.

Student Learning Outcomes Assessments

The 2009 revisions to the CACREP Standards ushered in a significant change in the process of measuring student learning outcomes. CACREP-accredited counselor education programs are now required to systematically and continuously use formative and summative measures to assess learning outcome throughout the program and in each program area. Some of these measures include case conceptualization, roleplays, tapings, papers, and formal exams. These measures are embedded as assignments, sometimes referred to as *signature assignments*, in specific courses requiring that students demonstrate mastery of the course content based on stated outcomes/competencies derived from the CACREP Standards.

Getting the Most Out of This Guide

This study guide covers content areas in relation to the roles and functions of the contemporary professional school counselor. Throughout the chapters of this study guide, you will view select ASCA position statements as they relate to the practice of school counseling and the domains of knowledge as defined by the ASCA National Model and School Counselor Competencies. The ASCA *Ethical Standards for School Counselors* are also weaved throughout this study guide as applicable to the topic of discussion.

The practice exams at the end of each chapter and at the end of the study guide mirror the format of the well-established NCSCE. Each simulation consists of three components: scenario, IG, and DM. There are five to eight sections following the scenario requiring a combination of IG and DM responses. A full-length (seven simulated school counseling cases) practice examination will be provided at the end of the text.

Learning is improved when you understand where your thinking may have gone astray. For this reason, responses are provided for chapter practice exams and the end of the text full-length exam. To optimize learning, explanations are provided to support correct responses, and explanations are provided to indicate why incorrect responses are incorrect for both the chapter practice exams and the full-length practice exam.

You will also be presented with case illustrations throughout the study guide that require conceptualization, effective client–counselor interactions, and content knowledge application, which are critical to obtaining a passing score on school counseling exams. Some will require a response in short answer/essay format, while others are formatted as multiple choice so that you might also be familiar with all school counseling exam formats. Appropriate responses and explanations for cases conceptualizations are provided at the end of each chapter in which the case was presented.

The guided reflection sections at the end of each chapter are grounded in Bloom's taxonomy to test you on a variety of levels: knowledge, comprehension, application, analysis, synthesis, and evaluation. You are encouraged to make use of this section to fully reflect on the material presented in each chapter. All the information you need to answer each item in the guided reflection sections is presented in this study guide.

Italicized words in this text represent key concepts related to the constructs presented. Those that are not already defined in sufficient detail in the body of the chapter are included in the glossary. The glossary of critical terms is provided to assist you in managing the material presented and to provide you with another learning tool.

This study guide presents the information using empirically supported strategies for enhancing learning and recall. The chapter practice tests, case illustrations, and guided reflection sections reinforce chapter content in a repetitive manner to aid in memorization. This study guide presents theories and other information in lists, clusters, or manageable pieces of information and charts for mapping main ideas, which isolates key points, thereby promoting movement from short-term memory to long-term memory and aiding in the recall of information.

I would encourage the use of a pencil when completing the practice exams and the guided reflection sections, or I would suggest making copies of those sections of the guide. My best advice is to take each exam repeatedly until perfect scores are achieved and to complete each item of the guided reflection sections until you have nailed it! Remember, writing and rewriting helps to commit information to memory.

Test-Taking Triumph

Without a doubt, taking and passing school counselor licensure, credentialing, and comprehensive exams are important milestones in your career. Consequently, by virtue of seeking these voluntary credentials, you are demonstrating a leadership quality that has been empirically supported as critical to the success of your school counseling program (leadership is discussed in Chapter 8).

The enormity of the information needed to prepare can be overwhelming. Keep in mind, however, that you have already been exposed to this information and, in many cases, you have already applied it in the school setting and during experiential learning activities in the classroom during your school counselor preparation program.

To help you prepare for all exams school counseling, consider these study basics and test-taking tips. Study skills and test-taking strategies can improve your score.

Time Management: A Waste of Time?

Most counselor education programs encourage students to study for certification, licensure, and comprehensive exams over time. While cramming has its value, it is not as effective and lasting as learning that takes place over time and builds on previous knowledge with thoughtful reflection and application.

For this reason, consider a timeline that allows you to control your study schedule. When it comes to control, I can help. Both a vice and a virtue, I can micromanage a minute, squeezing every ounce of life out of time. Try breaking up the information into manageable segments and pacing study sessions. Consider mastering one segment before moving on to the next segment, which will allow the information to move from short-term memory into long-term memory. This study guide provides you with a practice exams and chapter activities so that you can practice-practice-practice applying the material presented—repetition is key to retention.

Making Connections

Association has been linked to successful testing outcomes. Consider associating new information with familiar or easily remembered information. My favorite is using acronyms to represent the first letter of each piece of information. This is exemplified in Lazarus' assessment strategy known as BASIC ID (*B*ehavior, *A*ffect, *S*ensation, *I*magery, *C*ognition, *I*nterpersonal, *D*rugs/ *B*iological). BASIC ID is discussed in Chapter 4.

Concept mapping and cognitive mapping, or mental visualization, promotes learning and recall by connecting pieces of information and illustrating relationships. Isolating key facts and grouping concepts are additional avenues for enhancing memory and recall. This study guide presents critical information using a variety of empirically validated visualization strategies (e.g., charts, tables, figures, checklists) to enhance understanding and to promote success on school counseling exams.

No Veggie Left Behind

For some, studying is just not a part of their cultural or intellectual DNA. However, since you were unable to major in channel surfing, you have developed strategies to make studying ache less. Pairing study time with more desirable activities and studying in an environment that you find personally motivating and in clothing that is comfortable can make all the difference. For example, you may wish to study in your favorite room in the house with the glow of a scented candle, while wearing your favorite warm slippers and those sweat pants that you have rescued from the trash on multiple occasions. I have found that shamelessly plating up a scrumptious gallery of snacks to nibble on while enduring the permeation of knowledge is quite the reinforcer—behavioral counselors take note!

Oh, and by the way, studies have found that blueberries and caffeine boost memory. Also, cruciferous veggies (e.g., cabbage, carrots, broccoli, brussel sprouts, cauliflower, kale) improve cognitive functioning and memory. So, eat those super-veggies to maximize brain power—*buon appetito*!

Got People?

Sometimes it is helpful to have other people assist you in studying. Having another person quiz you after completion of each chapter can be helpful. You might want to consider having your study buddy turn each chapter's section headings into questions and cover topics that you have selected for focus. Afterward, review the material again, and again.

Flash cards are another great study strategy that you can do with others (or alone). You are encouraged to created flash cards from the glossary of terms provided in this study guide with an emphasis on how you would apply those concepts as a school counselor in a school setting.

The Square Root of Pi

There are some important constants that lend themselves to memorization. The square root of Pi is one of the most familiar and culturally significant of all constants that many have devoted countless hours to memorizing. However, the concepts and information related to school counseling are rarely, if ever, constant. So, keep in mind that while some of the material in this guide lends itself to memorization, much of your exam seeks to apply rather than recite.

With this said, applying knowledge and skills in the practice of school counseling is paramount, but it is also important to be able to identify specific tools, models, theories, and techniques that may be presented as options in a specific case, for example, academic and psychological assessments commonly used in the school setting, and career interest inventories and career information systems that you might wish to administer to a particular student at a particular grade level. Oh, by the way, the square root of Pi (3.14) is roughly 1.7725.

Occam's Razor

One of the biggest challenges for test takers is following directions. I believe Freud would agree that in our unconscious attempt to control the test-taking environment, we tend to distort the truth of the written word. Selecting the "single best response" becomes "what does the author want?" As triumphant test takers, we must take a minute to be sure that we understand exactly what it is that is being asked of us. Then, we must think in terms of what the "best" response is based on school counseling standards, best practices, ethics, law, school counselor roles and functions, and the scope of practice within the school setting. Read and carefully consider every response in these terms before making a selection.

Too often we tend to over-analyze exam questions. For this reason, we then tend to provide a response that is too complex, believing that more information is better. Responses that are unnecessary at a given time in the case simulation and that may cost the student and parent time, money, energy, and/or delay counseling process/outcomes will cost you points. Consider the logic of Occam's razor—do not make more assumptions than the minimum needed. That is, err on the side of less versus more—simplest versus more complex.

Less Is More

Examinees should anticipate appropriate responses before looking at the response choices and before writing essay responses. Consider the scenario from all angles and what you would realistically do as a school counselor in the moment with that student and within the scope of the practice of professional school counseling.

Not unlike other counseling specialties, school counselors act in the best interest of their clients. In doing so, are there other relevant individuals or agencies (e.g., parent, CPS) whose involvement may be needed or beneficial when counseling minors? What ethical and legal issues might need to be considered? Provide responses that are helpful, thorough, and relevant to the specific case presented at that given time in treatment—no more, no less. If you err, err on the side of less is more. No hasty choices.

Time Will Not Tell

Timed tests tend to heighten the anxiety experienced by testers. Do not allow time to tell you when to move to the next item on the exam. There will be some items on the test that you will blink right through, while others will need a bit more consideration. Do not allow yourself to become overly concerned with timing. In my many experiences with counseling and school counseling exams, I have found the time allotted to be ample, and I am a characteristically slow test taker. Stay focused and just recognize when you are spending an inordinate amount of time on one particular item.

When stress creeps up, counselor heal thyself. Use your positive self-talk. I have been known to hold entire conversations with myself—out loud. Yes,

I know, you may want to consider internal dialogue as to avoid a clinical enthusiast pegging you as schizophrenic. Of course in my case, this ship has sailed.

Anyway, self-talk, imagery, deep breathing exercises, and muscle relaxation techniques are quite helpful when you find yourself feeling anxious. Also, keep in mind that you are not expected to make a perfect score. There is room for error, and it is likely that you will not know the answer to every question or that every correct response will jump out at you. Although an appropriate amount of stress has been found to improve performance, research has also found that even short-term stress impedes recall and cognitive functioning, so prepare in advance and then relax on test-taking day.

Oh, the Places You'll Go

Relaxing and remaining positive about your ability to successfully complete the school counseling exam has been empirically validated. Use your cognitive behavioral counseling skills to engage in affirming self-talk and rational emotive behavior therapy (REBT) to debunk irrational thoughts destructive to success on the exam. Positive thinking does more than psych you up for exam success, remaining positive during study time improves memory and recall. During study time, reflect on what you will gain as a result of passing the exam, like earning your degree, adding a certification to your credentials, and/or becoming a practicing professional school counselor! Consider the inspirational words of Dr. Seuss—*oh, the places you'll go! (...and the students you'll help!)*

Delighted Synapses

Music, my personal favorite, has been found to enhance mood and cognitive abilities. So, consider playing music that is personally enjoyable to give study time a twist (and please exercise your freedom to get up and Dougie if you want to!). There is nothing like the smack of a workout to get the ole' cognitive juices flowing. Those delighted synapses will sing harmoniously while those dancing neurons will be firing a rate of a million dancing Umpa-Lumpas!

Carpe Diem!

It is time to prepare—*carpe diem!*

Chapter 1

The Foundations of School Counseling

School counseling exams weave in items that will test your knowledge of the foundations of school counseling. For this reason, it is important to know some basics with regard to the professions' roots, milestones, trends, and current direction.

The profession of school counseling has been largely shaped by its multidisciplinary heritage that encompasses both education and counseling. With one foot planted in each applied field, school counseling has slowly, but steadily, morphed into a profession unique it its own right.

The First Hundred Years

School counseling began as a vocational and moral curriculum developed by Jesse Davis, a high-school principal, in 1907. A year later, Frank Parsons, a man that one might consider a jack-of-all-trades—engineer, university professor, public school teacher, lawyer, author, and social activist—became interested in helping students transition from school to work and established the Vocation Bureau. Parsons' work paved the way for the trait and factor theory of career development and earned him the title of "father of vocational guidance."

In the 1920s and 1930s, guidance in the schools grew and became recognized as an area of specialty using a trait and factor model for identifying vocational direction. Together, the progressive education and mental health movements gave rise to vocational guidance and counseling. In the 1940s, Carl Rogers' focus on a nonmedical model for individual counseling resulted in individual counseling in high schools as a primary function of guidance.

In 1952, the American Personnel and Guidance Association (APGA) was established. The work of APGA was grounded in the philosophies of Carl Rogers (1961, 1969) well into the 1960s. The APGA created two divisions: the American School Counselor Association (ASCA) and the Association for Counselor Education and Supervision (ACES). These divisions provide leadership and promote *standards* for training programs and school counseling practices.

In 1957, Sputnik, a Soviet satellite, took a 98-minute celestial stroll around the earth that changed the world forever, catapulting our nation into the space age. The United States, perceiving the launch of Sputnik as a display of educational, technical, and political superiority, passed the National Defense Education Act. This legislation was the steroid that built the muscles of the school counseling profession, providing funds to enhance guidance counseling training programs and to hire more school counselors to provide career guidance and to identify students with a propensity toward science and math professions. To meet the volumes of post–World War II baby boomers, hiring more guidance counselors (as we were called) turned into the extreme sports version of recruitment and training. We were on our way, and like Sputnik, our elliptical path was uncertain as we explored the new universe.

Comprehensive developmental school guidance programs began to emerge to meet the needs of all K–12 students in the 1960s and 1970s. Developmental guidance became a global phenomenon, and in 1985, the APGA changed its name to the American Association for Counseling and Development (AACD).

The impetus behind the shift in paradigm currently underway in school counselor education and the practice of school counseling was prompted by an alarming treatise published in 1987 by the AACD, called *School Counseling: A Profession at Risk*. The undeniable realities regarding a profession that was being viewed as nice, but not necessary, by important stakeholders, incited immediate and unremitting action on the part of concerned school counselor educators and practitioners.

A few years later, with refocused fortitude, the AACD changed its name to the American Counseling Association (ACA). ASCA, taking paramedic responsibility for the resuscitation of a dying profession, created monographs, position statements, revised program philosophies, more clearly defined roles, and a series of recommendations to include school counselors as key players in educational reform. ASCA adopted National Standards (Campbell & Dahir, 1997) and a National Model (ASCA, 2005) and changed the title of *guidance counselor* to *professional school counselor* to more appropriately define renewed roles and practices that extend beyond the limited functions rooted in vocational guidance and *individual-focused* models. In 1997, the Education Trust with the support of ASCA, ACES, and the ACA introduced the *Transforming School Counseling Initiative* (TSCI).

The Transforming School Counseling Initiative

TSCI (Education Trust, 1997) was based on the belief that the prevailing and historically predominate individual- and mental health–focused model failed to align school counseling with the mission of schools and demonstrate an impact on academic achievement. TSCI balked at what they believed to be an outdated model responsible for the exclusion of school counselors from educational reform agendas. TSCI further contended that the model's ambiguous focus on academic achievement gave rise to the misconception that school counseling is an ancillary service in the schools.

TSCI, seeking to replace the traditional individual- and mental health–focused paradigm, introduced a new vision for school counseling that emphasizes the importance of school counseling *leadership* and support for a *systems-focused* and *academic-focused* paradigm. TSCI's *new vision school counseling* reflects the school counselor's dual roles of educator and counselor and aligns school counseling more closely with the academic mission of schools.

Changing the paradigm from mental health–focused to academic-focused and individual-focused to systems-focused was a bold move that positioned many within the profession nose-to-nose in opposition. For devout traditionalists and others who are just not hardwired to change, skepticism hit like a ballistic missile, creating an explosive divide. Nonetheless, as Julius Caesar declared to his army, *alea iacta est: the die is cast.*

TSCI, the brave scout, trudged forward, blazing a trail so that new vision school counselors could find their way in the uninhabited new frontier. Partnering with Metropolitan Life Insurance Company (MetLife) to fund the development of the NSCTI and the NCTSC, TSCI developed and distributed four modules to bridge previous thinking with new ways of conceptualizing the profession.

The modules describe how school counselors can contribute to high academic achievement and obtain educational equity for all students through both systemic and individual leadership, advocacy, and collaboration. Toward this end, ASCA, the Council for Accreditation of Counseling and Related Educational Programs (CACREP), and the new vision for school counseling emphasize the importance of addressing systemic inequities through accountable practices, technological competence, and cultural sensitivity and by promoting the tenants of *social justice*, to be discussed in Chapter 3 (Education Trust, 1997). Some are still chafing against the new vision and, therefore continue to practice from what is quickly becoming a Jurassic model that will only reemerge in an archeological dig into the proud beginnings of our profession.

We have traveled a great distance and gained much ground in the past hundred years, overcoming challenges and enduring periods of uncertainty and professional identity crisis. It says much about our profession that we did more than merely survive, but emerged stronger and with the vigor of ten Grinches, plus two, and a renewed vision for every Who in Whoville—the tall and the small.

School Counselor Preparation Programs

School counselor preparation programs are generally part of a university's school of education or school of counseling and human services. As a spice-of-life consequence to our multidisciplinary profession, school counselors take a variety of counseling, school counseling, and education courses.

ASCA's Position on School Counselor Preparation Programs

Professional school counselors are best prepared through master's- and doctoral-level programs … these programs emphasize training in the implementation of a comprehensive school counseling program promoting leadership, advocacy, collaboration, and systemic change to enhance student achievement and success.

Position statement adopted 2008

Counselor Education: CACREP

Committed to the advancement of counselor education and supervision, ACES began establishing accreditation standards for counseling programs to ensure the optimal preparation of counselors. ACES indissoluble efforts to standardize counselor education and training programs laid the foundation for its successor, CACREP.

In 1978, CACREP was formed to standardize training and function as the primary accrediting body for counselor education programs, under the prevailing school counseling pedagogy of the time, which was the mental health–focused model. In 2001, CACREP published standards that reflected the new vision's academic- and systems-focused paradigm.

In 2009, CACREP revised those standards (see Appendix IV) to continue reflecting the prevailing academic- and systems-focused school-counseling paradigm. These new standards place a stronger emphasis on professional identity and student learning outcome measures, particularly in specialty program areas (e.g., school counseling) with assessments tied to specific individual standards.

CACREP provides counselor education programs with unified, minimal competencies for the optimal preparation of school counselors. In addition to requirements specific to counseling in the schools, CACREP requires demonstrated knowledge in eight core areas of counselor education (i.e., professional orientation and ethical practice, social and cultural diversity, human growth and development, career development, helping relationships, group work, assessment, and research and program evaluation).

The CACREP standards specific to school counseling are covered in this study guide. Each chapter of the study guide reflects each of the eight school counseling specialty standards: the foundations of school counseling; counseling *prevention* and *intervention*; diversity and *advocacy*; assessment; research and evaluation; academic development; *collaboration* and *consultation*; and *leadership*.

These school counseling specialty standards emphasize education and training in developing a comprehensive, developmentally appropriate school counseling program using evidence-based prevention and intervention practices that meet the needs of diverse and *special needs students*. The standards further underscore the importance of using a program model (e.g., the ASCA National Model) in both school counselor education and school counseling practices. CACREP spotlights the importance of academic outcomes and demonstrates the use of *data-driven* and data-producing programs and *program evaluation* in school counseling practices. Additionally, the standards stress collaboration, consultation, leadership, and advocacy, and the identification and removal of personal and systemic barriers to academic achievement.

CACREP has become a university magnet with schools across the country seeking its stamp of approval. Indeed, if school counselor education was a religion, CACREP would be their Bible, with counselor educators striving to live by the word.

Teacher Education: NCATE

While CACREP is considered to be the primary accrediting body for counselor education programs, the NCATE is considered to be the primary accrediting body for teacher education programs. Because school counselors share the dual roles of educator and counselor, some school counseling programs are accredited by NCATE and/or CACREP. For this reason, this study guide addresses both CACREP School Counseling Specialty Standards and NCATE Standards 1e, 1f, and 1g (see www.ncate.org), which address the knowledge, skills, and professional dispositions of other school professionals (e.g., school counselors).

ASCA: Standards, Competencies, and the National Model

The ASCA is a division of the ACA, which is the largest professional counseling association in existence. ASCA is the national *professional association* for school counselors, with a membership of over 28,000 school counseling professionals. ASCA provides professional development, leadership, advocacy, research, publications, and resources to school counselor educators, preservice school counselors, and school counseling practitioners. In case you have not figured it out yet—when ASCA speaks, we listen!

The ASCA National Standards (see Appendix III) and the ASCA National Model (ASCA, 2005) define and unify the professional identity of school counselors and the practices of school counseling. The ASCA National Model is recognized by CACREP, NCATE, and the Department of Education as a framework from which to establish accountable, comprehensive, standards-based, developmental school counseling programs that align with academic achievement missions and emphasize systems-focused service delivery as an integral part of the total education program.

ASCA advocates for a balanced approach to school counseling. The balanced approach meets the developmental needs of students while also providing prevention and intervention services, which is reflected in the ASCA National Model. To fully implement the ASCA Model, ASCA recommends a counselor to student ratio of 1:250, but in reality the national average counselor to student ratio is 1:457.

The ASCA National Model has had an epic impact on the profession of professional school counseling. The model represents a developmental, comprehensive, and balanced approach to school counseling programming. The model is comprised of three operational levels that house four fundamental components: (1) foundation, (2) management, (3) delivery, and (4) accountability. The importance of school counselor skills and attitudes in promoting leadership, advocacy, collaboration, and systemic change for *universal academic achievement* and total student development is built into each of the four components.

The foundation component represents the first operational level of ASCA's model, addressing the "what" of the school-counseling program (ASCA, 2005, p. 27). The foundation comprises student standards with competencies and indicators (see Appendix III) for facilitating student development in three domains (i.e., academic, career, and personal/social). These standards and competencies provide a sound foundation upon which the school-counseling program is built and identifies what students will know and be able to do as a result of the school-counseling program. Foundation building involves (1) assessing student, district, and school needs, as well as program strengths and weaknesses, (2) creating a mission statement and program philosophy, (3) establishing program goals that are based on needs, and (4) identifying standards to be met over time. The foundation of your school counseling program must be strong since it is sitting on the San Andreas fault that is the scrutiny of our educational climate of accountability.

Program delivery, representing one of two components at the second operational level of ASCA's model, speaks to "how" the school-counseling program is implemented (ASCA, 2005, p. 39). ASCA identifies four methods of delivery used to implement the school-counseling program: guidance curriculum, individual student planning, *responsive services*, and systems support. School counselors blend these methods of delivery to share their knowledge and skills and to advocate for students, the profession, and systemic change. The delivery system involves curriculum design and implementation including closing the *achievement gap* activities, the creation of *action plan*s, and the identification of data collection methods for measuring program outcomes.

Sharing the second operational level of ASCA's building-block approach is the management system. This component of the model addresses the "when, why, who, and on what authority" the school counseling program is operating (ASCA, 2005, p. 45). Key components of the management system include securing administrative support, completing management agreements, establishing an advisory committee, developing a master calendar and timelines, and promoting the school counseling program. There are a variety of ways to promote the school-counseling program, including websites, brochures, school newsletters, and participation at PTA meetings, which is now often referred to, particularly at the secondary levels, as the PTSA.

Accountability makes up the third level and final level of ASCA's operational systems. Accountability has a direct impact on the foundation system. That is, information learned from the processes of the third level is used to improve the effectiveness of the school-counseling program.

Accountability is vital to the success of the school-counseling program, using measurable outcomes that are documented in *results reports* to answer the question, "How are students different as a result of the school counseling program?" (ASCA, 2005, p. 59). Components of the ASCA Model Accountability System include assessing program processes, perceptions, and results data to determine the program's effectiveness in meeting targeted student competencies, which may include the program's impact on attendance, behavior, academic achievement, and career development. Other tasks at this level involve developing results reports, making program decision based on results reports, and sharing results reports with *stakeholders*. The accountability system also includes school counselor performance standards that reflect new vision roles and functions.

School Counselor Roles and Functions

Professional school counselors are a special breed. I recall a counselor educator referring to a particular school counseling student in her course as possessing the inherent qualities of Saint Francis of Assisi. Specifically, that the student did not so much seek to be consoled as to console or to be understood as to understand. I have seen the same in so many school counselors whose hearts of service and passion for the profession are marked with an altruistic drive to make a difference in the world.

School counselors absolutely do make a difference in the world and the lives of children and adolescents by integrating their primary role of *counselor* with the role of *educator*. School counselors live by a succinct guiding philosophy that holds the healthy mind as an educable mind. A healthy mind does not necessarily mean that it is a mind free from physical, mental, emotional, social, and environmental distress.

Operating from this philosophy, school counselors recognize that we all have baggage that we haul around (some heavier than others). In other words, we are all merely a rubber band snap away from complete madness. Okay, so I am exaggerating just a bit. The point is that we cannot ignore academic needs in order to only address the baggage. School counselors make every effort to meet all needs simultaneously. Ignoring educational needs in the presence of other issues is detrimental to the student's academic success and perpetuates achievement gaps.

School counselors are trained to move fluently between the two roles of educator and counselor for optimal and total student development. Meeting the total development of students often requires that school counselors engage in a host of shared functions including *teaming*, consulting, informing, collaborating, leading, advocating, counseling, programming, assessing, referring, evaluating, coordinating, and reporting.

In unifying our roles and functions, ASCA has created the School Counselor Performance Standards (ASCA, 2005). In addition, ASCA collaborated with practicing school counselors, district school counseling supervisors, and counselor educators to develop the School Counselor Competencies (see Appendix IV) to ensure the adequate training of professional school counselors.

School Counselor as Educator

Education and training that distinguishes the school counselor as an educator includes pre-K–12 program design and delivery, classroom instruction, theories of learning, child and adolescent development, career preparation, standardized testing and assessment, use of technology, behavioral theory, disability and exceptional behavior, identifying student competencies and ways to achieve academic competency, identifying and removing barriers to academic achievement, developing effective learning environments, *needs assessment*, and educational program evaluation. School counselors work closely with stakeholders, namely teachers, engaging their skills as educators to provide the finest services to students and parents and to accomplish the academic mission of schools.

As educators, school counselors engage in instruction by way of guidance lessons and school-wide programs that provide information and resources to all participants. In addition to instruction, functions inherent in the school counselor's role of educator include applying academic standards, interpreting standardized testing score reports, engaging in standardized testing programs, developing *research-based* or research-supported curriculum, and creating and evaluating needs-based educational programs.

Because fulfillment of the school counselor's role of educator involves instruction, a few states still require a teaching background in order to become a school counselor. Decades of research have examined the question of whether or not school counselors should be teachers prior to becoming school counselors. The results of these studies indicate that school administrators and school counselor supervisors deem school counselors without teaching experience to be as effective as those with teaching experience. Unexpectedly, in some cases, the majority of school counselors without teaching experience were found to be more effective in their overall performance as school counselors than those with teaching experience (Beale, 1995; Dilley, Foster, & Bowers, 1973; Olson & Allen, 1993).

Based on this research, it appears that distinct differences between the functions of teachers and school counselors necessitate that the teacher unlearn previously held dispositions in order to acquire new dispositions that are in many ways contrary in nature. For example, the teacher judges, disciplines, and manages. The role of teacher is subject-focused and involves didactic teaching with little or no concern for confidentiality in teacher–student interactions. The school counselor is nonjudgmental and does not discipline students. The role of the school counselor is facilitative and change-focused and ensures confidentiality in school counselor–student interactions.

School Counselor as Counselor

In the role of counselor, school counselors meet with students individually and in small groups to provide both prevention and intervention services related to personal, social, and emotional development and well-being, directly and indirectly, removing barriers to academic achievement.

School counselors also develop and deliver programs in the classroom and school-wide that address issues related to the personal, social, and emotional well-being of students. School counselors also work with teachers to modify the classroom climate for optimal learning and to develop academic contracts and schedules of *reinforcement*. School counselors also serve as a resource and consult and collaborate with stakeholders, discussed in Chapter 7, to provide support, information, and referral sources as needed and promote equity and access to school programs, activities, and rigorous curriculum.

School counselors understand that the relationship between academic success and personal, emotional, social, and physical well-being is a door that swings both ways. As such, school counselors encourage students faced with issues related to personal, social, and emotional health and physical challenges to believe in their ability to change, grow, overcome challenges, and achieve academically. School counselors encourage impaired students to embrace academics as an avenue to a promising, self-directed future.

Academic-focused channeling can be therapeutic, motivational, and build competencies, self-esteem, and psychological *resilience*—epitomizing the specialty of school counseling. Challenges can be our greatest asset, pushing us onward and upward. For this reason, school counselors are dogmatic in their efforts to balance their roles of counselor and educator for optimal student development. While priority is given to the significant role of counselor, counselors embrace and fulfill their dual roles of counselor and educator. After all, this is the role that sets counseling in the schools apart from other counseling specialties and defines our profession.

NBCC and NBPTS Voluntary School Counseling Credentials

Gladding (2001) defines certification as the process by which an agency, government, or association officially grants recognition to an individual for having met specific professional qualifications that have been developed by the profession. School counselors are encouraged to secure advanced voluntary credentials and actively seek out opportunities for professional development, embracing a continuous state of learning in order to provide optimal counseling services and to strengthen professional identity.

ASCA's Position on Credentialing and Licensure

ASCA strongly supports a professional school counselor credentialing or licensing law in each state, which includes a definition of the profession, minimum qualifications for entry into the profession, and requirements for continuing professional development. ASCA encourages all state education certification or licensure agencies to adopt the School Counselor Performance Standards from the ASCA National Model and the ASCA School Counselor Competencies for professional school counselor credentialing or licensing.

Position statement adopted 1990; revised 1993,
1999, 2003, 2009

NBCC is the national professional certification board that monitors the certification system for counselors and maintains a national register of certified counselors. In addition to national credentialing, NBCC provides counselors with a code of ethics for guiding professional practices. NBCC examinations are used by more than 48 states to credential professional counselors on a state level. NBCC was created by the ACA, and both organizations work closely to advance the profession of counseling and maintain high standards of excellence.

The NBCC administers the Uncle Sam of national general counseling credentials—the one and only—NCC. Counselors who hold the NCC credential from the NBCC have demonstrated mastery of the CACREP Standards as well as the NBCC Standards. For this reason, counselors who hold the NCC have established equivalency to graduation from a CACREP-accredited program.

NBCC also administers several national specialty counseling credentials such as the NCSC credential, first awarded in 1991. School counselors who hold the NCSC have a master's degree and have demonstrated competence in areas specific to contemporary school counseling and demonstrate a high level of professional commitment that goes beyond required state licensing. Since the NCC is a prerequisite or corequisite to the NCSC, school counselors who hold the NCSC credential have established equivalency to graduation from a CACREP-accredited program as well as mastery of the high standards set by the profession. The credential is a result of a collaborative effort with professional associations, accreditation, and certification organizations in counseling and is governed by a board of counselors.

Holding the NCSC serves to inspire school and community confidence in the school counselor's clinical ability to meet the personal, social, and emotional needs of their children. This is particularly significant in a charged climate where the public's confidence in our educational system is already wavering if not waning. Parents are questioning not only the ability of public schools to successfully educate their child, but the ability of public schools to identify and effectively intervene in situations with troubled students who threaten the safety of their progeny.

As recognition mounts pertaining to the acceptance of the NCSC for state board credentialing, school counselors actively pursue the NCSC to enhance career mobility and credibility in the practice of counseling and to demonstrate an alignment with mental health counseling. Other benefits to certification by the NBCC are outlined on their website at www.nbcc.org.

The NBPTS also offers a national voluntary credential for school counselors along with School Counseling Standards (NBPTS, 2002). Like the NCSC, obtaining the credential demonstrates a high level of professional commitment that goes beyond required state licensing. Unlike the NCSC, the credential does not require a master's degree, nor is it a collaborative effort with all professional associations, accreditation, and certification organizations in counseling. The credential promotes the school counselor's identity as educator and counselor and is governed by a board of teachers and school counselors.

Ethical, Legal, and Professional Considerations

Personal ethics are moral principles guiding an individual's behavior; codes of ethics and ethical behavior are values that guide an entity with which members of that entity are bound (Remley & Herlihy, 2010; Stone, 2009). Ethical codes for the counseling profession steer the professional practices of counselors to ensure the safety and well-being of clients. Counselors' ethical standards, regardless of specialty, are grounded in five ethical principles (autonomy, nonmaleficence, beneficence, justice, and fidelity), which are described as follows (Kitchener, 1984):

Autonomy refers to the notion of independence, which encourages the client to exercise freedom of choice and behavior when those actions do not infringe upon the rights and beliefs of others. Autonomy is promoted versus dependence upon the counselor.

Nonmaleficence is often defined as "above all do no harm" and viewed by many as the most critical of the five ethical principles. In brief, this concept promotes the idea of avoiding any actions or intentions that may place the client at risk for harm.

Beneficence refers the counselor's responsibility to *do good.* Counselors contribute to the well-being of clients.

Justice should be conceptualized as treating others equally, but in relation to their individual differences. When treating clients differently in order to meet their unique needs, counselors operate from a sound rationale for such actions.

Fidelity refers to the trusting nature of the therapeutic relationship built upon a demonstrated reliability and authenticity toward the client. Counselors promote fidelity by honoring commitments and obligations to clients.

Primarily, school counselors follow the ASCA *Ethical Standards for School Counselors* (ASCA, 2010) located in Appendix II. School counselors also refer to the ACA *Code of Ethics* (ACA, 2005) for additional guidance related to the ethical practice of counseling. School counselors seeking the NCSC credential would be wise to be familiar with the NBCC *Code of Ethics* (NBCC, 2005) as well, which is located in Appendix V.

Some ethical guidelines are straightforward, others, well, not so much. There will likely be many times during the course of your life as a school counselor that you will encounter ethically laden situations, requiring tough decisions. Trust me, some will be real head scratchers and finger-drummers—perhaps even paving the way to baldness. For this reason, ACA and ASCA have introduced models for ethical decision making. School counselors will want to be familiar with both models. ACA suggests the following seven-step ethical decision-making model (Forester-Miller & Davis, 1996):

1. *Identify the problem*: Gather objective information (e.g., facts) and gain clarification of the problem.
2. *Apply the ethical standards (ACA and/or ASCA)*: Follow the course of action indicated by the standards or continue this model for more complex dilemmas.
3. *Determine the nature and dimensions of the dilemma*: Examine the problem from all angles and consider:
   a. The five moral principles for guiding ethical practices noted earlier in this section
   b. Professional literature
   c. Consulting with professional colleagues, supervisors, and/or professional associations.
4. *Generate potential courses of action*: Brainstorm possible solutions.
5. *Consider the potential consequences of all options and determine a course of action*: Assess each option and possible consequences to each option and then select the most promising option(s).

6. *Evaluate the selected course of action*: Consider any possible ethical issues associated with your option(s). If your course of action presents ethical issues, then reevaluate the initial problem and original options.
7. *Implement the course of action*: Carry out your plan and follow up on the situation.

ASCA adopted the Solutions to Ethical Problems in Schools (STEPS) model (Stone, 2001) which furthered ACA's seven-step model by addressing the specialty of counseling in the school setting (Stone, 2009). The STEPS model is included in Section G.3 of the *Ethical Standards for School Counseling Programs* (ASCA, 2010). The STEPS model includes the following nine steps to ethical decision making:

1. Define the problem emotionally and intellectually.
2. Apply the ASCA Ethical Standards and the law.
3. Consider the students' chronological and developmental levels.
4. Consider the setting, parental rights, and minors' rights.
5. Apply the moral principles.
6. Determine your potential courses of action and their consequences.
7. Evaluate the selected action.
8. Consult.
9. Implement the course of action.

THE SAME OR DIFFERENT?

The school counselor meets with a fifth-grade Caucasian female student, Rita, for issues related to social skills. The school counselor meets with a different fifth-grade student, Regina, an African American female, for issues related to social skills, but takes a different approach. The school counselor is applying which ethical principle in these two students' cases?

a. Fidelity
b. Nonmaleficence
c. Justice
d. Autonomy
e. Beneficence

Section A.1 of the ASCA *Ethical Standards for School Counselors* (ASCA, 2010) states that school counselors "are knowledgeable of laws, regulations and policies relating to students and strive to protect and inform students regarding their rights" (p. 1). Protecting the rights of children while those children are in our care during the school day is also emphasized in the common-law doctrine *in loco parentis.*

In addition to ethical guidelines, school counselors must be assiduously mindful of the legal issues related to the population for which they are providing services—minors. Minors are typically those students who are under the age of 18 and the population generally served by school counselors.

While school counselors follow fairly consistent national ethical standards created by our governing bodies and professional associations, a large variation exists in the law and policy from state to state, city to city, and school division to school division. Such differences necessitate that school counselors become familiar with legislation and policy as it pertains to counseling minors in their state and locality and impacting school division policy. There are times when division policy, ethical standards, and legal mandates conflict when entering into a counseling relationship with minors in a school setting. While it is not without complication, it is necessary for school counselors to find a way to balance ethical, legal, and school policy requirements. Heaven knows, sometimes it feels like walking a greased tightrope.

Although school counselors rely on school division policy to guide practices, school division policy does not substitute for knowing and abiding by the ethical guidelines of the profession and the law. In cases where ethical guidelines and the law conflict with school division policy, school counselors should advocate for change based on such knowledge. The simple fact is that in some cases, school administrators are unaware and unfamiliar with the law as it pertains to school counseling and that which may place school counselors in an unethical situation. And, since principals are vicariously responsible for the actions or inactions of the school counselors in their building, principals more often than not appreciate your expertise in relation to your job. Knowing your stuff allows them to take care of their own stuff, and keeps them from stumbling into bad lighting.

Confidentiality

Confidentiality, the hallmark of a trusting therapeutic relationship, is one of the most common areas of controversy. Perhaps, this is why the "Confidentiality" section in the ASCA *Ethical Standards for School Counselors*

(ASCA, 2010) is as long as the Mississippi River. Confidentiality is a concept grounded in ethical principles that refer to a client's right to privacy in the practice of counseling. A related construct, privileged communication, is a legal term that refers to the requirement to protect the privacy between counselor and student (Stone, 2009).

In many states, the school counselor and student relationship is not recognized by law as privileged. School counselors need to know if the state in which they practice recognizes privileged communication between the school counselor and student and under what circumstances. Perhaps privilege exists, but only with specific school counselors in the school (e.g., student assistance counselors).

ASCA's Position on Confidentiality

The professional responsibility of school counselors is to fully respect the right to privacy of those with whom they enter counseling relationships. Professional school counselors must keep abreast of and adhere to all laws, policies and ethical standards pertaining to confidentiality. This confidentiality must not be abridged by the counselor except when there is clear and present danger to the student and/or other persons.

Position statement adopted 1974; reviewed and reaffirmed 1980; revised 1986, 1993, 1999, 2002

School counselors are ethically and morally obligated to maintain a minor client's confidentiality except in circumstances of harm to self/others, abuse, court order, or when the client has provided written permission to share his or her disclosures made during counseling sessions. Keep in mind that harm to others can include property. Also, there are policies in some school divisions that require school counselors to breach confidentiality and to inform the parent if a child is engaging in sexual activity or drug use, or if the student is pregnant. Know your school division's policy.

When counseling minors, the law's perspective is often that counselors are obligated to the parents or guardians of their minor clients with regard to the disclosure of information shared in a counseling session. In short, school counselors have an ethical obligation to the minor client and a legal obligation to the parent or guardian.

On the other hand, if privileged communication exists between school counselors and minors in the state in which the school counselor is practicing, then it is illegal for the school counselor to disclose counseling session information without the consent of the minor student in the absence of clear and imminent danger. Also, some states have minor consent laws in place that allows minors, deemed *emancipated minors*, to enter into counseling relationships and make other decisions without the consent of an adult, which affords those students privileged communication (Remley & Herlihy, 2010; Stone, 2009).

ORDER IN THE COURT, HERE COMES THE JUDGE

A school counselor has been subpoenaed to appear in court in a state that does not recognize privileged communication between school counselors and students. The school counselor expresses her reluctance to answer the attorneys' questions regarding the case of Donna, the 15-year-old student that the school counselor has been providing individual counseling services to for the past four weeks. When the judge requires that the school counselor answer the attorneys' questions, the school counselor responds by attempting to explain the importance of maintaining counselor–student confidentiality and requesting a withdrawal of the requirement. What are the ethical implications in this case? Are Donna's actions in accordance with professional ethical standards?

When confidentiality must be breached, remind the student of the conversation held during the initial session pertaining to the limits to confidentiality. Then, explain the reasoning behind the need to break confidentiality. If it is a situation where the parent needs to be contacted, empower the student to be the one to make contact with the parent in your presence. Another option is to offer to be the one to initiate the communication with the parent in the student's presence. At a minimum, let the student know that you will be contacting the parent as legally/ethically required and discussed in the initial counseling session.

If the issue requires that contact be made to social services or the local police, the school counselor should make contact and keep the student involved as much as possible or prudent. School counselor continues to maintain sensitive and open communication with the students throughout the process. Whether or not it is appropriate or practical to allow the student to be present during mandatory contacts should be considered on a case-by-case basis.

In situations where parent involvement may be helpful to the student's progress, but is not ethically or legally required, the student's consent should be secured. In these cases, it is recommended that school counselors discuss with the student the reasons why parent involvement is desired and let the student know what information will be shared. The school counselor might encourage the student to be present to hear what is shared and encourage the student to speak freely during the communications. It has been this school counselor's experience that even the most reluctant students come around when they understand the school counselor's reasoning and trust that the school counselor will remain involved and supportive throughout the process. Parent involvement or knowledge of the student–school counselor relationship often results in (1) securing parent support for maintaining the confidential counseling relationship, and (2) effective counseling outcomes.

A primary and legitimate concern for parents is that counseling sessions will not be private. Parents express concern that teachers, staff, other parents, and students may overhear or somehow find out about personal information shared in the counseling session that may result in harm or embarrassment for their child. Having an open discussion with the parent and the student about confidentiality and its limits at the time that counseling is initiated is paramount to helping the parent and student to understand the nature of counseling.

If the student will be participating in group counseling, school counselors need to let students and parents know that confidentiality cannot be guaranteed in group counseling sessions. School counselors also let the parent and student know that there may be times when sharing confidential information with faculty and school administrators may be deemed in the best interest of the student in order to provide the student with additional supports and allies during times of stress. During these times, permission will be sought from the student, and perhaps the parent as well depending upon the developmental level of the student.

Section C.2.e of the ASCA *Ethical Standards for School Counselors* (ASCA, 2010) advises school counselors to "recognize the powerful role of ally that faculty and administration who function high in personal/social development skills can play in supporting students in stress, and carefully filter confidential information to give these allies what they 'need to know' in order to advantage the student" (p. 4). Seek *consultation* with other school counseling professionals when in doubt as to what constitutes a need-to-know basis.

Filtered confidential information is considered that which is true and accurate and shared in a sensitive and caring manner (Remley & Herlihy, 2010; Stone, 2009). Information that might be construed as an invasion of privacy or defamation of character may place the school counselor in a legally troubling situation.

ALLIANCES

Robert is an elementary school counselor. In an attempt to establish a partnership with parents toward the well-being of their children and to ease parents' concerns about their child having sessions with the school counselor, Robert announces during a PTA meeting and a school open house that he is happy to share information discussed during counseling sessions with their children. Robert emphasizes the importance of sharing information and working together in order to help students to be successful. What do you think about Robert's approach to promoting positive school counselor–parent relations? Are there ethical concerns to be considered here?

In cases of divorce, make every attempt to provide information to both parents that is objective and respectful unless, of course, explicitly prohibited by court order. Section B.2 of the ASCA *Ethical Guidelines for School Counselors* (ASCA, 2010) avows, "in cases of divorce or separation, school counselors exercise a good-faith effort to keep both parents informed, maintaining focus on the student and avoiding supporting one parent over another in divorce proceedings" (p. 4). What is Switzerland (for ten points)?

In the case of guardians and noncustodial parents, school counselors generally provide them with information that the school counselor deems helpful to the student and family with the custodial parent's knowledge. Section B.1 of the ASCA *Ethical Standards for School Counselors* (ASCA, 2010) encourages school counselors to be "sensitive to diversity among families and recognize that all parents/guardians, custodial and noncustodial, are vested with certain rights and responsibilities for their children's welfare by virtue of their role and according to law" (p. 3). With this said, school counselors are well advised to be aware of any restraining orders that may exist to ensure information is shared only with parents and guardians legally eligible to receive such information.

Confidentiality of Counseling-Related Electronic Communication

When using technology for counseling and counseling-related communications, and transmitting student records, school counselors are careful to consult the ethical guidelines with regard to the appropriate use of technology in counseling to ensure confidentiality is maintained. Parents and students often request that school counselors provide services via the Internet, e-mail, texting, or other forms of electronic communication. School counselors should know that they are in no way required to provide electronic counseling to students, parents, teachers, or other school personnel.

School counselors aflame with the desire to make use of the banquet of avant-garde (you may have to look that one up—got to keep you on your toes) modalities of communication need to be aware of the school's and the school division's policy on this issue, as well as relevant ethical and legal standards of practice. Even those school counselors who are not intending to provide technology-based counseling services should be aware of the legal and ethical implications involved. In this technologically driven world, unintentional electronic counseling may occur disguised simply as e-mail. Do not fall for the old e-mail disguise.

Section A.10 of the ASCA *Ethical Standards for School Counselors* (ASCA, 2010) emphasizes the need for school counselors to "take appropriate and reasonable measures for maintaining confidentiality of student information and educational records stored or transmitted through the use of computers, facsimile machines, telephones, voicemail, answering machines and other electronic or computer technology … understand the intent of FERPA and its impact on sharing electronic student records" (p. 3). School counselors, beware, e-mail has been considered in legal cases to be an educational record (see what I mean about the infamous e-mail masquerade) and therefore subject to the proviso of the FERPA of 1974, P.L. 93-380 (United States Department of Education, 2008). FERPA is discussed in greater detail later in this chapter.

NBCC, anticipating this growing trend, has created a guidance document titled *The Practice of Internet Counseling*. This document is available at www.nbcc.org, and it describes the different types of technology-assisted distance counseling tools and methods and provides Internet counseling standards.

With this said, in situations where sharing student information meets the need-to-know ethical guideline noted previously, school counselors must be mindful of the confidential nature of student information when using electronic mail, facsimile machines, the Internet and Intranet, voicemail, text messaging, flash drives, and other technological devices to transmit confidential information. In these cases, be sure that what is communicated is free of any identifying information (e.g., student name, social security number, student identification number) and that it is professional and aligned with the school counselor duties and responsibility to students and parents. A good rule of thumb is to only communicate electronically that which could be shared in a public forum. That is, if the National Educational Inquirer intercepted it, there would be no story.

There are also times when the electronic transfer of student information may not be appropriate (e.g., sensitive, personal information that may be linkable to a particular student). In such cases, a plan needs to be developed for the sharing of confidential information between professionals (e.g., school counselor to personal counselor).

Harm to Self or Others

School counselors have a duty to protect and a duty to warn in cases of harm to self or others (or their property). This duty requires a breach in confidentiality. When a student names an identifiable other to which they have a plan to do harm, then the school counselor needs to warn the identified victim. This may require more than parent notification, but police officer involvement as well to be sure protection can be obtained for the intended victim.

School counselors have a duty to protect in cases where students threaten harm to self. In such cases, school counselors should assess for clear and imminent danger. Most school divisions have policy, guidelines, and forms to aid school counselors in making such assessments—know your school division's policy, and review assessments used by the school counselors to be sure they accurately reflect current federal and state legislation. If it is believed that the student is at risk for self-harm, the proper authorities must be notified.

Section A.7 of the ASCA *Ethical Standards for School Counselors* (ASCA, 2010) necessitate that school counselors "inform parents/guardians and/ or appropriate authorities when a student poses a danger to self or others" (p. 3). It is important to spotlight "parent/guardians *and/or* appropriate authorities" in this statement. Because the student is a minor, the immediate reaction of some may be to contact the parent when a student threatens harm to self. This may not be the appropriate action in some cases.

If the parent is implicated by the student as a factor for suicidal thoughts, the parent would not be the first contact. In fact, the school counselor may not contact the parent at all in such cases. In most states, school counselors would contact CPS, a division of Social Services. The CPS personnel would make contact with the parent at their discretion based on a more detailed investigation and discussion with the student.

If parents are not implicated, they should be the first contact, and the student should remain under adult supervision until the parent or guardian arrives. School counselors should provide parents with a list of resources that provide counseling services to children, adolescents, and families. In some states, if parents indicate in any way that they will not be seeking professional counseling for their child or adolescent who is at risk of suicide or other behaviors harmful to self (e.g., cutting), this is viewed as child neglect. In such cases, generally, CPS would be contacted immediately.

In some cases, school counselors may not deem particular information shared by a student as constituting harm to self or others. In such cases, and where law or policy is not in place, school counselors may decide not to disclose particular information to a parent (e.g., risky behaviors, drug and alcohol use, issues related to eating/diet, sexual activity) to avoid a possible negative impact on the counseling relationship. In these situations, school counselors are assuming responsibility for the student's safety and well-being. Should any harm come to the student as a result of withholding such information, school counselors may be held legally responsible for those inactions. School counselors are strongly encouraged and supported by the ASCA *Ethical Standards for School Counselors* (ASCA, 2010) to consult,

THOUGHTS OF SUICIDE

Patrick, a ninth grader, was referred to you by a teacher who said Patrick expressed suicidal intentions because he is having some personal and family issues. You talk to Patrick long enough to assess that he is at imminent risk of suicide. Understanding that Patrick is a minor, the school counselor contacts the student's parent(s) and prints a resource list of community mental health counselors to give to the parent. Is this the best course of action, ethically and legally, on behalf of this student?

consult, consult with other counselors in the best interest of the student in instances where they may be uncertain about a course of action.

The reverse can also be true, in cases where the school counselor shares information with the parent or guardian that should not have been disclosed even in the absence of privileged communication and in the presence of clear and imminent danger. For example, if a student threatens to commit suicide and implicates their parent or guardian as a reason for their suicidal thoughts, disclosing this information to the parent could result in serious harm to the student at the hand of him or herself or an abusive parent. In this case, the school counselor may be found negligent and held liable if the law in the state in which they practice requires that school counselors contact CPS when parents are implicated.

Child Abuse and Neglect

The federal CAPTA established minimum standards, allowing each state to create its own definition of child abuse and neglect. CAPTA defines *child abuse* and *child neglect* as "any recent act or failure to act on the part of a parent or caretaker which results in death, serious physical or emotional harm, sexual abuse or exploitation, or an act or failure to act which presents an imminent risk of serious harm" (Child Welfare Information Gateway, 2009).

All 50 states have passed mandatory child abuse and neglect reporting laws. Legislation imposes penalties to school counselors who do not report suspected child abuse or neglect.

ASCA's Position on Child Abuse and Neglect

It is the professional school counselor's legal, ethical, and moral responsibility to report suspected cases of child abuse/neglect to the proper authorities. Recognizing that the abuse of children is not limited to the home and that corporal punishment by school authorities might well be considered child abuse, ASCA supports any legislation that specifically bans the use of corporal punishment as a disciplinary tool within the schools.

Position statement adopted 1981; revised 1985, 1993, 1999, 2003

As mandated reporters, school counselors must make verbal contact with CPS in cases of suspected child abuse or neglect generally within 48–72 hours. What constitutes abuse or neglect varies from state to state.

Some states still allow corporal punishment. I do not like this and never did. Not having been accused of being a woman of few words, let me say with the greatest conviction that I can muster—corporal punishment pollutes the very air that we seek to purify. ASCA supports the extermination of corporal punishment in the schools. School counselors remain diligent in reporting suspected child abuse that may be occurring within and outside of the school.

ASCA's Position on Corporal Punishment in the Schools

Professional school counselors advocate abolishing corporal punishment in schools. Corporal punishment is defined as "intentional infliction of pain or discomfort and/or use of physical force upon a student as punishment for an offense of behavior" (American Medical Association; Orentlicher, 1992).

Position statement adopted 1995; revised 2000, 2007

CHARLIE'S WORLD

Charlie is a 9-year-old student who went to the school nurse because his back was hurting. The school nurse did not see any visible signs of injury, but asked the school counselor to talk to Charlie because he said that while he was staying with his dad last weekend his dad punched him, so he called his mother crying to come and get him. The school counselor talked to Charlie and found out that his father was very angry and hit Charlie, repeatedly, in the stomach and back about a week ago. Charlie had been out of school for the past week while back with his mother, who told Charlie's teacher that he was playing and fell out of a tree. Since the school counselor knew that Charlie's parents were separated and this happened at the dad's house, the school counselor called the mother. Do you agree with the school counselor's actions in this case? Why or why not?

In most states, school counselors need only to have reasonable cause to suspect child abuse and/or neglect and do not need to see bruises, cuts, or marks of any kind in order to request CPS intervention on behalf of a child, adolescent, or the elderly (Child Welfare Information Gateway, 2009). If the school counselor suspects that the student may run or that the student is afraid to go home, this needs to be shared in the initial contact with CPS. Together, the school counselor and CPS intake specialist should determine an immediate course of action based on the information provided by the student.

Scope of Practice

Another area that is potentially problematic for school counselors involves the scope of practice and referrals. School counselors want to be careful not to practice outside of their areas of expertise and training. ASCA supports the use of referrals and a collaborative approach to meet the persistent and long-term needs of these students.

ASCA's Position on Meeting the Mental Health Needs of Students

Professional school counselors do not provide long-term therapy in schools to address psychological disorders; however, they must be prepared to recognize and respond to student mental health crises and needs, and to address these barriers to student success by offering education, prevention, and crisis and short-term intervention until the student is connected with available community resources.

Position statement adopted 1974; reviewed and reaffirmed 1980; revised 1986, 1993, 1999, 2002

It is important that school counselors know that providing ongoing counseling sessions with students whose issues are so severe, frequent, and enduring that they cannot be sufficiently addressed within the scope of school counseling and within the expertise of the school counselor is in violation of professional ethical guidelines. Section A.5.b of the ASCA *Ethical Standards for School Counselors* (ASCA, 2010) maintains that school counselors "help educate about and prevent personal and social concerns for all students within the school counselor's scope of education and competence and make necessary referrals when the counseling needs are beyond the individual school counselor's education and training. Every attempt is made to find appropriate specialized resources for clinical therapeutic topics that are difficult or inappropriate to address in a school setting such as eating disorders, sexual trauma, chemical dependency and other addictions needing sustained clinical duration or assistance" (p. 2).

MOONLIGHTING

Stuart is a school counselor and a licensed professional counselor. Since counseling students in the school setting for an indefinite period of time and providing diagnoses and therapy is outside of the scope of the practice of school counseling, Stuart has decided to offer his counseling services to students outside of the school day and school setting. Since these are students he serves in the schools, he is offering a reduced rate for these families. Are there ethical implications to consider here?

There are times when a school counselor and agency counselor may wish to collaborate to help the student. In such instances, all parties involved (i.e., parents, student, both counselors) should agree to the collaborative relationship, which will require the sharing of confidential information, communications, and student records. All parties will need to sign a release of information, which should include a statement that clearly defines and describes the nature of the collaborative relationship between all parties involved.

Another consideration with regard to scope of school counseling practice involves student evaluation, assessment, and interpretation. Psychological and *intelligence testing* by school counselors can be particularly problematic. Testing and assessment of this nature may be acceptable practices for school counselors in some school divisions, while unacceptable in others. Know your school division's policy. I realize by saying this yet again for about the sixth time in one chapter, I am running the risk of your having me committed for self-parroting behaviors (I believe the clinical term is echolalia). Just so you know, I am not answering the door to anyone wearing a white coat—although a sanitarium does offer something of a restful appeal.

School counselors only engage in evaluation, assessment, and interpretation when adequately trained. Section A.9.a of the ASCA *Ethical Standards for School Counselors* (ASCA, 2010) emphasizes that school counselors "adhere to all professional standards regarding selecting, administering and interpreting assessment measures and only utilize assessment measures that are within the scope of practice for school counselors and for which they are trained and competent" (p. 3).

Informed Consent

School counselors are not legally obligated to obtain parental permission prior to counseling unless there is a federal or state statute to the contrary (Remley & Herlihy, 2010; Stone, 2009). However, many school division policies require that school counselors obtain parental consent, particularly if counseling will extend beyond one or two sessions, as a matter of best practices (Stone, 2009).

School administrators, also intent on promoting positive relations and support for the school counseling program, are aware that judicial rulings have historically favored parental rights (Remley & Herlihy, 2010). For this reason, school systems generally have a policy in place with regard to parental consent for individual and small group counseling. Classroom guidance lessons, unless they are of a sensitive nature (e.g., sexual abuse), are viewed as part of the curriculum afforded to all students.

ASCA's Position on Parental Consent

The professional school counselor educates students, parents and the community about the school counseling program. Parental consent is obtained if state or local law or policy requires it.

Position statement adopted 1999; revised 2004

Many school systems include an "opt out" of counseling form in the student handbook. In this case, if a parent does not specifically opt a student out of counseling services, then professional school counselors are free to provide counseling services to students as needed. School counselors check with division supervisors for school counseling to stay abreast of school division policies pertaining to the provision of school counseling services.

SENSITIVE TOPICS

In an effort to be proactive in promoting child safety, an elementary school counselor conducted a classroom guidance lesson for all fourth- and fifth-grade students on Internet safety. The school counselor invited a community police officer to talk about a particular case where a boy was lured by a stranger over the Internet, abducted, and killed. The next day, a very upset parent called because their fifth grader, Kirbi, came home in tears as the program reminded her of what had happened to her brother, who had been taken by a stranger and killed. The parent said she had not been informed that this program would take place or she would not have allowed her child to participate. Are school counselors required to inform parents about the topics of the classroom guidance lessons and school-wide presentations? Should the parent have been informed about this classroom guidance lesson?

Some high schools now have student assistance counselors and student assistance programs (SAPs). Student assistance counselors are generally school counselors who specialize in working with students in crisis and those who are experiencing varying degrees of personal, social, and emotional distress and behavioral issues. Student assistance counselors often have advanced counseling credentials (e.g., NCC, NCSC, LPC). In some school divisions, while school counselors may be required to obtain parental consent for individual and small group counseling, student assistant counselors do not need to obtain parental permission to meet with students for multiple counseling sessions. School counselors need to be knowledgeable of the policy in their school division as it pertains to informed consent and counseling services provided by the student assistance counselor.

ASCA's Position on Student Assistance Programs

Professional school counselors play a key role in initiating and creating student assistance programs in the schools.

Position statement adopted 1994; revised 2000

Informed consent from parents and guardians should be in writing. It is not necessary to get informed consent in writing from the minor, although it is necessary to obtain agreement, or assent, from minor clients. School counselors use developmentally appropriate language to discuss counseling services so that students can make informed decisions about whether or not they wish to engage in a counseling relationship with the school counselor.

Student Records and Counseling Case Notes

Documenting counseling session information and storing such information is another consideration with regard to maintaining confidentiality. School counselor case notes, often referred to as "sole possession records" (p. 3), are not a part of the student's academic record (ASCA, 2010). School counselor's sole possession records are self-created case notes written as a memory aid documenting professional opinion and observations and not accessible or shared verbally or in writing with any other party.

Moreover, the school counselor's sole possession records are not to be kept in the student's school record, which is accessible to many other educators and could constitute a breach of confidentiality. In some states, general counseling case notes may be considered part of the educational record. In those states, school counselors are well advised to have a specific understanding of exactly what is required to be placed in the student's education records. Likely, it is no more than dates that the student visited the school counselor and whether the topic was personal, social, emotional, academic, or career related.

The advanced voluntary credentialing of school counselors (e.g., NCC, NCSC, LPC) requires that school counselors abide by the standards of practice of the credentialing agency. Many advanced voluntary credentials earned by school counselors have placed them in the category of mental health provider. Mental health providers are subject to compliance with HIPAA.

In brief, HIPAA established national standards related to the confidentiality and security of health information. Health records in the school setting are exempt from HIPAA because those are covered under FERPA. However, it is not entirely clear how school counseling case records may be viewed during litigation should there be a mighty clash of the titans—HIPAA versus FERPA. My advice is to keep two sets of counseling notes: sole possession records and formal counseling records. As the adage goes, better safe than sorry!

Therefore, even in the absence of HIPAA, demands for accountability in today's society necessitate the school counselor's diligence in maintaining factual and accurate information. Formal counseling case notes should be objective and include the following:

■ Dates of sessions
■ Number of sessions
■ Assessment data
■ Presenting problem
■ Treatment/counseling plan
■ Information related to collaboration and consultation with others
■ Session notes
■ Associated documents (e.g., informed consent, drawings, letters, referrals)

Case notes need to be stored in a secure location (e.g., locked in the school counseling office file cabinet) and maintained for several years and perhaps indefinitely in some cases (Remley & Herlihy, 2010; Stone, 2009). Section A.8 of the *Ethical Standards for School Counselors* (ASCA, 2010) suggests "shredding sole possession records when the student transitions to the next level, transfers to another school or graduates ... apply careful discretion and deliberation before destroying sole possession records that may be needed by a court of law such as notes on child abuse, suicide, sexual harassment or violence" (p. 3). Case notes can be quite valuable, confirming meeting dates and times, dates of conversations with relevant others, and actions taken. Case notes may demonstrate a school counselor's professional, ethical, and legal actions in a given situation.

Case notes are accessible under a subpoena or court order. If (I should say when) you are subpoenaed to appear in court regarding one of your students and you are uncertain about what to say or what information to provide, set up a meeting with your school division's attorney for guidance. In fact, it is just good practice to touch base with your school attorney when subpoenaed to court for school-related matters.

There may be times when a parent or guardian demands access to case notes or wants to know exactly what has been communicated in a counseling session. In these cases, first try to persuade the adult that it would not be in the best interest of their child to reveal such information without the student's knowledge. Explain your ethical obligation to the student as well as your desire to collaborate with the parent on the student's behalf.

Reassure the parent that had anything been shared by the student that the parent should know in order to help the student that you would have requested permission from the student to share the information. Encourage the parent to ask the student about the counseling sessions.

If the parent is still insistent, let the parent know that you would like to request the student's permission to share the session content in order to preserve not just the counselor–student relationship, but the parent–child relationship. If the student would like to maintain confidentiality, then encourage a meeting with the student and the parent to mediate a solution. If the meeting is not productive and you decide not to disclose the information to the parent, ensure that you have administrator support. The parent may decide to legally pursue the matter and may have a legal right to the information.

School counselors should gain an understanding of FERPA of 1974 P.L. 93-380, also known as the Buckley Amendment (United States Department of Education, 2008). It is important that school counselors know how this legislation applies to student records and accessing school counseling case notes. FERPA's arm extends far and wide. It is not only a legal mandate but an ethical one as well, safeguarding the rights of students and parents in relations to educational records (ASCA, 2010).

FERPA is a federal law that applies to all schools that receive funds from the U.S. Department of Education. FERPA protects the privacy of student records and provides parents (or students over 18 and/or postsecondary school students) with rights pertaining to record inspection, correction, copying, and general consent before release. Requests must be made in writing. Schools will provide the parent or student with access to the record within 45 days of the date of the request.

Unless a parent specifically requests a school not disclose directory information about the student, directory information may be disclosed. Directory information may be considered to be the following:

- Name
- Address
- Telephone number
- Grade level
- Sports activities
- Weight and height of members of athletic teams
- Enrollment status
- E-mail
- Date and place of birth

- Photograph
- Major field of study and degrees obtains
- Previous schools attended and dates of attendance
- Honors and awards

While disclosing information that is not considered directory information requires parental consent, like all good rules, there are exceptions to this as well. Consent is not required by the parent to disclose information contained in a student's record under the following circumstances:

- Judicial order/subpoena
- State law (local juvenile justice authority)
- School studies/audit/evaluation
- School safety/health emergency
- Student's financial aid advisor
- School officials with legitimate educational interest
- School transfer

School counseling sole possession case notes, as discussed earlier, are not part of the student's school record, even under FERPA. Thus, parents and guardians do not have access to the school counselor's sole possession records under FERPA.

WHEN TO SAY NO

Shirley is a school counselor in a very large inner-city school. Her principal has asked her to include a copy of her counseling notes in the student's educational record in file room. The principal believes this is the only place those case notes will really be secure, and he wants teachers and administrators to understand each student's issues and history to aid them in better meeting student needs. Shirley politely says "no," that these are official counseling records and might also be considered "sole possession" notes that are not intended to be part of the student's cumulative educational record in accordance with ethical guidelines and the law. Shirley further explains that should the counseling notes be included in the educational records of students, parents may have grounds for legal action based on a breach of confidentiality in the school counselor–student relationship. Do you agree with the school counselor's actions in this case? Why or why not?

IDEA and Section 504

The *IDEA* is civil rights legislation created to ensure equality in education for students with an identified *disability* under three major types of disorders: physical and neurological disabilities, sensory disabilities, and developmental disabilities (United States Department of Education, 2004). Students who are found eligible for services under IDEA will receive IEP, which entitles the student to accommodations and specialized services as decided upon by the IEP team and included in the student's IEP.

A civil rights law, the Rehabilitation Act of 1973 (*Section 504*), as amended (United States Department of Education, 2009), includes information about the *Americans with Disabilities Act of 1990* (ADA) and protects the rights of students with disabling conditions that limit one or more major life activities (e.g., vision, hearing, speaking, walking, learning). Students who do not qualify for special education services under IDEA are often eligible for services under Section 504. Students who are found eligible under Section 504 will receive a *504 plan*, which entitles the student to accommodations and specialized services as decided upon by the 504 team and included in the 504 plan.

Together, IDEA and Section 504 of the Rehabilitation Act are powerful tools that school counselors use to advocate for *equity and access* to rigorous and appropriate educational programming and services in the schools for all students. School counselors are often the first person parents, teachers, and administrators involve when a student is struggling. Early intervention is key, and knowing the process and resources available for these students is vital to their well-being and academic success.

Parents, teachers, administrators, school counselors, and just about anyone can refer a student to the *child study* team, if a disability is suspected, and the 504 committee, if a disabling condition is suspected. Most schools have an early intervention team that assumes many different names but have a similar purpose, which is to begin a plan of action to help students who are struggling academically, personally, emotionally, socially, physically, and/or behaviorally. School counselors are generally members, even chairs, of these teams that also include the parent, classroom teacher(s), a special education teacher, and upon invitation, the school psychologist/social worker.

The early intervention team develops an intervention plan, monitoring timelines and indicators of success. The intervention plan is distributed to all who work with the student and a copy is included in the student's educational record. An early intervention plan may be all a student needs to get back on track or to stay on track. If not, the team refers the student to the child study team or the 504 committee for possible *diagnostic testing* and/or additional intervention assistance.

Many schools are now requiring that teachers refer students to the early intervention team before a referral can be made to the 504 or child study team. This helps to reduce the number of students in special education because of an overreliance on child study versus other less restrictive forms of intervention. However, a parent who wishes to take their child directly to the child study team has a legal right to do so and is not required to go through the early intervention team first.

THE 504 PLAN

Kenneth is a third-grade student with a 504 plan. The plan allows Kenneth to have extended time, frequent breaks, and small group instruction and testing. The school counselor is creating a standardized testing schedule for their school for special needs students. Kenneth's teacher tells the school counselor not to worry about pulling Kenneth out of the classroom since she has not really been doing this through-out the school year and Kenneth is doing just fine without those accommodations. The school counselor pulls the student out of the class on the day of statewide standardized testing to adhere to the accommodations listed on the student's 504 plan. What issues do you view as problematic in this case? Do you agree with the school counselor's actions in this case? Do you agree with the teacher's actions in this case? What are the implications for Kenneth?

Homelessness

According to the National Law Center on Homelessness and Poverty (2007), each year 1.35 million children are identified as homeless. Students who are homeless have a higher incidence of developmental delays, behavioral problems, poor academic performance, and depression, which makes poverty a pervasive risk factor (Amatea & West-Olatunji, 2007; Hernandez, Jozefowicz-Simbeni, & Israel, 2006).

School counselors collaborate with stakeholders to remove the barriers to school success perpetuated by homelessness. School counselors need to be aware of the McKinney-Vento Act of 1987 (United States Department of

Education, 2000), which defines homelessness as lacking a fixed, regular, and adequate nighttime residence, and provides federal money for homeless shelters.

ASCA's Position on Homelessness

Professional school counselors recognize the effects homelessness/displacement has on children's mental and physical health and academic functioning. Professional school counselors collaborate with community stakeholders, advocate to remove barriers to academic success, and implement educational and prevention programs to promote successful performance and interactions within the school environment.

Position statement adopted 2010

Research

It is important for school counselors to consider the ethical and legal issues associated with conducting research in the schools. Section F.1 of the ASCA *Ethical Standards for School Counselors* (ASCA, 2010) states that school counselors "conduct appropriate research, and report findings in a manner consistent with acceptable educational and psychological research practices ... and advocate for the protection of individual students' identities when using data for research or program planning" (p. 6). Issues to consider include

- Obtaining parental and student informed consent
- Confidentiality of assessment data
- Culture and gender bias in the selection of measures
- Withholding treatment
- Providing treatment for all students in experimental groups

In addition to a review of the ACA's *Code of Ethics and Standards of Practice* (ACA, 2005) and the ASCA *Ethical Standards for School Counselors* (ASCA, 2010), the following resources are beneficial when conducting studies in the public school setting: *Competencies in Assessment and Evaluation for School Counselors* (Association for Assessment in Counseling and Education, 1998); *Counseling and Educational Research* (Houser, 1998); *Guiding*

Principles for Evaluators (American Evaluation Association, 1994); *Program Evaluation: Methods and Case Studies* (Posavac & Carey, 2003); and *Code of Fair Testing Practices in Education* (Joint Committee on Testing Practices, 2004). Chapter 5 discusses research and program evaluation in the schools.

Dual Relationships

Maintaining professional distance is sometimes more difficult for the school counselor, as opposed to a private practitioner or community counselor. School counselors are often asked by administrators to serve as coach or sponsor the *SCA* or they are requested to take on any number of extracurricular program sponsorship roles. Also, some school counselors live in communities where everybody knows your name.

When dual relationships are unavoidable, continuously examine your professional and ethical behaviors as a school counselor by asking yourself, "Whose needs are being met by my behaviors?" (Stone, 2009). And, since dual relationships are often about personal gain (e.g, extravagant gifts, money, emotional, personal, or social need, recognition, popularity), ask yourself, "Am I doing this for personal gain or reasons?" If the answer is yes, then, in the words of our former first lady, Nancy Reagan—*just say no*!

Section A.4.a of the ASCA *Ethical Standards for School Counselors* (ASCA, 2010) cautions school counselors to "avoid dual relationships that might impair their objectivity and increase the risk of harm to students (e.g., counseling one's family members or the children of close friends or associates). If a dual relationship is unavoidable, the school counselor is responsible for taking action to eliminate or reduce the potential for harm to the student through use of safeguards, which might include informed consent, consultation, supervision and documentation."

Supervision

ASCA recommends that school counselors receive regular supervision in order to maintain and enhance professional and ethical practices. Section E.1 of the ASCA *Ethical Standards for School Counselors* (2010) states that "effective school counselors will seek supervision when ethical or professional questions arise in their practice" (p. 5).

Supervision at the division level may be thought of as program supervision and is provided by a division level/central office administrator. The other two types of supervision are administrative and clinical supervision.

Administrative supervision is generally provided at the building level by the school counseling director or principal. The director or principal provides the school counselor with general guidance pertaining to the daily operations of the school counseling program and evaluates the school counselor's professional performance.

Clinical supervision provides school counselors with consultation and supervision as it pertains to improving counseling skills and providing needed professional support, yet it is the least received type of supervision for school counselor. School counselors may obtain clinical supervision from local counselor educators and professional counselors in community agencies and private practice. Individual and group peer supervision or consultation by fellow practicing school counselors are the most commonly used methods of school counselor supervision, often using a developmental model or some integrated approach that includes various aspects of the developmental model.

Developmental models of supervision allow school counselors to meet peers where they are in their developmental process as a practicing counselor. Developmental models posit that counselors move through qualitatively different stages that require qualitatively different levels of supervisor involvement (e.g., less, moderate, or highly structured) and roles (e.g., teacher, trainer, colleague, consultant) to meet the unique needs of the supervisee (Bernard & Goodyear, 2004).

Peer supervision or consultation as a type of clinical supervision aids school counselors in case conceptualization and working through complex ethical and legal issues that often arise when counseling minors, while also providing an medium for shared feedback, exploration of thoughts and emotions, and the validation and support critical to self-care (Bernard & Goodyear, 2004; Page, Pietrzak, & Sutton, 2001).

We do not need Nostradamus to tell us what the future holds for school counselors who do not find ways to distress, reenergize, and maintain our own well-being. How can we effectively meet the needs of others in the lingering presence of our own unmet needs? School counselors are like the cobbler with no shoes. We get so busy fashioning shoes for all of our students, teachers, and parents, that we do not make time to create a pair for ourselves. It is time to design our own shoes. Now, before your heart starts hammering too quickly with excitement, I did not say designer shoes—I said—design our own shoes.

It is no longer just our personal and professional responsibility to prevent our own impairment that often results from professional burnout. ACA (2003), recognizing the growing number of counselors suffering from professional burnout, created the Taskforce on Counselor Wellness and Impairment to provide counselors with strategies, self-assessments, and resources to address burnout (www.counseling.org/wellness_taskforce/index.htm).

ACA recognizes burnout as an impairment that may impact our professional counseling ability and result in harm to the client, making it our ethical responsibility to address self-care. ACA provides a long list of strategies to reduce burnout and maintain personal health and well-being that fall into the following categories:

- Clinical supervision (peer consultation/supervision, supervision by a professional counselor)
- Involvement in professional associations
- A balanced lifestyle that attends to the holistic self, mind, body, and spirit
- Identifying and maintaining a support system
- Identifying and removing the barriers to self-care
- Making time for fun and socialization

Human Development, Learning, and Motivation

Human development, simply stated, is the change that occurs in human beings over the course of the lifespan. The process, however, is not so simple. Human development is multidimensional and complex. For these reasons, it is not appropriate to generalize developmental processes and stages across cultures or ethnicities because some developmental characteristics are socially engineered or thwarted by culturally engendered developmental processes. This section will look at key developmental theories and general developmental characteristics of elementary, middle, and high school students.

Understanding the characteristics and processes of a student's psychological, social, cognitive (including learning, motor skills, and language development), spiritual, and moral development during the school-age years is necessary to distinguishing between what may be considered normal developmental characteristics and minor to serious developmental impediments. Knowledge of the multifaceted aspects of human development is also essential to designing developmentally appropriate strategies for successful intervention with specific populations such as students with physical, mental, and emotional disabilities and/or advanced functioning students.

An understanding of human development across the lifespan enables school counselors to adjust language, approaches, and techniques to meet the unique needs of school-age children. It is also important that school counselors consider those biological and environmental forces that impact human development.

Theorists continue to ponder the impact of nature versus nurture on human development. That is, to what extent do genetic factors (i.e., nature) and environmental factors (i.e., nurture) and their interactions influence human development? To date, the topic has been widely researched, and data indicates that both play a significant role in determining our attitudes, beliefs, and behaviors. For this reason, school counselors are encouraged to consider both nature and nurture when working with children, adolescents, and adults.

The fundamental nature of counseling, thus school counseling, and human development is change. Meeting students where they are when prevention and intervention is needed is critical. School counselors achieve this with an understanding of human development theories. The human development theories discussed in this section are categorized as follows: psychosocial development, cognitive development and learning theories, and moral and spiritual development. Figure 1.1 presents this information in a fashion that aids learning and recall.

Psychosocial Development

Psychosocial development theories seek to explain personality development and the acquisition of social skills and social attitudes. The three primary psychosocial theorists discussed in this chapter are Erik Erikson, Robert Havighurst, and Sigmund Freud. Eric Berne's theory of personality development, *transactional analysis*, is also are because it is often applied in the school setting.

Erik Erikson (1950, 1959) is best known for his eight stages of psychosocial development. Erikson postulates that each stage held a developmental task that needed to be successfully resolved in order to experience healthy personality development. When the task was successfully resolved, a *psychosocial strength*, or *virtue*, would emerge. Table 1.1 presents Erikson's eight stages, corresponding ages, the conflict to be resolved, and the resulting virtue in a manner that will aid in learning and recall.

Erikson is credited for coining the term *identity crisis*, which he suggests occurs during adolescence. Identity crisis is used to describe a period of role confusion whereby the individual explores roles, questions authority, strives to find his or her own unique self or identity, and struggles with social relationships and social and moral issues. When the individual commits to an identity, role confusion ends and role achievement is reached. *Role diffusion* is the result when an individual has not experienced identity crisis or commitment.

Psychosocial development

Explains personality development and the acquisition of social skills and social attitudes.

Erik Erikson

Development driven by stage-related task resolve. Eight stages of psychosocial development: trust vs. mistrust; autonomy vs. shame and doubt; initiative vs guilt; initiative vs. inferiority; identity vs. role confusion; intimacy vs. isolation; generativity vs. stagnation and eco; integrity vs. despair.
Key constructs: identity crisis; virtues

Robert Havighurst

Development driven by stage-related task resolve. Six stages of personality development: infancy; early childhood; middle childhood; adolescence; early adulthood; middle adulthood; and later maturity.
Key constructs: sources of developmental tasks (physical maturation, personal values, and societal pressures).

Sigmund Freud

Development driven by sexual pleasures and interactions of the id, ego, and superego. Five psychosexual stages: oral, anal, phallic, latent period, and genital stage.
Key constructs: conscious, unconscious; Oedipus and Electra complexes; libido; fixation; erogenous zones; pleasure principle.

Cognitive development and learning theories

Explains the development of thought, intelligence, and problem solving abilities.

Jean Piaget

Development is a continuous process of achieving balance between assimilation and accommodation (i.e., equilibrium) and the resulting modification of schemas.
Four stages of cognitive development: sensorimotor; preoperational; concrete operational; and formal operational.
Key constructs: egocentrism; sociocentrism!

B. F. Skinner

Learning driven by operant conditioning. Key constructs: behavior modification; stimulus; response; positive and negative reinforcement and punishment; schedules of reinforcement.

Lev Vygotsky

Learning is contextual and driven by culture, environment, and social interactions.
Key constructs: guided participation; zone of proximal development; scaffolding; cultural mediation; internalization.

Albert Bandura

Learning driven by modeling.
Key constructs: motivation; observational learning; reciprocal determinism.

Moral and spiritual development

Explains the development of attitudes and behaviors toward others, and the meaning and nature of our existence, grounded in cultural and societal norms/laws.

Jean Piaget

Moral reasoning develops from cognitive structure and social relationships in two stages. Individuals construct/reconstruct their perceptions of the world based on their interactions with environment and others.
Key constructs: heteronomy; autonomy; goodness; evil.

Lawrence Kohlberg

Moral thinking is developed through an understanding of and exposure to concepts such as justice, human rights and welfare, and equality. Three levels containing six stages of moral reasoning: Level 1(preconventional), Level 2 (conventional), and Level 3 (postconventional).
Key constructs: justice operation; moral universalism; formalism; relativism.

James Fowler

Faith development occurs in six stages and involves cognition, emotion, and imagination: intuitive projective; mythic literal; synthetic conventional; individuative reflective; conjunctive faith; universalizing (or enlightenment).
Key constructs: transcendence.

Figure 1.1   Human development theories.

Table 1.1 **Erikson's Eight Stages of Psychosocial Development**

Stage/Age	Task to be Resolved	Characteristics	Virtue
Infancy/ages 0–1	Trust vs. mistrust	Need for reliable care (e.g., feeding) from caregiver	Hope
Toddler/ages 2–3	Autonomy vs. shame and doubt	Need for sense of control over physical tasks (e.g., toilet training)	Determinism/will
Preschool/ages 3–5	Initiative vs. guilt	Need for control over environment (e.g., exploration)	Courage/purpose
School age/ages 6–11	Industry vs. inferiority	Need to successfully navigate social and educational demands (e.g., school)	Competence
Adolescence/ages 12–18	Identity vs. role confusion	Need to develop a personal identity and sense of self (e.g., peer relationships)	Loyalty/fidelity
Early adulthood/ ages 19–40	Intimacy vs. isolation	Need for intimacy and love (e.g., social relationships)	Love
Middle adulthood/ ages 40–65	Generativity vs. stagnation	Need to create and nurture (e.g., work/ parenthood)	Caring
Late adulthood/ ages >65	Ego integrity vs. despair	Need for a sense of fulfillment (e.g., reflection on life)	Wisdom

DEFIANCE

Kelly is in middle school, and his parents are worried that he is exhibiting defiance that could lead to more serious behaviors. His parents say that he just does not listen to a thing they say or comply with what they ask him to do. His grades are good as well as his relationships with peers. His teachers report that he is respectful but questions everything they ask him to do. Developmentally, what might Kelly be experiencing?

Robert Havighurst (1972) applied Erikson's concept of stages of psychosocial development, postulating six different stages and an emphasis on the successful achievement of each task at each stage, which derive from three sources: physical maturation (e.g., motor skills, walking and talking, adjusting to menses and menopause), personal values (e.g., spirituality/philosophical beliefs, selecting an occupation), and societal pressures (e.g., learning to be responsible, citizenship). Table 1.2 presents Havighurst's six stages of personality development along with the developmental tasks associated with each stage. Havighurst believed that introducing students to these developmental tasks at the *ripe time* creates a teachable moment.

Sigmund Freud believed that personality development was driven by sexual interests or pleasures that focused on specific *erogenous zones* (i.e., mouth, anus, and genital area) at particular stages of development (Nye, 1975). Like other stage theorists, Freud emphasized the importance of resolving developmental conflicts at each stage. Freud proposes that unresolved conflicts at each stage results in *fixation*, thereby leaving a part of the child's *libido* (i.e., psychic energy of the mind) fixed at that stage, impacting personality into adulthood. One wonders at which stage Freud developed his rumored fear of ferns—things that make you go hmmm? Nonetheless, Freud's brilliant mind conceptualized five stages of psychosexual development quite influential to this day. Each stage and the characteristics of each stage are listed in Table 1.3.

Freud further believed that personality was driven by the interactions of the mind, or psyche made up of the id (i.e., primal instinct), ego (i.e., realistic, organized part of the mind), and superego (i.e., moralistic part of the mind). The id is our unconscious and driven by the *pleasure principle*—if it feels good do it, if it doesn't don't do it! The ego, mainly but not entirely conscious, operates on the *reality principle*, which has us delay gratification and endure

Table 1.2 Havighurst's Stages of Personality Development

Stage/Age	Developmental Tasks
Infancy and early childhood/ages 0–6	Learning to talk, crawl, and walk; learning to control bowels; learning concepts; learning gender differences
Middle childhood/ages 6–12	Learning interpersonal skills and daily living concepts; developing attitudes about self, others, social groups, institutions, and society; developing a conscience, values, and morality; learning masculine or feminine social roles; achieving independence/ autonomy
Adolescence/ages 13–18	Continued development of independence and relationships with males and females; adjusting to one's physique; securing a job; adjusting to physiological changes
Early adulthood/ages 19–30	Selecting a mate; starting a family; becoming a caregiver; achieving social responsibility, values, and morality; selecting an occupation
Middle age/ages 30–60	Achieving occupational satisfaction; developing leisure activities; adjusting to physiological changes; assisting aging parents
Later maturity/ages >60	Adapting to living arrangements and declining physical strength/health; adjusting to retirement and reduced income

necessary pain when needed, meeting the needs of the id in a realistic way. The superego mainly but not entirely unconscious, seeks perfection, discerns right from wrong, and acts as the conscience.

To illustrate, imagine you are sitting in class and your belly begins to grumble and rumble with hunger. Your immediate instinct is to "go now seek sustenance" (id). But, before you can stand up, you hear, "Dude, you can't just get up and leave right in the middle of the professor's lecture, but we may be able to leave early and go get three or four tacos and a couple of burrito supremes" (ego). Now, at this point, superego would be the cloaked

Table 1.3   Freud' Stages of Psychosexual Development

Stage/Age	Characteristics
Oral stage/ages 0–1	The mouth is the child's primary interaction with the world and derives pleasure from oral stimulation (e.g., sucking and tasting). If gratification is not achieved, fixation on oral stimulus is the result into adulthood (e.g., nail biting, thumb-sucking, overeating, smoking).
Anal stage/ages 1–3	The primary focus is on bowel control. Too much emphasis can result in excessive need for organization or order and cleanliness into adulthood, whereas too little emphasis can result in sloppiness and destructive behavior into adulthood.
Phallic stage/ages 3–6	The genitals are the child's primary focus. Children develop an attraction to the opposite sex parent. Freud termed this the *Oedipal complex* (boy's attraction to mother) and *Electra complex* (girl's attraction to father).
Latent stage/ages 6–11	The primary focus is on the development of social skills, peer relationships, and values. The superego continues to develop while the id is suppressed.
Genital stage/ages 11–18	Physiological changes due to puberty, again create a focus on the genitals, and an interest in the opposite sex develops. Individual continues healthy development if progression through the stages have been successful to this point.

voice from deep within that chimes in now and says (depending upon our individually developed conscience), "For crying out loud, you can wait until the end of class and then go to Taco Bell."

Eric Berne (1961), largely influenced by the work of Freud, is best known for his theory of personality development known as TA. According to TA, to understand personality we must analyze the interpersonal interactions.

During a personal encounter, one individual will act toward the other in some fashion (*transactional stimulus*) and the other will respond in some manner (*transactional response*). TA holds that individuals take on one of three ego states: parent, adult, and child. In the parent ego state, individuals are either critical or nurturing, acting in a manner consistent with that of their parents. In the adult ego state, individuals act in a manner that illustrates self-discovered thinking and behavior. In the child individuals act as their true, unencumbered self for better (e.g., endearing) or worse (e.g., disobedient). TA also emphasizes the importance of attention in shaping our personalities and interactional patterns. Attention, or *strokes*, which can be nonexistent (i.e., no strokes, ignoring), negative (i.e., strokes that feel bad), or positive (i.e., strokes that feel good) impact our thoughts, feelings, and behaviors.

EDDIE'S EGO STATE

You are the middle school counselor meeting with a group of four seventh-grade males. The students were referred to you because of behavioral problems. Eddie, one of the group members, continued during the first group session to do just as the teacher described observing during class—he put others in the group down with hurtful and unsolicited remarks. Together, the school counselor and the other group members helped Eddie to explore his motivation for those behaviors. Eddie realized that this is how his father interacted with him. According to TA, what ego state is Eddie incorporating when he interacts with others?

Moral and Spiritual Development

Moral and spiritual development theories seek to explain the development of attitudes and behaviors toward the self and others and the meaning and nature of our existence. Morality and spirituality are largely determined by cultural and societal norms and laws and form the foundation of ethical behavior (Matsumoto & Juang, 2008). Three theorists, Jean Piaget, Lawrence Kohlberg, and James Fowler, have made a lasting impact of our understanding of moral and spiritual development.

Jean Piaget (1932), most widely known for his theory of cognitive development, discussed in the next section, suggested that moral thinking develops from cognitive structure and social relationships. Piaget studied the moral development of children using exercises of judgment based

Table 1.4   Piaget's Stages of Moral Development

Stage/Age	Characteristics
Heteronomy/birth to ages 9 or 10	Children do not understand rules or morality. Children at this stage depend on those in authority to reinforce or punish what is considered to be right (goodness) or wrong (evil).
Autonomy/ages 9 or 10+	Children begin to understand behaviors of right and wrong and allow principles and ideals to guide behavior, which are largely determined by that which was reinforced during the heteronomy stage and by their own maturing perspectives.

on the goodness or evil of storybook characters. Piaget's theory of moral development involves two stages: *heteronomy* and *autonomy*. Piaget's stages, ages, and primary characteristics for each stage of moral development are described in Table 1.4.

Lawrence Kohlberg (1967, 1969), inspired by Piaget's work and agreeing with his contention that moral development is a reflection of cognitive development, expanded on Piaget's stage model of moral development. Kohlberg contended that advanced cognitive functioning was necessary, but not sufficient for advanced moral reasoning.

Kohlberg proposed three sequential levels and six stages of moral reasoning, emphasizing the need to experience each stage—no stage skipping—in order to advance to the subsequent higher level of moral reasoning. The *preconventional* level (level one) consists of stage one, *obedience and punishment* (ages 5–7), and stage two, *instrumental relativist*. The *conventional level* (level two) consists of stage three, *interpersonal relationships* or *good boy, nice girl orientation*, and stage four, *law and order*. The postconventional level (level three) consists of stage five, *social contract and individual rights*, and stage six, *universal principles*. Kohlberg's levels, stages, ages, and characteristics at each stage of moral reasoning are illustrated in Table 1.5.

James Fowler (1981) is credited for his significant contributions toward our understanding of the development of faith. In his model, Fowler views faith not as a particular religion but in terms of one's relationship to the universe and to a transcendent power. Fowler's model, illustrated in Figure 1.2, is hierarchical, with each stage building upon the other. The stages of Fowler's mode include undifferentiated, intuitive–projective, mythic–literal, synthetic–conventional,

Table 1.5 Kohlberg's Levels and Stages of Moral Reasoning

Level	Stage (Age)	Characteristics
Level I, preconventional	Stage one (ages 5–7), obedience and punishment	Obey rules to avoid punishment/gain reward
	Stage two (ages 8–12), instrumental relativist	Can break rule for reciprocal gain or to meet needs
Level II, conventional	Stage three (ages 13–16), interpersonal relationships or good boy, nice girl	Actions intended to gain approval of others (be nice)
	Stage four (ages >16), law and order	Actions intended to please society; follow rules and obey the law; respect authority
Level III, postconventional	Stage five (adult), social contract and individual rights	Rules important for an orderly society but should be decided on by all based on differing values/beliefs
	Stage six (adult), universal principles	Actions begin to reflect internalized morality even if conflicts with rules and the law

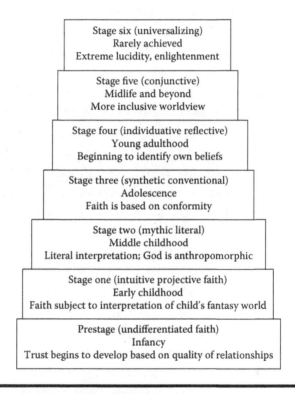

Figure 1.2 Fowler's stages of faith development.

individuative–reflective, conjunctive, and universalizing. Although Fowler believes that all individuals have the capacity for faith development, he points out that not all individuals make it to all stages of the developmental model.

School counselors use a variety of clever strategies to teach morality. School counselors use character education activities, bibliotherapy, ethical case discussions, current and past events, positive role models, and role plays to help students to understand the impact of our actions and inactions on others. School counselors promote moral development by encouraging reflection, reasoning, self-esteem, positive social interactions, peaceable schools, respect for others, and appreciation for differences.

Cognitive Development and Learning Theories

Cognitive development theories seek to explain the development of thought, intelligence, and problem-solving abilities. The most prominent cognitive development theorists include Jean Piaget, B. F. Skinner, Albert Bandura, and Lev Vygotsky. Each of these theorists has contributed significantly to our understanding of learning, information processing, and the development of language and reasoning skills.

Considered to be educators, moreover theorists, Benjamin Bloom and Robert Marzano have also contributed significantly to our understanding of student learning. For this reason, their educational philosophies and instructional strategies widely used in today's educational environments are covered in this section as well.

Piaget (1963) proposed four stages of cognitive development: sensorimotor, preoperational, concrete operational, and formal operational. Piaget's stages encompass birth to adolescence, describing a child's cognitive evolution from egocentrism (i.e., orientation to self) to sociocentrism (i.e., orientation to society). Table 1.6 presents Piaget's stages and the thinking and reasoning characteristics associated with each stage of a child and adolescent's development.

GRANDMA WILL BE BACK

Caryn is an elementary school student whose grandmother just passed away. Caryn is not upset because she said that grandmother will wake up and come back over to play with her soon. Which of Piaget's stages of cognitive development is representative of Caryn's thought processes in this situation?

Table 1.6 Piaget's Stages of Cognitive Development

Stage/Age	Thinking and Reasoning Characteristics
Sensorimotor/ages birth to 2	Primarily motor and reflex actions; sucking; grasping; kicking; understands the world through senses; speech is single utterances
Preoperational/ages 2–7	Personifies objects; play important for exploring self and world; present orientation; little perception of time; judgment based on perceptions; egocentric thinking (self the center of all things); egocentric speech (speech said aloud, but to self) to more socialized speech (speech that depicts thought and language as separate functions)
Concrete operational/ages 7–12	More organized, logical thought; good inductive logic (specific to general); sequencing and categorizing; problem solving; understands concept of reversibility; thinking less egocentric and more sociocentric (orientation toward society); socialized speech
Formal operational/ages >12	Ability to understand abstract and hypothetical concepts; good deductive logic (general to specific); socialized speech and vocabulary continue to develop

As one of the most influential psychologists of the twentieth century, Skinner's behavioral concepts are still widely used by school counselors in the twenty-first century. This study guide highlights the most salient concepts of Skinner's behavior modification and learning theory. Skinner contended that our behavior is determined by environmental factors, dismissing the notion of individual freedom (Skinner, 1971; Nye, 1975).

Skinner introduced the process of *operant conditioning*, which is grounded in the belief that behavior is learned. Voluntary behaviors, also referred to as responses, that are followed by a reinforcing stimulus are repeated as the result of desirable consequences and behaviors that are followed by a punishing stimulus and are not repeated as the result of undesirable consequences. The behavior reinforcements or punishments may be *positive* (e.g., applied after the response) or *negative* (i.e., removed after the response). Skinner promoted the use of *schedules of reinforcement* (i.e., multiple reinforcements over time) to modify, or shape, behavior.

School counselors most often use schedules of reinforcement to either increase or decrease the frequency of specific child and adolescent behaviors. This often takes on the form of a *behavior contract* or classroom management strategies in which the school counselor identifies expected behaviors (responses) and consequences based on the removal or application of a punishment or reinforcement (stimulus).

By the way, behavioral counseling, discussed in Chapter 2, is the approach most often used with the growing number of children and adolescents diagnosed with ADHD during the school years. Also, a little piece of trivia to keep in mind: Skinner advocated for reinforcement over punishment unless repeated attempts using schedules of reinforcement were unsuccessful.

DR. CANTHOLDEM

You are a school counselor and a teacher, Dr. Cantholdem, comes to you to ask for guidance. She is having a problem with attendance in her class. You ask her how she feels about exempting students from the final exam if they have perfect attendance. This is an example of:

a. Negative reinforcement
b. Positive reinforcement
c. Positive punishment
d. Negative punishment

Vygotsky (1934, 1978) suggests a sociocultural approach to human development, or social development theory, which holds thought, language, and reasoning development as contextual and driven by culture, environment, and social interactions. Vygotsky's key premise is *cultural mediation* (i.e., interactions between a child and the cultural group as well as individuals of the culture that develops cognitive constructs such as speech patterns, written language, and symbolic knowledge), which occurs during the process of *internalization* (e.g., the acquisition of specific and shared knowledge of a culture).

Vygotsky believed that cognitive development occurs within the *zone of proximal development*, which he defines as the difference between what a child can do without assistance (i.e., actual development) and what a child can do with assistance (i.e., potential development). In the process of assisting the child in mastering new skills, the adult adjusts to the child's level of development, which Vygotsky termed *scaffolding*. *Guided participation* may be used, whereby students help each other (e.g., peer tutoring) under the general guidance of a teacher.

Bandura (1969, 1977), the originator of social learning theory, believed that behavior was the result of a reciprocal relationship between the world and the person, which he termed *reciprocal determinism*. Bandura postulated that individuals learn through *modeling* (i.e., imitating another), or *observational learning*, driven by a rationalization or perceived reward (e.g., motivation).

WATCHING MOMMY

Starr is 7 years old and spends much time watching mommy. Every evening Starr watches her mother tuck a dishtowel into her slacks right before she washes the dishes. A few days ago, Starr's father said, "Starr, lets do the dishes so we can surprise mommy with clean dishes when she comes home today." Excited, Starr rushes over to the drawer and pulls out a dishtowel and tucks it into the front of her jeans. Starr's action is an example of learning by observation. This is the foundation of:

a. Operant conditioning
b. Social learning theory
c. a and b
d. None of the above

Benjamin Bloom (1953) introduced six classifications of learning levels progressing from the most basic to the most complex in the following hierarchical order: knowledge, comprehension, application, analysis, synthesis, and evaluation. In the past decade, Bloom's taxonomy has been revised (Anderson & Krathwohl, 2001) to associate specific verbs that represent ways to promote the development of higher-level thinking skills at each level illustrated in Figure 1.3.

Robert Marzano introduced instructional strategies that have been empirically validated as approaches that build background knowledge and improve student achievement across grade levels (Marzano, 2004). These strategies are listed in Table 1.7.

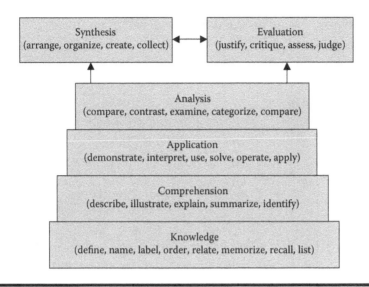

Figure 1.3   Bloom's taxonomy and associated verbs.

Table 1.7   Marzano's Nine Instructional Strategies

Instructional Strategy	Characteristics
Identifying similarities and differences	Breaking concepts into similar and dissimilar pieces; representing concepts in graphic forms (e.g., Venn diagrams, charts, analogies).
Summarizing and note taking	Conceptualizing presented material then restating it in one's own words; when note taking, more notes are better and allow time to process.
Reinforcing effort and providing recognition	Show the connection between effort and achievement (e.g., share success stories, underscore student's achievements); recognize individual accomplishments and personalize recognitions.
Homework and practice	Amount of homework should vary by grade level; homework schedule and setting should be consistent; homework provides practice; provide feedback on homework in a variety of ways.
Nonlinguistic representations	Use with linguistic representations; nonlinguistic representations stimulate and increase brain activity; use tangible models, physical movement, and apply symbols to represent words/images.

(Continued)

Table 1.7   Marzano's Nine Instructional Strategies (*Continued*)

Instructional Strategy	Characteristics
Cooperative learning	Positive impact on learning; vary group sizes and objectives.
Setting objectives and providing feedback	Provides direction for learning; students should personalize goals; use contracts; feedback should be timely, specific, and rubric based.
Generating and testing hypothesis	Use general rules to make a prediction; student should explain their predictions.

The theory of learning style suggests that individuals have a propensity toward receiving and storing information using one or more of the three sensory modalities: visual (e.g., pictures, written word), kinesthetic (e.g., body movement, tactile), and auditory (e.g., spoken word). It is not only important for school counselors to gain an understanding of learning styles and teach to all learning styles but also important for students to help students to identify their learning styles—students learning how to learn.

Generally speaking, individuals also have a preference for particular learning environments and times of day where conditions are optimal for learning. School counselors help students to understand their individual learning preferences and how those preferences can change over time. This self-knowledge enables students to adapt to a variety of teaching environments, selecting a preferred approach to the assigned task.

Motivation

Theories of motivation are often categorized under three broad schools of thought: behavioral, cognitive, and humanistic. In addition to understanding the behavioral, cognitive, and humanistic interpretations of motivation, it is important for school counselors to be familiar with a fourth force—achievement motivation theory and its implications for motivating student learning.

Albert Bandura and B. F. Skinner are considered to be the two of the most influential behavioral theorists on the topic of motivation. Both Bandura and Skinner were discussed earlier in some detail. To recap, Bandura holds modeling as having a considerable impact on student learning and motivation. In light of Bandura's suppositions, it is paramount that parents, educators, and important others in a student's life serve as positive role models, illustrating the significance of education and learning. Skinner's behavioral learning theory interprets motivation toward learning as a result of reinforcement. That is motivation occurs on the basis of extrinsic rewards and punishments.

The cognitive view of motivation, significantly influenced by Jean Piaget, also discussed earlier in this chapter, contends that learning is motivated when dissonance occurs. That is, when students recognize a gap in their knowledge (e.g., inconsistency between newly presented information and what is already known), they experience cognitive discomfort, or disequilibrium, thus motivating them toward learning in order to regain balance, or equilibrium. Sort of like the impact that this study guide may be having on some of you—hey, just keeping it real.

Human *motivation* is believed to be intrinsic and extrinsic. Piaget emphasized the importance of intrinsic motivation. *Intrinsic motivation* rests within the individual, who derives pleasure from accomplishment of the task itself and an interest in the content. Intrinsic motivation is considered to be the highest level of self-regulated behavior that drives individuals to pursue higher learning and new challenges, even when it is not required (Scheel & Gonzalez, 2007). For example, connecting life to academics often piques students' inquisitiveness and interest in learning, perhaps even unearthing a deeply buried and now unremitting passion that takes up permanent residence in the student.

Extrinsic motivation rests outside of the individual, driven by reward or threat of punishment. School counselors are careful not to overuse extrinsic rewards (e.g., money, treats, praise), which have often been associated with temporary change and may result in the reduction of intrinsic motivation (Deci, Koestner, & Ryan, 2001). School counselors seek to "promote the learning process" (ASCA, 2005, p. 22) through the application of intrinsic/extrinsic motivation within the three developmental domains of personal–social, academic, and career. Research demonstrates that students who "perceive school activities as personally relevant and contributing to their futures are generally more academically motivated" (Scheel & Gonzalez, 2007, p. 55).

Although research to date demonstrates the superiority of intrinsic motivation on student success, extrinsic rewards such as praise have been shown to produce lasting change when provided in an explicit manner. For example, there is sound research to support the positive impact of praise when the praise is specific and spontaneous and attributes accomplishment to effort. Under these conditions, praise has been found to increase motivation and self-esteem in students. Praise matters—even to adults!

INTRINSIC MOTIVATION

You are a school counselor conducting a classroom guidance lesson in a second-grade classroom. One of the activities is to draw a picture. While the students are sharing their completed pictures, you are providing praise as a means of recognition. When you get to Ronnie's picture, which of the following statements would be considered specific praise that attributes success to effort?

■ Ronnie, what a beautiful picture; you worked really hard!
■ Ronnie, you finished your picture so quickly and it is very nice!
■ Ronnie, your picture is so beautiful!
■ Ronnie, your picture has such a beautifully yellow, smiling sun, your hard work really shows!

Abraham Maslow's theory of motivation (1970), a humanistic view of motivation, may well be the single most influential theory of motivation to date. Maslow suggests that the most basic human needs must be met before an individual will actively seek out, or be motivated toward, higher levels of need. The simplicity of Maslow's brilliance is undeniable.

Maslow's hierarchy of needs consists of five levels and is illustrated in Figure 1.4. The most fundamental needs are portrayed at the bottom level with progression up the hierarchy to the top level, which depicts

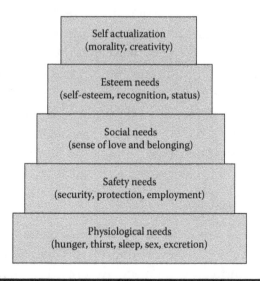

Figure 1.4   Maslow's hierarchy of needs: A theory of motivation.

an individual's need to reach his or her full potential. Maslow's levels in order from bottom to top include physiological needs, safety needs, social needs, esteem needs, and self-actualization. Maslow theorizes that a needs deprivation at any level can result in grave consequences. For example, an imbalance of physiological needs can obviously result in death. An imbalance at the safety level may result in a sense of insecurity that will interfere with motivation toward the next level of need. When social needs and/ or esteem needs are not met, the intensity can be so overwhelming as to ignore more basic physiological and safety needs. In the absence of feelings of acceptance, intimacy, and belonging, individuals may experience extreme loneliness, anxiety, distress, crippling esteem issues, and feelings of inferiority, resulting in clinical depression, anorexia, and a number of other disorders.

We can understand, then, how the development of disorders at these levels prevents further progression on the hierarchy. We can understand, too, how death can be the ultimate result of imbalances at the higher levels when physiological and safety needs are disregarded. The journey to self-actualization, which might be viewed as meeting one's full potential, is an internally driven human development process. Needs at all the levels must be mastered in order to achieve the upper most level of self-actualization.

The implications of Maslow's work are clear with regard to student learning. As educators, we must help to ensure through school and community collaboration, advocacy, counseling, and the promotion of safe and equitable environments, that a student's basic needs are met in order for the student to be available to learn and so that students are motivated to achieve to their full potential.

There are a multitude of family and community issues that may negatively impact a student's need for achievement and their development and functioning, such as abuse, neglect, poor peer relations, divorce, parenting styles, crime, homelessness, and poverty, to name a few. Chapter 2 focuses on counseling theories and school counseling prevention and intervention services delivered by school counselors to mitigate issues related to student development and well-being.

Lastly, achievement motivation theory (McClelland, 1961, 1985) is grounded in the belief that individuals are driven toward success, or avoidance of failure, which is influenced by varying levels of need for achievement and values. Once success is experienced, more success is desired, much like a snowball effect, resulting in self-sustaining desires toward continued achievement (while enhancing self-esteem).

We can understand how the environment in which a student lives and works can either positively or negatively impact a student's need for achievement. Although research is limited, the following areas for attention and training are promising for instilling achievement motivation (i.e., the need for achievement) in both students and adults (McClelland, 1965):

■ Provide clear feedback on performance
■ Accept responsibility for performance
■ Establish realistic and achievable goals
■ Provide opportunities whereby the individual can succeed

MOTIVATING JOHN

John is an academically average eighth-grade student who has not generally demonstrated evident motivation toward school and learning. John's parents encouraged him to enter his graphic design work in a school competition. John received first place among 100 entries. For the first time that John's parents can recall, John was excited about learning more about digital imagery and graphic design. According to achievement motivation theory, what would be John's parents' next-best course of action if they wish to keep John motivated toward learning?

a. Celebrate with John.
b. Work with John's school counselor to get him enrolled in related elective courses for next year (high school) and supporting core courses.
c. Encourage John to enter city- and statewide competitions.
d. Do not get overly excited about John's accomplishment, which might set him up for future disappointment.
e. a, b, and c.
f. b and c.

Chapter 1: Case Conceptualization Responses

Ethical Standards and Legal Considerations

The Same or Different?
The correct response is "c." The school counselor is applying the ethical principle of justice, meeting the unique needs of each student in relation to individual differences.

Confidentiality

Order in the Court, Here Comes the Judge
The school counselor is supported by section A.2.(c, d, and g) of the ASCA *Ethical Standards for School Counselors* (2010), when requesting that the court withdraw the requirement to divulge counseling session information without the consent of Donna, the 15-year-old minor client. Respecting the confidential nature of the school counselor and minor client relationship and the information disclosed by the student in counseling sessions adheres to a critical ethical principle—nonmaleficence. Should the judge order disclosure despite Donna's request, Donna should submit to the court order.

Alliances
Although school counselors are diligent toward establishing alliances and partnerships with parents and make it clear that they understand and respect parental rights, school counselors do not divulge the content of counseling sessions to parents. Instead, school counselors explain to parents the need for confidentiality in counseling sessions for establishing a trusting relationship with their children, reassuring parents that confidentiality will be breached if needed in order to protect the child or others. Also, sharing with parents that you encourage students during counseling sessions to talk to parents about the issues shared in order to promote family communications and to help students to identify and make use of their support systems.

Harm to Self or Others

Thoughts of Suicide
Patrick's reason for suicidal intentions included his "family," which may indicate that his parent(s) are implicated. The school counselor should explore this area more deeply. If Patrick's parents are implicated, many, if not all,

state guidelines would warrant a call to social services instead of a call to Patrick's parents. It would also be important to find out if Patrick was afraid to go home, in which case social services would likely come to the school before the end of the school day to talk with Patrick.

Child Abuse and Neglect

Charlie's World

Since it appears that Charlie's mother knew the truth about what happened to Charlie even though the incident occurred at his father's home, CPS should have been contacted. The school counselor would be wise to directly ask Charlie if he told his mother that his father struck him. If Charlie had said "no" that he did not tell his mother, then asking the student what stopped him from sharing this important information with his mother would be important and could lead to additional critical information (e.g., perhaps both parents are striking the child). Or, perhaps, the child dislikes dad and is not telling the truth in order to stay with mom all the time? In either case, however, contacting CPS based on the existing information provided by the child is warranted and essential—err on the side of child safety. Another important piece of information here is that school counselors and school nurses do not have to see scars, bruises, or cuts in order to report suspected child abuse.

Scope of Practice

Moonlighting

Section F.1 (g) of the ASCA *Ethical Standards for School Counselors* (2010) make it clear that school counselors do not recruit or gain clients for his or her private practice to gain goods or services.

Informed Consent

Sensitive Topics

The nature of the school counselor's classroom guidance lesson, while seemingly not so sensitive based on the title of "Internet safety," contained graphic content that is considered to be sensitive in nature, particularly for some students, depending on past experiences. Although school counselors do not generally need to seek parental consent for classroom guidance lessons that are intended to be educational in nature and afforded to all students school-wide, the topic's content warranted informed consent from parents, or at the very least, the opportunity for the parent to opt the student out of the classroom guidance lesson by providing information about the program and when it was to occur.

Student Records and Counseling Case Notes

When to Say No
The school counselor's actions are appropriate.

IDEA and 504 Plan

The 504 Plan
The school counselor's actions are appropriate and in compliance with the student's 504 plan—a legal document entitling the student to these *accommodations* as agreed upon by a 504 committee that included the parent/legal guardian. The school counselor would want to discuss their intended actions in advance of testing day, to ensure that the teacher and others involved in testing understand the process and placement of students with special needs. The school counselor should also consult with the teacher to understand why the accommodations are not being followed in the classroom and to encourage either going back to the 504 committee if the teacher believes accommodations are no longer needed or to begin compliance. Another point is to be made here: If a student is not being given the small group testing accommodation outlined in a 504 plan or IEP and is given this accommodation on the day of standardized testing, this could adversely impact the student's performance on the test. Nonetheless, the school counselor is acting in the best interest of the student by following the currently active and legally binding 504 plan.

Human Development, Learning, and Motivation

Psychosocial Development

Defiance
Kelly is experiencing the developmental stage of adolescence, possibly struggling with identity crisis by resisting authority and questioning adults in an effort to explore and discover his individual self, thoughts, ideas, and

behaviors. School counselors can help Kelly's parents to understand this sensitive developmental stage and encourage Kelly's self-development by providing answers to Kelly's questions, which helps to reassure Kelly's sense of self and self-worth. Planned family activities and meal times are great mediums for encouraging exploration of Kelly's own thoughts, ideas, and communications.

Eddie's Ego State

According to TA, Eddie is acting in the parent ego state when he says hurtful things to others. Eddie has discovered during the group process that he is treating others in the same critical manner that his father treats him while also realizing how he has internalized those influential communications.

Cognitive Development and Learning Theories

Grandma Will Be Back

Caryn is likely between the ages of 2 and 7 years old. According to Piaget's stages of cognitive development for this age, Piaget would consider Caryn to be in the preoperational stage of development since she views death as reversible.

Dr. Cantholdem

The correct response is "a." The school counselor is attempting to apply negative reinforcement in Dr. Cantholdem's class, that is, removal (negative) of the final exam (stimulus) in an effort to increase attendance (desired behavior/response).

Watching Mommy

The correct response is "c." Starr is learning by observing, which is the foundation upon which both operant conditioning and social learning theory are grounded.

Motivation

Intrinsic Motivation

The correct response is "d." The school counselor's praise is attached to a very specific part of the picture. The school counselor also makes it very clear to Ronnie that his success is due to his hard work or effort.

Motivating John

The correct response is "d." It is important to celebrate the accomplishments of others, particularly those of your children. According to achievement motivation theory, John's parents should continue to fuel this flame ignited in John by connecting work he enjoys to academics and working. Now is a good time to work with the school counselor to establish a high school academic plan that supports John's talent and interest (e.g., digital photography, graphic art, computer science, multimedia, and web technologies). Also, encouraging John to continue to showcase his talent and enter competitions, whether his work places or not, will provide John with additional opportunities to experience successes and to grow from valuable feedback and exposure to others' work.

Chapter 1: Simulation

Early Intervention

Brief Case Description

You, the school counselor, are the chair of the elementary school's early intervention team. The team is meeting today with the parent (biological mother) of a fifth-grade student, Ernesto, who is failing multiple subjects. The teacher also reports a lack of motivation on the part of the student toward school and learning over the past few months. The teacher has not observed any issues socially, that is, the student appears to get along well with peers.

Section A: Early Intervention

What information would be important to obtain at the beginning of the first meeting of the intervention team to help the committee to gain a greater understanding of Ernesto's case?

(Select as many as you consider indicated in this section.)

_____A−1.	Relationship with peers
_____A−2.	Interventions applied previously
_____A−3.	Academic history
_____A−4.	Psychological history
_____A−5.	Subject areas of struggle
_____A−6.	Amount of time spent watching television
_____A−7.	Interests and hobbies
_____A−8.	Information Ernest has shared with teacher and parent
_____A−9.	Amount of time spent on the computer
_____A−10.	Recent changes in Ernesto's life

Section B: Early Intervention

After sharing a variety of information and gaining some insight into Ernesto's situation, the parent reveals that Ernesto has been crying at home for the past 2–3 months while doing his homework. When she asks him what is wrong, he says that the math is just too hard and he does not understand it. Ernesto's mother expressed her concern because although Ernesto has experienced many transitions in his young life and struggled with schoolwork before, she has never seen him cry, which was why she was very happy about this academic intervention meeting at school. Which of the following questions might yield the most beneficial information at this time?

(Select as many as you consider indicated in this section.)

_____B—1.	Has Ernest reported feeling poorly lately?
_____B—2.	What else did Ernesto name as the reason for crying?
_____B—3.	What other behaviors have the teacher and parent noticed in the past 3 months?
_____B—4.	What has changed in the past 3 months?
_____B—5.	How is Ernesto's relationship with his father?
_____B—6.	Does Ernesto currently receive tutoring?

Section C: Early Intervention

Further communication during the intervention meeting reveals that Ernesto has a good relationship with his father, who has been deployed for the past year. Ernesto's father is very involved in Ernesto's life and, generally, is the parent who attends the school functions and helps in the classroom when he is not deployed. Ernesto has shared with his mother that he misses his father very much, although they write to each other often. At this point in the meeting, what would be the best course of action by the committee?

(Select as many as you consider indicated in this section.)

_____C—1.	Have the teacher and parent talk alone
_____C—2.	Request the assistance of an administrator
_____C—3.	Develop an academic intervention plan
_____C—4.	Come up with rewards for Ernesto when he completes his classwork and homework
_____C—5.	Request that Ernesto join the school counseling small group for students with parents/guardians who are deployed
_____C—6.	Table the meeting until Ernesto's father can be present

Section D: Early Intervention

Over the next week, the teacher reports to the parent that Ernesto is beginning to push and yell at fellow students, and he gets angry very easily. The parent and teacher agree to send Ernesto to you for individual counseling sessions. During the first session, Ernesto becomes very emotional and shares that he overheard his mother telling his grandmother that she was planning to divorce his father when he returned to the states. Your most immediate courses of action with Ernesto should be:

(Select as many as you consider indicated in this section.)

_____	D—1.	Discuss divorce
_____	D—2.	Discuss deployment
_____	D—3.	Work on securing a support system
_____	D—4.	Discuss involving his mother
_____	D—5.	Discuss feelings
_____	D—6.	Work on strategies for managing emotions
_____	D—7.	Work on strategies for reducing stress

Section E: Early Intervention

Ernesto comes to your office first thing in the morning immediately after getting off the bus. He is shaking and crying. As you calm Ernesto and sit down to talk, he reveals that his mother has a boyfriend who has been touching him when mom is not around. He has been telling Ernesto that they are just "wrestling." He said that last night, mom's boyfriend came into his bedroom. Ernesto describes the sexual acts. He said he yelled for his mother, but she did not come into the room. What is the most essential course of action?

(Choose ONLY ONE in this section.)

_____	E—1.	Ask questions to determine the mother's knowledge and involvement
_____	E—2.	Contact the local police
_____	E—3.	Call the mother

_____E—4.	Contact CPS	
_____E—5.	Request that the school nurse examine Ernesto	
_____E—6.	Make contact with the father	

Section F: Early Intervention

Two weeks later, you receive a letter in the mail that says the case is "unfounded." The following week, Ernesto comes to your office, again, right off the bus, shaking and crying, saying that his mother's boyfriend did it again. Ernesto's mother shows up at your door with the principal while Ernesto is in your office. Ernesto's mother very calmly taps on your door and walks in. She said she is there to take Ernesto to a doctor appointment and that he was not supposed to get on the bus this morning. You express your concern and ask Ernesto if he would like to tell his mother what he just told me. Crying, he nods his head and tells his mother. Calmly, she said, "Ernesto, you know this is a lie, and this is why the social services people dismissed it." What is the best course of action?

(Select as many as you consider indicated in this section.)

_____F—1.	Call CPS	
_____F—2.	Contact the local police department	
_____F—3.	Make contact with the father	
_____F—4.	Tell the parent that she cannot take Ernesto	
_____F—5.	Call in the boyfriend and talk with all three (i.e., mother, boyfriend, and Ernesto)	
_____F—6.	Be stern with Ernesto and ask him for the truth	

Chapter 1: Simulation Answers

Early Intervention

Brief Case Description

You, the school counselor, are the chair of the elementary school's early intervention team. The team is meeting today with the parent (biological mother) of a fifth-grade student, Ernesto, who is failing multiple subjects. The teacher also reports a lack of motivation on the part of the student toward school and learning over the past few months. The teacher has not observed any issues socially, that is, the student appears to get along well with peers.

Section A: Early Intervention

What information would be important to obtain at the beginning of the first meeting of the intervention team to help the committee to gain a greater understanding of Ernesto's case?

(Select as many as you consider indicated in this section.)

A—1.	Relationship with peers No Peer relations have already been addressed by the teacher sufficiently at this time.
A—2.	Interventions applied previously Yes Knowing what has been done in the past and what has or has not been effective is helpful toward understanding Ernesto's case better. It can also assist in identifying present and future interventions.
A—3.	Academic history Yes Gaining a better understanding of past and present academic functioning provides insight into academic change and patterns over time, specific subjects of challenge and strength, and the scope and magnitude of academic problems.
A—4.	Psychological history Yes It is a good idea to find out what psychological issues, if any, may be a contributing factor when conceptualizing the student's case.

A—5.	Subject areas of struggle Yes Difficulties across subject areas may be indicators of broader issues related to learning disabilities or other special needs (e.g., attention-deficit/hyperactivity disorder). Difficulty in isolated subjects may simply indicate an area of challenge that can be remediated with interventions such as additional study.
A—6.	Amount of time spent watching television No The student's struggles are not limited to home. This may be warranted later depending on other information shared.
A—7.	Interests and hobbies No This information would not be helpful, at this time, in gaining an insight into Ernesto's struggles.
A—8.	Information Ernest has shared with teacher and parent Yes It is very important to hear what the student identifies as the struggle.
A—9.	Amount of time spent on the computer No The student's struggles are not limited to home. This may be warranted later depending on other information shared.
A—10.	Recent changes in Ernesto's life Yes This is particularly important considering the teacher's referral to the intervention team is based on changes in the student's academic-related behavior over the past few months.

Section B: Early Intervention

After sharing a variety of information and gaining some insight into Ernesto's situation, the parent reveals that Ernesto has been crying at home for the past 2–3 months while doing his homework. When she asks him what is wrong, he says that the math is just too hard and he does not understand it. Ernesto's mother expressed her concern because although Ernesto has experienced many transitions in his young life and struggled with schoolwork before, she has never seen him cry, which was why she was very happy about this academic intervention meeting at school. Which of the following questions might yield the most beneficial information at this time?

(Select as many as you consider indicated in this section.)

B—1.	Has Ernest reported feeling poorly lately? Yes It is a good idea to rule out possible medical reasons for Ernesto's lack of motivation toward school and learning.
B—2.	What else did Ernesto name as the reason for crying? Yes Exploring the conversation between Ernesto and his mother may lead to more information about what is particularly related to the student's struggle.
B—3.	What other behaviors have the teacher and parent noticed in the past 3 months? Yes This is particularly important since the teacher indicates the onset of the academic difficulties as beginning a few months ago.
B—4.	What has changed in the past 3 months? Yes It is important to fully explore this area, particularly since the teacher indicates the onset of the academic difficulties as beginning a few months ago.
B—5.	How is Ernesto's relationship with his father? Yes Exploring Ernesto's relationship with others in the family is important, particularly since his father has not been brought up as of yet, and there is much research on the correlation between family interpersonal relations and academic performance.
B—6.	Does Ernesto currently receive tutoring? No Asking about what interventions may have been successful or unsuccessful in the past is appropriate. However, it is not warranted to specifically target tutoring to elicit information that may provide insight into Ernesto's lack of motivation toward school and learning.

Section C: Early Intervention

Further communication during the intervention meeting reveals that Ernesto has a good relationship with his father, who has been deployed for the past year. Ernesto's father is very involved in Ernesto's life and, generally, is the parent who attends the school functions and helps in the classroom when he is not deployed. Ernesto has shared with his mother that he misses his father very much, although they write to each other often. At this point in the meeting, what would be the best course of action by the committee?
(Select as many as you consider indicated in this section.)

C—1.	Have the teacher and parent talk alone
	No
	This is a committee meeting where the parent and teacher are encouraged to talk openly with the committee so that a plan of action can be created with the team's input in the best interest of the student. If the parent and teacher wish to talk after the meeting, this is encouraged.
C—2.	Request the assistance of an administrator
	No
	Administrators hire licensed professionals, who they appoint to interdisciplinary intervention teams to make good informed decisions about the educational needs of students in their absence and, often, outside of their area expertise (e.g, school counselor, school psychologist, nurse).
C—3.	Develop an academic intervention plan
	Yes
	Now is a good time to establish an intervention plan based on current information. The plan will have progress review dates and be redesigned if it is not being effective or if new information is presented and new developments occur.
C—4.	Come up with rewards for Ernesto when he completes his classwork and homework
	No
	Ernesto's academic struggles require more than rewards for work completion. A comprehensive action plan with multiple strategies is warranted. Also, extrinsic motivation has been linked to reducing intrinsic motivation and must be used sparingly and carefully and not in the absence of more concrete, research-supported, individualized academic supports.

C—5.	Request that Ernesto join the school counseling small group for students with parents/guardians who are deployed Yes In addition to an academic intervention plan, Ernesto has clearly indicated a need for involvement in small group counseling with other students who experience issues related to parent deployment.
C—6.	Table the meeting until Ernesto's father can be present No School counselors and other educators meet students' needs in the presence and/or absence of parents. Although parental permission and informed consent are required in some circumstances, this is not the case here.

Section D: Early Intervention

Over the next week, the teacher reports to the parent that Ernesto is beginning to push and yell at fellow students, and he gets angry very easily. The parent and teacher agree to send Ernesto to you for individual counseling sessions. During the first session, Ernesto becomes very emotional and shares that he overheard his mother telling his grandmother that she was planning to divorce his father when he returned to the states. Your most immediate courses of action with Ernesto should be:

(Select as many as you consider indicated in this section.)

D—1.	Discuss divorce No There is no substantial evidence to support the notion that Ernesto's parents are divorcing. Also, if a school counselor wants to meet with elementary students to discuss parental divorce, parental permission is warranted. This is not to say that the counselor should not listen and validate Ernesto's concern about his belief.
D—2.	Discuss deployment No This is not the topic Ernesto has indicated. Not warranted at this time.
D—3.	Work on securing a support system Yes It is important to help Ernesto to identify important others, particularly adults that he can talk to about what he overheard and his beliefs.

D—4.	Discuss involving his mother
	Yes
	It is important to help Ernesto to understand the importance of involving his mother, who can talk to him about what he overheard her say to his grandmother.
D—5.	Discuss feelings
	Yes
	Allow Ernesto to express his thoughts and emotions, and offer validation.
D—6.	Work on strategies for managing emotions
	Yes
	Helping Ernesto to express his emotions appropriately and to develop an understanding that he does not have to be a puppet to his emotions is an important life skill.
D—7.	Work on strategies for reducing stress
	Yes
	Helping Ernesto to understand what he is feeling and to teach him strategies for managing the stress he is experiencing.

Section E: Early Intervention

Ernesto comes to your office first thing in the morning immediately after getting off the bus. He is shaking and crying. As you calm Ernesto and sit down to talk, he reveals that his mother has a boyfriend who has been touching him when mom is not around. He has been telling Ernesto that they are just "wrestling." He said that last night, mom's boyfriend came into his bedroom. Ernesto describes the sexual acts. He said he yelled for his mother, but she did not come into the room. What is the most essential course of action?

(Choose ONLY ONE in this section.)

E—1.	Ask questions to determine the mother's knowledge and involvement
	No
	At this time, it is in the best interest of Ernesto to assume the mother had knowledge of the incident and seek immediate safety for Ernesto.

E—2.	Contact the local police
	No
	The local police will likely request that you contact CPS, or they will contact CPS.
E—3.	Call the mother
	No
	The mother may be involved.
E—4.	Contact CPS
	Yes
	You are suspecting child abuse. Although the suspected sexual abuse is not by a family member, a family member (i.e., the mother) may be involved. The best course of action to protect Ernesto is to call CPS, and they can assess the mother's involvement.
E—5.	Request that the school nurse examine Ernesto
	No
	This can be humiliating for a child or adolescent (even adults), particularly when care is not taken in the manner in which this may be accomplished. You can report suspected abuse without personally seeing any physical signs or in the absence of physical signs.
E—6.	Make contact with father
	No
	The father is deployed. Contact CPS.

Section F: Early Intervention

Two weeks later, you receive a letter in the mail that says the case is "unfounded." The following week, Ernesto comes to your office, again, right off the bus, shaking and crying, saying that his mother's boyfriend did it again. Ernesto's mother shows up at your door with the principal while Ernesto is in your office. Ernesto's mother very calmly taps on your door and walks in. She said she is there to take Ernesto to a doctor appointment and that he was not supposed to get on the bus this morning. You express your concern and ask Ernesto if he would like to tell his mother what he just told me. Crying, he nods his head and tells his mother. Calmly, she said, "Ernesto, you know this is a lie, and this is why the social services people dismissed it." What is the best course of action?

(Select as many as you consider indicated in this section.)

F—1.	Call CPS Yes Again, call CPS with an additional report.
F—2.	Contact the local police department No The mother has every legal right at this point to take Ernesto unless she is intoxicated. If so, you may contact the police so that the student is not put in harm's way (e.g., driving under the influence). Police involvement may be warranted, too, if the parent is behaving in a manner that is disruptive in the school.
F—3.	Make contact with the father No The father is deployed. The mother, too, is custodial parent and, so, can pick up her child for a doctor's appointment.
F—4.	Tell the parent that she cannot take Ernesto No The parent has a legal right to take Ernesto under the current circumstances.
F—5.	Call in the boyfriend and talk with all three (i.e., mother, boyfriend, and Ernesto) No Do not involve the boyfriend, who has no legal rights in the case of Ernesto and is the alleged perpetrator.
F—6.	Be stern with Ernesto and ask him for the truth No Assume Ernesto is giving you the truth.

Chapter 1: Guided Reflection

Identify key events, people, associations, trends, and movements, and discuss their significance in the history of the school counseling profession.

Describe and support the importance of CACREP and NCATE for a school counselor education program.

Explain the purpose of ASCA with regard to the school counseling profession.

Examine and summarize key components of the ASCA National Model.

Identify the three developmental domains. Then, create *one* activity that integrates one ASCA National Standard from *each* of the three domains.

Identify the dual roles of the professional school counselor. Then, summarize the functions inherent in each role.

List critical ethical and legal considerations associated with each construct:

Confidentiality

Confidentiality of counseling-related electronic communication

Harm to self or others

Child abuse and neglect

Scope of practice

Informed consent

Student records and counseling case notes

IDEA and Section 504

Homelessness

Research

Supervision

Match the following theorists to one of the primary categories of human development. It is possible that one theorist could be connected to multiple theories. Then, identify key constructs of the theory, and summarize the theory.

Jean Piaget

Erik Erikson

Lev Vygotsky

Fowler

Freud

Kohlberg

Skinner

Havighurst

Bandura

Support the use of Bloom's taxonomy in school counseling.

Discuss the importance of Marzano's nine instructional strategies, and explain how an understanding of those strategies would be useful in school counseling.

Compare and contrast intrinsic and extrinsic motivation.

Relate the premise of achievement theory by creating a case scenario to illustrate the concept.

Convince me of the importance of Maslow's theory in relation to student learning and motivation. Use one example in your persuasive argument.

Chapter 2

Counseling, Prevention, and Intervention

School counselors engage in prevention and intervention activities for a variety of purposes related to personal–social, academic, and career development. Prevention is aimed at stopping a problem or problematic situation before it starts, while intervention, also referred to as responsive services, occurs post-onset or after a particular problem or disorder has been identified.

ASCA's Position on Prevention and Intervention of Behaviors That Place Students at Risk

Professional school counselors make a significant contribution toward the academic, career and personal/social success of all students. Professional school counselors work in a leadership role with other student services professionals including social workers, psychologists and nurses, in liaison with staff and parents, to provide comprehensive school counseling programs that focus on prevention and intervention of behaviors that place students at risk.

*Position statement adopted 1989–1990;
revised 1993, 1999, 2004*

Prevention can be primary prevention, secondary prevention, and tertiary prevention (Baker & Gerler, 2004). *Primary prevention* focuses on programming for the entire student body using education to ward off any potentially at-risk behavior or problematic situations. *Secondary prevention* is aimed at mediating a specific behavior or problem identified as a potential threat for a specific population deemed at risk. *Tertiary prevention* targets a specific population to reduce or eliminate a problem or behavior that is already occurring. Later in this chapter, all three levels of prevention are illustrated as they relate to substance use, abuse, and addiction. The three levels of prevention are illustrated again in Chapter 7 in relation to consultation and collaboration.

School counselors embrace the proverb, "An ounce of prevention is worth a pound of cure," providing students with primary and secondary preventative programs. The school counselor also provides resources and conducts workshops that spotlight at-risk behaviors and teach parents, teachers, and the community what to look for when identifying students who may be contemplating suicide or homicide or both and who are experiencing depression, severe anxiety, or other debilitating conditions.

However, we must be honest about what we are dealing with here— complex human beings. So, no matter how diligent we are as school counselors, teachers, parents, administrators, and community members, we cannot always head off all problems before onset using primary prevention. For this reason, school counselors engage in tertiary prevention and intervention to meet the needs of students and families using a comprehensive school counseling program.

Comprehensive School Counseling Programs

The ASCA National Model described in Chapter 1 is the only recognized national comprehensive developmental school counseling program (CDSCP) model that defines our profession. Many states have their own comprehensive, developmental models. However, most are designed using ASCA's National Model and Standards (see Appendix III) as a framework, which was the intention of the model; it is understand able that school divisions develop programs based on the varying needs and unique school communities.

Although preventative in design, CDSCPs provide developmentally appropriate prevention and intervention services that support the academic achievement mission of schools. The hallmark of a CDSCP is its focus on providing career, academic, and personal–social development to all students in addition to support services for teachers, parents, administrators, and the community as an integral part of the educational system.

ASCA's Position on Comprehensive School Counseling Programs

Professional school counselors design and deliver comprehensive school counseling programs that promote student achievement. These programs are comprehensive in scope, preventative in design and developmental in nature. *The ASCA National Model: A Framework for School Counseling Programs* outlines the components of a comprehensive school counseling program. The ASCA National Model® brings professional school counselors together with one vision and one voice, which creates unity and focus toward improving student achievement.

Position statement adopted 1988; revised 1993, 1997, 2005

A recent meta-analysis of 150 studies revealed the effectiveness of school counseling interventions across all levels—elementary, middle, and high school. Research shows that school counseling interventions result in cognitive, behavioral, and affective improvements, as well as reductions in disciplinary referrals and enhanced problem-solving abilities (Whiston, Tai, Rahardja, & Eder, 2011). To continue to ride the waves of positive student outcomes, careful consideration is given to the varied needs of each developmental level, school community, and student population.

For example, limited language development at the elementary level calls for the use of more expressive approaches such as *play therapy* to communicate and promote interaction between the student and school counselor. I recall one of the first times I engaged in play therapy as a new elementary school counselor. I was sitting with the smallest most adorable first grader on the planet. She was beaming with pure delight while describing her adventures in collecting fireflies in a jar. As we squeezed and manipulated play doh, I could hear in the background the sound of joyous students singing completely out of harmony, the most beautiful version of "We Are the World" that I had ever heard as they rehearsed for that evening's PTA performance. At that frozen moment in time, I felt as if I was in that wondrous place somewhere between waking and dreaming, when I recall thinking, "And they pay me to do this—suckers!" A few days later, the monsoon hit Utopia! Sparing you the details, I recall thinking (I may have even said it under what little breath I had at that moment), "They don't pay me enough to do this—I'm such a stooge." As you, my esteemed colleagues know, this is the ebb and flow of professional school counseling that we would not trade for a million chocolate frogs.

The majority of the elementary school counselor's time is spent facilitating small groups and classroom guidance lessons and responding to students' immediate needs with responsive services strategies and programming. The elementary student's developmental level limits the application of counseling models to the more active approaches that do not require significant insight and self-awareness. Behavioral approaches are more often used at the elementary level while students are beginning to learn appropriate behavioral patterns and expectations.

Students at the elementary level are more closely supervised and sheltered because of their developmental level. Therefore, parents tend to be more actively involved during the elementary school years. Parents are a fabulous resource, and it is important to find ways to involve parents and make them feel welcomed in the classrooms and schools. The school counselor and parent have a major commonality—you both want the best for their children!

During the middle school years, students demonstrate much-improved language skills and heightened individuality and self-exploration. The need to begin high school academic preparation and postsecondary career decision making increases the demand for individual counseling and individual planning during the middle school years. Although the delivery of individual services increases at the middle school level, the majority of the middle school counselor's time, like the elementary school counselor, is used delivering responsive services, conducting classroom guidance lessons, and facilitating small groups.

Behavioral approaches that may have dominated the school counselor's repertoire at the elementary level are now supplemented with counseling approaches that make use of the more sophisticated cognitive processes developmentally available during adolescence. Adolescents, too, have the relational ability to connect with the counselor and engage in self-analysis. Counseling approaches that encourage responsible living, decision making, and problem solving, and the impact of cognitions on emotions and behavior are particularly beneficial for the adolescent.

Developmentally, elementary and middle school students are in two very different places. Although elementary students generally aim to please, treating us like a celebrity when spotted in the grocery store, the adolescent will make every effort to avoid us, as though we are merely annoying creatures to be endured. Keep in mind the adolescent's unique developmental issues and personal characteristics when selecting counseling approaches and techniques. Developmental constructs are important guides but not all-inclusive, so be careful not to use a cookie-cutter approach based on widely recognized developmental characteristics and milestones of adolescence.

Parent involvement at the middle school level is often dependent upon the adolescent. Developmentally, adolescents are seeking independence from parents, and may, therefore, be apprehensive about having their parent in the school. Nonetheless, school counselors continue to encourage parents to engage in their adolescent's education both at home and at school, while negotiating responsibility and independence. There is an abundance of research linking parent involvement with improved academic achievement and attendance, as well as reduced dropout rates (Wright & Stegelin, 2002).

The high school counselor spends the majority of his or her time with high school students implementing responsive services and providing individual counseling and student planning. Their primary responsibilities include student scheduling, administration of assessments, providing career and college information, and addressing individual student concerns and assisting with the decision-making process, primarily as it relates to school and postsecondary opportunities.

Generally speaking, high school students will tend to view the school counselor as their friend and equal. Some will even attempt to call us by our first names. Keeping boundaries while maintaining an effective school counselor–high school student relationship can be a challenge, particularly for school counselors from a neighboring generation.

Assuming normal developmental levels, high school students are fully capable of understanding abstract concepts, analyzing, synthesizing, and relating. Advanced developmental levels allow school counselors to apply virtually any counseling approach appropriate to the school setting and fitting to the student and the presenting issue.

Parent involvement is generally low compared to the family's involvement at the elementary and middle school levels. Developmentally, high school students have established their independence, for the most part, and are making many of their own decisions. School counselors are called upon to continue to encourage parent involvement at the high school level because research connecting academic achievement to parent involvement pertains to the high school and college years as well as the earlier school years.

THE PARENTS DO NOT TRUST ME

A school counselor is in a professional development program at his school. A teacher sitting beside him is experiencing her first year at the elementary level. The teacher had just served 5 years at the high school level. The teacher is concerned because she is getting so many visits and calls from parents to help in the classroom. The teacher remarks to the school counselor that perhaps she has done something that has caused the parents not to trust her with their children or perhaps they believe because she came from the high school level that she will not be able to relate to the children. How might you respond to the teacher's concerns?

Personal–Social Development

One of the three developmental domains of a CDSCP is *personal–social development*. School counselors help students to overcome personal and social challenges so that they can focus on learning, and develop the personal, social, and emotional fortitude for wellness and to become contributing members of society.

The following topics related to personal–social development are covered by school counselors as a part of a CDSCP at the elementary and secondary school levels. The ASCA National Standards (ASCA, 2005) provide school counselors with competencies and indicators for each of the following areas within the personal–social domain:

- *Self-knowledge*: values, attitudes, beliefs, personal, social, and family roles, behavior, boundaries, personal strengths, self-control, self-esteem
- *Interpersonal skills*: rights, respect for others' views, appreciation of differences and cultural diversity, communication skills, friendship

- *Decision making, problem solving, and goal setting*: consequences, coping skills, alternative solutions, resources, conflict resolution, peer pressure, perseverance
- *Personal safety*: rules, laws, individual rights, inappropriate contact, when and how to seek adult help, manage stress/life events, make healthy choices

School counselors work collaboratively with other professionals within and outside of the school system to provide optimal services that place the safety and well-being of children first while supporting academic achievement. School counselors may work with the *school psychologist, school social worker, school nurse*, special education teachers, resource teachers, and the 504 committee, early intervention team, and child study team to effectively meet the personal and social needs of students.

Collaboration with outside agencies is a growing trend in today's schools. School counselors often partner with community mental health agencies to provide optimal services to students and families. School counselors provide parents with information related to psychosocial development and community resources that include specialized counseling, psychological and psychiatric services, social services, childcare services, and support groups.

School counselors implement interventions and consult with teachers and parents to provide strategies for implementation at home and in the classroom. School counselors assist students in identifying support systems to combat unhealthy levels of stress and reduce feelings of isolation. Section A.1 of the ASCA *Ethical Standards for School Counselors* (ASCA, 2010) encourages school counselors to "consider the involvement of support networks valued by the individual student" (p. 1).

School counselors, who partner with families, teachers, and community members, are better able to identify supports that strengthen protective factors and enhance resilience, empower students, and help students to discover unique personal strengths (Bryan & Henry, 2008). Developing students' resilience enables them to overcome threats to educational success and to successfully engage life's challenges. CDSCPs that include interventions that place responsibility for success within the student are educational, empowering, and help develop coping skills that can be accessed into adulthood (Gilchrist-Banks, 2009).

School counselors assist teachers, parents, and administrators in developing behavioral interventions and classroom management strategies. School counselors do not engage in the discipline of students (ASCA, 2005).

ASCA's Position on Discipline

The professional school counselor works with school personnel and other stakeholders to establish and maintain policies
that encourage appropriate behavior so schools can be a safe
place where teaching and learning can be effectively accomplished. Such policies promote the use of the school counselor as
a resource person with expertise in the area of discipline plans.
The professional school counselor is not a disciplinarian.

Position statement adopted 1989; revised 1993,
1999, 2001, 2007

Personal–social needs at the elementary level primarily revolve around
the child's egocentric nature, adjustment to the concept of attending school,
establishing a sound academic, personal–social, and career development
foundation, and the transition to middle childhood. Personal–social programming is generally focused on cooperation, taking turns, making friends,
sharing, character education, caring, resolving conflict, and helping.

Classroom guidance and small groups are the primary methods of program
delivery at the elementary level. These systems-focused delivery methods are
ideal during middle childhood for promoting positive peer interactions and
healthy personal development in a social context that is facilitated and closely
monitored by the school counselor. The development of social skills and positive peer relationships during middle childhood enhances the likelihood of
positive peer relationships during adolescence, which has been identified as
critical to prosocial personality development (Schellenberg, 2000).

The middle school years are a time of intense emotions associated with
rapid physical changes and identity development. The adolescent is no longer a child, but not yet an adult, growing away from the family of origin and
into the family of man. Peer relationships are extremely influential in the
development of identity, self-esteem, and positive interpersonal functioning.

Responsive to this challenging developmental stage, the personal–social
domain of a comprehensive school counseling program focuses programming on the transition to middle school from elementary school and from
middle school to high school. The school counseling program also focuses
on dealing with emotions, bullying, problem solving, responsible decision
making, conflict resolution, interpersonal relationships, violence, and

Internet safety. In addition, school counselors may include prevention programming that addresses teen dating, teen pregnancy, sexually transmitted disease, and chemical dependency.

Personal–social programming and counseling services for high school students are a continuation of the areas of focus noted for middle school students. High school counselors continue to focus on a successful transition into high school from middle school, providing services for incoming freshmen to promote personal–social and academic success in high school.

Transitioning

I do not know who said that "the one constant in our lives is change," but I totally agree with this shrewd proclamation that has earned just attention. Change does not sit idle, and the vast number of personal, social, physical, and development changes that take place, particularly in the lives of children and adolescents, can be anxiety producing. Even welcomed change upsets homeostasis with some discomfort experienced until balance is regained. Helping clients to change, and to work through change, is the heart of counseling.

Transitioning has been conceptualized in a variety of ways. There are, however, three common points of agreement among specialists in transitioning theory: (1) transition involves grieving the loss of the old and finding stability in the new, (2) successful transition is generally achieved when approached intentionally and with an understanding of the associated challenges, and (3) transition is more likely to succeed when a support system is in place to aid in overcoming challenges and adjusting to the new (Turner, 2007).

Transitions, both welcome and unwelcome, have been identified as a source of stress for children and adolescents—and adults. Developing the attitudes and skills for successful transitioning at an early age is critical to continued health and well-being during periods of change. Framing the experience of transition and change (and life!) as largely dependent upon our attitudes helps student to understand that they control the process and outcome of their internal experiences and are victims or victors of their attitudes.

School counselors begin by helping students to normalize change, that is, to view change as a necessary characteristic of life. School counselors offer programming that identifies and helps students to develop competencies essential to successful transitions and continued growth, including support systems, self-care, stress management, decision making, problem solving, communication, and positive attitude.

School counseling programs and activities include transition programs for those students, who are entering middle school and high school. Successful transitioning programs invite parent participation, highlight positive aspects of the new setting, underscore increased freedoms and choices associated with maturity, and address the following frequently identified fears of students entering secondary school (Akos, 2002):

- Bullying by older students
- New rules
- Forgetting locker combinations
- Switching classes
- Getting lost
- Not succeeding academically
- Increased responsibility
- Understanding class scheduling

Transition programs also provide students with faculty, staff, and school information as well as a map of the school. This information helps students to identify who to go to and how to get there. New students are often reluctant to ask for help. For this reason, during the transition program, school counselors present the concept of asking for help as a positive and strength-building characteristic, reminding students that even the greatest of men recognize and confess that "no man is an island" (Donne, n.d.). School counselors collaborate with students to establish and coordinate peer-mentoring programs for transfer students. This is particularly helpful for students who are coming from culturally and linguistically different backgrounds.

School counselors encourage parents and teachers to look for maladaptive behaviors or behaviors that are not typical for the student (personal, emotional, social, and academic), which may be indicators of unsuccessful transitioning. School counselors work individually with students who are experiencing transition difficulties using a variety of counseling techniques and approaches, as well as family and peer support systems.

Crisis Management

School counselors include *crisis* management as part of a comprehensive school counseling program. School counselors prepare for the unexpected, defining and documenting their roles during student, family, and school-wide crisis situations. School counselors provide information and conduct workshops for faculty addressing appropriate responses and intervention during a human crisis (e.g., accidental death, suicide and homicide, terrorism) and natural disaster (e.g., hurricane, earthquake, tornado).

ASCA's Position on Crisis/Critical Incident Response

The professional school counselor is a leader in the successful development and implementation of a response plan with respect to the needs of both students and staff during any school- or student-related incident and serves primarily as an advocate for students' safety and well-being. The professional school counselor is a pivotal member of a school's/school district's crisis/critical incident response team collaborating with other school staff members to implement a comprehensive response to any such incident.

Position statement adopted 2000; revised 2007

School divisions generally have established crisis-management plans mandated by state/local policy that clearly define the chain of command, school personnel roles, collaboration with community services (e.g., fire, police, medical), media and community responding guidelines, and follow-up procedures. Schools also have crisis-management teams that involve the school counselor. The school counselor provides guidance to the committee with regard to meeting the psychological and emotional needs of students, faculty, and parents during a crisis.

In times of crisis, school counselors occupy an important role that includes leadership, collaboration, and advocacy. School counselors' response to crisis can be summarized in three significant, systematic steps: (1) assess students' level of risk, (2) stabilize the situation with counseling intervention, and (3) follow-up to assess well-being and determine the need for further intervention (Kerr, 2009).

When evaluating level of risk, school counselors quickly assess for further threat (physical or psychological) and identify immediate security methods and coping mechanisms. During the process of crisis counseling, school counselors establish a trusting and positive therapeutic relationship in what is often a very limited amount of time. Using basic attending skills (e.g., active listening, *paraphrasing, summarizing*), school counselors foster a safe climate that invites students to identify and express emotions and thoughts and make sense of the traumatic experience. School counselors aid students in identifying copying strategies by exploring past coping successes and promising support systems. The very nature of crisis, and unexpected tragic event, calls for diligence on the part of the school counselor to identify students and members of the school community who may be grieving, traumatized, and experiencing suicide ideation. Suicide assessment is discussed in Chapter 4.

When working with grieving children and adolescents, it is important to understand (1) the child's developmental level, (2) the child's level of maturity, (3) the family's values, perceptions, and rituals related to death and burial, and (4) the factors surrounding the death (sudden, anticipated, relationship). School counselors also look for behaviors that are out of the ordinary and impact on academic, social, and emotional functioning. It is also important to be familiar with the stages of grieving (i.e., denial/isolation, anger, bargaining, depression, acceptance) to identify the difference between the normal grieving process and possible post-traumatic stress (Kubler-Ross, 1969).

Often, parents consult with the school counselor about whether or not to allow their child to participate in a funeral. After fully explaining to a child what a funeral entails, allowing the child to attend based on his or her level of maturity and desire to attend provides the child with an understanding of a customary practice and the opportunity to grieve, say good-bye, and experience closure.

Postcrisis follow-up and the provision of resources are critical because stress reactions are not always immediate (Kerr, 2009). Follow-up is recommended at intervals (e.g., 1 month, 4 months, crisis anniversaries). Follow-up after a crisis will help to identify those students who are experiencing symptoms of post-traumatic stress, prolonged grief-loss reactions, and/or unresolved issues that require more intense counseling services.

KYLEIGH'S MOTHER

Kyleigh, a second grader, is meeting with the school counselor due to the death of her mother, which occurred during a natural catastrophe 1 week ago. Kyleigh has been uncharacteristically quiet since the tragedy. What might be your primary focus during this first session with Kyleigh?

a. Reassuring Kyleigh that everything will be okay
b. Assisting Kyleigh in identifying and expressing her feelings appropriately
c. Sharing your own experience with death
d. Having Kyleigh recall the experience

Dropout

Dropping out of school is a national issue of growing concern. Recent data from the U.S. Census Bureau (2008) reports 4%–6% dropout rates nationally. It is essential that school counselors continue to act as programming pit bulls to reclaim the graduation march for our nation's challenged students— pomp and circumstance for all!

ASCA's Position on Dropout Prevention

Professional school counselors at all levels make a significant, vital and indispensable contribution toward the mental wellness of "at-risk" students. School counselors work as a member of a team with other student service professionals including social workers, psychologists and nurses, in liaison with staff and parents, to provide comprehensive developmental counseling programs for all students including those identified as being potential dropouts or at-risk.

Position statement adopted 1989–1990; revised 1993, 1999

Understanding the causes of dropout is the first step to developing creative programming to keep our students in school. The risk factors identified for dropping out of school are as diverse as the student body and become more salient predictors of dropout when found in combination. These risk factors, which can be indicators of dropout as early as elementary school, include poor academic performance; negative attitude toward school; hostile school climate; low parental involvement; low student involvement; behavioral problems; poor teacher–student relationships; low socioeconomic status; educational levels of parents; and personal, social, and emotional issues (Suh & Suh, 2007).

Addressing these barriers to graduation requires programming that (1) supports student and parent involvement in the school, (2) enhances academic performance with supplemental knowledge and skill building, (3) promotes a more encouraging school climate, (4) links school to career and life after high school, (5) provides counseling services to mediate life's challenges, (6) mediates behavioral problems, (7) addresses the needs of students in financially challenged homes, and (8) focuses on early intervention. Programming to keep students in school requires collaboration within and outside of the school with a variety of stakeholders.

School Violence and Bullying

Safe and prosocial school environments are essential to academic success and student safety. However, aggressive student interactions often permeate a school's culture and create hostile learning environments that stifle the academic productivity and success of students (Guetzloe, 1999; Olweus, 1995; Schellenberg, 2000).

ASCA's Position on Bullying, Harassment, and Violence Prevention

Professional school counselors recognize the need for all students to attend school in a safe, orderly and caring environment. To promote this type of environment, comprehensive school counseling programs include violence-prevention activities and programs fostering a positive school climate.

Position statement adopted 1994, 2000; revised 2005

School counselors seek to implement programs that foster a positive climate and optimal learning environment that respects diversity to promote peaceable schools. One of the most widely used programs for promoting peaceable schools and prosocial behavior is character education. *Character education* involves, first and foremost, modeling. Educators impact the character development of their students through their own attitudes, expectations, and behaviors. Character education involves shaping students thoughts, emotions, and behaviors to reflect core values of caring citizenship, which may include characteristics such as responsibility, respect, courage, perseverance, fairness, trust, integrity, honesty, cooperation, empathy, and acceptance.

ASCA's Position on Character Education

Professional school counselors endorse and support character education programs. The professional school counselor promotes the inclusion of character education in the school curriculum and takes an active role in promoting character traits within the comprehensive school counseling program.

Position statement adopted 1998, revised 2005

Another approach that is often used in the schools is *conflict resolution*. ASCA calls for conflict resolution as a vital component of a comprehensive school counseling program. *Peer mediation*, a *peer-helping* program, is a form of conflict resolution that aids students in resolving interpersonal problems peacefully. Peer mediation provides students with a safe place in which to resolve interpersonal conflict peacefully while learning effective communication, conflict resolution, problem solving, appreciation for differences, and relationship building.

ASCA's Position on Conflict Resolution Programs

The professional school counselor recognizes the need for all students to have access to a conflict-resolution program that is part of a comprehensive developmental school counseling program. Such programs foster a positive campus climate and promote lifelong skills enabling individuals to resolve conflict in a positive manner. Comprehensive conflict-resolution programs combine peer mediation, the incorporation of conflict-resolution principles into the academic curriculum and the education of all members of the school community in applying methods for alleviating conflicts.

Position statement adopted 2000

Research identifies a link between peer mediation programs and school-wide violence reduction. Development of students' knowledge and skills related to conflict resolution strategies and prosocial behaviors paves the way for increased academic performance (Bell et al. 2000; Schellenberg, Parks-Savage, & Rehfuss, 2007).

Bullying, too, often unresponsive to peer mediation and conflict resolution, poses a threat to school safety and to the physical and emotional well-being of others. Let us not forget that bullies are victims unto themselves, requiring intervention that disrupts the self-destructive path and aids in charting a new course. School counselors work with teachers, administrators, and law enforcement officers to create programs that deliver strong anti-bullying messages using everyday examples of the paralyzing atrocities and life-destroying impacts of bullying on named children and adolescents. School counselors educate students regarding bullying and teach strategies for dealing with bullies, such as maintaining a confident demeanor; making eye contact; delivering strong, assertive, nonemotional communication to the bully; and confiding in a trusted adult.

Internet Safety and Cyberbullying

Advances in technology have heightened the need for school counselors to educate students on issues related to Internet safety, *cyberbullying*, and the misuse of cell phones. Programming pertaining to Internet and cell phone use and safety should include Internet addictions, illegal download of music and clipart, stalking and luring, access to illicit drugs, inappropriate chat rooms, invasion of privacy, safeguarding personal information, identity theft, sexting (e.g., the texting/transmission of sexually explicit language/materials), the misuse of personal pictures and information, and school policies pertaining to cyberbullying during and outside of school (Chibbaro, 2007).

ASCA recommends that school counselors provide educators and parents with guidelines for the appropriate use of technology by students, for example, keeping computers (with electronic filtering and monitoring programs installed) in a room that is clearly visible by responsible adults; strongly encouraging children and teens to discuss anything they have received that is confusing, uncomfortable, or frightening; and establishing rules for the use of available technologies. School counselors also arm parents with information about how to recognize "secretive behaviors surrounding the computer" (p. 67), such as immediate screen switching and acronym deciphering (Chibbaro, 2007). It is also critical that parents understand and relay to their children and adolescents the ethical and legal implications of electronic actions and words and the dangers of giving out personal information and photographs in an electronic environment that is often permanent and irreversible.

ASCA's Position on Internet Safety

ASCA recognizes both the democratic rights of all citizens in regard to freedom of speech and access to information. These freedoms must be balanced with the need for appropriate guidance, protection and security through students' development stages. Professional school counselors advise parents and school personnel in determining age-appropriate materials and resources for children. This important information may be disseminated as part of the school's comprehensive developmental school counseling program. Professional school counselors are cognizant of the benefits of accessing programs and materials for students as well as the need to ensure the safety of students with regard to online threats, privacy, access to personal information and consent.

Position statement adopted 2000

School counselors include cyberbullying as an essential topic when discussing Internet safety. Cyberbullying is a disturbing issue of grave concern with dire consequences. Cyberbullies often perceive themselves to be invisible, believing that their communications are anonymous and that they will not be caught or held responsible in cyberspace. Ensuring that students understand that all communications online can be tracked may have an immediate and lasting impact on the reduction of cyberbullying.

It is also important that students understand that cyberbullying is considered by law to be a criminal offense when it (1) involves repeated or excessive harassment with or without threats, (2) encourages/suggests suicide, (3) threatens harm to a person or their property, (4) threatens to commit a crime, and/or (5) posts private information in a public forum (Willard, 2006). Actions that can be taken by students to defend against cyberbullies include blocking the sender, avoiding chat rooms where the attacks occur, saving and sharing communications with parents and law enforcement, and changing passwords/accounts. As with other types of bullying, students are encouraged to send a strong, assertive, nonemotional message to the bully along with the action to be taken if the messages continue.

WILL I GO TO JAIL?

Steven, a high school junior, comes to you very upset because he was angry with his best friend. He said that he sent a nude picture of his girlfriend to his best friend's cellphone because his friend did not believe that Steven's girlfriend would ever take her clothes off for him. His friend spread the picture around, and someone loaded it to Facebook, and his girlfriend's parents called the police. He said, "It isn't fair—she said I could take the picture, and I'm not the one who spread the picture around school or created the Facebook page." The student asks, "Will I go to jail"? If you were Steven's school counselor, how would you respond?

Substance Use, Abuse, Addiction

Addiction can be categorized as process addiction and substance addiction (Capuzzi & Stauffer, 2012). Process addiction refers to behavioral patterns, and addictions may include gambling, shopping, Internet, eating, working, sex, and more. Substance addiction refers to the ingestion of mood-altering substances such as alcohol and other drugs, including anabolic steroids, which is a growing concern in high school athletic circles.

There are many models, noted below, that attempt to explain the etiology of addiction (Capuzzi & Stauffer, 2012). Psychological models look to cognitive-behavioral, psychodynamic, personality, and learning models for explanations for addiction. Sociocultural models suggest that addiction is contextual and related to the social and cultural environment in which an individual interacts. The disease model holds the addiction as an incurable and progressive disease that one is powerless over, once contracted. Family models suggest that addiction is behaviorally based, with the family interactions and members reinforcing the addiction, either consciously or unconsciously. Biological models hold genetics and our brain's chemical reactions as creating predispositions to addiction. Finally, the moral model holds addiction as a matter of personal choice. As a society, we have now, for the most part, rejected the idea that addiction is the result of immorality. At the present time, our society and our public health system embraces a multicausal model that considers the interaction of the individual, environment, and the substance or process.

School counselors do not treat addiction. In the school setting, the primary emphasis is on understanding addiction, identifying and referring students who may be suffering from addiction, and providing primary prevention, secondary prevention, and tertiary prevention programming described earlier in this chapter and illustrated below. School counselors develop primary prevention programs to prevent drug use. School counselors also coordinate existing nationally recognized campaigns such as Just Say No and Drug Abuse Resistance Education (DARE) programs within the schools. To date, there is no significant research to support the effectiveness of the Just Say No and DARE programs (Birkeland, Murphy-Graham, & Weiss, 2005).

Founded in 1983, the DARE program is the most widely used drug prevention program in our schools today. The DARE program's mission is to provide students with skills and education to live drug and violence free. The program is focused on abstinence from drug use and is generally delivered by law enforcement officers during the school day with a curriculum that is sequentially designed for grades K–12. The program now offers community-based programs as well to promote parent involvement and to provide after school activities and support for families.

The Just Say No to Drugs campaign was championed by then First Lady Nancy Reagan in the 1980s in response to the War on Drugs movement. This primary prevention program, grounded in the prevention efforts of the National Institutes of Health, enlists the support of other nationally recognized organizations such as the Girl Scouts of America and the Kiwanis Club. The program is intended to educate and inoculate students on the negative impact of drug use and to provide students with skills for resisting peer pressure and drug experimentation.

School counselors collaborate with local police officers, community agencies, and other school personnel (e.g., school nurses, coaches, and school psychologists) to implement a variety of primary prevention strategies aimed at promoting healthy and drug-free lives. Primary prevention may also include parent and teacher education aimed at recognizing the signs and symptoms of addiction and resources for treatment. In-home drug testing is fast becoming a commonly practiced strategy in the homes of our families, aiding parents in early identification of *substance use* and *substance abuse*.

School counselors also implement secondary prevention strategies that target students who may be at risk for substance use, abuse, and addiction. School counselors are in an ideal position to identify students who are already demonstrating negative attitudes and risky behaviors. Like in-home drug testing, in-school drug testing is a growing strategy in today's schools, resulting in early treatment for students who test positive. There are legal considerations, including parental consent, and schools will need community support before implementing drug-screening strategies. Secondary prevention programs may include small groups on topics related to living responsibly, health and *wellness*, the effects of drug consumption, healthy choices, and Internet addiction.

Recognizing the signs and symptoms of addiction is essential to tertiary prevention, which involves identifying students who are already ingesting chemical substances and are displaying behavior patterns associated with process addiction. Signs and symptoms of addiction include neglecting responsibilities, increased tolerance, preoccupation with the substance or behavior, engaging in risky behaviors such as stealing and driving under the influence, changes in levels of social interaction or a change of friends, abandonment of hobbies and activities that use to be enjoyable, mood swings, paranoia, irritability, interference with daily functioning (e.g., sleep, diet, hygiene), and a general change in what was considered typical behavior for the individual.

THE BEST FOOTBALL PLAYERS

You are the high school counselor at Crossroads High School. The physical education (PE) teacher has asked you to meet with a group of six male students on the football team because he overheard them chatting about giving anabolic steroids a try to build muscles and be the best football players on the team. The PE teacher said he already spoke to the parents of the students, who are in agreement with the students meeting with the school counselor. How should you proceed, and is this an example of primary, secondary, or tertiary prevention?

Once identified, school counselors work with parents and community agencies to secure appropriate counseling services for the student and family. Some schools now have student assistance counselors, discussed in Chapter 1, who collaborate with community agencies to help students with substance abuse and other addictive behaviors.

Divorce

Divorce is a growing trend in our society. Nearly 1.5 million children and adolescents are affected by parental divorce each year in the United States, where the divorce rate is the highest in the world (Haine et al. 2003).

Generally speaking, research suggests that children of divorce adjust well if divorce is accompanied by amiable parental interactions, quality parenting, and reassurance of continued contact after separation and divorce and if the divorce does not substantially impact lifestyle (e.g., finances, discipline, transitions). Other characteristics that are linked to positive adjustment after divorce include level of resiliency and preexisting personal assets (discussed in greater detail in the "Strengths-Based Counseling" section of this chapter). Age and gender, too, are associated with the level of adjustment for children of divorce; however, the link is largely contextual.

On the other hand, compared to children and adolescents from intact healthy functioning families, children of divorce often demonstrate a variety of issues (DeLucia-Waack & Gerrity, 2001; Peris & Emery, 2004; Ruschena, Prior, Sanson, & Smart, 2005). These issues include

■ Sadness and depression
■ Anxiety and fear
■ Rejection

- Anger
- Insecurity
- Drug and alcohol use
- Misbehavior
- Feelings of grief and loss
- Poor academic performance
- Interpersonal problems
- School dropout

The issues listed above can last well into adulthood. Children of divorce generally achieve less education and earn less income than those from intact families (Amato & Cheadle, 2005).

School counselors help children and adolescents to adjust to divorce with a variety of interventions that build protective factors and resilience and allow students to express and work through emotions, share experiences, resolve self-blame, and accept divorce. Small group counseling for children of divorce provides mutual support and allows students to normalize divorce (Corey, 2008). Also, encouraging students to engage in positive school and community activities and build relationships with trusted adults outside of the home helps to build protective factors. School counselors assist parents by providing community resources, including family counseling services, and the research noted above depicts the factors that have been associated with positive adjustment for children of divorce.

Parenting Style

Parenting is not instinctual but requires specific knowledge and skills to raise a well-adjusted adult and contributing member of society. Parenting style has a profound impact on child and adolescent development.

The four widely recognized parenting styles with which school counselors are knowledgeable are authoritative (collaborative, respectful, reasonable consequences), authoritarian (strict, demanding, harsh punishment), permissive (lenient, indulgent), and uninvolved (detached, neglectful). The authoritative parenting style has been found to be the most beneficial to the child, resulting in a well-adjusted, confident, self-controlled, and academically successful child. Inconsistency, ignoring, and intimidation associated with the permissive, uninvolved, and authoritarian parenting styles, respectively, have been linked to the development of emotional, social, psychological, behavioral, and academic problems (Rothrauff, Cooney, & Shin An, 2009).

School counselors provide parental consulting and parenting workshops identifying different parenting styles and the impact of each on child development. Additionally, they help parents to realize that each sibling is an individual and so what works for one may not work for another. Also, they help parents to realize that a child's performance is not an indicator of self-worth and that mistakes are a part of learning and misbehavior a part of childhood, and they prepare the parent for the realities of parenthood. Parenting is a job—likely the most difficulty and high-stress job on the planet.

Career Development

Like the personal–social domain, *career development* standards and student competencies guide school counselors in creating activities that are career specific and developmentally appropriate. The following topics related to career development are covered by school counselors as a part of a CDSCP at the elementary and secondary school levels. The ASCA National Standards (ASCA, 2005) provide school counselors with competencies and indicators for each of the following areas within the career development domain:

- *Career awareness*: nontraditional occupations; knowledge of interests, skills, and abilities; decision making and goal setting; working cooperatively; knowledge of career search information systems and strategies
- *Employment readiness*: time management, resume writing, employability skills, knowledge of workplace, work ethic, employee–employer rights, dependability, responsibility, punctuality
- *Career planning, orientation, preparation*: course selection; relating personal interest, skills, and abilities to career choice; knowledge of career planning process; occupational classifications; use of Internet and career information systems; relationship between work, economy, and society
- *Career goals*: knowledge and skills to establish and achieve career goals, knowledge of education/training required for career choice, relationship between educational achievement and career, relationship between work and personal satisfaction/lifestyle, equity and access, function of job shadowing/internships

There are three fundamental differences in career development at each level of K–12 education: career awareness, career exploration, and career planning. At the elementary level, school counselors promote career awareness. *Career awareness* activities might include exposing students to diverse occupations through career day/week guided activities. These activities might include speakers from a variety of occupations, displays of books in the library dedicated to diverse occupations, dressing like a favorite occupation, and mystery career games whereby students guess the occupation based on a description. Any activity that supports the student's curiosity and develops their sense of self and the world of work is appropriate at the elementary level.

Career exploration is the focus at the middle school level, while *career planning*, also referred to as career orientation or career preparation, is the focus at the high school level. Secondary school counselors engage students in career development activities that typically combine counseling, education, and the administration and interpretation of *career development inventories* (e.g., interests, skills, work values). This comprehensive approach to career development at the secondary level emphasizes the importance of going beyond trait and factor theory to understand the whole person and explore the many internal and external variables that influence a student's career decision making.

Delivering effective career development programs in the schools necessitates that the school counselors apply *career counseling* and *career development* theories and strategies; stay abreast of relevant legislation, research, trends, and resources; identify and administer interest, values, and skills inventories, and other career-related assessments; and understand the influences on career development.

Influences on Career Decision Making

Helping students to identify personally satisfying career paths requires the application of career development theory, techniques, sound counseling practices, and information. School counselors blend career counseling, assessment, and career education to aid students in (1) understanding and preparing for transition into the world of work, (2) selecting a career path that will be meaningful and satisfying, and (3) ultimately becoming productive members of society.

School counselors engage in career counseling with a sound understanding of the diverse influences on career choice. School counselors aid students in understanding these influences to make informed decisions about their future. Career choice influences include, but are not limited to, family of origin, access to career information, socialization (beliefs and values), personality (including multiple intelligences discussed in Chapter 6), parent's employment and educational status, early work experiences, economy, socioeconomic status, gender, ethnicity, and development level of functioning.

Research indicates that children begin to limit their career aspirations as early as first grade based on gender, ethnicity, race, and social class (Porfeli, Hartung, & Vondracek, 2008). For example, let us consider the impact of socialization on career choice with regard to gender. Traditionally, women have been guided toward occupations such as teacher, cosmetologist, and nurse, while males have been encouraged to pursue careers such as doctor, mechanic, and scientist.

For this reason, school counselors are now developing programs that educate students with regard to these historical trends, who may not realize how early social interactions have influenced their career decision making. As a result, males are beginning to pursue careers in nursing, accounting, and other occupations that have historically been occupied by females. Females are beginning to pursue careers in science and math and in occupations that have traditionally been dominated by males. There is now a growing trend toward promoting *nontraditional occupations* at every level of education.

In addition to promoting nontraditional career paths, school counselors promote a variety of postsecondary career paths. Our society has come to realize that college is not for everyone and that because a student does not want to attend college it does not mean that the student will not have a successful and fully satisfying career. Student's career choices may take them on a journey down one of five paths after high school: apprenticeship, college (2 or 4 year), technical/trade school, employment, or military service. Well, there is always couch-warming and channeling surfing—oh, how parents will rejoice!

Career Development Theory and Career Counseling

School counselors apply career development theory to help students make sense of their experiences and how those experiences influence career decision making. Career counseling grounded in sound theoretical principles, offers education, insight, and alternatives during the process of career planning. Like counseling theories, there are a multitude of career development and career counseling theories, models, and approaches. This section highlights the major theories, theorists, and key constructs. Figure 2.1 is provided to promote the learning and recall of this material.

In general, there are two camps to consider when conceptualizing career development theories (Savickas, 2000): objectivist and constructivist. The objectivist school of thought may also be referred to as the traditional ideology, the positivistic approach, or the established theoretical view, depending upon the company of career theorists you are keeping. The objectivist

Objectivist ideology (traditional) Traits and work environment match Administers assessment instruments Objective reasoning and/or measurement are key	Constructivist ideology (emerging models) Socially constructed, dynamic, ever-changing Individuals' interactions and experiences Subjective intention and perspectives in context
[a]Frank Parson: Trait and factor Matches individual traits to job factors Focuses on three-step process: understanding self, diverse occupational characteristics, and relationship of the two	**[b]David Tiedeman: Career construction** Career choice based on evolving ego/self-development—total cognitive development and processes of decision making Focuses on differentiation (evaluating self and self in the world) and integration (find congruence in world of work); parallels Erikson's stages of development
John Holland: Typology Individuals express self through career Focuses on assigning individuals and work environments into six categories	**Larry Cochran: Narrative** Individual "tells story" about past and present career experiences and related interactions; counselor assists in creating future career story Focuses on phases, episodes, plots: making meaning out of narrative, enacting the role, and crystallizing a decision
Donald Super: Life span-life space Career choice is an expression of self concept and changes across life span Focuses on five major life stages, career maturity, career determinants, role of self-concept	**Mark Savickas: Narrative** Individual "tells story" about past and present career experiences and related interactions; counselor assists in creating future career story Focuses on four areas: vocational personality (uses Holland's typology), developmental tasks (use Super's life stages), adaptability, life themes (mattering)
Linda Gottfredson: Self-creation Career choice based on social-psychological self, created by heredity-biological factors Focuses on self-concept, cognitive maps, circumscription, and compromise	
Anne Roe: Personality development Career choice based on psychological needs derived from parent–child relationships Focuses on relating six attitudes of parent–child interactions to specific occupational groups	**Duane Brown: Values-based** Work values influence occupational choice Focuses on the importance of cultural values and differences
Susan Phillips: Developmental-relational Career choice based on relationships with important others—family, friends, teachers Focuses on two themes: actions of others and self-directedness	**John Krumboltz: Social learning** Career choice based on cumulative interactions and experiences with people and environment Focuses on behavior and cognitions; teaching career decision making techniques

[a]Parson is considered father of vocational guidance.
[b]Tiedeman is considered the author/engineer of the first post-modern career theory.

Figure 2.1 Career development theories: objectivist and constructivist schools of thought.

ideology, as the name implies, is an objective and measurable construct that matches individuals to occupations based on personality and occupational work environment. The constructivist school of thought, also known in certain circles as the emerging postmodern ideology, views career development as an ever-changing, contextual, and dynamic process that is driven by personal perceptions, interactions, and experiences. Figure 2.1 places the variety of career development theories in the respective categories to aid you in the cognitive organization of the many career theories.

The objectivist school of thought began with Frank Parsons. Parsons (1909), who became known as the father of vocational guidance, developed the trait and factor theory, which matches individual traits (e.g., aptitudes, interests, and abilities) to job factors. The trait and factor theory has dominated the field of career development since its inception some one hundred years ago.

John Holland's (1966, 1985) typology is an example of a trait and factor approach that is still widely used today. Holland's constructs include six broad occupational environments. RIASEC is the acronym used to represent Holland's work place environments and points on his well-known hexagon. Holland theorizes that individual personalities can be matched to work place environments for a "good occupational fit." For example, "R" represents the "Realistic" environment, which is the more physically demanding jobs working with tools, machines, automobiles, animals. Realistic personality types are those who enjoy working with their hands and interacting with things versus people. "I" represents "Investigative" environments, requiring scientific and mathematical problem solving. Investigative personalities enjoy solving puzzles and researching for solutions. "A" or "Artistic" work environments prize creativity and match to personalities that enjoy free expression often inherent in occupations associated with music, art, theater, and writing. "S" represents the "Social" work environment that involves interaction with other individuals. Social environments often appeal to those who wish to help and provide human services to others, which may include teaching, counseling, and medical professions. "E" encompasses the "Enterprising" work environments that attract those who wish to lead, persuade, sell, and gain positions that provide a level of power. Enterprising individuals are drawn to politics, real estate, business, insurance, and the stock market. "C" is the "Conventional" work environment, which are often office positions. Individuals who enjoying organizing and performing tasks related to accounting, clerical, and record keeping are good fits for the conventional work setting. It is important to note that no one work environment fits one specific type, but involves a combination of types. Therefore, no one personality type fits squarely into one work environment. Instead, an individual's personality may be well-suited to multiple occupational environments. Holland created a career interest inventory known as the *self-directed search* (SDS) for this purpose (Holland, 1974). The SDS is discussed later in this chapter in the section titled "Assessment Instruments and Career Information Delivery Systems."

Donald Super's (1949, 1970, 1980) work in career development may be the most extensive of all the career development theorists, particularly pertaining to the career development of children and adolescents. Major constructs defining Super's lifespan–life space approach includes life stages, career maturity, life-career rainbow, self-concept, and the archway of career determinants. Super's model of career development in children contends that, driven by curiosity, children explore the environment and interact with others, thereby maturing and developing self-control and time perspectives that lead to planful career decision making and implementation of self-concept. Super provides school counselors with a sound theoretical foundation from which to plan and implement developmentally appropriate career activities.

Linda Gottfredson (1981), too, emphasized self-concept in her theory of career development, which focused on childhood and adolescence. Gottfredson's theory of self-creation through interactions with the environment underscores the role of prestige, gender, and cognitive development in career decision making. Other theoretical constructs include circumscription (i.e., eliminating alternatives perceived as inappropriate due to societal expectations, prestige, gender) and compromise (i.e., giving up desired alternatives for those that are more accessible). Gottfredson's views magnify the need for school counselors to address historical trends in career development programming and to explore with students what might be perceived and self-imposed and obstacles to desired careers.

I WANT TO BE A NURSE

You are the elementary school counselor delivering a career awareness classroom guidance lesson to first graders. You are holding up pictures of an array of people dressed in attire that depicts specific occupations. You hold up a card of a male who is dressed in a nursing uniform, and the class begins to guess the occupation. Some of the students shouted out "doctor." You said, "Well, it could be that this person is a doctor, but the card said that he is a 'nurse.'" One of the male students said quietly, "I wanted to be a nurse, but my father said that I could not be a nurse because that was a job for girls." According to Gottfredson's theory, is this an example of compromise or circumscription?

Anne Roe (1957) provides school counselors with a career development theory that is grounded in personality development. Roe suggests that there are six parent attitudes toward, or away from, their children that impact a child's personality development. As such, Roe contends that a child's career choice is based on psychological needs derived from these early interactions. School counselors can help students to identify how early interactions with parents may have impacted their career development.

Broadening Roe's parent–child interactions, Susan Phillips postulates that career choices are grounded in interactions with all important others (Phillips, Christopher-Sisk, & Gravino, 2001). Phillips created categories of relational responding, suggesting that others impact our career choices either by inviting themselves into our career decision making (i.e., actions of others) or our inviting others into our career decision making (i.e., self-directedness). It is important to help students identify the strengths and weaknesses of career decision-making influences.

In this section, we have covered the key career theories from the objectivist school of thought. The theories that follow are grounded in the ideologies of the constructivist school of thought.

David Tiedeman (1961) has been credited for engineering the constructivist ideologies, earning himself the title of author, or engineer, of the first postmodern career theory. Tiedeman broke away from traditionalist thought, declaring that career decision making is far more personal and subjective because it is created from an individual's unique perceptions and *worldview*. Tiedeman's theory holds career decision making as an evolving process across developmental stages that parallel those of Erikson. Tiedeman's major constructs included differentiation (i.e., evaluating self and self in the world) and integration (i.e., finding congruence in the world of work). School counselors use Tiedeman's developmental perspectives and theory of the evolving ego, or self, to encourage students at specific developmental stages to consider how this unique self would fit into a variety of occupations.

Larry Cochran (1997), following Tiedeman's theory of the evolving self, provides school counselors with a constructivist approach that allows students to tell their story about career and related interactions. Together, the school counselor and student create a future career story that is a more ideal career narrative, which Cochran refers to as crystallizing a decision. Major theoretical constructs include phases, episodes, plots, narratives, characters, and enacting a role.

Mark Savickas (1997, 2000) also supports the narrative approach in career counseling, believing that clients construct their own career in unique, subjective, and complex ways. He departs a bit from Cochran in his integration of objectivist theories such as Super's life stages and Holland's typology. Savickas focuses on four areas in his theory of career development: vocational personality, developmental tasks, adaptability, and life themes. Savickas integrates Holland's typology in vocational personality and Super's life stages in his developmental tasks. Mattering is a key construct of Savickas' life themes, that is, Savickas explores life themes to determine that which matters to an individual. Mattering, according to Savickas, brings purpose and meaning to work, while adaptability melds the vocational self with an occupational role.

Duane Brown (2002) presents a theory that focuses on the impact of contextual variables on career decision making, satisfaction, and success. Brown's contextual variables include values, gender, family, socioeconomic status, and discrimination. Key constructs are Brown's values-based theoretical propositions.

John Krumboltz (1994) presents a career theory that is grounded in social learning theory. Krumboltz contends that career decisions are made based on an interaction of genetic endowment, learning experiences, environment (e.g., conditions and events), and task approach skills. School counselors who conceptualize career development using Krumboltz theory will likely use traditional behavioral interventions in career counseling, such as role playing, simulation, reinforcement, and role modeling.

TED'S FUTURE

You are a high school counselor meeting with Ted, who is uncertain about his career path. During your session you are focused on teaching Ted career decision-making strategies. Which of the career development theories discussed in this section are you implementing?

Career and College Transitions

Although career development and college preparation has remained a primary function of the school counselor since the guidance movement, there has been a resurgence in popularity and support over the past two decades. Many school systems are hiring school counselors to specifically serve as career counselors at the high school level with an emphasis on preparing today's students for tomorrow's world of work.

Primary legislation pertaining to the school-to-work movement includes *Goals 2000 (1994): Educate America Act, National Skills Standards Act*, and the *School-to-Work Opportunities Act of 1994*. This legislation, simply stated, promotes the development of occupational standards and an integration of vocational and educational competencies so that students will be well prepared to enter and be successful in our multifaceted and technologically advanced workforce.

School counselors are creative in meeting school-to-work initiatives using a variety of strategies to integrate occupational information and college readiness activities using classroom guidance, small groups, and individual counseling/planning. Activities at the elementary level designed to introduce students to the world of work and college may include career day/week, videos, activity sheets, books, skits, fieldtrips, and tutoring at local colleges. Activities at the secondary level designed to assist students in exploring and planning for college and career include job shadowing and internships; college and career fairs; financial aid workshops; scholarship application process and resources; athletic eligibility; college entrance exams, dates, and procedures; college essay writing; mock interviewing; college tour fieldtrips; and panel presentations by former high school students sharing career and college success stories.

Many high school counselors partner with community colleges to offer students the opportunity to take the ACT-sponsored WorkKeys assessments. Students who pass the three WorkKeys assessments (i.e., applied mathematics, locating information, and reading for information) earn the national Career Readiness Certificate. The certification is gaining recognition as a viable screening, hiring, and promotion tool among prospective employers.

Students can now earn industry certifications in many high schools. Industry certifications are generally attached to specific elective courses. For example, students taking culinary arts may be eligible to take the National Occupational Competency Testing Institute (NOCTI) assessment, leading to certification in commercial foods. Students taking marketing classes may be eligible to take the NRF assessments, leading to certifications in customer service and sales. Industry certifications are also available in a variety of software packages and linked to business and technical education courses (see Chapter 8).

School counselors make students aware of WorkKeys and industry certifications during course scheduling. School counselors often go to the classrooms to promote the benefits of these voluntary certifications, which may include course credit and additional diploma seals. Certifications also demonstrate a commitment on the part of the student toward a specific occupation and earnestness about postsecondary employment and/or education.

School counselors adhere to the professional competencies and ethical issues involved in providing career counseling services to minors. School counselors are well advised to become familiar with the Multicultural Career Counseling Minimal Competencies (National Career Development Association [NCDA], 2009) provided by the NCDA, a division of ACA, as well as the ASCA Model's student competencies for the career development domain.

Section A.3. of the ASCA *Ethical Standards for School Counselors* (ASCA, 2010) emphasizes the responsibilities of school counselors to work with all students to develop personalized academic and career goals that will lead to postsecondary opportunities of their choice. This may necessitate collaboration with recruiters to provide students with information related to postsecondary education and career options while ensuring the protection of students' personal information in accordance with FERPA.

ASCA's Position on Postsecondary Student Recruitment

Professional school counselors encourage and promote positive and equitable reception of career and postsecondary educational institution recruiters into the school setting. These recruiters may include individuals from organizations such as

- Apprenticeship programs
- Athletic programs
- Branches of the military
- Career and technical education institutions
- Colleges and universities

Position statement adopted 2004; revised 2009

Most states have adopted requirements pertaining to the formal creation of an academic and career plan. The plan, generally, begins in middle school and is updated annually through the senior year of high school. The plan identifies the courses, specialized programs, and steps needed for the student to attain their desired career and postsecondary education and training.

ASCA's Position on Academic and Career Planning

Professional school counselors recognize that each student possesses unique interests, abilities and goals that will lead to many future opportunities. Collaborating with students, parents, educational staff, and the community, the professional school counselor works to ensure that all students develop an academic and career plan that reflects their interests, abilities and goals and includes rigorous, relevant coursework and experiences appropriate for the student.

Position statement adopted 1994; revised 2000, 2006

Transitioning from school to work or to any of the other postsecondary career options presents unique challenges for young adults. In addition to the general transitioning support noted earlier in this chapter, school counselors can help students to make successful transitions to work and college by offering programming on topics such as workplace skills, job market trends, resume and cover letter writing, interviewing, application completion, networking, securing mentors, managing time and money, and balancing social and academic/work life.

Assessment Instruments and Career Information Delivery Systems

School counselors will often begin the career development process with career-related inventories that assess student's interests, work values, and skills. Information gleaned from these assessments aids in the career planning process, providing both the counselor and student with valuable information from which to identify possible career paths and establish career goals. Like other student appraisal instruments, however, school counselors do not rely on the results of career assessment alone to guide students' career planning because such instruments do not provide a comprehensive conceptualization of individual complexities. Additionally, some of these instruments lack cultural validity, that is, not all appraisal instruments consider worldviews that differ from the dominant culture.

The three most commonly used career inventories in the schools are the *SDS*, the *SII*, and the *KOIS*. All three inventories are based on John Holland's theory of typology and yield Holland codes. The SDS (Holland, 1974) helps students to identify preferences for specific activities, matching personality type with six workplace environments using the three-letter Holland code. Information about the SDS is available at www.self-directed-search.com. The SII (Strong & Campbell, 1974) provides information about careers that match students' codes and is available at www.cpp.com/products/strong/index.asp. The KOIS (Kuder, 1964) suggests occupations and college majors based on students' interest patterns. Information about the KOIS is available at www.kuder.com.

It is not necessary to memorize all the different types of assessment instruments and tests. It is important, however, for the purpose of school counseling exams, to know the difference between career assessments, personality assessments, intelligence test, aptitude tests, and other types of assessments, inventories, and tests, as well as situations in which you might administer a particular type of assessment over another. Assessments are discussed in greater detail in Chapter 4.

Career development instruments are often included in career information delivery systems (CIDS), also referred to as *computer-assisted career guidance systems* (CACGS), to aid students in career planning. The Association of Computer-Based Systems for Career Information (ACSCI, 1999) defines CIDS as a computer-based, user-supported, career information system that provides assessment and search functions that link to career and educational information. This Internet-based career development tool is available 24-7 to help students plan postsecondary careers and education.

There are many CIDS available for school counselor and student use. Some of the most widely used systems in school counseling include Choices Explorer, Choices Planner, SIGI Plus, DISCOVER, Bridges' Paws in Jobland, and Career Trek. In brief, Bridges' Paws in Jobland is used with elementary school students. Career Trek is primarily used for grades four through middle school. Choices Explorer is generally used with middle school students. Choices Planner is appropriate for career planning at the high school level. DISCOVER is used at both the middle and high school levels, and SIGI Plus is often used for college-bound juniors and seniors, students in 2- and 4-year colleges, and adult populations.

There is often some overlap with regard to the developmental level within which these systems are used. For example, although DISCOVER is often used at the middle school level, it may also be used by some school counselors at the high school level. For this reason, selection of one particular system over another is often a matter of school counselor and student preference.

Nationally recognized resources include the *Occupational Outlook Handbook* (OOH) and *Occupational Information Network* (O*Net).

The OOH provides information about the job market and specific information about hundreds of occupations. O*Net is a national, interactive database that allows you to explore and search hundreds of occupations and to participate in assessment instruments to aid in career decision making.

Card sorts, too, are an informal and fun way to gain insight into possible occupational choices and can be used with students of all ages. School counselors provide students with a stack of cards. Each card identifies a specific occupation. The student begins placing cards in categories such as (1) "I might consider," (2) "I would not consider," and (3) "I am not sure if I would consider." Once the student sorts the stack of cards, the school counselor explores the student's reasons for the selections (e.g., education, training, characteristics of the job, salary).

Academic Development

The domain of *academic development* has evolved over the past decade. Efforts to change the direction of school counseling have placed considerable emphasis on academic-focused practices in school counseling. The following topics related to academic development are covered by school counselors as a part of a CDSCP at the elementary and secondary school levels. The ASCA National Standards (ASCA, 2005) provide school counselors with competencies and indicators for each of the following areas within the academic development domain:

- *Academic self-concept*: pride in work, positive attitude and interest in learning, acceptance of mistakes as learning process, express sense of competence
- *Learning skills*: knowledge of learning styles, importance of effort and persistence, time/task management, critical thinking skills, motivation, resources, application of information, becoming a self-directed learner
- *School success*: dependability, initiative, productivity, developing interests and abilities, working independently and cooperatively, responsibility
- *Achieve goals*: use of assessment results for educational planning, identify postsecondary options, develop plan of study, relate classroom performance to school success, problem solving, and decision making
- *Relate learning to life*: transition from student to member of society; cocurricular experiences; balance school, leisure, and family; understand value of lifelong learning; understand relationship between school success and career opportunities

Topics related to academic development during the elementary school years emphasize paying attention, focusing, following directions, listening, completing classwork and homework, organization, goal setting, study and test taking skills, and test anxiety. School counselors at the secondary level generally focus on goal setting, time management, study skills, test taking skills, test anxiety, identifying learning styles, course selection, college admission success, post–high school athletic programs, financial aid for college, college testing requirements, and identification of academic programs at the postsecondary level. Academic development is covered in greater detail in Chapter 6.

Delivery

Studies support the effectiveness of all school counseling methods of service delivery (Gerrity & DeLucia-Waack, 2007; Whiston et al., 2011), recommending a balanced approach to school counseling that provides classroom guidance for all and responsive services to meet the immediate needs of students. The sections that follow describe the varying methods of school counseling program delivery.

Classroom Guidance and Group Work

Classroom guidance lessons and small groups allow school counselors to provide services to meet the unique needs of all students, supporting the developmental domains of a CDSCP. These methods of service delivery are the mainstay of systems-focused practices (ASCA, 2005). Both methods are used primarily for educational and psychoeducational purposes covering a broad range of topics.

Classroom guidance and group counseling are often used for academic skills enhancement, career and academic planning, and personal–social skills development. Academic skills enhancement may include study habits, test taking, time management, and organization. Career and academic planning may entail identifying interests, work values and skills, college and job application processes, job search strategies, interviewing, and resume writing. Personal–social skills development often includes resisting peer pressure, interpersonal relations, anger management, communication, problem solving, and decision making. There is significant evidence documenting the effectiveness of small groups and classroom guidance as a delivery method for both prevention and intervention (Whiston et al., 2007).

The classroom guidance curriculum is primarily preventative in nature and comprised of structured, written lessons that address student knowledge, skills, and attitudes using differentiated instructional strategies as discussed in Chapter 6. Classroom guidance is the mainstay of school counseling, deeply rooted in the teaching profession during the vocational guidance movement. Although classroom guidance is effective at all grade levels, an extensive, current review of school counseling interventions found classroom guidance to be more effective than individual and group counseling at the middle and high school levels (Whiston et al., 2011).

Classroom guidance is implemented as a part of a CDSCP. One classroom guidance lesson may be implemented to cover a singular topic, or multiple lessons may be conducted as a classroom guidance unit over a specified period of time to cover a singular, multifaceted topic. Often, classroom guidance is conducted at the request of the classroom teacher to supplement specific course material and/or to address pressing sensitive issues or issues that have surfaced unique to the needs of their classroom and interfering with classroom instruction.

Classroom guidance lessons may be 20–90 minutes, determined by the developmental level of the student. Kindergarten and first grade lessons are likely to be about 20–25 minutes to accommodate the shorter attention spans of young children. Classroom guidance lessons for the upper elementary level students and middle school students (i.e., grades 3–8) are generally 30 minutes to an hour. Classroom guidance for high school students can take an entire class period, even 90-minute block schedules, as long as the teacher's schedule permits.

Like classroom guidance, group counseling has a history of positive student outcomes related to a variety of topics including, but not limited to, eating disorders, anger management, pregnancy prevention, bullying, and social skills (Gerrity &Waack-DeLucia, 2007). Group work has also gained considerable attention as a useful delivery method for transforming the school counseling profession (Paisley & Milsom, 2007).

ASCA's Position on Group Counseling

Group counseling is vital in the delivery of the ASCA National Model to students and should be supported by school districts as part of an effective comprehensive school counseling program.

Position statement adopted 1989; revised 1993, 2002, 2008; reviewed 1999, 2008

Psychoeducational groups, considered both educational and thera-peutic, are the most widely used in the schools. Psychoeducational groups are time limited, impart information, and offer opportunities for self-development. For example, psychoeducational groups in the school may include study skills, social skills, test-taking strategies, conflict resolution, organization, time management, problem solving, and anger management. Psychoeducational groups are also used to respond to the needs of students experiencing difficult life situations such as the deploy-ment of a military family member, death, adoption, divorce, and family transitions (e.g., leaving for college, moving, remarriage, and blending families).

One of the most significant concerns with group work is that despite the school counselor's vigilance in protecting the psychological and physi-cal well-being of group participants during member interactions within the group, confidentiality cannot be guaranteed due to the nature of group work. For this reason, school counselors are just as vigilante in ensuring that parents and students understand the limits of confidentiality in group counseling.

Group counseling unites students with shared issues; promotes sup-portive relationships, healthy personal development, team problem solving, and cooperative behaviors; and provides opportunities for building com-munication, knowledge, and coping skills. The group experience may also enhance students' ability to empathize with others, to more fully understand the behavior of others, and to develop insight into themselves and into the unique and common aspects of their problems. For example, *dyadic coun-seling*, a form of group counseling that is popular in the schools, involves pairing two children in a relationship that revolves around play. In dyadic counseling, these children are paired based on opposing interpersonal ori-entations and guided by the school counselor toward more developmentally mature social interactions.

The Association for Specialists in Group Work (ASGW), a division of the ACA, as well as ASCA, promotes the value of group work in the school setting at the elementary, middle, and high school levels. The Council for Accreditation of Counseling and Related Education Programs (CACREP) and ASCA underscore the need for school counselors to develop professional competencies in group work. Section A.6 of the ASCA *Ethical Standards for School Counselors* (ASCA, 2010) calls for school counselors to "develop pro-fessional competencies and to maintain appropriate education, training and supervision in group facilitation and any topics specific to the group" (p. 3).

The process of group counseling coordination and facilitation for school counselors may look like this: (1) selecting/screening group members, (2) defining the group's purpose based on student need, (3) securing parent, teacher, and student permissions, (4) identifying meeting space, (5) determining length and number and days and times of meetings, (6) developing group activities, (7) facilitating group movement through the four stages of the process (i.e., initial stage, transition stage, working stage, and termination), (8) evaluating the effectiveness of the group intervention, and (9) providing for group follow-up. While planning small groups, the school counselor also considers whether or not the group will be an *open group* (i.e., new members are accepted after the group facilitation process in underway) or a *closed group* (i.e., new members are not accepted after the initial group meeting).

When screening, group members look for appropriate fit and aligned goals in relation to the group's purpose and focus. School counselors may elect to create small groups that are homogeneous (i.e., members share a variety of common characteristics), heterogeneous (i.e., diverse membership), or a combination of the two.

An example of a homogeneous group would be a self-esteem group for sixth-grade African American male students with similar backgrounds, experiencing low self-esteem. An example of a heterogeneous group would be a study skills group for grades 3–6 students, who may or may not be experiencing study skills issues, who represent a mix of race, gender, age, backgrounds, ethnicity—a microcosm of society. An example of group members that may be both heterogeneous and homogeneous is a social skills group at the elementary level may be homogeneous in that all members are having some issues with social skills and that they are all in third grade. However, the group may be heterogeneous in that the group is cross-cultural and includes both male and female students.

The number of group sessions and the length of the group sessions generally vary by school, often dependent upon teacher and administrator support because students will miss class time to take part in counseling. ASCA recommends that groups be brief and solution-focused. Generally speaking, small groups in the school setting meet once or twice a week for a total of four to eight sessions. Groups are typically 30 minutes in length for students at the elementary level and 40–60 minutes for students at the secondary level.

Individual Student Planning

Individual student planning entails the coordination of activities designed to aid students in establishing unique personal, academic, and career goals. Studies indicate that individual student planning is generally related to education and career planning and conducted most frequently by high school counselors (Gysbers & Henderson, 2006).

Relating learning to students' career aspirations and providing students with opportunities for success and involvement in courses perceived as interesting have been linked to enhanced academic motivation, discussed in Chapter 1 (Scheel & Gonzalez, 2007). Additionally, individual planning teaches students problem-solving skills that transfer to real life into adulthood (Whiston et al., 2011).

ASCA's Position on Educational Planning

The professional school counselor works with administrative, curricular and instructional staff to ensure all students have the opportunity to design academically challenging programs of studies.

Position statement adopted 1994; revised 2000

Individual student planning activities may be delivered on an individual basis or in a small group setting and may include immediate, short-term, and long-term planning. Individual student planning topics may include postsecondary educational and career planning, transitioning from school to postsecondary training/employment, test review and score interpretation, career-related assessment, success strategies, action plan development, promotion/retention, course selection, financial aid, and college/job application. During individual student planning, school counselors often discuss the student's performance progress by examining the average of all their grades, referred to as the student's grade point average (GPA). The importance of GPA in relation to college entrance and scholarships is also discussed.

Individual Student Counseling

School counselors engage in individual counseling with students for a variety of reasons that have resulted in personal–social, career, and academic success (Whiston et al., 2011). Referrals to the school counselor may be self-initiated or initiated by an important other (e.g., parent, teacher, administrator, friend). Individual counseling, unlike individual student planning, is often reactive, rather than preventative. The student is generally experiencing some kind of difficulty (e.g., family issue, friendship issue, bullying, depression, chronic illness, pregnancy, abuse, truancy, substance abuse) that requires clinical intervention, information, community agency referral, problem solving, and/or decision making.

Individual counseling in the schools requires that the school counselor draw upon the counseling theories and techniques noted earlier in this section. School counselors understand the importance of establishing and maintaining effective counseling relationships throughout the counseling process, from goal setting to termination.

Responsive Services

Responsive services may entail counseling, consultation, referral, education, mediation, problem solving, and/or community intervention. Responsive services meet students' pressing developmental or situational needs and are typically self-initiated through student referral or by a referral from a concerned teacher, parent or guardian, school administrator, or as a response to school-wide crises.

Although research is limited on the effectiveness of responsive services, to date, interventions considered to be responsive services have been effective (Whiston et al., 2011). Responsive services generally include small group counseling, individual counseling, peer helping, and mentoring, while classroom guidance and school-wide interventions may be considered responsive services when implemented in response to an immediate student need. Methods of delivery will depend on the number of students in need of intervention and the nature and scope of the expressed difficulty or crisis situation.

Individual and group counseling are ideal methods of delivery for individuals or small populations of students. School counselors determine the best method of program delivery on a case-by-case basis, which involves assessing the student's current functioning; the nature of the presenting issue, including severity, frequency, and immediacy; and the student's desired level of privacy.

Responsive services like individual and small group counseling services are short-term. "Short-term" should be emphasized because school counseling alone is not in the best interest of children and adolescents experiencing severe, persistent, and progressive issues. Additionally, to provide ongoing counseling sessions with students whose issues cannot be sufficiently addressed within the scope of school counseling and within the expertise of the school counselor is in violation of professional ethical guidelines (see Chapter 1). School counselors can best meet the specific personal, social, and emotional needs of these students using referral services and a collaborative model.

A school counselor's most valuable resources for helping students are students. There is much research to support the positive outcomes of peer-to-peer helping/support programs (Whiston et al., 2011), which are also encouraged by ASCA. Section A.11 of the ASCA *Ethical Standards for School Counselors* (ASCA, 2010) addresses peer-to-peer programs to ensure that student welfare is safeguarded by emphasizing the importance of proper training and supervision of peer helpers by school counselors.

ASCA's Position on Peer-Helping Programs

ASCA believes that peer-helping programs are one means of helping students reach a higher level of maturity and accepting responsibility. Peer-helping programs are implemented to enhance the effectiveness of school counseling programs by increasing outreach and the expansion of available services.

Position statement adopted 1978, revised 1984, 1993, 1999, 2002, 2008

Peer-to-peer programs might also include transition/orientation programs, whereby a more senior student serves as an escort and friend to new individual students and groups of students (i.e., elementary students transitioning to middle school and middle school students transitioning to high school) to promote a successful transition. Another type of peer-helping program would include peer tutoring, whereby a student who is adept in a particular subject coaches a student who is struggling in that subject.

SMALL GROUP COUNSELING

You are a middle school counselor creating a school counseling intervention that targets special education students in eighth grade who are performing below average in mathematics. After careful data analysis, you have identified 20 students. You are creating small groups to work with these students on test taking and study skills while also crosswalking the school counseling standards with mathematics standards as a part of the structured small group curriculum. Your intervention is considered to be

    a. Small group method
    b. Responsive services
    c. a and b
    d. None of the above

Systems Support

Systems support generally involves school counseling program management activities that promote systemic change, covered in Chapter 8. These activities include the following in support of the entire school community: consultation and collaboration with stakeholders, maintaining *advisory councils*, participating in committees, analyzing data, budgeting, conducting research, developing resources, community outreach, and participating in professional development opportunities.

Theories and Techniques for the School Setting

Several years ago, Corsini and Wedding (1995) reported more than 250 counseling and psychotherapy theories, models, and approaches. The theoretical approach(es) a school counselor elects to use will depend on the topic and goals of counseling, student characteristics (e.g., culture, developmental level), and the comfort level of the school counselor with a specific approach.

School counselors are well advised to consider the principle of reductionism when considering the complexities of a student's case, that is, the child is but one part of an intricate system of multiple interacting parts. Systems theory necessitates that school counselors consider students in the context of their relationship to other family members because each part (individual) influences the whole (family). When there is evidence of a family dysfunction, school counselors strongly encourage parents to consider counseling by a licensed marriage and family therapist.

Deemed critical to the personal, social, and cognitive development of a healthy child, incorporating play therapy techniques into counseling services is another consideration for school counselors (Santrock, 2010). Play therapy may be directive, nondirective, or a combination of approaches. Play therapy has been associated with enhanced social skills, communication, attention, self-control, and self-esteem, as well as reduced levels of *aggression*, depression, anxiety, and *antisocial* and delinquent behaviors. Play therapy has also helped many children and adolescents to work through emotional, personal, and interpersonal issues associated with trauma (e.g., grief, abuse, disaster) and family issues (e.g., divorce, adoption, deployment). Play therapy also enhances cognitive and psychosocial functioning in students with disabilities and is used as a diagnostic tool to appraise psychosocial functioning (Kottman, 2003).

During play therapy, the school counselor systematically applies one or more of the theoretical approaches covered in this chapter. Toys are used and often represented in categories such as nurturing, aggressive, scary, expressive, and pretend. Some of the toys may fit into several categories, which are listed in the following paragraphs (Kottman, 2003). Nurturing toys help students to express and act out relationships and past, present, or future events. School counselors are careful to include dolls that represent different cultures for exploring differences and similarities. Nurturing toys may include the following:

- Dolls or people puppets (some with anatomical parts and removable clothing)
- Child-size furniture (e.g., kitchen sink, stove, refrigerator)
- Kitchenware (e.g., plates, pots, pans, cups)
- Doll clothing
- Blankets
- Stuffed animals

Aggressive toys help children and adolescents to express feelings of anger appropriately or symbolically. School counselors often elect not to include aggressive toys in their office, preferring to avoid conveying a message that violence of any kind is acceptable. Aggressive toys may include

- Punching bag
- Rubber mallet
- Soft boxing gloves
- Foam bats

Scary toys help children and adolescents to express fear; to symbolically represent abusive, frightening, or past traumatic situations; and to practice ways in which they can keep themselves safe. Scary toys may include

- Plastic insects
- Rubber snake
- Plastic dinosaur, shark, rat, alligator
- A variety of puppets and stuffed toys representative of scary animals (e.g., lion, gorilla, bear, wolf, tiger)

Toys that allow children to pretend, or fantasize, promote behavioral and emotional expression, communication, role exploration, and the reenactment of past and present life events. Students use these toys for metaphorical expression of ideas and experiences. These toys may include

- Clothing
- Jewelry
- Telephones and computers
- Puppets and puppet stage
- Blocks
- Masks
- Kits (e.g., doctor, geologist)
- Hats
- Magic wands
- Fantasy creatures (e.g., unicorn, leprechaun, witch, troll, fairy princess)
- Superheroes (e.g., Superman, Spiderman, Batman)
- Villains (e.g., Joker, Riddler, Dr. Doom)

Expressive toys help students to communicate difficult emotions through actions and symbols while finding the appropriate vocabulary for verbal expression of emotions. Expressive toys also help students gain a greater understanding of themselves, their environment, and the self in relation to others. Use of expressive toys with children has been linked to enhanced problem solving, self-confidence, creativity, self-control, and emotional and cognitive expression. Expressive toys include

- Games
- Musical instruments
- Paint
- Play dough
- Blocks
- Books
- Sand and water trays
- Stuffed animals
- Beads
- Construction paper, tape, scissors, pencils, glue sticks, markers
- Yarn

PLAY THERAPY

Yasmin is an 8-year-old female student whose grandfather died suddenly last week. Yasmin's teacher reports that Yasmin is very quiet and withdrawn. Also, her classwork is not completed, which is not typical for Yasmin. The parent and teacher have asked the school counselor to meet with Yasmin. What toys might be particularly helpful to Yasmin at this time?

a. Scary
b. Nurturing
c. Expressive
d. Aggressive
e. Pretend

The sections that follow will cover nine of the most widely used theories and associated techniques for counseling children and adolescents in the schools. For ease of learning and recall, each theory will be summarized in a chart that includes the following: theorist and philosophy, therapeutic relationship, key concepts and techniques, and multicultural responsiveness. The following theories are covered in this section:

- Adlerian
- Behavioral

- Cognitive behavioral
- Gestalt
- Person-centered (also called Rogerian and humanistic)
- Rational emotive behavior therapy (REBT)
- Reality
- Solution-focused brief counseling
- Strength-based counseling

Adlerian

Developed by Alfred Adler (1925), Adlerian counseling, also referred to as individual psychology, is defined by its encouraging, goal-driven approaches that focus on immediate behavioral change (Table 2.1). School counselors with Adlerian orientations often rely on play therapy methods to induce communication, interaction, and problem solving while acting out appropriate responding and behavioral expectations (e.g., differentiating good behavior from bad behavior).

Table 2.1 Adlerian Counseling

Theorist and philosophy	Alfred Adler's theoretical philosophy holds internalized feelings of inferiority/inadequacy and resulting frustration and discouragement as the source of difficulties and misbehavior. The underlying belief is that social interest/inherent human desire for success drives behavior. Counseling is directive.
Therapeutic relationship	School counselor is supporter, encourager, facilitator.
Key concepts/ techniques	Self-awareness is encouraged. Using structured questions, confrontation, and *play therapy*, students share perceptions of their lives, family history, and social interactions. Students identify unconstructive behaviors by catching oneself and more constructive alternatives. Together, goals are established toward creating a desired lifestyle that gives students a sense of equality. *Inferiority complex* (an advanced sense of inability and inequality in meeting life's demands) is a concept born out of Adler's work.
Multicultural responsiveness	Focus on individuality is not compatible with some cultures; individualized approach is culturally sensitive and accommodates the student's frame of reference/ worldview; focus on the holistic approach and social responsibility is compatible with some cultures; focus on shared goal setting is culturally sensitive.

Behavioral

B. F. Skinner (1971) developed behavioral counseling. The defining characteristics of behavioral counseling (see Table 2.2) involve identifying behavioral influences and helping students to eliminate problematic behavior and learn more functional behaviors. School counselors who practice from a behavioral orientation view behavior as learned and therefore focus on teaching new behaviors.

Three approaches are generally associated with behavioral theory. The first, *stimulus–response*, which applies to involuntary behaviors illustrated by the classical experiments with Pavlov's dog, is not covered in this study guide. The stimulus–response method is rarely, if ever, applied in the school setting because educators are more concerned with voluntary behaviors. The

Table 2.2 Behavioral Counseling

Theorist and philosophy	B. F. Skinner philosophy holds environmental factors responsible for creating dysfunctional behaviors. Behavior is learned; therefore, behaviors can be unlearned and modified. Counseling is directive.
Therapeutic relationship	Counselor is teacher, collaborator, advisor, facilitator, and reinforcer.
Key concepts/ techniques	Operant conditioning using a behavior modification technique that involves introducing a *stimulus* (activating event), applying (positive) or withdrawing (negative) a reinforcer or punisher to elicit a desire or undesired *consequence* that changes behavior (extinguishes undesired/promotes desired), particularly when using schedules of reinforcement (repeated over time). Other techniques used toward collaboratively established goals include *behavioral rehearsal* (practicing desired behavior), *assertiveness training* (reducing anxiety in appropriate emotional expression), and *contingency* or *behavioral contracts* (identifies target behavior and rewards/punishments involved).
Multicultural responsiveness	Focus on behavior versus feelings is compatible with many cultures; focus on shared goal setting is culturally sensitive; focus on collaboration is empowering for many cultures; the definition of "appropriate" behavior may differ across cultures; passivity is revered in some cultures.

other two approaches, *operant conditioning* and *social-cognitive*, are covered in this study guide and are often used by school counselors to bring about behavioral change.

Operant conditioning, more recently referred to as applied *behavioral analysis*, applies punishment or reward to specific behaviors to reduce or eliminate undesirable behaviors and to promote desirable behaviors. Operant conditioning is exemplified when the school counselor applies intrinsic and extrinsic rewards in an attempt to modify behavior. Chapter 1 describes the process of *behavior modification* using operant conditioning and the use of intrinsic and extrinsic rewards in greater detail.

The social-cognitive approach is grounded in the concept of *modeling*, that is, that students learn new behaviors by observing the behaviors of others. Observational learning is a powerful phenomenon that has a lasting impact on a student's behavior. School counselors apply the social-cognitive approach in peer-helping programs, mentor programs, and by exposing students to prominent current and historical figures and community participants during career week.

LEARNING TO RESOLVE CONFLICT

During a small group session, an elementary school counselor introduces the students to a conflict resolution strategy and names several historical figures who used conflict resolution to deflect war and improve lives. Members of the group take turns role-playing the strategy. This is referred to in behavioral counseling as

a. Teaching new behavior
b. Rehearsal
c. Social cognitive learning
d. All of the above

Cognitive Behavioral

Aaron Beck (1979) developed cognitive behavioral counseling, "also referred to as cognitive behavioral theory/therapy (CBT). Beck has been referred to in cerebral circles" as the father of cognitive therapy. Beck developed a banquet of self-report measures related to the assessment of thoughts and feelings associated with depression, hopelessness, anxiety, and suicide. The defining characteristics of cognitive behavioral counseling (see Table 2.3) involve viewing counseling as learning and emphasizing the role of cognitions and internal dialogue (i.e., thinking) in bringing about emotional and behavioral responses (i.e., doing). In other words, our emotions and behaviors are slave to our thoughts. School counselors used this structured and time-sensitive approach to teach and practice new skills and behaviors, problem-solving approaches, and to promote self-control.

Table 2.3   Cognitive Behavioral Counseling

Theorist and philosophy	Aaron Beck's philosophy holds that one's thoughts determine one's feelings and behaviors. Dysfunction is a result of faulty cognitions. Directive approach to counseling.
Therapeutic relationship	Counselor is teacher and collaborator.
Key concepts/ techniques	*Cognitive restructuring* (replacing maladaptive thoughts with more functional thoughts) is a core technique in this psychoeducational model that is direct, goal driven, and structured. Other techniques include identifying faulty thinking that leads to self-defeating behaviors; using *reframing* (alternative perceptions), cognitive modeling (self-talk), *Socratic dialogue* (how questioning); and *thought stopping* (yelling STOP or visualizing a STOP sign when the target thought surfaces) to change thought patterns. *Stress inoculation* (teaching cognitive and physical skills for heading off future stress and identifying automatic thoughts—triggers), *guided imagery* (mental picture—past, present, or future), and problem-solving (step-by-step process) aid in reducing stress, relieving anxiety, and gaining alternative perceptions of events and direction. Homework is often assigned as a strategy to change and practice new thought processes and behaviors.
Multicultural responsiveness	Focus on thinking versus feelings is compatible with many cultures; focus on teaching and learning is better suited to cultures that hold a negative view of mental health counseling; challenging belief systems may not be compatible with some cultures.

Gestalt

Gestalt theory, developed by Fritz Perls (1969), focuses on here-and-now processes (i.e., thinking, perceiving, feeling, acting) of the whole (Table 2.4). The whole is considered more than the sum of its parts but the unification of those parts as observed by the relationship between those parts. School counselors help students to identify what they are doing and how they can change while gaining insight and learning to appreciate of self.

School counselors may rely on gestalt theory to assist students in crisis and to help students get in touch with their emotions through self-exploration and in-the-moment experiencing. School counselors might use gestalt techniques to aid students in resolving past problems so that they

Table 2.4   Gestalt Counseling

Theorist and philosophy	Fritz Perls' philosophy holds that disturbance may be due to any number of issues such as overintellectualizing (i.e., out of touch with emotions); unresolved or unfinished business; loss of contact with environment or overinvolved in the environment and loss of contact with self; pulled in too many directions; conflict between what one wants to do and what one feels like they should do.
Therapeutic relationship	The therapeutic relationship is considered critical to successful outcomes; counselor is caring, warm, accepting, and nonjudgmental.
Key concepts/ techniques	Counselor helps students to resolve current life problems; to meet needs to achieve homeostasis; to become more self-aware; to develop holistically (mind, body, emotions, sensations); and to identify, clarify, and take responsibility for behaviors using direct experiencing with techniques such as *psychodrama* (enacting conflicts), *empty chair* (enacting dialogues), *I Take Responsibility* (student completes sentences pertaining to an issue with "I take responsibility for it"), and *confrontation* (counselor challenges student's actions or words).
Multicultural responsiveness	Working within students' values and acceptance of uniqueness and diverse worldviews appreciates cultural differences; focus on holistic development is compatible to some cultures.

might move toward the future, to meet needs as they arise in order to regain a sense of balance, and to recognize that the future is impacted by our choices in the present.

Person-Centered

Carl Rogers (1961, 1969) developed person-centered counseling, also referred to as humanistic and Rogerian counseling. The defining characteristics of person-centered counseling (see Table 2.5) involve viewing the student as having the capacity for growth and self-direction, as well as the potential to understand and resolve life problems.

School counselors may apply person-centered counseling to help students gain a greater understanding of self and daily experiences and work through brief, situational stress and anxiety. School counselors rely on the person-centered approach to establish positive, nurturing counselor–student relationships that allow for the incorporation of more directive counseling techniques and approaches.

Rational Emotive Behavior Therapy

Ellis and Dryden (1997) developed rational emotive behavior therapy (REBT), born out of cognitive behavioral theory. The defining characteristics of REBT

Table 2.5   Person-Centered (Humanistic) Counseling

Theorist and philosophy	Carl Rogers' philosophy holds that disturbance is due to incongruence between the real and ideal self. Nondirective approach to counseling.
Therapeutic relationship	Therapeutic relationship is considered essential to effective outcomes; counselor is nurturing, warm, and genuine and exhibits unconditional positive regard for the client.
Key concepts/ techniques	Counselor promotes self-exploration in a safe climate with *active listening*, reflecting feelings, *paraphrasing*, and clarifying so that client recognizes barriers to performance and growth and identifies new aspects of self.
Multicultural responsiveness	Working within students' values appreciates cultural differences; focus on feelings may not be compatible to some cultures; some cultural populations desire more activity.

Table 2.6   Rational Emotive Behavior Therapy

Theorist and philosophy	Albert Ellis' cognitive-behavioral theoretical philosophy holds that faulty/irrational thinking is the cause of dysfunction. Directive approach to counseling.
Therapeutic relationship	Collaborative.
Key concepts/ techniques	Use the A-B-C Model to debunk irrational thinking. The process involves identifying the activating event and the faulty belief about the event that contributes to the consequence, or self-defeating behavior. Counselors challenge faulty assumptions using questioning and identify alternatives to change internal dialogues and previously held beliefs, and, consequently, emotional and behavioral responses.
Multicultural responsiveness	Working within the student's values appreciates cultural differences.

(see Table 2.6) involve encouraging clients to confront and gather evidence to dispute irrational beliefs and faulty assumptions that are believed to result in negative emotional and behavioral consequences.

MEAN GIRLS

Elijah comes to you, the elementary school counselor, very upset. He said that a group of girls on the playground were teasing him, so he is never going to talk to girls again because girls are so mean. Which counseling approach might best describe Elijah's thoughts in this case, and how might the school counselor apply this approach to help Elijah?

School counselors use REBT to promote change and choice by helping students to better understand their thought processes and the relationship between those processes and emotional and behavioral responding. School counselors seek to ultimately empower students to apply REBT in daily living for self-regulation of emotions and behaviors.

Table 2.7   Reality Counseling

Theorist and philosophy	William Glasser's theoretical philosophy holds unmet needs due to unproductive/ineffective behaviors as the source of dysfunction and that all behavior is an attempt to control the environment to meet our needs. Directive approach to counseling.
Therapeutic relationship	Facilitator.
Key concepts/ techniques	Focusing on responsibility, choice, and doing, the counselor asks the student: (1) *What do you want?* (2) *What are you doing to get what you want?* (3) *Is it working?* Counselor challenges current behaviors and encourages students to self-evaluate and judge quality of their behaviors toward getting what they want. Together, a workable plan is established to change unproductive behaviors to more productive behaviors that guide future direction and meet needs/desires.
Multicultural responsiveness	Focus on students' evaluation of self within their own cultural frame of reference prizes diversity and accommodates differing worldviews; focus on personal responsibility for change does not account for external factors of discrimination and racism; individualized approach is culturally sensitive.

Reality Counseling

William Glasser (1998) developed reality therapy, also referred to as *control* or *choice* theory, to promote effective decision making and responsible living. The defining characteristics of reality counseling (see Table 2.7) involve helping students to identify inappropriate decisions and honestly evaluate and take responsibility for their current self-defeating behaviors. As Shakespeare proclaimed—*to thine own self be true!*

School counselors may find reality counseling helpful for students who have a pattern of making poor choices, exhibiting an external locus of control, and lacking realistic goals. School counselors use choice theory to help students to understand that they are in control of their lives and possess the ability to change, grow, and achieve, using self-evaluation and relevant planning (Gilchrist-Banks, 2009).

Solution-Focused Brief Counseling

Solution-focused brief counseling (SFBC), introduced by Steve de Shazer (1985), is a growing and promising approach particularly suited to school counseling because of its brief nature. SFBC has been vigorously inducted into the no-so-secret society of positive psychology discussed in the next section. The defining characteristics of solution-focused brief counseling (see Table 2.8) involve focusing on solutions versus problems based on what the student is already doing that works, nurturing internal assets, and involving important others (e.g., teachers, parents).

In addition to brevity, SFBC is particularly useful with children and adolescents because of its focus on developmental stages, social support,

Table 2.8　Solution-Focused Brief Counseling

Theorist and philosophy	Steve de Shazer's solution-focused brief counseling focuses on a student's strengths and abilities rather than weaknesses and inabilities and on solutions rather than problems. Time-limited, directive approach to counseling.
Therapeutic relationship	Collaborative.
Key concepts/ techniques	Students' inner and external resources with attention to developmental level are accessed. The counselor identifies what has worked for the student in the past and focuses on goals. Techniques may include the *miracle question* (if magic happened and the problem was gone, what would be different), *exceptions* (identify times where the problem is not present— what does it look like), *scaling* (on a scale of 1–10, with 10 being the hardest day and 1 being after the miracle, where would you be right now), *mindmapping* (e.g., identify what you did that made you successful in the past), *reframing* (viewing problems in more positive terms), and *assigning behavioral tasks* (e.g., doing more of the exceptions).
Multicultural responsiveness	Compatible to some cultures that prefer time-limited, practical applications; viewing the student as the expert and working within the student's frame of reference are culturally sensitive and accommodate differing worldviews; using developmentally appropriate, flexible interventions congruent to students' culture is culturally responsive.

appropriate use of humor, and active techniques. School counselors identify developmental struggles and help students to identify internal and external resources to create realistic solutions germane to the developmental stage.

Strengths-Based Counseling

Strengths-based counseling, an emerging positive psychology pioneered by Martin Seligman, accesses inherent strengths to identify the student's resources and supports for addressing the problem. The strengths-based approach underscores the value of protective factors in combating *risk factors* and enhancing resilience, embracing the philosophy that treatment is not just about fixing what is broken, but nurturing what is best within ourselves (Seligman, 2004). Defining characteristics of strengths-based counseling (see Table 2.9) involve identifying current and past successes to address future challenges.

Unlike many theories focused on deficit reduction, school counselors use strengths-based counseling to build on students' unique assets to empower, strengthen, instill hope, and strengthen resilience. The Search Institute (2007) has developed lists of development assets for early childhood, middle childhood, and adolescence. These lists are available at

Table 2.9   Strengths-Based Counseling

Theorist and philosophy	Strengths-based counseling is a therapeutic approach that is grounded in the belief that personal strengths enable individuals to achieve, change, and grow. Counseling is directive.
Therapeutic relationship	Collaborative; counselors are guides.
Key concepts/ techniques	Accesses students' unique, inherent strengths and builds upon those strengths to empower, promote change, and encourage self-help. This is often found in what has generally been identified as a weakness. For example, being very talkative and opinionated is viewed, instead, as having great passion, conviction, and being communicative.
Multicultural responsiveness	Working within the clients values appreciates cultural differences; focusing on inner strengths, assets, and resources is compatible to many cultures.

www.search-institute.org/developmental-assets/lists. Each list depicts 40 developmental assets considered to be building blocks for healthy development, which include eight categories:

1. Support
2. Empowerment
3. Boundaries and expectations
4. Constructive use of time
5. Commitment to learning
6. Positive values
7. Social competencies
8. Positive identity

In turn, developmental assets will aid in preventing and mediating problems and promote change. School counselors may find strengths-based counseling particularly helpful for students with low self-esteem, marginal academic performance, and a lack of self-confidence and motivation.

THE MEANING OF LIFE

Kafi is a middle school student whom you meet for issues associated with low motivation and poor self-esteem. During today's session, Kafi remarks, "My life just has no meaning... who am I... what can I do about anything anyway... what kind of future could I possibly have?" Which category of the developmental assets likely needs to be the focus of this counseling session?

Chapter 2: Case Conceptualization Responses

Comprehensive School Counseling Programs

The Parents Do Not Trust Me
The school counselor explains to the teacher that parent involvement at the elementary level is far greater than at the high school level and that due to their child's developmental level parents tend to be much more protective and engaged in the elementary school child's school years.

Personal–Social Development

Crisis Management

Kyleigh's Mother
The correct response is "b." Children of Kyleigh's age may experience difficulty labeling and expressing the emotions they are experiencing as a result of the death of a loved one. School counselors can help Kyleigh to identify, label, and express what she is feeling. As counselors, we do not tell clients "everything will be okay" (response option "a"). Everything may not be okay.

Internet Safety and Cyberbullying

Will I Go to Jail?
Steven's school counselor cannot comment on what the law may or may not do in his case. The school can educate Steven, by letting him know that what he did is considered "sexting" and that sexting is against the law with some state prosecutors charging teens with felonies, including child pornography. It is important that Steven explores his actions, assumes responsibility for his actions, and considers the consequences of his actions on others.

Substance Use, Abuse, Addiction

The Best Football Players
Although the PE teacher has touched base with the parents, the school counselor, too, will want informed consent from the parents due to the

sensitive nature of the topic and the limited confidentiality of a counseling group as a matter of best practices. Meeting with the students to determine their motivation toward group participation is critical as well. Participating in the group to merely satisfy the coach is not sufficient. If the students are motivated and give assent to counseling, they should be given signed consent forms for parental approval to participate in counseling related to this topic. The group would be considered secondary prevention because the students are currently at risk for engaging in the behavior.

Career Development

Career Development Theory and Career Counseling

I Want to Be a Nurse
According to Gottfredson, this is an example of circumscription. The first-grade student is ruling out nursing because his father has signified the occupation as socially unacceptable based on gender.

Ted's Future
You are applying Krumboltz's social learning theory, which focused on actions and cognitions and teaching career decision-making techniques.

Academic Development

Delivery

Classroom Guidance and Group Work

Responsive Services

Small Group Counseling
The correct response is "c." This is both a small group (i.e., method of delivery) and a responsive service (i.e., responding to the immediate needs of students).

Theories and Techniques for the School Setting

Play Therapy

The correct response is "c." Yasmin would likely benefit from expressive toys that will allow her to work through a variety of emotions. The school counselor can explore metaphorical and symbolical expressions of emotions that may be associated with grief, helping Yasmin to identify emotions and work through difficult emotions.

Behavioral

Learning to Resolve Conflict
The correct response is "d." All the possible responses in this scenario are examples of behavioral counseling. *Behavioral rehearsal* involves teaching new behaviors (i.e., conflict resolution) and having students practice those behaviors in some fashion (i.e., role play). Introducing historical figures as models of a specific behavior is a social-cognitive learning approach used in behavioral counseling.

Rational-Emotive Behavior Therapy

Mean Girls
Albert Ellis might describe Elijah's thoughts as irrational. Elijah is overgeneralizing the behavior of girls based on the behavior of a few select girls in one situation. Debunking Elijah's irrational thoughts using the A–B–C model of REBT might be helpful for Elijah.

Strengths-Based Counseling

The Meaning of Life
The school counselor should focus on the developmental assets category of "positive identity," empowering Kafi and encouraging her to be an explorer of her world and all the possibilities.

Chapter 2: Simulation

High School Career Development

Brief Case Description

You are a high school counselor creating a career development classroom guidance unit to target ninth grade students. Your lesson objectives include (1) increasing student knowledge of self in relation to career, (2) enhancing knowledge of resources available for career exploration and decision making, and (3) creating a career and academic plan.

Section A: High School Career Development

What information about the ninth grade student population would be helpful to know when developing your curriculum?

(Select as many as you consider indicated in this section.)

_____A−1.	Gender
_____A−2.	Attendance
_____A−3.	Developmental level of functioning
_____A−4.	Retentions
_____A−5.	Ethnicity
_____A−6.	Discipline
_____A−7.	Grades
_____A−8.	Course selections

Section B: High School Career Development

Which Internet-based career information system might you consider most appropriate to introduce to ninth grade students in your classroom guidance lesson?

(Choose ONLY ONE in this section.)

_____B—1.	WISC
_____B—2.	Choices Planner
_____B—3.	MBTI
_____B—4.	SDS
_____B—5.	Stanford-Binet

Section C: High School Career Development

You want to include an activity in your career development program curriculum that will aid students in developing an understanding of how they come to make career decisions over time, including developmental interests and self-control. Which career theorist's model or approach would be the most useful in helping you to develop your activity?

(Select ONLY ONE in this section.)

_____C—1.	Parsons
_____C—2.	Super
_____C—3.	Krumboltz
_____C—4.	Savickas
_____C—5.	Holland
_____C—6.	Gottfredson

Section D: High School Career Development

When delivering culturally sensitive career development programs to a diverse student population, school counselors consider the following influences on career choice.

(Select as many as you consider indicated in this section.)

_____D—1.	Allocentrism
_____D—2.	Social relationships
_____D—3.	Availability of occupation information

_____D—4.	Beliefs and values	
_____D—5.	Favorite meal	
_____D—6.	Gender	
_____D—7.	Personal appearance	
_____D—8.	Job factors	
_____D—9.	Socioeconomic status	
_____D—10.	Developmental level of functioning	

Section E: High School Career Development

What other strategies might be introduced in your curriculum to aid students in exploring diverse careers?

(Select as many as you consider indicated in this section.)

_____E—1.	Resume and cover letter writing
_____E—2.	Community service
_____E—3.	Job shadowing
_____E—4.	Developing a career portfolio
_____E—5.	Informational interviewing
_____E—6.	Creating a career and academic plan
_____E—7.	Obtaining a part-time/summer job

Section F: High School Career Development

Which interest inventory might you consider including in your curriculum to aid students in understanding self and the work environments for which they may be best suited?

(Choose ONLY ONE in this section.)

_____F—1.	SDS
_____F—2.	Connors scale
_____F—3.	ASVAB

_____F—4.	Career beliefs inventory
_____F—5.	WISC
_____F—6.	Vineland

Section G: High School Career Development

Once your unit is implemented, your principal, who emphasizes accountability and outcomes, would like to know how effective you were in meeting lesson objectives aimed at enhancing student development and career readiness. What information would you provide?

(Select as many as you consider indicated in this section.)

_____G—1.	The number of students who participated in the lessons
_____G—2.	Pre–post measure of knowledge of career resources
_____G—3.	Pre–post measure of student attendance and participation
_____G—4.	Feedback from students' about the lessons' usefulness
_____G—5.	The number of students who completed a career and academic plan
_____G—6.	Pre–post measure of students' knowledge of self related to career
_____G—7.	Measure of academic performance pre- and postlesson implementation

Chapter 2: Simulation Answers

High School Career Development

Brief Case Description

You are a high school counselor creating a career development classroom guidance unit to target ninth grade students. Your lesson objectives include (1) increasing student knowledge of self in relation to career, (2) enhancing knowledge of resources available for career exploration and decision making, and (3) creating a career and academic plan.

Section A: High School Career Development

What information about the ninth grade student population would be helpful to know when developing your curriculum?

(Select as many as you consider indicated in this section.)

A—1.	Gender
	Yes
	Gender is applicable when considering the promotion of nontraditional occupations and the enhancement of student knowledge of self in relation to career. It is also critical that school counselors understand and provide information to students related to gender and the world of work (e.g., gender-role stereotyping, gender segregation, bias in occupational information). Such information enhances student knowledge for career decision making and understanding self in relation to career, two of the objectives identified for this classroom guidance lesson.
A—2.	Attendance
	No
	Attendance is not a factor for consideration because it has no bearing on the objectives identified for this classroom guidance lesson.
A—3.	Developmental level of functioning
	Yes
	Students' levels of social and cognitive functioning is important to consider when creating and delivering a developmentally appropriate educational curriculum. Otherwise, students may not be capable of grasping the material presented, and the school counselor is unable to meet the objectives of the lesson.

A—4.	Retentions
	No
	Knowing which students have been retained or the number of students with retentions is not a factor for consideration because it has no bearing on the objectives identified for this classroom guidance lesson.
A—5.	Ethnicity
	Yes
	Ethnicity is a consideration when creating any curriculum that is sensitive to the needs of a diverse population. It is important for school counselors to understand how ethnicity impacts career decision making and critical that school counselors provide students with information related to culturally diverse individuals and the world of work (e.g., stereotyping, discrimination, affirmative action, bias in occupational information). Such information enhances student knowledge for career decision making and understanding self in relation to career, two of the objectives identified for this classroom guidance lesson.
A—6.	Discipline
	No
	Discipline is not a factor for consideration because it has no bearing on the objectives identified for this classroom guidance lesson.
A—7.	Grades
	No
	Grades are not a factor for consideration because they have no bearing on the objectives identified for this classroom guidance lesson.
A—8.	Course selections
	No
	Although students will be identifying courses and programs as part of the curriculum for this classroom guidance lesson (e.g., creating a career and academic plan), knowing students' current course selections is not a factor for consideration because it has no bearing on the objectives identified for this classroom guidance lesson.

Section B: High School Career Development

Which Internet-based career information system might you consider most appropriate to introduce to ninth grade students in your classroom guidance lesson?

(Choose ONLY ONE in this section.)

B—1.	WISC
	No
	The WISC is often used in schools for diagnostic testing to assess level of intelligence.
B—2.	Choices Planner
	Yes
	Choices Planner is a comprehensive career information system for career planning at the high school level and the single best selection for this item.
B—3.	MBTI
	No
	The MBTI, although sometimes used in career counseling, it is considered a personality test.
B—4.	SDS
	No
	The SDS is a career interest inventory.
B—5.	Stanford-Binet
	No
	The Stanford-Binet is an intelligence test often used in the schools for diagnostic testing.

Section C: High School Career Development

You want to include an activity in your career development program curriculum that will aid students in developing an understanding of how others influence career decision making. Which career theory, model, or approach would be the most useful in helping you to develop your activity?

(Choose ONLY ONE in this section.)

C—1.	Cochran's narrative career counseling theory
	No
	This theory focuses on one's narrated story based on perceived interactions with the world. Although one's story may include important others in the individual's life, the instructions stated to select "only one" and this is not the most relevant response among the choices provided.

C−2.	Super's lifespan theory Yes This model demonstrates how childhood career development evolves.
C−3.	Krumboltz's social learning theory No Social learning theory emphasizes the role of behavior and cognitions in career decision making. Important others may have served as role models or important reinforcers of behavior, however, relationship is not the single most applicable construct for this theory or response for this item.
C−4.	Savickas' career construction approach No Seeks to identify meaningful life themes and one's adaptation to the environment and unique situations.
C−5.	Cognitive information-processing approach No Emphasizes how one's thoughts influence career development.
C−6.	Gottfredson's theory of circumscription and compromise No Focus is on developmental processes in career decision making.

Section D: High School Career Development

When delivering culturally sensitive career development programs to a diverse student population, school counselors consider the following influences on career choice.

(Select as many as you consider indicated in this section.)

D−1.	Allocentrism Yes It is important to understand the way the student views career selection.
D−2.	Social relationships Yes Career choice is influenced by important others in student's life.

D—3.	Availability of occupation information Yes Students from low-socioeconomic environments do not have the same access to career information and career development tools.
D—4.	Beliefs and values Yes Understanding how one's general and work-related beliefs and values impact occupational choices is critical to aiding individuals in making decisions that result in satisfying careers.
D—5.	Favorite meal No This would not be relevant to career decision making.
D—6.	Gender Yes Gender influences career selection. Encouraging students to consider nontraditional careers is a growing trend in today's schools.
D—7.	Personal appearance No A student's appearance does not impact career decision making. However, it is important to consider that how students feel about themselves (e.g., appearance, intelligence) may impact career decision making.
D—8.	Job factors Yes Job factors (e.g., salary, environment, physical ability, education, and training) influence career decision making.
D—9.	Socioeconomic status Yes Students may rule out particular careers (ruling in others) based on socioeconomic status. Also, students from low socioeconomic backgrounds may not be knowledgeable of all the different career opportunities due to limited career resources and information.
D—10.	Developmental level of functioning Yes A student's ability to perform the occupation of choice must be considered.

Section E: High School Career Development

What other strategies might be introduced in your curriculum to aid students in exploring diverse careers?

(Select as many as you consider indicated in this section.)

E—1.	Resume and cover letter writing
	No
	Resumes and cover letters are important tools for applying for colleges, jobs, military, apprenticeships, and technical schools. However, students will not find these tools useful for exploring diverse careers.
E—2.	Community service
	Yes
	Community service is a valuable way for students to learn about different occupations while also providing a valuable service to the community.
E—3.	Job shadowing
	Yes
	Job shadowing allows students to observe, first-hand, the characteristics of specific occupations from which to further development career interests.
E—4.	Developing a career portfolio
	No
	Career portfolios are important tools for enhancing application to colleges, jobs, military, apprenticeships, and technical schools. However, students will not find this tool useful for exploring diverse careers.
E—5.	Informational interviewing
	Yes
	Informational interviewing provides students with relevant and real world information about specific occupations. Informational interviews allow students an opportunity to ask valuable questions that might not be asked in a job interview for fear of revealing a lack of knowledge to a prospective employer.
E—6.	Creating a career and academic plan
	No
	Creating a career and academic plan is an objective of the career development program. However, it is not a strategy that will aid students in exploring diverse careers. It will aid students in identifying future course selections and programs based on identified careers of interest.

E—7.	Obtaining a part-time/summer job
	Yes
	Part-time and summer jobs are excellent ways for students to explore a variety of occupations and work environments.

Section F: High School Career Development

Which interest inventory might you consider including in your curriculum to aid students in understanding self and the work environments for which they may be best suited?

(Choose ONLY ONE in this section.)

F—1.	SDS
	Yes
	Holland's SDS assigns individuals and work environments into six categories using a three-letter code.
F—2.	Connors Scale
	No
	The Connors Scale is an instrument used to assess for ADHD.
F—3.	ASVAB
	No
	The ASVAB, often used to identify areas of strength, can drive career decision making, but it does not yield information about self and the work environment.
F—4.	Career beliefs inventory
	No
	Krumboltz's career beliefs inventory identifies problematic self-perceptions and worldviews.
F—5.	WISC
	No
	The WISC is often used in schools for diagnostic testing to assess level of intelligence.

F—6.	Vineland
	No
	The Vineland measures levels of personal and social functioning and is considered to be a personality test.

Section G: High School Career Development

Once your unit is implemented, your principal, who emphasizes accountability and outcomes, would like to know how effective you were in meeting lesson objectives aimed at enhancing student development and career readiness. What information would you provide?

(Select as many as you consider indicated in this section.)

G—1.	The number of students who participated in the lessons
	No
	The number of participants does not indicate the lesson's effectiveness in meeting the identified objectives for this career development program.
G—2.	Pre–post measure of knowledge of career resources
	Yes
	Pre- and postlesson assessments of knowledge gains related to career resources measure one of the lesson's objectives (i.e., enhancing knowledge of resources available for career exploration and decision making) and would be valuable information to submit to your principal in a results report.
G—3.	Pre–post measure of student attendance and participation
	No
	Student attendance and participation does not indicate the lesson's effectiveness in meeting identified objectives for this career development program.
G—4.	Feedback from students about the lessons' usefulness
	No
	Feedback from students' pertaining to their perceived value of the lesson is useful information for program improvement and/or continuance. However, it is not useful information to submit to your principal, who is requesting outcome data related to meeting the program's objectives.

G—5.	The number of students who completed a career and academic plan
	Yes
	Creating a career and academic plan is an objective of the program. For this reason, providing your principal with the number of students who created a plan is appropriate to his or her request. In this situation, it would be appropriate to provide the number of participants as well because participation provides a point for comparison (i.e., number of participants and number of participants who completed a career and academic plan).
G—6.	Pre–post measure of students' knowledge of self related to career
	Yes
	Increasing student knowledge of self in relation to career is an objective of the program. For this reason, providing your principal with this outcome data is appropriate to his or her request.
G—7.	Measure of academic performance pre- and postlesson implementation
	No
	Enhanced academic performance is not an objective of this program.

Chapter 2: Guided Reflection

Describe in your own words a comprehensive school counseling program.

Explain the significance of personal–social development in school counseling.

The following are critical issues/incidents associated with the personal–social development of students in the school setting. Define each critical incident and identify related constructs and its significance to school counseling.

Transitioning

Crisis management

Dropout

School violence and bullying

Internet safety and cyberbullying

Substance use, abuse, addiction

Divorce

Parenting style

The following are critical issues/incidents associated with the career development of students in the school setting. Define each critical incident and identify related constructs and their significance to school counseling.

Influences on career decision making

Career development theory and career counseling

Career and college transitions

Assessment instruments and career information systems

Describe, compare, and provide examples as needed for clarification for each of the following methods of service delivery used by school counselors.

Classroom guidance and group work

Individual student planning/counseling

Responsive services

Systems support

The following are the most widely used counseling theories in the school setting. For each theory identify the theorist and associated techniques and constructs, and summarize the theory. Last, provide one example for each theory of a situation in which the theory might be selected over another and why.

Adlerian

Behavioral

Cognitive behavioral theory

Gestalt

Person-centered

Rational emotive behavior therapy

Reality counseling

Solution-focused brief counseling

Strengths-based counseling

Chapter 3

Diversity and Advocacy

Never in the history of school counseling have our student populations been more lusciously diverse than they are at the present time. Multilingual, multiethnic, and multicultural students are expected to become the majority by the close of the next decade (Holcomb-McCoy, 2004). In order to continue to practice effectively, professionally, and ethically, school counselors must be culturally competent with a sound commitment to understanding how unique student characteristics impact learning and educational experiences.

School counselors advocate for the acceptance, respect, and fair and equal treatment of all people (ASCA, 2005). The Tucson shootings and the youth camp massacre in Norway are recent reminders of the international scope and magnitude of the need for a call to arms of the people to advocate for one another—in our homelands and across oceans.

School counselors actively challenge oppressive conditions, teach social responsibility, promote climates of acceptance and safety, and seek to remove barriers to success for all individuals. Advocacy is driven by the school counselor's compassion for others and conviction to promoting social justice. *Social justice* is an ideological approach to the professional and ethical practice of professional school counseling. Section E.2.a of the ASCA *Ethical Standards for School Counselors* (ASCA, 2010) states that school counselors "monitor and expand personal multicultural and social justice advocacy awareness, knowledge and skills" (p. 5).

Six key elements have been identified as key to implementing a social justice approach in school counseling. The following six

Cs of school counseling encompass the life-force of social justice (Holcomb-McCoy, 2007):

■ Counseling and intervention planning
■ Consultation
■ Connecting schools, families, and communities
■ Collecting and utilizing data
■ Challenging bias
■ Coordinating student services and support

Section E.2.g of the ASCA *Ethical Standards for School Counselors* (ASCA, 2010) reiterates school counselors' responsibility "work as advocates and leaders in the school to create equity-based school counseling programs that help close any achievement, opportunity and attainment gaps that deny all students the chance to pursue their educational goals" (p. 5). The ACA adopted *Advocacy Competencies* (Lewis, Arnold, House, & Toporek, 2003), which aid school counselors in better understanding our roles associated with advocacy and how Advocacy Competencies apply vis-a-vis school counseling. Table 3.1 provides a brief overview of the Advocacy Competencies for each of the six domains. For a detailed listing of the competencies for each domain go to the ACA website at www.counseling.org.

School counselors are the rock stars of advocacy, belting out the lyrics of equity and access for quality curriculum and educational and career resources for all. Data and evaluation are the instruments used to identify and remove obstacles to student success and to challenge oppressive policies and practices. Emphasis is placed on social justice, empowerment, and equality, creating opportunities to promote students' strengths and academic, career, and personal–social development. School counselors apply systems-focused practices and leadership while collaborating and consulting with important others both within and outside of the school on behalf of students and families.

Barriers to academic success are identified by disaggregating data from a variety of sources by race, ethnicity, special needs, gender, and teacher. (ASCA, 2005, 2010; Erford, 2011; Schellenberg, 2008) provides a list of whole-school data elements, which have been embellished to provide you with a comprehensive listing of school wide data sources that when examined can identify access, attainment, and achievement gaps (see Table 3.2).

Table 3.1 Advocacy Competencies

Community collaboration	Their ongoing work with people gives counselors a unique awareness of recurring themes. Counselors are often among the first to become aware of specific difficulties in the environment.
	Advocacy-oriented counselors often choose to respond to such challenges by alerting existing organizations that are already working for change and that might have an interest in the issue at hand.
	In these situations, the counselor's primary role is as an ally. Counselors can also be helpful to organizations by making available to them our particular skills: interpersonal relations, communications, training, and research.
Systems advocacy	When counselors identify systemic factors that act as barriers to their students' or clients' development, they often wish that they could change the environment and prevent some of the problems that they see every day.
	Regardless of the specific target of change, the processes for altering the status quo have common qualities. Change is a process that requires vision, persistence, leadership, collaboration, systems analysis, and strong data. In many situations, a counselor is the right person to take leadership.
Public information	Across settings, specialties, and theoretical perspectives, professional counselors share knowledge of human development and expertise in communication.
	These qualities make it possible for advocacy-oriented counselors to awaken the general public to macrosystemic issues regarding human dignity.
Social/political advocacy	Counselors regularly act as change agents in the systems that affect their own students and clients most directly. This experience often leads toward the recognition that some of the concerns they have addressed affected people in a much larger arena.
	When this happens, counselors use their skills to carry out social/political advocacy.

Source: Adapted from Lewis, J., Arnold, M., House, R., & Toporek, R. (2003). *Advocacy competencies*. Retrieved March 7, 2011, from www.counseling.org/resources.

Table 3.2   School-Wide Data for Gap Identification

Access (or Opportunity)	Enrollment patterns and participation in: • AP, IB, honors, college preparation, and enrichment classes • Special education programs • 504 Plans • Gifted and talented programs • Student Council • Governor's School • ESL/ELL learner classes/programs
Attainment	• Attendance • Dropout rates and graduation rates • Promotion and retention rates • Homework completion rates • Course completion and pass rates • Non-traditional program tracks (GED, Job Corps) • In-school and out-of-school suspensions and expulsion rates • Study abroad • Parent participation rates • GED attainment rates • College/postsecondary acceptance patterns • College application completion • FAFSA completion • Scholarship submissions • Participation in Individual Planning with the School Counselor • Rates of participation in interest inventories, career development activities, college entrance testing, industry certifications, learning style inventories, academic portfolios development.
Achievement	• Grade point averages • Scores on classroom assignments end-of-course tests • Scores on standardized achievement tests • Scores on homework assignments • Scores on aptitude tests • Course grades in all subjects

Equity and Access

As advocates, school counselors are rock stars promoting the equity and access tour for quality curriculum and educational and career resources for all. School counselors use data and evaluation to identify and remove obstacles to student success, challenging oppressive policies and practices and emphasizing social justice, empowerment, and equality. Systems-focused practices and leadership are also paramount to equity and access, collaborating and consulting with important others both within and outside of the school on behalf of students and families.

Equity and access begins with compassion. School counselors advocate for an appreciation of diversity and understand that issues related to diversity impact learning and academic achievement as well as students' personal–social and career development. Advocating for an appreciation of diversity (e.g., socioeconomic background, family and community, culture, gender, ethnicity, levels of intelligence and functioning). The goal is to create encouraging learning environments perfumed with social consciousness and compassion for all regardless of race, culture, gender, sexuality, religion, family and community, levels of intelligence and functioning, and socioeconomic standing or status.

ASCA's Position on Equity for All Students

Professional school counselors recognize and distinguish individual and group differences and strive to value all students and groups equally. Professional school counselors advocate for the equitable treatment of all students in school and in the community.

Position statement adopted 2006

Diversity has many faces and has been defined as the range of cultures and subcultures that characterize attitudes, values, beliefs, rituals, norms, symbols, conventions, customs, ideologies, and behaviors (McDevitt & Ormond, 2002). School counselors spread the aroma of respect and value for diverse individuals and groups, seeking to eliminate hostility and inappropriate language. Inclusive language, too, is modeled to foster a nonjudgmental environment where diversity is embraced and celebrated.

ASCA's Position on Cultural Diversity

Professional school counselors promote academic, career, and personal/social success for all students. Professional school counselors collaborate with stakeholders to create a school and community climate that embraces cultural diversity and helps to remove barriers that impede student success.

Position statement adopted 1988; revised 1993,
1999, 2004, 2009

Resolving identified inequities may involve reviewing and making suggestions for more inclusive classrooms, curriculum, instructional strategies, textbooks, classroom management approaches, and spearheading changes to local and state policy. Challenging the system in this manner may result in resistance and disequilibrium, necessitating that the school counselors aid the system in working through difficult changes and rediscovering new balance.

HELP ME TO REACH MY POTENTIAL

Jameel, a tenth-grade student, comes to you, his new school counselor, to discuss college opportunities. You notice that Jameel's classes are not rigorous and may limit his college options, while his GPA is consistent with a high-functioning student. Upon further investigation, you notice that students from low socioeconomic backgrounds and ethnically diverse students are underrepresented in rigorous courses. This is an example of:

a. Access gap
b. Attainment gap
c. Achievement gap
d. None of the above

National legislation, enacted under the Rehabilitation Act of 1973, also referred to as Section 504, and the IDEA, ensures that all students receive *free appropriate public education* (FAPE). Additionally, students who are LEP or use ESL are entitled to specialized instructional and testing accommodations. Students with special needs are guaranteed access to general and specialized educational aids and services to meet their individualized learning needs.

ASCA's Position on Students with Special Needs

Professional school counselors encourage and support all students' academic, personal/social, and career development through comprehensive school counseling programs. Professional school counselors are committed to helping all students realize their potential, and make adequate yearly progress regardless of challenges resulting from disabilities and other special needs.

Position statement adopted 1999
revised 2004, 2010

School counselors ensure that instructional strategies include accommodations for students with special needs (i.e., students with an IEP, 504 plan, *medical plan*, and/or LEP students). Accommodations may include alternative testing programs; extended time on classwork, homework, and tests; the use of translators and bilingual or multilingual instruction; resources in a variety of languages, large print, or Braille; reduced assignments and homework; special seating arrangements; and specialized equipment.

The promotion, retention, and placement of students are monitored by the school counselor by participating on committees (e.g., child study, student assistance, early intervention) that review individual student needs and provide specialized instruction to meet those needs. School counselors create programs and classroom guidance lessons and facilitate small groups designed to close gaps identified through data sources, observation, and established research.

ASCA's Position on Retention, Social Promotion, and Age-Appropriate Placement

Professional school counselors recognize that decisions on student retention, promotion and placement are best made when the needs of the student are at the forefront of the decision and after multiple factors have been considered. Professional school counselors oppose laws or policies that require social promotion or retention without considering the needs of the individual student.

Position statement adopted 2006

Equity and access for all students also applies to those students who are advanced functioning. Students who are more advanced cognitively need to be intellectually challenged. Advanced functioning students benefit from participation in gifted and talented programs such as Governor's School and/or advanced placement and summer enrichment classes, discussed in Chapter 6.

When school counselors hear "gifted student," our antennas begin to flail and hum in readiness to pick up on any frequency of distress, because cognitively advanced students are often the suffer-in-silence type. Gifted students may experience a host of social, emotional, and behavioral difficulties unique to the characteristics of giftedness calling for both preventive and responsive services that take into consideration the academic pressures, intellectual excitabilities, and heavy commitments that may lead to stress, depression, and career uncertainty (Peterson, 2006).

ASCA's Position on Gifted and Talented Student Programs

The professional school counselor is an integral part of the educational team that delivers a comprehensive school counseling program to meet the needs of all students. Because gifted and talented students have some unique and diverse needs professional school counselors collaborate with other educators within the context of the comprehensive school counseling program to assist in meeting these needs.

Position statement adopted 1988; revised 1993, 1999, 2001, 2007

Low SES poses unique challenges for schools, families, and communities. Low SES can have a negative impact on family structures, housing, individual identity, self-esteem, health, and access to educational and career resources. School counselors act as advocates for social change, social responsibility, and social justice in the school and community, providing students from low SES and impoverished backgrounds with much-needed consideration to ensure equity and access to programming and services. Advocating for equity and access necessitates active participation, action, and unity. Toward this end, school counselors coordinate and engage in community efforts to combat poverty, empower, support, and give a voice to diverse student populations and the family system.

Confronting barriers to academic achievement and student wellness may also involve helping parents and students to identify and access resources, communicate needs, and advocate for themselves. School counselors can take the lead in establishing strategies that will help to remove some of the more common barriers to parents' participation in school activities, such as

- Brainstorming ways to welcome parent participation
- Providing child care during school meetings and events
- Arranging school bus transportation to school events
- Developing needs assessments
- Coordinating car pools
- Providing information regarding bus transportation
- Offering multiple times for program presentations including weekends

Admittedly, during my years as a practicing school counselor, the fierce growl of my inner bear would emerge in the face of injustice. Hey, it happens. Plus, most of the snarls were equivalent to a quake of no more than a 2.0 in seismic energy on the Richter scale. So, with about 8000 quakes of this size each day across the nation, at times, the growl was barely noticeable. When the bear is riled, we simply (and sometimes not so simply) keep the explicatives to ourselves as if performing a soliloquy, ask for strength, and stay mindful that the bear, too, works responsibly, professionally, and ethically with others to affect change. That is, we show our teeth, but we are careful not to bite anybody!

Section G.2 of the ASCA *Ethical Standards for School Counselors* (ASCA, 2010) reminds us that when working in situations or faced with policies that do not reflect the ethics of the profession, school counselors collaborate with others, acting "responsibly through the correct channels to try and remedy the condition" (p. 7). School counselors labor under the philosophy that it really does *take a village*—and sometimes a bear.

FAPE

You are a school counselor and member of the child study team at your school. During today's meeting, a parent became quite upset and roared, "I am going to seek legal advisement ... you are denying my child a free and appropriate education." The parent is likely referring to which legislation:

a. IDEA
b. ADA
c. FERPA
d. McKinney-Vento Act

Multicultural Competence

School counselors understand how students' self-perceptions and world-views (e.g, conceptualization of the world) are shaped by culture and cultural experiences. As such, culturally sensitive responsive services and competent *multicultural counseling* are used to clarify feelings, promote self-understanding and self-esteem, and develop the personal, social, and emotional well-being of students from all cultures and backgrounds.

To promote equitable practices, school counselors are culturally competent and seek to improve the cultural competence of others with whom they interact. CACREP (2009) defines multicultural as "the diversity of racial, ethnic, and cultural heritage; socioeconomic status; age; gender; sexual orientation; and religious and spiritual beliefs, as well as physical, emotional, and mental abilities." (p. 60).

Section E.2 of the ASCA *Ethical Standards for School Counselors* (ASCA, 2010) emphasizes that "school counselors strive for exemplary cultural competence by ensuring personal beliefs or values are not imposed on students or other stakeholders" (p. 5). In striving for this competence, school counselors need to become familiar with the Multicultural Counseling Competencies and Standards developed by the AMCD, a branch of the ACA. The Multicultural Counseling Competencies and Standards are available at www.amcdaca.org.

School counselors who wish to gain a greater understanding of the knowledge and skills areas needed to provide culturally competent counseling should refer to the *School Counselor Multicultural Competence Checklist* (Holcomb-McCoy, 2004). The checklist is also helpful in heightening self-awareness of current levels of cultural competence and assessing the school's policies, procedures, and programs for cultural competence. As noted above, Section E.2 of the ASCA *Ethical Standards for School Counselors* (ASCA, 2010) underscores the importance of the school counselor's self-knowledge and an understanding of oppression and the development of racial identity and worldviews as key to multicultural competence.

Reducing and, moreover, eliminating issues associated with *encapsulation* and developing the ability to provide students from diverse backgrounds with the optimal environment for success call for a keen sense of one's cultural self (dominant and minority cultures) and the affirmation of nondominant cultures, which involves

- Awareness of one's own assumptions, racial biases, and attitudes
- Awareness of the environmental forces that have impacted minority students
- Understanding the importance of worldviews and the similarities and differences between the school counselor and the culturally different student and how those characteristics impact counseling process
- Understanding differences in language, terminology, and communication styles
- Possessing an empathetic attitude
- Possessing a knowledge of a variety of counseling theories and techniques and their strengths and weaknesses with diverse cultures
- Possessing a knowledge of racial identity development
- Learning a variety of languages
- Participating in multicultural development workshops
- Staying abreast of current literature on topics related to counseling the culturally different
- Participating in cultural immersion experiences

School counselors realize that racial identity development is a multifaceted process, and are careful not to conceptualize students within a universal grouping based on culture or subculture. In other words, they avoid stereotyping. Individuality is multifaceted and influenced by numerous personal and environmental factors. Models of racial identity development affirm varying levels of enculturation among members of a particular race or culture. That is, on the basis of social and cultural influences, some students feel a stronger identification with their culture than others, which, in turn, impacts acculturation, which is the individual's personal struggle to adapt to a new and unfamiliar culture (Matsumoto & Juang, 2008). Schools are agents of encultura-tion reflecting societal organization and views that support a particular culture.

School counselors are aware that students who enter a school where the dominant culture is different from their own will experience varying levels of adjustment based on the strength of their enculturation. The internal process of acculturation is influenced by assimilation, a process external to the individual and determined by the dominant cultures' acceptance of the individual from a new and unfamiliar culture (Matsumoto & Juang, 2008).

THE FISH MARKET

Kwame, a new student from Ghana, is sitting in his new American fifth-grade elementary school class. While the teacher is teaching the mathematics lesson, she notices that Kwame appears confused and asks him if he understands what she is teaching. He responds that he does not understand and that this is really different from the way he learns in his country. He goes on to say that he learned math by selling fish. The class laughs, and the teacher, taking Kwame's remark as a per-sonal affront, tells him that math instruction is not the time to be joking around. The teacher's response is an example of:

a. Assimilation
b. Acculturation
c. Encapsulation
d. Enculturation

Recognizing that culture impacts a student's thoughts, beliefs, view of self, problem-solving and decision-making processes, orientation to time, and verbal and nonverbal communications—their very being—school coun-selors are students and teachers of multiculturalism. In addition to becoming culturally competent, school counselors teach cultural sensitivity to teachers and to students using systemic approaches such as classroom guidance les-sons, school-wide presentations, transitioning programs, and small groups. The following topics are recommended when teaching others to be sensitive to those from culturally diverse backgrounds (Erford, 2011):

■ Affirming differences
■ Using accurate multicultural terminology
■ Exploring one's own biases

- Learning about ethnic and racial identity models
- Understanding diverse worldviews
- Challenging oppression
- Understanding the dangers of stereotyping
- Exploring racial, ethnic, and cultural histories

Affirming cultural diversity within and outside of the school setting aids students of the nondominant culture in developing a strong racial identity. A strong racial identity is a protective factor that promotes resiliency. The importance of resilience and additional ways that school counselors can build resilience in children and adolescents is discussed in Chapter 2.

LOOK AT ME WHEN I AM TALKING TO YOU

Maya, an Asian high school student, comes to you, her alphabet counselor, because the student assistance counselor is out with the flu. She discusses an important family issue with you, hoping to make some critical decisions related to the issue. When the student assistance counselor returns, you let her know about your brief session with Maya. The student assistance counselor immediately knows who you are referring to and says that she, too, met with Maya once for about 10 minutes, and adds, "Did you notice how little eye contact she makes with you—it's a cultural thing." The alphabet counselor replies, "I did not notice." The student assistance counselor is making a generalization based on Maya's culture, which is considered

    a. Acculturation
    b. Encapsulation
    c. Assimilation
    d. Stereotyping

Spirituality

Spirituality has been a taboo topic in the public school system as a result of the separation of church and state. However, heightened emphasis on the importance of spirituality in the ethical and culturally competent practice of counseling is opening the school doors for the return of spirituality as a topic crucial to holistic student development.

Spiritual development is a critical aspect of human development, a cultural agent, and a natural component for exploration in the counseling process that significantly impacts the student's worldview and the counseling relationship (Ingersoll & Bauer, 2004; Rayburn, 2004). How can you study Naples, Italy, and disregard the pizza pie? ASCA committed an entire special issue in the June 2004 journal *Professional School Counselor* to aid school counselors in understanding the importance and appropriateness of spiritual development as part of a comprehensive school counseling program and approaches for promoting the spiritual development of students without espousing our values on students.

Section A.1 of the ASCA *Ethical Standards for School Counselors* (ASCA, 2010) states that school counselors "respect students' values, beliefs and cultural background and do not impose school counselor's personal values on students or their families." Uncertain as to how to address the sensitive topic of spirituality in a manner that would be considered by parents, students, and administrators to be ethical, professional, and legal, school counselors have elected to avoid the topic.

Like the path to multicultural competence, becoming a school counselor competent in addressing matters of spirituality begins with identifying personal biases with regard to spiritual and religious beliefs and traditions and a commitment to learning more about the spiritual and religious practices of others. Socrates, a Greek thinker and architect of Western philosophies, is viewed by some as a martyr for moral virtue. Socrates emphasized the importance of not being blind to our own (and others') deeply seeded beliefs and presuppositions. Like Socrates, school counselors are heartened to live by the truism "To know thyself," seeking a path for ourselves and our students in what Italians refer to as living *la dolce vita*, or the good life.

Helping students to gain insight into their worldviews and working within the worldviews of students necessitates cultural diplomacy. That is, having a dialogue about how religious or spiritual beliefs, as well as tradition, lifestyle, ideas, beliefs, and values, may impact the student's personal–social, academic, and career decisions. For example, it is virtually impossible to understand Indians apart from their religion because it is so deeply ingrained in everyday personal and public living.

Allow teaching versus preaching to be the guiding philosophy (Wolf, 2004). That is, objectively educate students about spirituality and religion by (1) being descriptive and unbiased in the information presented, (2) teaching respect and appreciation of diversity, and (3) introducing literature or current events that involve spirituality, religion, personal beliefs, and values for class or group discussion. Discussing issues related to spirituality is both constitutional and ethical in accordance with the First Amendment of the Constitution and the ASCA Code of Ethics, respectively (Wolf, 2004). Just as Michelle Obama has the right to bare arms, school counselors have the right to remove the sleeves that cover critical areas of human development in our efforts to provide culturally competent counseling services.

Maintaining objectivity in school counseling activities related to spirituality and religion begins with an understanding of the differences between spirituality and religion. Religion is more of an organized practice that involves specific beliefs. Religion generally involves worship by groups of individuals in a ritualized fashion and in a brick-and-mortar establishment such as a church. Spirituality is broad, unstructured, and focused on the individual's essence of being in relation to nature and the universe and may include religion. Fundamental principles of spirituality include hope, meaning in life, and compassion.

In addition to teaching, school counselors might also consider participating in student-initiated spiritual and religious events such as the annual See You at the Pole prayer meeting. Section 9524 of the Elementary and Secondary Education Act (ESEA) constitutionally protects prayer in public schools (United States Department of Education, 2003). School counselors who explore issues of spirituality with students are engaging in both ethically responsible and culturally sensitive counseling practices.

AN INTERNATIONAL BROUHAHA

Michelle Obama's reaching out to shake the hand of the conservative Indonesian government official has been viewed as a culturally insensitive gesture grounded in a lack of knowledge pertaining to the Indonesian culture. This would also demonstrate the profound impact of the following religious beliefs in shaping the cultural customs and identity of many Indonesian people:

a. Muslim
b. Christian
c. Protestant
d. None of the above

Chapter 3: Case Conceptualization Responses

Diversity and Advocacy

Equity and Access

Help Me to Reach My Potential
The correct response is "a." Jameel has not been given access to rigorous coursework despite his ability to succeed in advanced placement classes. School counselors consider the student's ability and aptitude based on past academic performance and take future career and college desires into consideration when determining core and elective course placements.

FAPE
The parent is referencing the language used in the IDEA, which ensures that students receive a FAPE.

Multicultural Competence

The Fish Market
The correct response is "c." The teacher's response is demonstrative of encapsulation and a lack of cultural sensitivity. The teacher is encapsulated in the Western culture whereby mathematics is taught in a formal educational institution and classroom. In Ghana, many children learn math in the community, through the elderly, and in trades such as marketing fish.

Look at Me When I Am Talking to You
The correct response is "d." The student assistance counselor is stereotyping. Generally speaking, the Asian culture views direct eye contact with elders and with those in authority as rude and confrontational. Maya's lack of eye contact could be related to culture and her way of showing the school counselor respect. However, it may not be related to culture; the alphabet counselor did not notice a lack of eye contact when speaking with Maya. Consequently, some secondary schools divide school counselor load by alphabet, and those school counselors are often referred to as the alphabet counselor. Other schools may assign students to school counselors by grade level, in which case the school counselor is often referred to as the grade level counselor.

Spirituality

An International Brouhaha

The correct response is "a." Many, if not most, of the people of Indonesia practice the Muslim faith. This real-world case drives home the importance of spirituality and religion in shaping the practices and worldview of individuals, which must not be ignored in counseling and in the specialty of school counseling as well as in the teachings in our schools. Whether we are of the majority or minority population of a Western or non-Western culture, we need to learn about (or in this case, be advised on) the cultures with whom we are interacting to develop positive relations.

Chapter 3: Simulation

The Newbie

Brief Case Description

You are a newly practicing elementary school counselor developing your first classroom guidance lesson for fifth graders.

Section A: The Newbie

One of the teachers informs you that the principal requires that special education students be pulled out of class to be with resource teachers for academic tutoring during the school counselor's classroom guidance lessons. The teacher said the principal announced this practice during a faculty meeting a few years ago, as a way to provide special education students with extra academic support and improve test scores. What is your response?

(Select ONLY ONE in this section.)

_____A−1.	Comply with the principal's requirements and develop the curriculum for the general education student population at that grade level.	
_____A−2.	Go to the principal and explain how this practice is not equitable and limits access to important programming for special education students.	
_____A−3.	Strongly encourage the teacher to keep special education students in the class during classroom guidance.	
_____A−4.	Talk to the special education teachers to ensure classroom guidance by the school counselor is a part of the students' IEP so that students are included in the lessons.	

Section B: The Newbie

Now that classroom guidance lesson will be delivered to both general education and special needs students, which of the following applies?

(Select as many as you consider indicated in this section.)

_____B—1.	Curriculum should be developed based on the grade level of the student regardless of special needs status to ensure access to rigorous, age-appropriate curriculum.
_____B—2.	Curriculum should be modified to meet the special needs of each student in the classroom.
_____B—3.	Because it is impossible to meet the special needs of all students, develop a curriculum that meets the needs of the majority.
_____B—4.	Make every effort to ensure special needs students sit grouped together so that you can better monitor their understanding of the lesson's content.
_____B—5.	Teachers need to inform school counselors of the needs of the special education students in their class because school counselors are not privy to this information.

Section C: The Newbie

One of the teachers who is receiving your classroom guidance lesson informs you that one of her students, Sabrina, will not be a part of the classroom guidance lesson because she is an ESL student and her translator is out on the day of the lesson. Your response is:
   (Select ONLY ONE in this section.)

_____C—1.	All students need to be present for the lesson, so you will reschedule the lesson.
_____C—2.	You will meet with Sabrina and her translator individually on another day to deliver the content of the lesson.
_____C—3.	Have Sabrina participate in the lesson without her translator to ensure equity and access to all programming.
_____C—4.	Identify others in the building who can translate for Sabrina and see if he or she can translate on the day of the lesson while also talking to the principal about getting a substitute.
_____C—5.	Tape the classroom guidance lesson so that Sabrina and her translator can watch it together when the translator returns.

Section D: The Newbie

During the classroom guidance lesson, a female student sitting by herself answers a question you posed. You notice that the student has an olive complexion, is very soft-spoken, and has an accent. Her response is uncommon, so you let her know that her response is interesting and offers a unique perspective. Another female student blurts out in a sarcastic tone, "Yea, you mean a weird perspective," and she and the girl next to her laugh along with the rest of the class. How would you respond?

(Select as many as you consider indicated in this section.)

_____D—1.	Continue the lesson, careful not to give the girls an audience.	
_____D—2.	Stop the lesson and have the two girls removed from the class.	
_____D—3.	Reassure the student that the response she gave was appropriate and worthwhile.	
_____D—4.	Tell the girls that those comments are unacceptable and mean-spirited, redirecting the lesson to one of diversity appreciation, respect, and the power of words.	
_____D—5.	Continue the lesson, and ask to see the two girls after class.	
_____D—6.	Tell the girls that those comments are unacceptable and mean-spirited and then continue the planned lesson.	
_____D—7.	Come back the following week to teach a lesson on appreciation of diversity.	

Section E: The Newbie

The day after the lesson, the student comes to you to thank you and lets you know that the girls have been nicer to her. She begins to share some family and personal issues that are bothering her. As a culturally sensitive counselor, how might you proceed?

(Select ONLY ONE in this section.)

_____E—1.	Let the student know that you are not familiar with her culture, express your interest in learning about her culture, and ask her to educate you.	
_____E—2.	Sensitive not to make the student uncomfortable about her culture, just listen and reflect her feelings.	

_____E—3.	Ask her to identify her culture and to come back later, so you can find out more about her culture before she returns.
_____E—4.	Let the student know that you are not familiar with her culture, so she should talk to her parents about her concerns to ensure cultural sensitivity.
_____E—5.	Let her know that you are not familiar with her culture, and share with her how the dominant culture handles those types of issues.
_____E—6.	Let her know that you are unfamiliar with her culture, but offer your thoughts and beliefs on the issues.

Chapter 3: Simulation Answers

The Newbie

Brief Case Description

You are a newly practicing elementary school counselor developing your first classroom guidance lesson for fifth graders.

Section A: The Newbie

One of the teachers informs you that the principal requires that special education students be pulled out of the class to be with resource teachers for academic tutoring during the school counselor's classroom guidance lessons. The teacher said the principal announced this practice during a faculty meeting a few years ago, as a way to provide special education students with extra academic support and improve test scores. What is your response?

(Select ONLY ONE in this section.)

A—1.	Comply with the principal's requirements and develop the curriculum for the general education student population at that grade level.
	No
	School counselors advocate for equity and access in educational programming.
A—2.	Go to the principal and explain how this practice is not equitable and limits access to important programming for special education students.
	Yes
	School counselors advocate for equity and access in educational programming.
A—3.	Strongly encourage the teacher to keep special education students in the class during classroom guidance.
	No
	This puts the teacher in the position of disobeying the principal's directives.

A—4.	Talk to the special education teachers to ensure classroom guidance by the school counselor is a part of the students' IEP so that students are included in the lessons.
	No
	Access to general education programming for special education students does not need to be in their IEP. It is the right of all students to participate in this programming.

Section B: The Newbie

Now that classroom guidance lesson will be delivered to both general education and special needs students, which of the following applies?
    (Select as many as you consider indicated in this section.)

B—1.	Curriculum should be developed based on the grade level of the student regardless of special needs status to ensure access to rigorous, age-appropriate curriculum.
	No The school counselor needs to consider the special accommodations of special needs students in the classes for which they are conducting classroom guidance lessons.
B—2.	Curriculum should be modified to meet the special needs of each student in the classroom.
	Yes
	Like teachers, school counselors must follow students IEP's, 504 plans, and the accommodations afforded to those students whose primary language is not English. Also, there may be students in the class who are under a temporary medical plan (e.g., broken finger).
B—3.	Because it is impossible to meet the special needs of all students, develop a curriculum that meets the needs of the majority.
	No School counselors create curriculum to meet the needs of all students to whom the curriculum is being implemented.
B—4.	Make every effort to ensure special needs students sit grouped together so that you can better monitor their understanding of the lesson's content.
	No School counselors and teachers do not segregate students based on ability, disability, gender, ethnicity, and so on.

B—5.	Teachers need to inform school counselors of the needs of the special education students in their classes because school counselors are not privy to this information.
	No
	School counselors may ask teachers to identify special needs students so that they can pull those students' IEP, 504 plan, or ESL plans for compliance. Many school counselors have access to the special needs status of students in every classroom via student information systems.

Section C: The Newbie

One of the teachers, who are receiving your classroom guidance lesson, informs you that one of her students, Sabrina, will not be a part of the classroom guidance lesson because she is an ESL student and her translator is out on the day of the lesson. Your response is:

(Select ONLY ONE in this section.)

C—1.	All students need to be present for the lesson, so you will reschedule the lesson.
	No
	All students cannot always be present for every classroom guidance lesson.
C—2.	You will meet with Sabrina and her translator individually on another day to deliver the content of the lesson.
	No
	School counselors do not meet with students individually to make up a classroom guidance lessons missed. The swollen counselor-to-student ratio makes it virtually impossible to provide this service to students unless mandated by student IEP and 504 plan or is a part of Sabrina's LEP services plan.
C—3.	Have Sabrina participate in the lesson without her translator to ensure equity and access to all programming.
	No
	It is not equity and access to have Sabrina participate without the accommodations she needs to comprehend the material presented.

C—4.	Identify others in the building who can translate for Sabrina and see if he or she can translate on the day of the lesson while also talking to the principal about getting a substitute.
	Yes
	Advocating on behalf of the student for her rightful accommodations in order to access programming is an important function of the school counselor.
C—5.	Tape the classroom guidance lesson so that Sabrina and her translator can watch it together when the translator returns.
	No
	Viewing the lesson as a spectator is not the same as interacting with other students and being a part of the lesson. However, in the event that a translator is not made available to Sabrina, then this would be an alternative to her missing the lesson entirely.

Section D: The Newbie

During the classroom guidance lesson, a female student sitting by herself answers a question you posed. You notice that the student has an olive complexion, is very soft-spoken, and has an accent. Her response is uncommon, so you let her know that her response is interesting and offers a unique perspective. Another female student blurts out in a sarcastic tone, "Yea, you mean a weird perspective," and she and the girl next to her laugh along with the rest of the class. How would you respond?

(Select as many as you consider indicated in this section.)

D—1.	Continue the lesson careful not to give the girls an audience.
	No
	This is bully behavior and needs to be addressed.
D—2.	Stop the lesson and have the two girls removed from the class.
	No
	This action would not teach the girls appropriate behavior.
D—3.	Reassure the student that the response she gave was appropriate and worthwhile.
	Yes
	This is appropriate in addition to intervention in the moment.

D—4.	Tell the girls that those comments are unacceptable and mean-spirited, redirecting the lesson to one of diversity appreciation, respect, and the power of words.
	Yes
	Use this as an immediate opportunity (a teachable moment) to demonstrate a zero tolerance for bullying and to promote a climate of compassion and acceptance.
D—5.	Continue the lesson, and ask to see the two girls after class.
	No
	This is a teachable moment for all, and counselors address behavior but not as disciplinarian.
D—6.	Tell the girls that those comments are unacceptable and mean-spirited and then continue the planned lesson.
	No
	Chances are, the girls already know that what they are saying and doing is bullying. Continuing with your lesson as planned after pointing out the obvious will not eliminate the problem or appeal to the support of the group or to the human compassion of the "mean" girls.
D—7.	Come back the following week to teach a lesson on appreciation of diversity.
	No
	The teachable moment will have passed. School counselors are flexible.
	You may be able to cover your intended lesson as well as the unexpected lesson.

Section E: The Newbie

The day after the lesson, the student comes to you to thank you and lets you know that the girls have been nicer to her. She begins to share some family and personal issues that are bothering her. As a culturally sensitive counselor, how might you proceed?

(Select ONLY ONE in this section.)

E—1.	Let the student know that you are not familiar with her culture, express your interest in learning about her culture, and ask her to educate you.
	Yes
	This is the culturally sensitive response. The student will recognize that you want to help and appreciate your honesty.

E—2.	Sensitive not to make the student uncomfortable about her culture, just listen and reflect her feelings.
	No
	This will only take you so far, and you risk the student misinterpreting your lack of knowledge about her culture as not being genuine or worse.
E—3.	Ask her to identify her culture and to come back later, so you can find out more about her culture before she returns.
	No
	The student is asking for assistance now, and it may have taken much courage to come to you on her own. Now is the moment.
E—4.	Let the student know that you are not familiar with her culture, so she should talk to her parents about her concerns to ensure cultural sensitivity.
	No
	The student came to you, not her parents. She may not want her parents to know because what she is experiencing is contrary to deeply held cultural beliefs.
E—5.	Let her know that you are not familiar with her culture, and share with her how the dominant culture handles those types of issues.
	No
	You are espousing your personal beliefs onto your client. This is against our code of ethics.
E—6.	Let her know that you are unfamiliar with her culture, but offer your thoughts and beliefs on the issues.
	No
	You are espousing your personal beliefs onto your client. This is against our code of ethics.

Chapter 3: Guided Reflection

Define diversity and describe its importance in school counseling.

Define advocacy, and describe its importance and function in school counseling.

Examine the concept of equity and access and explain the construct and the function of the school counselor toward achieving equity and access.

Compare and contrast access, attainment, and achievement gaps. Give one example of each and a corresponding strategy to address the gap based on your example.

Describe what it means to be a multicultural-competent school counselor.

Recommend several approaches a school counselor can use to appropriately address spirituality in the public school setting.

Chapter 4

Assessment

The legacy of student *appraisal* is rooted in the vocational guidance movement whereby school counselors used standardized tests to assess student knowledge, skills, abilities, and aptitudes in order to make the most advantageous occupational choices. The movement gained popularity and school counselors began coordinating and administering assessments to make school placement decisions and to monitor student achievement. *Assessment* in educational practices has a long history. In this educational climate of accountability and results-based outcomes, a secure shelf life is certain—death and taxes.

As such, the colossal influx of broadened assessment demands left school counselors feeling our way, as though in the midst of a blinding sandstorm of assessment requirements in the Taklamakan Desert—you know—the one that legend says you can enter but you can never leave. As usual, the cavalry, that is ASCA, brought camels and guides! Consequently, the nostalgia for our assessment roots may not find its way out of that desert.

Recognizing the rapidly growing demands of assessment assigned to the duties of school counselors, ASCA, in collaboration with the Association for Assessment in Counseling (1998), now the Association for Assessment in Counseling and Education (AACE), identified the following nine assessment competencies to guide school counselors:

1. Selecting appropriate assessment strategies
2. Identifying, accessing, and evaluating the most commonly used assessment instruments

3. Administering and scoring assessments
4. Interpreting and reporting assessment results
5. Using assessment results for decision making
6. Interpreting and presenting statistical information about assessment results
7. Evaluating school counseling practices and programs
8. Developing assessments (e.g., surveys, questionnaires) to meet local needs
9. Observing professional and ethical standards related to assessment

Student Appraisal

School counselors use data from individual student appraisals to identify and target prevention and intervention strategies. While engaging in student appraisal, school counselors carefully consider the use of both formal and informal assessments and appropriate procedures for assessment administration in a variety of situations with diverse populations (e.g., language proficiency, special needs). A combination of both formal and informal approaches are recommended as best practices for school counselors for assessing individual needs and academic and counseling progress. Together, informal and formal assessments ensnare all the senses and sensibilities, capturing the whole essence of the individual.

School counselors are vigilant in evaluating assessments for cultural bias (no one assessment instrument is entirely bias-free), applying basic principles for scoring assessments, interpreting the results, and relaying assessment outcomes to students, parents, and important others. Section A.9 of the ASCA *Ethical Standards for School Counselors* (ASCA, 2010) dedicates an entire section to student evaluation, assessment, and interpretation. Read it, learn it, live by it. Table 4.1 describes specific measurements concepts with which school counselors need to be familiar in order to adequately interpret assessment outcomes: measures of central tendency, norms, rank, percentile rank, grade equivalents, standard deviation, standards scores, raw scores, derived scores, criterion-referenced scores, correlation, reliability, validity, and norm-referenced assessments.

Often shared responsibilities with the school psychologist, school social worker, educational diagnostician, and teachers, formal and informal assessments are useful tools that provide a deeper understanding of students'

Table 4.1 Measurement Concepts

Correlations are the degree to which two measures/constructs are related (e.g., the examination between a class of students' test scores in mathematics and their level of self-esteem).
Criterion-referenced assessments are those that compare an individual's score to a preestablished standard.
Derived scores are scores that are drawn from raw scores by comparing the raw score to those of a norm group; sometimes referred to as norm-referenced scores.
Grade/age equivalents are a type of developmental score that compares an individual student's raw score with that of others of a certain grade/age level.
Measures of central tendency, known as *mean, median,* and *mode*, are representative of averages. The mean is the mathematical average of a set of scores; the median is the middle score below which, and above which, half of the scores of a set of scores will fall; the mode is the score that appears the most frequently in a set of scores.
Norm-referenced assessments are those that compare an individual's score to that of a norm group.
Norms are representative of a distribution of scores obtained through the administration of an instrument to a standardized sample against which all other scores are assessed.
Percentile rank is the percentage of scores that are at or below a named score.
Rank is the relative position, standing, or degree of a specific grouping, often used at the secondary and postsecondary levels of education to describe a student's standing in relation to others based on GPA.
Raw scores are original scores that have not yet been converted into a meaningful score.
Reliability refers to the consistency with which an instrument measures that which it purports to measure (i.e., does the instrument yield the same or similar results at each administration for the same individual?)
Standard deviation is a measure of variability in a given set of data.
Standard scores represent the distance between a given score and the mean and are used in norm-referenced (see norms above) assessments to compare a student's performance to that of his or her peers.
Validity refers to the extent to which an instrument measures that which it purports to measure (i.e., can meaningful inferences be made based on the instrument's results?)

JENNIFER'S SCORE

Jennifer is a high school student who obtained a raw score of 73 on her mathematics exam. Her score was compared to a norm group in order to obtain a derived score. Jennifer must have taken:

a. A nonstandardized assessment
b. A norm-referenced assessment
c. A criterion-referenced assessment
d. An informal assessment

issues in relation to their personal, social, environmental, developmental, and cultural worlds. Assessments are used to:

- Identify student strengths and challenges.
- Develop targeted interventions.
- Provide optimal learning environments.
- Provide important information to parents, students, and school personnel.

In some school divisions, formal assessment is conducted by school psychologists, school social workers, and educational diagnosticians.

Formal Assessment

Standardized tests, or assessments, are objective, often norm-referenced (e.g., compare scores against an average), generally quantitative in nature, and ensure consistency in content, administration, scoring, and interpretation. Standardized tests are frequently referred to as *formal assessments*.

It is essential that school counselors be able to identify a variety of formal assessments based on type or purpose. There are generally five categories: achievement, aptitude, intelligence, interests, and personality. The assessments most often used in the schools within each category are summarized in Table 4.2. School counselors become familiar with the validity, reliability, limitations, bias, and characteristics of the assessments they plan to administer. While committing this information about each individual assessment is not necessary, it is important to understand the appropriate uses of each category of assessment in a given situation with a specific

Table 4.2   Summary of Key Assessments Used in Schools

Assessment Category	Assessments
Achievement evaluates general knowledge/performance in a variety of subject areas.	Woodcock–Johnson Test of Achievement (Woodcock–Johnson) PIAT Stanford Achievement Test Series ACT—college entrance
Aptitude evaluates potential or ability to learn, assessing a variety of specific areas.	ASVAB GATB Kaufman Assessment Battery for Children PSAT—practice for SAT SAT—college entrance
Intelligence evaluates general cognitive ability.	WISC WAIS Stanford–Binet Intelligence Scales (Stanford–Binet)
Interests identify preferences for specific activities, matching personality type with six workplace environments.	SDS SII KOIS
Personality identifies attitudinal, emotional, interpersonal, and motivational characteristics.	Vineland Adaptive Behavior Scales (Vineland) MBTI

population and possess the ability to identify specific assessments and the category to which they belong.

School counselors are aware of the options available to students with special needs (e.g., Braille print, large print, tape-recorded tests). Also, students whose primary language is not English may need bilingual test administration, test administration by a translator or interpreter, and/or a version of the test written in the students' primary language.

The most well-known and controversial formal assessments are the academic achievement tests. These tests are designed to measure a student's knowledge of subject content based on core academic standards up to the date of test administration. Achievement tests vary by name across states but are often referred to as *high stakes testing*. They are high stakes because in most states, students cannot graduate without passing scores on these tests, and school and teacher performance is often measured by student performance on these tests.

While serving as an elementary school counselor, I coordinated school-wide standardized achievement testing for 8 years—SOL in Virginia. Over the years, I became consumed with admiration and respect for class-room teachers who instead of kicking and screaming gazed fearlessly into the eyes of achievement tests as Ahab into the eyes of the massive Moby Dick.

ASCA's Position on High Stakes Testing

Professional school counselors recognize that standardized test results are one of many measures that can be used to assess student performance and learning. Professional school counselors advocate for the use of multiple criteria when educational decisions are made about student performance and oppose the use of a single test to make important educational decisions affecting students and their schools.

Position statement adopted 2002; revised 2007

In addition to academic standards-driven achievement tests, other achievement tests, often used in the schools to assess students in kindergarten to grade 12 for gifted or special education, include the Woodcock–Johnson Test of Achievement (Woodcock–Johnson) and the PIAT. The Woodcock–Johnson and the PIAT reveal present levels of performance compared to peers and identify students' academic areas of strengths and weaknesses.

The Stanford Achievement Test Series is often used in the schools as a measure of achievement from kindergarten to grade 12. It is a general test of knowledge in a variety of subjects including math, English, science, and writing for each grade level. The test yields national percentile bands that illustrate how a student scores in relation to others students at that grade level.

The ACT is one of the most widely used achievement tests taken by high school students to satisfy college entrance requirements. Total composite scores for all core subject areas covered (English, math, reading, science) by the test range from 1 to 36. The ACT writing test is optional.

MY STUDENT MAY HAVE A DISABILITY

A third-grade teacher comes to you, the elementary school counselor and child study chair, to arrange for a child study meeting because she suspects that one of her students may have a learning disability based on low academic functioning in math and writing. Which of the following would be useful in assessing the student?

a. Peabody
b. Standardized grade-level tests in math and writing
c. Classroom and homework assignments
d. All of the above

Aptitude assessments are designed to evaluate an individual's potential or ability to learn. Aptitude tests measure a variety of specific areas such as art, music, mechanical, verbal, spatial, reasoning, critical reading, writing, and coding. Aptitude tests are primarily used in schools for the purpose of career decision making, special education screening, and entrance into the military. The most widely used aptitude tests in the schools are the ASVAB, the GATB, and the Kaufman Assessment Battery for Children. The ASVAB and GATB assessments are intended for students at the high school level. The Kaufman is used for children ages 3–18.

The SAT is the most widely used college entrance test and is often used with the ACT test to assess academic readiness for college. The test yields scores in three subject areas (critical reading, writing, and mathematics), with 800 being the highest possible score for each section for a total score of 2400. The average score is 1500. The SAT is most often taken during the spring of the junior year of high school and again in the fall of the senior year of high school. Many students take the PSAT as a practice test to the SAT during the ninth and tenth grade years, although some students take it during the fall of their junior year of high school. The PSAT is also used to make scholarship awards.

Intelligence assessments are used in the schools to determine a student's general cognitive ability. Intelligence tests yield a single *intelligence quotient* (IQ) score. The majority of individuals have an IQ score between 85 and 115, with 100 being the average. IQ scores above 115 are considered to depict superior intelligence, whereas IQ scores below 85 indicate borderline deficiency with a score of 70 or less signifying retardation. IQ scores are often used to determine student placement in gifted and special education programs and aid educators in identifying a variety of cognitive challenges.

THE COLLEGE DREAM

The mother of Carolyn, one of your 11th-grade high school students, is in your office expressing concern about Carolyn's ability to be successful in college. She shares that they do not have the money to pay for Carolyn's college just for Carolyn to "flunk out." She said that Carolyn told her that she does not qualify for any scholarships that are listed in the scholarship binder at school. You notice in the student information system that Carolyn has a GPA of 3.9 and is not showing any scores for college entrance testing. You ask the parent if Carolyn has taken any college entrance assessments as of yet. The parent said no because those, too, are expensive and she just is not sure about the whole college thing. The parent begins to cry, stating that it is just she and Carolyn, and the only income is her disability check. She said she feels lost because she nor anybody else in her family has ever gone to college. What other information might you want to find out in this case? How would you help this parent and Carolyn?

The most widely used intelligence tests in the schools are the WISC, ages 6–16, and the WAIS, ages 16–19. Individuals who are 16 can take either the WAIS or the WISC. Each assessment yields a verbal IQ, performance IQ, and full IQ (total cognitive development) score with a standard deviation of 15 and a 95% confidence level. Also widely used in schools is the Stanford–Binet Intelligence Scales (Stanford–Binet). The assessment can be administered on individuals ages 2 to 90 and yields a verbal IQ, a nonverbal IQ, and a full-scale IQ with a standard deviation of 15 and a 95% confidence level.

Interest assessments, often referred to as interest inventories, discussed in Chapter 2, are primarily used for career development purposes. Generally, results obtained from interest inventories are derived by comparing student responses with individuals who have been successful in specific occupations or by comparing student responses to those of their peers. The most widely used interest inventories in the schools include the SDS, the SII, and the KOIS.

Standardized personality assessments provide information about a student's attitudinal, emotional, interpersonal, and motivational characteristics. Personality assessment may be used for (1) gaining insight into students' thoughts and behaviors, (2) placement into specialized programs (e.g., gifted, special education), and (3) career decision making. The most widely used personality assessments in the schools include the Vineland Adaptive

Behavior Scales (Vineland), which measures levels of personal and social functioning, and the MBTI, which identifies patterns of behavior and preferences for relating to ideas, others, and the environment.

MEETING ANDRE'S NEEDS

Andre is a third-grade student whose misbehavior at school has become increasingly persistent. Andre has been consistently achieving academically at higher grade levels than third grade in all subject areas. Andre scored 5.3 (grade equivalent score) on his mathematics achievement test. How would you interpret this score for Andre's parents? What programs might you want to recommend that would help to further develop Andre's academic knowledge and skills and ensure that Andre remains challenged with a rigorous program to meet his special needs? How might you address Andre's misbehavior at this time?

Informal Assessment

Nonstandardized assessments are subjective, are not norm-referenced, are generally qualitative in nature, and may be variable in their content, process, administration, scoring, and interpretation procedures. Nonstandardized tests are often referred to as *informal assessments.*

School counselors are careful to consider context, developmental level, and students' cultures and worldviews when using both formal and informal assessments. School counselors are also keenly alert to the subjective nature of informal assessment, exercising caution during implementation and interpretation. Additionally, school counselors do not rely on any single assessment but use a variety of informal assessments when appraising student functioning, which may include:

■ Records review
■ Observation
■ Case study
■ Role play
■ Checklists
■ Storytelling and story completion
■ Student self-assessment and self-monitoring
■ Portfolio
■ Work samples and writings
■ Consultation with teachers, parents, and other school personnel

Informal interviews are often used by school counselors in the initial counseling sessions and as a means for assessing student progress on a continuous basis. In addition to fully exploring the issues that brought the student to counseling, school counselors may find helpful information when exploring the student's attitude, emotionality, thought processes, academic progress, school attendance and experiences, and relationships with family and home, school, and virtual friends.

Clinicians from outside the school system will often request a release of student records and call upon teachers, school nurses, and school counselors to collaborate and consult with regard to student functioning in order to assist in diagnosing disorders such as ADHD. A widely used informal student appraisal instrument for this purpose is the *Connors Scale*, which is also referred to as the Connors Test and the Connors Checklist. The Connors Scale is completed by educators and others who work closely with the student, documenting observations to aid clinicians in making a diagnosis. The Connors Scale is generally associated with assessment related to the diagnosis of ADHD.

A commonly used method for informal student appraisals was developed by Lazarus (1976) and referred to as the BASIC ID approach (see Table 4.3).

Table 4.3   BASIC ID

(B)ehavior
Fine and gross motor skills and activities
(A)ffect
Observed or client self-reported emotions
(S)ensation
Sensory experiencing: taste (gustatory), touch (kinesthetic), sight (visual), smell (olfactory), hearing (auditory)
(I)magery
Mental pictures that have an impact on the client
(C)ognition
Client thoughts and beliefs
(I)nterpersonal relationships
Observed or self-reported interactions with others
(D)rugs/diet
Biochemical and/or nutritional impact on the client

Table 4.4 SOAP Notes

(S)ubjective observations
Counselor perceptions of client thoughts, attitudes, emotions, and dispositions during sessions and the client's self-reported experiencing/observations (e.g., hopelessness, depression, client perceptions, anger).
(O)bjective observations
Directly observed behaviors and emotional experiencing during the counseling sessions (e.g., crying, posture, hygiene, orientation to time/place, physical appearance).
(A)ssessment
Appraisal based on counselor's general impressions of the client's psychological, social, and emotional functioning.
(P)lan
Treatment strategies to mediate presenting client concerns, which may include individual, small group counseling, and/or family counseling and a variety of theoretical approaches and counseling techniques. The plan might also include referral and further information gathering strategies.

The acronym represents seven interdependent categories, or modalities, (behavior, affect, sensation, imagery, cognition, interpersonal relationships, and drugs/diet) that aid school counselors in organizing case notes, identifying the individual's preferred modalities, clarifying problems, creating counseling interventions, and assessing the effectiveness of interventions and the progress of treatment.

SOAP notes (Cameron & Turtle-Song, 2002), too, are used by school counselors to organize case notes and develop case conceptualizations. Table 4.4 describes the characteristics of each of the four components of SOAP notes: (1) subjective observations, (2) objective observations, (3) assessment, and (4) plan.

Life-Saving Assessment

Assessing the needs of individual students is important to identifying levels of academic performance as well as barriers to academic performance. Identification and removal of barriers that impede a student's ability to be successful in school and in life is a goal of the school counseling program. There are times when appropriate individual student appraisal can save the life of a child. Children and adolescents live at the maximum pace of wide open. School counselor must go Mach 2 with our hair on fire, just to keep up (a pilfered line from *Top Gun*). At this speed, things can get very real, very fast.

When conducting student appraisals, school counselors look for the signs and symptoms associated with physical, verbal, and emotional child abuse and neglect, violence, substance abuse, depression, eating disorders, and attention deficit disorder in children and adolescents. Changes in behavioral, emotional, and attitudinal patterns are often clues alerting school counselors to the possibility of problematic issues in the student's life. One or more changes, unexplained by developmental stages, and the frequency, duration, and magnitude of behaviors noted as follows should be explored (Morrison, 2007):

- Periods of disinterest
- Flat affect
- Interpersonal conflicts
- Sense of worthlessness or guilt
- Passivity
- Agitation or irritability
- Significant weight loss or weight gain
- Fatigue
- Changes in sleeping patterns (e.g., hardly sleeping, wanting to stay in bed)
- Trouble concentrating and following directions
- Inattentive
- Decline in academic performance
- Excessive absences
- Frequent/unexplained injuries
- Flinching
- Withdrawn
- Unattended medical conditions
- Emotionality
- Does not care to (or want to) go home

Child Abuse and Neglect

Conversations with parents and observations of parent–child interactions may expose additional signs of possible child abuse or neglect, or other problems related to family functioning. The following signs portrayed by a parent or guardian may signal child abuse or neglect (Child Welfare Information Gateway, 2007):

■ Showing little concern for the child
■ Indifference toward the child
■ Apathy or depression
■ Abusing alcohol or other drugs
■ Irrational or bizarre behavior
■ Being secretive or isolated
■ Being overly protective, severely limiting child's contact, especially with opposite gender
■ Being jealous or controlling
■ Denying the existence of, or blaming the child for, problems at home or school
■ Asking the teacher to use harsh punishment on the child for misbehavior
■ Viewing the child as entirely bad, burdensome, or worthless
■ Demanding a level of physical or academic performance that the child cannot achieve
■ Looking primarily to the child for care, attention, and satisfaction of emotional needs
■ Parent and child rarely touch or look at each other
■ Parent and child view their relationship as entirely negative
■ Parent and child state that they do not like each other

There are also additional signs that warrant further exploration into possible sexual abuse. Students who are being sexually abused may exhibit one or more of the following as well as any of the signs and symptoms noted above (Bauman, 2008; Child Welfare Information Gateway, 2007):

■ Nightmares
■ Bed wetting
■ Difficulty sitting or walking
■ Sophisticated sexual knowledge or bizarre sexual behaviors
■ High-risk behaviors
■ Running away
■ Early pregnancy
■ Change in appetite
■ Refusal to change for gym class

- Thoughts of suicide
- Substance abuse
- Frequent medical conditions
- Anxiety/stress
- Depression
- Interpersonal relationship difficulties

School counselors are mandated reporters of suspected child abuse and neglect, discussed in Chapter 1. Additional information on violence prevention and child abuse and neglect along with mandated reporting requirements and Child Abuse and Neglect Training Modules are available at www.childwelfare.gov/preventing/developing/training.cfm.

AYMEE'S BASIC ID

Aymee is a middle school student who is seeing you, her school counselor, because of social issues that she is experiencing in school. You are assessing Aymee's progress and determine interventions using BASIC ID, which is considered to be which type of assessment?

   a. Standardized
   b. Objective
   c. Formal
   d. Informal

Substance Abuse

Substance abuse, too, often involves specific signs and symptoms. For example, children and adolescents who are using or abusing substances may exhibit one or more of the following behaviors (Capuzzi & Stauffer, 2012):

- Withdrawal from responsibility
- Increased secretiveness
- Wearing sunglass inappropriately
- Wearing long sleeves in hot weather
- Stealing money
- Having associations with known substance abusers
- Taking risks

- Avoiding family members
- Talking excessively about drug/alcohol use
- Getting into legal trouble

Duration, frequency, and intensity are important factors to consider when making student appraisals along with information shared during counseling sessions. When in doubt, consult, consult, consult, and err on the side of student safety. That is, make the call to the parent, legal system, or child protective services, as deemed appropriate. School counselors balance students' rights to privacy and confidentiality with duty to warn and duty to protect while also considering parental rights in the cases of minors, discussed in Chapter 1.

During assessment, school counselors may find that a recent death of an important other, a family transition, and/or a crisis situation have occurred in the student's life that accounts for observed changes. In such cases, school counselors explore the student's thoughts and emotions for possible *suicide ideation* because risk factors for child and adolescent suicide include recent losses or other events perceived as distressing by the student (McWhirter, McWhirter, McWhirter, & McWhirter, 2007).

Self-Harm

Intervening in cases where students are presenting self-injurious behaviors and/or suicide ideation is critical. Assessment is warranted when a student is experiencing an intense affective disturbance (e.g., rage, guilt, hopelessness, fear, depression, abandonment, anxiety), particularly when the precipitating event/issue is vague. Assessing for suicide is also warranted when a student is engaging in self-mutilating behaviors and/or is having thoughts of suicide, writing about suicide, has made comments about wanting to die, or has implied that others would be better off as a result of his or her death. Risk factors for suicidality in children and adolescents include (McWhirter et al., 2007)

- Negative family and/or peer interactions
- Loneliness/isolation
- Impulsivity
- Low tolerance for frustration
- Poor self-esteem
- Lack of problem-solving skills

- Faulty cognitions/negative beliefs
- Substance use
- A tendency toward risk-taking reactions to distress

Once the school counselor feels confident that *suicide assessment* is needed, ask the student plainly, "Are you having thoughts about committing suicide now, or recently?" Depending on the developmental level of the child, the question may need to be, "Are you thinking about hurting yourself on purpose?" or "Are you thinking about killing yourself?" School counselors should assess for a plan and a means for following through on the plan. However, as noted above, err on the side of caution—above all else protect the child or adolescent; in this case, from the self.

While safeguarding the student until the parent or CPS arrives (see Chapter 1), school counselors should consider creating a no-suicide contract with the student, which can be verbal (with a hand shake) or written (a document with a signature) affirming that the student will not harm himself or herself intentionally. Additionally, school counselors can help students by

- Establishing a positive relationship (the crux of counseling)
- Assisting the student in identifying support systems and internal strengths to build protective factors
- Exploring and validating emotions
- Identifying problems; teaching and engaging the student in problem-solving strategies

Schools counselors provide teachers and staff with suicide awareness training as a part of a comprehensive approach to preventing student suicide. Elements of the training include recognizing the suicide risk factors noted previously and identifying behavioral and verbal warning signs and steps for intervention.

Behavioral warning signs may include giving possessions away, declining academic performance, a change in social interactions, and an increase in school absences. Verbal warning signs may include statements such as "I can't go on," "I can't stand living anymore," and "Life is meaningless" (Gibbons & Studer, 2008). Steps for intervention may include a formal written policy and outlines the process for referring students who may be at risk of suicide to the school counselor.

There are mixed views among school administrators and school counselors with regard to screening students for suicide ideation and implementing student programs aimed at suicide prevention education. Those who are against the screenings and prevention education believe that these strategies draw attention to suicide and may result in increased suicide attempts. Those who are in favor of these strategies believe that education will reduce the incidence of suicide. Because of this confluence of conflicting views, school counselors work closely with school administrators when planning suicide prevention programming.

Students at risk of suicide need mental health counseling and possibly hospitalization. Some schools will not allow students to return to school until parents or guardians have secured such counseling because students experiencing this level of emotional disturbance are deemed harmful to themselves and possibly others.

THE DIVORCE OF GEOFFREY'S PARENTS

Geoffrey, a 13-year-old student, expressed to you, his middle school counselor, that he is angry because of his parents' recent divorce. This was the second time Geoffrey came to you, but this time he seemed much more unkempt and upset. His hair was disheveled and his clothes were dirty. During this second session, Geoffrey sat slumped over with his hands clinched and began to cry, saying that his mother must now work so he never sees her, and his dad does not care enough to even visit on the days he has visitation. Geoffrey said that sometimes he just feels numb and other times he is so angry he could explode. He went on to say that he feels all alone and just wants to quit school because he does not understand the point of it all.

Use SOAP notes to conceptualize this case.

Self-mutilation (e.g., cutting, burning, interfering with wound healing, biting, scratching) has been identified as a reaction and coping mechanism associated with feelings of depression, anger, frustration, and hopelessness and resulting in feelings of guilt, shame, and regret (Moyer & Nelson, 2007). Research has identified the importance of allowing students engaging in self-mutilating behaviors the opportunity to talk about the experiences—"to be heard" (p. 47) and to ask questions in a nonjudgmental environment.

Self-mutilation is viewed by the school counselor as an imminent risk and treated in the same fashion as suicide ideation with regard to involving parents or child protective services and providing referral resources. Some students try to convince school counselors that their self-mutilating behaviors are self-decoration. Avoid succumbing to deception by staying abreast of current developments in these areas of high-risk behavior. Training oneself, as well as teachers, parents, and administrators, in understanding the difference between self-mutilation and self-decoration is critical. In the end, when in doubt, err on the side of protecting the student from his or herself.

Symptoms consistent with *anorexia* and *bulimia* are also viewed by the school counselor as imminent risk and should be brought to the attention of parents or child protective services. School counselors will also have resources ready to share as a part of their ever-evolving resource listing for parents. The growing number of adolescents with eating disorders is alarming, calling for systemic prevention efforts on topics related to body image and the all too real natural consequences of eating disorders and anabolic steroid use.

To promote a continued trusting relationship with students for whom you must break confidentiality, remind the student of your legal and ethical responsibility to protect. You will have covered the limits of confidentiality earlier in the session or in your initial session with the student.

Assessment and Diagnosis

School counselors are careful not to offer diagnoses. Even those school counselors who hold advanced licensure and national credentialing are discouraged from diagnosing students' mental health issues in the school setting. Clinical diagnosis is more often than not considered to be outside the scope of the practice of school counseling. Instead, when deeper issues are presented that are outside of the expertise of the school counselor or scope of school counseling practices, school counselors strongly encourage parents and guardians to seek the assistance of a mental health counselor, psychologist, psychiatrist, physician, or family therapist.

Instead of a diagnosis, school counselors may wish to share observations as being "consistent with symptoms that are associated with _____" and provide parents with a list of counseling resources that address a broad range of services (e.g., family counseling, parenting education, mental health counseling, counseling for victims of abuse or sexual abuse, substance abuse counseling, support groups for children and parents, crisis–suicide intervention centers and numbers).

Needs Assessment

Unlike formal and informal individual student assessments, needs assessments are generally used to systematically identify the needs of broader populations (e.g., student body, teachers, parents, community agencies) and subpopulations (e.g., special education students, fifth-grade teachers, parents of gifted students, mental health agencies). Information obtained from needs assessments aids school counselors in designing or redesigning programs for targeted populations and topics and continuous program improvement.

Needs assessment may be conducted using existing data or by gathering data in the form of participant perceptions from the target population using a needs assessment technique or instrument. Needs may be assessed using a selection of data or a selection of participants from the population to be served. An exhaustive list of existing data sources are provided in Chapter 5. When using existing data sources to assess need, school counselors look for patterns and inconsistencies. Assessing needs based on participant perceptions is not generally considered standardized but can take a more formal tone versus an informal tone. They may be written (e.g., survey, questionnaire) or oral (e.g., interview) and conducted in person, on the telephone, via the Internet, or by mail.

When assessing needs based on participant perception, the school counselor might also elect to use focus groups, community forums, and/or key informants. School counselors who elect to use focus groups select several individuals representative of the population to be served—like apple picking. Collectively, in a structured or semistructured format, differing needs are discussed and together the group prioritizes needs. If you picked any bad apples, this is where you will find out. Community forums have merit in that any stakeholder wishing to be involved may participate. School counselors announce the community forum meeting and the topic of discussion, and those interested participate in much the same fashion as the focus group. Key informants are selected by the school counselor based on their vast knowledge of the target population but may not necessarily be a member of the population. Key informants are generally surveyed individually or in small groups.

Needs assessments that seek participant perceptions may include any number of questions deemed important by the school counselor. The following sampling of questions would be considered appropriate for assessing the needs of upper elementary school students, adults, and students at the high school level:

- What school counseling services do you find helpful?
- What additional school counseling services would you find helpful?
- What are the strengths of the school counseling program?
- What suggestions do you have for possible improvements to the school counseling program?

Needs assessments for children may be read aloud with interpretations dependent upon developmental level. Needs assessments that make use of the check system are ideal for children and special needs populations. The following is a sample that illustrates how students would simply place a check in the box beside the topic(s) of interest:

- ◾ Dealing with bullies
- ◾ Making and keeping friends
- ◾ Dealing with anger
- ◾ Getting along with others
- ◾ Making good choices
- ◾ Doing more chores (tossed it in to see if you are still listening)

DR. DATARULES

Dr. Datarules, your school principle, has asked you, the school counselor, to provide him with data other than what is already available to him (e.g., school report cards, standardized testing results, classroom assessment results) that identifies instructional strategies that are both enjoyed by students and effective in producing higher levels of academic achievement. You decide to administer a needs assessment. Who would be the target of your assessment?

Translating Needs: Developing Program Goals and Objectives

Once the school counselor has identified stakeholder needs, those needs are converted to goals that are supported by measurable objectives. For example, a goal based on need might be to manage school-wide conflict. The goal does not lend itself to measurement, that is not its job. That is the task of the objective. Therefore, once a goal(s) is (are) established, specific and measurable objectives that support the achievement of the goal(s) are developed.

One objective supporting this goal might be "Students will be able to identify four problem-solving strategies." We conclude, then, that there must be at least four problem-solving strategies covered in the curriculum content—are not we the brainiacs! Curriculum development is discussed in Chapter 6. Understanding how to translate stakeholder needs into goals and measurable learning objectives is critical to creating program content that meets stakeholder needs. Measurable objectives are prerequisite to evaluating program effectiveness.

ASCA provides school counselors with broad goals (e.g., standards) and objectives (i.e., student competencies) that cover the three broad domains

Table 4.5   Who? How? What? of Objectives

(W) *Who* are the participants receiving the program/intervention?
Who examples:
"Students will"
"Teachers will"
"Parents will"
(H) *How* will we know the behavior is achieved?
How examples:
"Students will identify"
"Parents will be able to"
"Teachers will develop"
(W) *What* is the desired behavior?
What examples:
"Students will identify five study skills strategies"
"Parents will be able to define ADHD"
"Teachers will develop five auditory teaching strategies"

CAN THIS BE MEASURED?

You are a school counselor facilitating a small group on the topic of anger management. The goal of the group is to learn how to express anger in a healthy way. This is a fine goal, to be sure; however, it is not measurable as it is. Which of the following would be a possible measurable objective to support this worthy group goal?

a. Students will learn healthy ways to express anger.
b. Students will express anger in ways that are not hurtful to others.
c. Students will complete an anger management worksheet.
d. Students will identify three anger management strategies.

for a developmental comprehensive school counseling program. However, school counselors must also develop their own more specific and measurable objectives based on stakeholder need. Table 4.5 describes a method for creating measurable objects using a (W)ho, (H)ow, (W)hat process.

Chapter 4: Case Conceptualization Responses

Student Appraisal

Jennifer's Score

The correct response is "b." Jennifer took a norm-referenced assessment, which is a standardized, formal assessment.

Formal Assessment

My Student May Have a Disability

The correct response is "d." School counselors advocate for student appraisal that draws from multiple sources of both formal and informal assessments to promote practices that reduce premature or inaccurate diagnoses of learning disabilities.

The College Dream

Carolyn's GPA would indicate that she is academically successful. For this reason, the school counselor may wish to inquire as to why the parent believes her daughter will "flunk out" of college. It is important for the parent to know that the SAT is an aptitude test as well as a college entrance exam, which aids in predicting Carolyn's future performance as a college student. Also, providing the parent with an SAT fee waiver may help with the financial burden. Finally, walking the parent through the steps needed to complete and submit the Free Application for Federal Student Aid, or providing her with a contact that will assist her is crucial to guiding the parent of a first-generation college student. This parent could also use some college preparation and financial aid information. Finally, considering the family's financial challenges and Carolyn's GPA, there may be scholarships available, so offering to assist Carolyn with the scholarship search and identifying colleges of interest is critical to helping Carolyn to realize the college dream. It would also be prudent to explore Carolyn's thoughts regarding attending college.

Meeting Andre's Needs

Andre's grade equivalent score on the mathematics test indicates that he has performed at the level of an average fifth-grade student, 3 months into the school year. Andre's persistent achievement in all subject areas indicates the need for a more rigorous or advanced curriculum to keep Andre motivated toward academics. The school counselor may want to recommend Andre for accelerated learning and enrichment programs such as the school's gifted

and talented program and the Governor's School, as well as summer enrichment experiences. The school counselor may want to reassess Andre's need
for intervention pertaining to his misbehavior until he has engaged in these
extracurricular activities. Andre's misbehavior may be due to boredom or
frustration with the nondescript pace of the on-grade-level curriculum.

Informal Assessment

Aymee's BASIC ID
The correct response is "d." BASIC ID is a comprehensive, nonstandardized,
informal, and subjective assessment method that identifies student's specific
strengths and needs, which allows the school counselor to tailor counseling
to meet those needs.

The Divorce of Geoffrey's Parents
(S)ubjective Observations
Anger (self-report), helplessness/depression (counselor observed).
(O)bjectives Observations
Poor hygiene, sitting slumped over, hands clinched, crying.
(A)ssessment
Geoffrey appears to be somewhat depressed and anxious as a result of his
parents' divorce. He also appears to be experiencing a sense of hopeless-
ness about the future based on his statement that he wants to quit school
because he does not understand the point of it.
(P)lan
The school counselor might provide Geoffrey with anger management techniques and combat possible depression with cognitive behavioral strategies. The
school counselor might also offer strengths-based counseling to build resiliency
and identify internal and external resources. Person-centered counseling, too,
will allow Geoffrey the opportunity to express his emotions and gain insight
into his emotional experiencing. Geoffrey would likely benefit from the support
of a small group with other students whose parents are divorcing or already
divorced. It would also be prudent to suggest parent involvement with Geoffrey.

Needs Assessment

Dr. Datarules
Creating a needs assessment(s) that could be administered to both teachers
and students would be warranted in this case. Teachers are in the best position to identify instructional strategies that work; students are in the best

position to identify instructional strategies that are enjoyable. You can use a comparative analysis to provide Dr. Datarules with data that identifies instructional strategies that are both effective and enjoyed by students.

Translating Needs: Developing Program Goals and Objectives

Can This Be Measured?

The correct response is "d." This option will demonstrate that the student has learned strategies for expressing anger in a healthy way, which is the goal of the group. The objective is also written using the (W)ho, (H)ow, (W)hat for creating measurable program objectives. Options "a" and "b" cannot be measured as written, reading more like goals than objectives. Option "c" is an activity that will take place to support the goal, but completing the worksheet does not demonstrate that the student has learned healthy ways to express anger. This option does not provide the "what" of the desired behavior (i.e., healthy ways to express anger) is to be accomplished.

Chapter 4: Simulation

Student Appraisal

Brief Case Description

Timmy, a fifth-grade male, has been referred to the Child Study Team by his teacher because of both behavioral concerns and academic performance. You are the school counselor and chair of the Child Study Team. Based on the information presented in the meeting, the team decides testing is needed. The school counselor explains to Timmy's mother, who is present at the meeting, that the team will administer a series of assessments that will include assessing personality, achievement, aptitude, intelligence, and adaptive and social functioning.

Section A: Student Appraisal

The parent inquires as to how personality tests will get to the root of Timmy's behavior. The school counselor responds that understanding Timmy's personality is important to helping the team to more fully understand Timmy's behavior because the assessment reveals the following information:

   (Select as many as you consider indicated in this section.)

_____ A—1.	Emotional functioning
_____ A—2.	Level of knowledge
_____ A—3.	Motivation
_____ A—4.	Social functioning
_____ A—5.	Skills
_____ A—6.	Attitude
_____ A—7.	Abilities
_____ A—8.	Level of achievement

Section B: Student Appraisal

The parent asks the school counselor to identify the personality assessment that will be administered to her son. The school counselor identifies the following standardized personality test for the school setting at the elementary level:

(Choose ONLY ONE in this section.)

_____ B—1.	SII
_____ B—2.	Kuder
_____ B—3.	SAT
_____ B—4.	Vineland
_____ B—5.	ACT

Section C: Student Appraisal

The parent also asks which achievement test will be used. The school counselor replies, identifying the following standardized achievement test:

(Select ONLY ONE in this section.)

_____ C—1.	MBTI
_____ C—2.	Woodcock–Johnson
_____ C—3.	Vineland
_____ C—4.	Stanford–Binet
_____ C—5.	SDS
_____ C—6.	ASVAB
_____ C—7.	SAT

Section D: Student Appraisal

The parent requests that the team also includes an aptitude test because she is worried about her son's potential for learning. The school counseling identifies the following standardized aptitude test appropriate for Timmy's age:

(Select ONLY ONE in this section.)

_____ D—1.	ACT
_____ D—2.	Kaufman Assessment Battery

_____ D–3.	Vineland
_____ D–4.	Woodcock–Johnson
_____ D–5.	WISC
_____ D–6.	GATB

Section E: Student Appraisal

The team decides that meeting with the school counselor individually would also be beneficial. The school counselor gathers information using the following nonstandardized approaches to better understand Timmy and his situation:

(Select as many as you consider indicated in this section.)

_____ E–1.	Observation
_____ E–2.	WISC
_____ E–3.	Portfolio
_____ E–4.	ACT
_____ E–5.	Counseling notes
_____ E–6.	Consulting with teachers
_____ E–7.	School records
_____ E–8.	SAT
_____ E–9.	GATB

Section F: Student Appraisal

After four sessions, the school counselor becomes concerned about Timmy's increasingly flat affect, sense of worthlessness, excessive absences, inability to focus, lack of personal hygiene, and frequent injuries. The school counselor cannot get Timmy to communicate. The school counselor calls a meeting with Timmy and his mother. When his mother arrives, she is agitated and expresses what a terrible inconvenience this is, reiterating that she was just here a month ago. During the meeting, the school counselor identifies the following behaviors, coupled with the information she already has, as indicators of child abuse or neglect:

(Select as many as you consider indicated in this section.)

_____ F—1.	Mother smells of alcohol
_____ F—2.	Mother asks school counselor to be sensitive to her son
_____ F—3.	Mother and son rarely make eye contact
_____ F—4.	Mother is apathetic
_____ F—5.	Mother allows son to control the conversation
_____ F—6.	Mother is indifferent toward son
_____ F—7.	Mother and son appear secretive
_____ F—8.	Frequent touch between mother and son
_____ F—9.	Son flinches when mother turns in his direction

Section G: Student Appraisal

After the meeting, the school counselor suspects that Timmy is being neglected and abused. The school counselor should take the following course of action:

(Select ONLY ONE in this section.)

_____ G—1.	Contact local police
_____ G—2.	Contact Timmy's dad
_____ G—3.	Contact the emergency contact on Timmy's health card
_____ G—4.	Contact CPS
_____ G—5.	Ask the principal for appropriate course of action
_____ G—6.	Inform the mother of her suspicions, and say if it continues she will report her

Chapter 4: Simulation Answers

Student Appraisal

Brief Case Description

Timmy, a fifth-grade male, has been referred to the Child Study Team by his teacher because of both behavioral concerns and academic performance. You are the school counselor and chair of the Child Study Team. Based on the information presented in the meeting, the team decides testing is needed. The school counselor explains to Timmy's mother, who is present at the meeting, that the team will administer a series of assessments that will include assessing personality, achievement, aptitude, intelligence, and adaptive and social functioning.

Section A: Student Appraisal

The parent inquires as to how personality tests will get to the root of Timmy's behavior. The school counselor responds that understanding Timmy's personality is important to helping the team to more fully understand Timmy's behavior because the assessment reveals the following information:

   (Select as many as you consider indicated in this section.)

A—1.	Emotional functioning
	Yes
	The personality assessment provides this information.
A—2.	Level of knowledge
	No
	The personality assessment does not provide this information.
	Tests of achievement and intelligence tests measure knowledge.
A—3.	Motivation
	Yes
	The personality assessment provides this information.
A—4.	Social functioning
	Yes
	The personality assessment provides this information.

A—5.	Skills
	No
	The personality assessment does not provide this information.
	Aptitude tests measure skills.
A—6.	Attitude
	Yes
	The personality assessment provides this information.
A—7.	Abilities
	No
	The personality assessment does not provide this information.
	Aptitude tests measure abilities.
A—8.	Level of achievement
	No
	The personality assessment does not provide this information.
	Achievement is measured using achievement tests such as Stanford tests of achievement.

Section B: Student Appraisal

The parent asks the school counselor to identify the personality assessment that will be administered to her son. The school counselor identifies the following standardized personality test for the school setting at the elementary level:

(Choose ONLY ONE in this section.)

B—1.	SII
	No
	The SII measures career interest.
B—2.	Kuder
	No
	The Kuder is used for career exploration and planning.
B—3.	SAT
	No
	The SAT is an aptitude test.

B—4.	Vineland
	Yes
	The Vineland measures levels of personal and social functioning and is considered to be a personality test.
B—5.	ACT
	No
	The ACT is a test of achievement.

Section C: Student Appraisal

The parent also asks which achievement test will be used. The school counselor replies identifying the following standardized achievement test:

(Select ONLY ONE in this section.)

C—1.	MBTI
	No
	The MBTI is a personality test.
C—2.	Woodcock–Johnson
	Yes
	The Woodcock–Johnson is a test of achievement.
C—3.	Vineland
	No
	The Vineland is considered a personality test/test of adaptive behavior.
C—4.	Stanford–Binet
	No
	The Stanford–Binet is a test of intelligence.
C—5.	SDS
	No
	The SDS is a career interest inventory.
C—6.	ASVAB
	No
	The ASVAB is an aptitude test.
C-7.	SAT
	No
	The SAT is an aptitude test.

Section D: Student Appraisal

The parent requests that the team also includes an aptitude test because she is worried about her son's abilities and potential for learning. The school counseling identifies the following standardized aptitude test appropriate for Timmy's age:

(Select ONLY ONE in this section.)

D—1.	ACT
	No
	The ACT is an achievement test.
D—2.	Kaufman Assessment Battery
	Yes
	The Kaufman Assessment Battery is an aptitude test often used in the schools for ages 3–18.
D—3.	Vineland
	No
	The Vineland is considered a personality test/test of adaptive behavior.
D—4.	Woodcock–Johnson
	No
	The Woodcock–Johnson is a test of achievement.
D—5.	WISC
	No
	The WISC is often used in schools for diagnostic testing to assess level of intelligence.
D—6.	GATB
	No
	The GATB is an aptitude test, but it is intended for students in grades nine and higher.

Section E: Student Appraisal

The team decides that meeting with the school counselor individually would also be beneficial. The school counselor gathers information using the following nonstandardized approaches to better understand Timmy and his situation:

(Select as many as you consider indicated in this section.)

E—1.	Observation
	Yes
	School counselors gain valuable information by observing students and their interactions with peers and adults in the classroom, on the playground, at lunch, and so on.
E—2.	WISC
	No
	This is a standardized test for intelligence.
E—3.	Portfolio
	Yes
	Portfolios provide a chronicle of information about a student's interests, strengths, and challenges.
E—4.	ACT
	No
	This is a standardized measure of achievement.
E—5.	Counseling notes
	Yes
	School counselor case notes provide a means by which to follow a student's progress from initial session to final session.
E—6.	Consulting with teachers
	Yes
	Consultation with other school personnel is a valuable means by which to learn more about a student by someone who may know the student better and/or in a different capacity.
E—7.	School records
	Yes
	A thorough review of the student's cumulative record provides the school counselor with insight into the student's health, personal–social, academic, and possibly psychological, social, and emotional functioning.
E—8.	SAT
	No
	The SAT is a standardized measure of aptitude.

E—9.	GATB
	No
	The GATB is a standardized aptitude measure.

Section F: Student Appraisal

After four sessions, the school counselor becomes concerned about Timmy's increasingly flat affect, sense of worthlessness, excessive absences, inability to focus, lack of personal hygiene, and frequent injuries. The school counselor cannot get Timmy to communicate. The school counselor calls a meeting with Timmy and his mother. When his mother arrives, she is agitated and expresses what a terrible inconvenience this is, reiterating that she was just here a month ago. During the meeting, the school counselor identifies the following behaviors, coupled with the information she already has, as indicators of child abuse/neglect:

(Select as many as you consider indicated in this section.)

F—1.	Mother smells of alcohol
	Yes
	Alone this would not be an indicator. However, coupled with other indicators this is considered.
F—2.	Mother asks school counselor to be sensitive to her son
	No
	Generally, abusive parents will encourage the school counselor to use stern punishment.
F—3.	Mother and son rarely make eye contact
	Yes
	Alone this would not be an indicator. However, coupled with other indicators this is considered.
F—4.	Mother is apathetic
	Yes
	Alone this would not be an indicator. However, coupled with other indicators this is considered.
F—5.	Mother allows son to control the conversation
	No
	Generally, the abusive parent will control the conversation.

F—6.	Mother is indifferent toward son
	Yes
	Alone this would not be an indicator. However, coupled with other indicators this is considered.
F—7.	Mother and son appear secretive
	Yes
	Alone this would not be an indicator. However, coupled with other indicators this is considered.
F—8.	Frequent touch between mother and son
	No
	Generally, the abusive parent will not openly display intimacy.
	Frequent touching and inappropriate or questionable touching could be an indicator of sexual abuse. All to be considered in context and in relation to other signs.
F—9.	Son flinches when mother turns in his direction
	Yes
	This behavior may be associated with physical and sexual abuse.

Section G: Student Appraisal

After the meeting, the school counselor suspects that Timmy is being neglected and abused. The school counselor should take the following course of action:
   (Select ONLY ONE in this section.)

G—1.	Contact local police
	No
	The local police may refer the child to CPS, or make contact with CPS themselves.
G—2.	Contact Timmy's dad
	No
	The school counselor cannot be sure that Timmy's dad is not involved or will protect Timmy.
G—3.	Contact the emergency contact on Timmy's health card
	No
	School counselors have a legal responsibility to report suspected child abuse to appropriate authorities (i.e., CPS).

G—4.	Contact CPS
	Yes
	This is the professional, ethical, and legal course of action.
G—5.	Asks principal for appropriate course of action
	No
	Principals depend upon school counselors to know the appropriate and legal course of action in these situations. Principals generally like to know when calls are made to CPS because social workers often visit the child at the school and go through the front office.
G—6.	Inform the mother of her suspicions, and say if it continues she will report her
	No
	This could anger the parent, who, if she is abusive, may take it out on Timmy. Instead of protecting Timmy, you may have placed him in harm's way. The responsible, ethical, and legal course of action is to report suspected child abuse to CPS.

Chapter 4: Guided Reflection

Compare individual and program assessment. Then, describe the differences between assessing individual needs (or student appraisal) and assessing program needs.

Discuss the importance of assessment (both individual and program) in identifying needs and creating a needs-driven school counseling program.

Compare and contrast formal and informal assessments. Give examples of each.

After examining the construct, summarize (rewrite in your own words) what is meant by life-saving assessment. Then, discuss the importance of assessment in the following critical incidents:

Child abuse and neglect

Substance abuse

Self-harm

Describe how the school counselor generally engages in assessment in the school setting.

Describe how the school counselor generally engages in diagnosis in the school setting.

Explain what a needs assessment is, and create one item that might be on a needs assessment for each of the following developmental levels: (1) elementary students, (2) middle school students, and (3) parents.

Compare goals and objectives. What are the differences? Give an example of a goal. Then, create one supporting objective for that goal.

Chapter 5

Research and Evaluation

School counselors make use of research and engage in research, particularly program evaluation, to create a cycle of research consumption and production. The importance of accountable practices cannot be overstated. The fundamental fact is, a tried-and-true school counseling intervention can forever change the direction of a student's life.

Research and program evaluation are the school counselor's bread and butter. Data gleaned from the analysis of research and program evaluation are essential in order to

- Identify practices that contribute to academic success and the personal–social and career development of students.
- Develop empirically supported curriculum.
- Engage in professional advocacy.
- Provide reliable consultation services.
- Make programming decisions.
- Enhance accountability.
- Shape policy in the schools and at the local, state, and federal levels.
- Inform and sustain the profession.

Research

School counselors are savvy consumers of professional literature and research. Unlike the scratchings of graffiti and murmurs of idle gossip, research communicates factual information. Information shared through published research identifies evidence-based techniques, models, and approaches, identifying what works and with whom, that is, *best practices*.

Best practices are the compass for school counselor prevention and intervention programs, techniques, and methods of service delivery. Best practices are easily located but require that school counselors know their way around professional peer-reviewed education and counseling journals. The application of best practices requires the ability to identify and critically evaluate important components of relevant studies such as (1) theoretical orientation, (2) target population, (3) intervention used, (4) method of data collection and analysis, and (5) results.

School counselors plan curriculum targeting students' needs as indicated by an analysis of data derived from needs assessment and/or existing school sources. During program planning, school counselors determine ways in which they will measure the program's effectiveness in meeting the stated goals and objective(s), discussed later in this chapter. In this regard, school counselors are creating and delivering research-supported curriculum that is both data driven and data producing.

The ACA has a list of counseling-related peer-reviewed journals on their website at www.counselor.com. There are two primary professional school counseling journals available that identify innovative methods and research for promoting effective practices in school counseling. *Professional School Counseling* (PSC) is American School Counselor Association (ASCA's) award-winning, peer-reviewed journal published five times a year and free of charge to ASCA members. PSC is available in print on online. The peer-reviewed *Journal of School Counseling* (JSC) sponsored by the College of Education, Health, and Human Development at Montana State University is an online journal dedicated to the practice of school counseling (www.jsc.montana.edu/index.html).

The National Technology Institute for School Counselors at www.tech counselor.org houses research-supported information and resources. The *ASCA Scene* at www.schoolcounselor.org/SCENE is loaded with research-supported programs and interventions. *Cultivating Performance* at www.thenewschoolcounselor.com introduces culturally sensitive research-supported crosswalking strategies to close the achievement gap and enhance total student development. *Cultivating Performance* also intro-duces interactive action plan (SCOPE) and results report (School Counseling Operational Report of Effectiveness, or SCORE) templates that walk school counselors through programming from conception to evaluation. SCOPE is illustrated in Chapter 6, and SCORE is illustrated later in this chapter in the section titled "Documenting Outcomes with Results Reports."

DROPOUT PREVENTION

A high school counselor designed a program using attendance and graduation reports to identify specific populations of students, who for a variety of reasons are not coming to school. He designed a program to meet the needs of these students with the goal of reducing truancy and school dropout rates and improving school attendance. The school counselor just evaluated the program to find that the program has been effective in meeting the established goals. Which of the following would best describe the practices used by this school counselor?

   a. Data-producing program
   b. Data-driven and data-producing program
   c. Research-based programming
   d. None of the above

Center for School Counseling Outcome Research and Evaluation

The Center for School Counseling Outcome Research and Evaluation (CSCORE) was established by a diverse group of counselor educators to aid school counselors in identifying school counseling practices that result in positive student outcomes. CSCORE provides international leadership that focuses on research-supported systemic programming and evaluation to support families and communities and students to achieve academically. To access CSCORE go to www.umass.edu/schoolcounseling.

School Counseling Analysis, Leadership, and Evaluation

ASCA established the School Counseling Analysis, Leadership, and Evaluation (SCALE) Research Center to aid school counselors in identifying best practices that demonstrate how a comprehensive school counseling program is connected to student success. The SCALE Research Center helps to connect school counselors with counselor educators for collaborative research design, implementation, evaluation, and publication. The center also provides school counselors with professional development opportunities grounded in accountable research-supported programming and practices as well as training related to data collection and analysis. To access the SCALE Research Center go to http://scale.schoolcounselor.org.

Program Evaluation

Section F.1.c of the ASCA *Ethical Standards for School Counselors* (ASCA, 2010) states that school counselors "conduct appropriate research and report findings in a manner consistent with acceptable educational and psychological research practice. School counselors advocate for the protection of individual students' identities when using data for research or program planning" (p. 6). Program evaluation is the most widely used method of research in the schools, providing school counselors with information about what works, demonstrating *evidence* over *effort*—and answering the pressing question: "How are students different as a result of the school counseling program?" Program evaluation keeps us out of the shadows and in the sunlight.

It is the professional responsibility of the school counselor to "systematically collect and analyze data for the purpose of program improvement and accountability and to demonstrate the effectiveness and outcomes of school counseling practices" (ASCA, 2005, p. 59). Effective practices sustain and strengthen the school counseling profession. For these reasons, there is a resounding call to school counselors from school counseling and educational leaders to engage in program evaluation as a primary and critical area of *action research* (ASCA, 2004; Erford, 2011). Program evaluation is also the ethical responsibility of school counselors. Section D.1.g of the ASCA *Ethical Standards for School Counselors* (ASCA, 2010) calls for school counselors to develop "a systematic evaluation process for comprehensive, developmental, standards-based school counseling programs" (p. 4).

Just as research-supported practices necessitate that school counselors become savvy consumers of research, demonstrating results-based practices and accountability to stakeholders requires that school counselors become efficient producers of research. As an essential competency, legislative mandate, and ethical responsibility, it is important that program evaluation becomes an integral component of the school counseling program's research, review, and feedback structure.

Historically, service logs have been used to document time on task and illustrate the numerous and diverse duties and levels of responsibilities of the school counselor. For example, service logs include how often or how much time school counselors spend doing the following:

- Community and parent contacts
- Teacher and colleague consulting and collaboration
- Referrals to outside agencies
- Committee meetings

- Individual counseling
- Small group counseling
- Classroom guidance
- Program coordination

Although services delivered has its value in identifying *what* it is that school counselors do from day to day, it is inadequate in an outcome-driven educational environment. As the axiom goes, "We are drowning in information, but starved for knowledge." Ongoing evaluation satisfies that hunger by collecting and analyzing data that increases knowledge. That is, program evaluation demonstrates outcomes pertaining to the effectiveness and/or successful implementation of services in measurable terms.

TROY

You are a seasoned elementary school counselor mentoring Troy, your itinerant, first-year elementary school counselor. Troy wants to demonstrate the helpfulness of the small group intervention he created because it has become so popular and many students are asking to be a part of future groups. He asks you what method he should use to demonstrate how the groups have helped students. You reply

a. Program evaluation to demonstrate effectiveness in meeting objectives
b. Service logs to demonstrate the how many students and groups have been conducted
c. Both a and b
d. None of the above

Data collected through program evaluation demonstrates how school counselors are contributing to positive student outcomes. Stakeholders review data collected through program evaluation to assess the value of the school counseling program in meeting student needs and the needs of the collective. School administrators use this data to justify resource allocations and the existence of school counseling programs and to demonstrate accountability, which is permeating every molecule of the school counseling profession. Program evaluation may very well be the lifeline for school counseling programs hovering on the brink of extinction. Program evaluation does not equal accountability but precedes it as a means by which to demonstrate credible professional practices. Accountability also includes data-driven practices and prevention and intervention programming that are supported by standards and research.

ACCOUNTABILITY

Principal Sorretusay requires that all the high school counselors in her building implement programs that demonstrate accountability. One of the school counselors conducted a program evaluation on the current transitioning program being used for incoming freshmen. The principal said she was pleased, but that she was sorry to say that this was not enough. Principal Sorretusay commented that she believed that school counselors should be evaluating their programs on an ongoing basis as a matter of professional practice. What is the assumption, or misconception, on the part of the school counselor in this case?

Outcome and Process Evaluations

Program evaluations that measure outcome, that is, the effectiveness of the program in achieving intended goals and objectives, are important to establishing a causal link between school counseling programs and student change. *Outcome evaluations*, sometimes referred to as summative evaluations or quantitative evaluations, seek to answer a significant question: "Did it work?"

PRINCIPAL SHOME

Your principal, Dr. Shome, is not convinced that interrupting a teacher's instructional time with classroom guidance lessons is beneficial. He has come to you requesting data that shows "how" your school counseling classroom guidance lessons are making a positive difference in the lives of students. Which of the following types of program evaluation methods would be most useful in responding to your principal's request?

  a. Results of a student and teacher survey assessing their perceptions of a classroom guidance lesson.
  b. Results of a forced-choice, pre–post classroom guidance lesson measure created from lesson content.

c. Results of a preclassroom guidance lesson measure that asks students what they hope to learn from the lesson, and a postlesson measure that asks students what they learned from the lesson.

d. A postclassroom guidance measure that asks students to describe what they liked about the lesson and their suggestions for how the program may have made more of a positive difference for them.

Program evaluations can also measure process. *Process evaluations* assess program functioning, strengths, weaknesses, and the extent to which the program meets the expectations of and serves the target population. Process evaluations, also known as formative evaluations and qualitative evaluations, are useful for program decision making and program improvement. Process evaluations seek to answer questions such as: How did it work? How or with what population did it work best? Is the program proceeding as planned?

Although the call from educational and school counseling leaders is focused on outcome measures, the importance of process measures cannot be underestimated. For example, should a program evaluation present data that does not demonstrate positive outcomes, process data may provide school counselors with information for program changes that may improve outcome. Additionally, even when outcome measures are positive, additional program data might provide knowledge that can be used to strengthen program outcomes, uncover further needs and unexpected benefits of the program, and identify additional target populations.

OUTCOME OR PROCESS?

You are the middle school counselor at Sunflower Middle School in Pratt, Kansas. You have been facilitating a peer mediation program for the past two years, and you want to determine whether or not the program is meeting the established goals and gain information that will identify areas of strengths and weaknesses for improving the program. What type of evaluation would be the most useful?

a. Process evaluation
b. Outcome and process evaluations
c. Outcome evaluation
d. None of the above

Proximal and Distal Evaluations

Proximal evaluation measures student characteristics immediately before and after the program or intervention. The administration of proximal evaluations allows school counselors to establish correlations and, in some cases, depending upon the strength of the research design, a causal link between school counseling interventions and outcomes.

Distal measures do not generally take place immediately following the program or intervention, but it is possible depending upon research design. Distal evaluation outcomes alone do not definitively link school counseling programming to student change because of the great number of factors (i.e., extraneous variables) that impact student development over time (i.e., between phases of evaluation).

There has been some debate over the significance of proximal (immediate) versus distal (over time) program evaluation in linking school counseling program activities to what students know and can do as a result of the intervention or program. However, since measuring the effectiveness of school counseling programs is the professional *zeitgeist*, then proximal outcome evaluation takes priority. Proximal evaluation methods, then, are primarily used to establish correlation, if not causality, whereas distal evaluations are often used as a means of cross validation to further support, or call into question, proximal evaluation outcomes.

DARE TO SAY NO

A middle school counselor created a classroom guidance unit that involves two visits to the health and PE classrooms over a period of 2 weeks to cover a drug and alcohol prevention program to supplement the DARE and Just Say No programs at their school. During the first visit, the school counselor administered two questionnaires developed from the content of the curriculum. One of the questionnaires included items that would be covered during this first lesson; the other questionnaire included content that would be covered in the entire 2-day program. On the second visit, the school counselor administered a questionnaire that included items that would be covered during this second lesson. One week following the unit, the school counselor returned to the classrooms to administer a questionnaire that was identical to the one administered during the first lesson, which included content that would be covered in the entire 2-day program. This is an example of the following type of program evaluation:

a. Proximal
b. Distal
c. Outcome
d. Proximal and distal

Methodology

Program evaluation is a type of field-based outcome study, or applied research. There are many other types of outcome research designs that could be used to measure any number of research questions. In fact, an infinite number of possibilities exist. Table 5.1 lists the three most commonly used designs (i.e., non-experimental, quasi-experimental, and true experimental) by school counselors when conducting outcome research in the school setting (Breakwell, Hammond, & Fife-Schaw, 2001; Erford, 2011).

Table 5.1 **Frequently Used Outcome Research Methodologies**

Non-experiemental (or Pre-experimental)
Pretest–posttest (one group only)
Case study (examination of one individual or group)
Quasi-experimental
Pretest–posttest (two or more groups)
Non-equivalent control group (use of a control group and a pre–post measure to understand similarities and differences of groups prior to intervention).
Time series design (no control group; one sample with multiple measures on three or more occasions).
True experimental
Randomized pretest–posttest with control group
Randomized posttest only with control group

There are basic differences in the three designs. The true experimental design uses random sampling and control groups; the quasi-experimental design shares similar characteristics of the true experimental design but does not use random assignment. The quasi-experimental design involves multiple groups or multiple measures. Non-experimental designs are generally one-time surveys and single observations. The true experimental design is the strongest for assessing cause and effect, with non-experimental designs having the least value for determining cause and effect between the intervention and the outcome.

IS PEER HELPING—HELPING?

A school counselor conducts a program evaluation that assesses the impact of a peer-helping program in five classrooms over a 4-week period of time. This methodology is considered to be

a. True experimental design
b. Non-experimental design
c. Quasi-experimental design
d. All of the above

Non-experimental and quasi-experimental designs do not allow school counselors to absolutely conclude that observed changes were due to their intervention. Nonetheless, these designs are invaluable in the educational setting where true experiments are extremely difficult because of vast uncontrollable variables and the ethical concerns of randomly assigning children and adolescents to treatment conditions and control groups. In the educational setting, the non-experimental and quasi-experimental pre–post program evaluation is the most widely used research design.

Program evaluations that use *triangulation* (i.e., the incorporation of multiple sources of data), in addition to both proximal and distal measures, strengthen confidence in observed changes. Figure 5.1 is an example of such a design, illustrating the evaluation questions, data sources, and methods of data analysis of a comprehensive and collaborative peer mediation program evaluation conducted by a school counselor in collaboration with counselor educators (Schellenberg, Parks-Savage, & Rehfuss, 2007).

Do peer mediation sessions result in the successful resolution of student conflict?

Data Source: Peer mediation session records over one academic year.

Data Analysis: Percentages

Do the number of schoolwide out-of-school suspensions decrease with the implementation of the Peace Palprogram?

Data Source: Out-of-school suspension data over a 5-year period.

Data Analysis: Frequencies and percentages

Do disputing students who participate in peer mediation sessions view the sessions as valuable?

Data Source: Peer mediation session records over one academic year.

Data Analysis: Percentages

Do peer mediators perceive the Peace Pal program as valuable?

Data Source: Process questions 5 years postprogram.

Data Analysis: Percentages and qualitative

Figure 5.1 Evaluation question, data sources, methods of data analysis (quasi-experimental design). (Adapted from Schellenberg, R., Parks-Savage, A., & Rehfuss, M. (2007). *Professional School Counseling*, 10, 475–481.)

Role of Data

While presenting in certain circles, just my mentioning the word *data* elicits a stomach-knotting panic response that is transparent on anguish-stricken faces. It is as though I just tried to pickpocket their superhero powers. My compassion runs deep on this issue, and I find myself wanting to say it in the most sincere way that I can muster: "Relax superman, it is not kryptonite." If you relate to this remark, as I once did—yes, I admit it—then the time is now to square with data. Because the thing is, as the tide of accountability rises, so too does the demand for data. Data-based decision making in education has been defined as the "process of collecting, analyzing, reporting, and using data for school improvement" (Poynton & Carey, 2006, p. 121). Best practices necessitate that school counselors use data to create needs-driven programs and to assess the effectiveness of school counseling programs and practices.

Table 5.2 Essential Data Skills for School Counselors

- Ability to identify existing data sources within and outside of the school
- Ability to collect process and outcome data related to individuals, groups, and programs
- Ability to disaggregate data and identify inequities and barriers to student success
- Ability to analyze and interpret data to identify and prioritize needs and develop appropriate programming
- Ability to establish baselines and create measurable goals and action plans based on data
- Ability to assess counseling progress and evaluate programs to determine effectiveness of practices
- Ability to use data to create a continuous cycle of program improvement
- Ability to create results reports from program outcome data`

The study of data is a powerful process that reveals not only stakeholder needs but inequities and barriers to academic achievement and other information essential to targeted, goal-focused programming and continuous improvement. Data, data, everywhere—and it requires effective management in order to organize critical information about the past and the present while guiding the future to ensure the continued life of the school counseling program. Table 5.2 lists data skills considered essential to effectively managing data in the school counseling program (Erford, 2011; ASCA, 2005; Isaacs, 2003; Schellenberg 2008).

School counselors can visit the state department of education website and/or school and school division websites for detailed local data that depicts the unique needs of the population they serve. The warehouse of local data may include school reports cards, accreditation studies, school improvement plans, and assessment outcomes.

School counselors, who make use of the robust sources of data on hand in their schools, have a foundation for accountable program construction. As discussed earlier, it is prudent to capture data from multiple sources in order to clearly identify needs and level of needs, and to strengthen confidence in observed changes demarcated by outcome data. The following list includes a few possible data sources for needs identification and program evaluation generally available to school counselors within the school in which they practice.

- Attendance rates
- Career assessments
- Classroom performance data

- College acceptance rates
- Course enrollment
- Demographic data
- Discipline records
- Dropout rates
- Expulsion records
- GED-track records
- Gifted education placement records
- Grade reports
- Graduation rates
- Program placement
- Promotion and retention rates
- Scholarship records
- Special rducation placement records
- Standardized assessment data
- Suspensions (in school)
- Suspensions (out of school)

Documenting Outcomes with Results Reports

School counselors share the outcomes of program evaluations in order to inform the profession and to demonstrate program effectiveness. Inquiring minds want to know *how* we make a difference in the lives of students. *Results reports* are the medium used to accomplish this communication. Results reports document program effectiveness in meeting stated goals and objectives.

Student change and the level of change as a result of the application of school counseling program interventions and strategies are demonstrated on the results report. For example, the report may indicate that the students' test scores improved as a consequence of participation in small group counseling on the topic of test-taking strategies. The immediate and long-term impact of the outcome and the implications for the school counseling program are also included. Results reports include a minimum of the following components (ASCA, 2005):

- Grade level of participants
- Content/curriculum (sometimes listed in accompanying action plan)
- Process data (number of lessons or sessions and number of participants)
- Knowledge gains (or other short-term perception data)
- Impact on behavior, attendance, achievement (or other long-term results)
- Implications for the school counseling program

Figure 5.2 illustrates *SCORE* (Schellenberg, 2008). SCORE illustrates the outcomes of a responsive, crosswalking intervention that is culturally sensitive and aimed at closing the achievement gap (Schellenberg & Grothaus, 2009).

SCORE
School Counseling Operational Report of Effectiveness

School Virginia School **Counselor** Schellenberg **Date** March 07

Activity Title

Enhancing Self-Esteem, Language Arts, and Mathematics

Goal(s)-Objective(s)

To enhance self-esteem and academic achievement for all group members.

Data Collection and Evaluation

Number of Program Participants: 6   Grade(s): 3   Other: AA-Male

Type of Evaluation: ☒ Outcome   ☐ Process   ☒ Proximal   ☒ Distal

Data Source(s): pre-post measure.

Details:

Method(s) of Data Analysis

☒ Percentages   ☒ Means/Averages   ☐ Frequencies   ☐ Counts   ☐ Statistical Testing   ☐ Other

Details:

Evaluation Outcome/Program Impact

The program was effective in meeting the program goal(s) and targeted objective(s) in the following area(s):

☒ Academic   ☒ Personal/Social   ☒ Career   ☒ Closing the Achievement Gap

Details: Knowledge development occurred on both the school counseling and academic curriculum for the entire group per session (Math, 56-80%; Language Arts, 65%; School Counseling, 35-133%). Pre- and post-group measures indicated knowledge development on both the school counseling (115%) and academic curriculum (Math, 80%; Language Arts, 65%) for the entire group.

Directions for Future Programming

☒ Continue Implementation of Current Activity   ☐ Modify Activity Based on Results

Details:

**Pre- and Post-Group Measures
for Each Student**

Pre-Post Data Worksheet

Figure 5.2   SCORE. (From Schellenberg, R. (2006). *The New School Counselor: Strategies for Universal Academic Achievement*. Lanham, MD: Rowman Littlefield Education.)

Chapter 5: Case Conceptualization Responses

Research

Dropout Prevention

The correct response is "b." The school counselor is demonstrating school counseling practices that are both data driven (e.g., he or she reviewed data to identify and create a program based on student need) and data producing (e.g., he or she evaluated the program to obtain data that supports the effectiveness of the program).

Program Evaluation

Troy

The correct response is "a." Troy wants to demonstrate how his small group has helped students. Service logs will only show the number of times the group has been facilitated. Demand for the group does not mean that it is effective. Student may just really like Troy, the group experience, or getting out of class. Troy needs to conduct program evaluation to determine the outcome of his efforts.

Accountability

The assumption, or misconception, on the part of the school counselor is his or her belief that program evaluation equals accountability. Program evaluation is a component of accountability, but accountable school counseling programs also include needs assessment based on collected or existing data and programming and interventions that are grounded in research and standards. School counselors use actions plans and results reports to document and share accountable practices with stakeholders.

Outcome and Process Evaluations

Principal Shome

The correct response is "b." Dr. Shome is asking for *outcome* data. By administering a forced-choice (e.g., multiple choice, true–false) prelesson measure and postlesson measure created from lesson content and lesson objectives, you can objectively measure your lesson outcome. Because you are administering the measure immediately before and immediately following the lesson (proximal evaluation), you can claim with some certainty that change is due to your intervention.

Outcome or Process?

The correct response is "b." Both outcome and process evaluations would be most useful based on your purposes for evaluation. Outcome evaluation will provide you with what is needed to determine effectiveness toward meeting program goals. To determine whether or not the program is being implemented as planned and to determine which components are responsible for the program's success or lack of success, process evaluation is needed.

Proximal and Distal Evaluations

DARE to Say No

The correct response is "d." This is an example of both proximal (immediate) and distal (over time) evaluations.

Methodology

Is Peer Helping—Helping?

The correct response is "c." This is an example of a quasi-experimental design because the methodology of the evaluation examines multiple groups as well as multiple measures.

Chapter 5: Simulation

Program Evaluation

Brief Case Description

You are the school counselor at an elementary school. The principal wants to ensure that you are implementing a data- and needs-driven, comprehensive school counseling program. As such, she has requested that you present her with a 5-year plan for meeting the needs of stakeholders and evaluating the school counseling program.

Section A: Program Evaluation

What strategies would you include in your plan to ensure that the school counseling program is appropriately evaluated?

(Select as many as you consider indicated in this section.)

_____A—1.	Preprogram surveys	
_____A—2.	Student names for interview by the principal	
_____A—3.	Needs assessment	
_____A—4.	Postprogram surveys	
_____A—5.	Teacher names for interview by the principal	
_____A—6.	Teacher program perception surveys	
_____A—7.	Parent reports to the principal	
_____A—8.	Student program perception surveys	
_____A—9.	Community member names for interview by the principal	
_____A—10.	Statistical testing of pre–post data	
_____A—11.	Committee meeting involvement	
_____A—12.	Website development	

Section B: Program Evaluation

The principal likes the strategies you have designed to include in your 5-year plan for accountable school counseling practices. She is uncertain as to how you would objectively measure each classroom guidance lesson and small group activity to ensure that you are making a positive difference in the lives of the students. She is focused on data that will demonstrate how well you have met stated goals, objectives, and standards. Which of the following types of evaluation will yield this data?

(Choose ONLY ONE in this section.)

_____B—1.	Process evaluation using a pre- and postmeasure
_____B—2.	Formative evaluation using a pre- and postmeasure
_____B—3.	Outcome evaluation using a pre- and postmeasure
_____B—4.	Pre- and postquestionnaire of participants' perceptions of the program
_____B—5.	Program review by teachers

Section C: Program Evaluation

In a recent faculty meeting, your principal stressed the importance of developing research-supported curriculum. You are about to develop a small group for second-grade students on social skills. What information do you need from the research to develop a research-supported curriculum?

(Select as many as you consider indicated in this section.)

_____C—1.	Previous successful social skills programs
_____C—2.	Age–grade-specific social skills activities
_____C—3.	Correlation between social skills and academic achievement
_____C—4.	Effectiveness of small group programs for enhancing social skills
_____C—5.	Definition of social skills
_____C—6.	Use of recognized interventions for social skills improvement

Section D: Program Evaluation

Which of the following resources would be most useful in providing research pertaining to school counseling and school counseling interventions?

(Select as many as you consider indicated in this section.)

_____D—1.	ASCA Scene
_____D—2.	Wikipedia
_____D—3.	*Counseling Today*
_____D—4.	National Technology Institute for School Counseling
_____D—5.	Peer-reviewed journals
_____D—6.	Center for School Counseling Outcome Research
_____D—7.	Webster Dictionary Online
_____D—8.	NBCC Newsletter
_____D—9.	PSC

Section E: Program Evaluation

The data collected from your social skills group indicated that the group intervention was not effective in meeting the stated objectives. What type of program evaluation would have been useful to determine the program's strengths and weaknesses and provide information that could be used for program improvement?

(Choose ONLY ONE in this section.)

_____E—1.	Process evaluation
_____E—2.	Formative evaluation
_____E—3.	Outcome evaluation
_____E—4.	Program evaluation
_____E—5.	Student evaluation

Chapter 5: Simulation Answers

Program Evaluation

Brief Case Description

You are the school counselor at an elementary school. The principal wants to ensure that you are implementing a data- and needs-driven, comprehensive school counseling program. As such, she has requested that you present her with a 5-year plan for meeting the needs of stakeholders and evaluating the school counseling program.

Section A: Program Evaluation

What strategies would you include in your plan to ensure that the school counseling program is appropriately evaluated?

(Select as many as you consider indicated in this section.)

A—1.	Preprogram surveys Yes Preprogram measures provide school counselors with a baseline for assessing change.
A—2.	Student names for interview by the principal No Principals do not have time to interview students about their perceptions of the effectiveness of the school counseling program. Also, principals are generally more interested in data that identifies the outcome of school counseling practices.
A—3.	Needs assessment Yes Needs assessments are a time-honored means for collecting data from stakeholders for needs-driven program decision making.
A—4.	Postprogram surveys Yes Postprogram assessment provides program outcome data. School counselors combine pre- and postprogram measures to assess academic and behavioral change.

A—5.	Teacher names for interview by the principal
	No
	Principals do not have time to interview teachers about their perceptions of the effectiveness of the school counseling program. Also, principals are generally more interested in data that identifies the outcome of school counseling practices.
A—6.	Teacher program perception surveys
	Yes
	Although program outcome data is necessary in today's educational climate that asks how school counselors are making a difference in the lives of students, process data from perception surveys depicts how the school counseling program is viewed by others and may identify areas of strength and weakness for program improvement.
A—7.	Parent reports to the principal
	No
	Principals do not have time to read parent reports or receive visits from parents of all the students regarding the school counseling program.
A—8.	Student program perception surveys
	Yes
	Program outcome data is critical to answering the important question "How do school counselors make a difference in the lives of students?"; however, process data from perception surveys are helpful in identifying areas of strength and weakness for program improvement.
A—9.	Community member names for interview by the principal
	No
	Principals do not have time to interview community members about the effectiveness of the school counseling program.
A—10.	Statistical testing of pre–post data
	Yes
	Statistical tests of program data are useful in understanding if changes related to program implementation are significant, which can be documented in results reports to school administrators and stakeholders.

A—11.	Committee meeting involvement
	No
	Although school counselors are encouraged to participate in committees and collaborate with others within and outside of the school, membership does not offer insight into the effectiveness of the school counseling program.
A—12.	Website development
	No
	School counselors are encouraged to have a presence on the Web. However, having a website does not offer insight into program effectiveness.

Section B: Program Evaluation

The principal likes the strategies you have designed to include in your 5-year plan for accountable school counseling practices. She is uncertain as to how you would objectively measure each classroom guidance lesson and small group activity to ensure that you are making a positive difference in the lives of the students. She is focused on data that will demonstrate how well you have met stated goals, objectives, and standards. Which of the following types of evaluation will yield this data?

(Choose ONLY ONE in this section.)

B—1.	Process evaluation
	No
	Process evaluation yields formative information that identifies program strengths and weakness.
B—2.	Formative evaluation
	No
	Formative evaluation, also referred to as process evaluation, provides information about program strengths and weaknesses.
B—3.	Outcome evaluation
	Yes
	Outcome evaluation yield objective data that demonstrates the effectiveness of the program in meeting stated goals and objectives.

B—4.	Pre- and postquestionnaire of participants' perceptions of the program
	No
	Perceptions will not objectively measure program effectiveness. The principal is requesting objective outcome data.
B—5.	Program review by teachers
	No
	Teacher reviews will yield perception data, which will not objectively measure program effectiveness.

Section C: Program Evaluation

In a recent faculty meeting, your principal stressed the importance of developing research-supported curriculum. You are about to develop a small group for second-grade students on social skills. What information do you need from the research to develop a research-supported curriculum?

(Select as many as you consider indicated in this section.)

C—1.	Previous successful social skills programs
	Yes
	Understanding what social skills interventions have worked in the past is helpful to present planning.
C—2.	Age–grade-specific social skills activities
	Yes
	Understanding what social skills interventions have worked in the past for a particular age group is helpful when considering the application of those interventions to the age group of the target population.
C—3.	Correlation between social skills and academic achievement
	Yes
	A brief statement in a school counseling action plan about how social skills connect to academic achievement demonstrates how your intervention relates to academic achievement.
C—4.	Effectiveness of small group programs for enhancing social skills
	Yes
	The school counselor wants to demonstrate with research that small group interventions are effective methods of delivery for social skills development.

C—5.	Definition of social skills
	No
	Defining social skills does not contribute to a research-supported curriculum.
C—6.	Use of recognized interventions for social skills improvement
	No
	"Recognized" interventions may not be research-supported interventions.

Section D: Program Evaluation

Which of the following resources would be most useful in providing research pertaining to school counseling and school counseling interventions?

   (Select as many as you consider indicated in this section.)

D—1.	ASCA Scene
	Yes
	The ASCA Scene provides school counselor with an abundance of resources, which may include research and research-supported interventions.
D—2.	Wikipedia
	No
	Wikipedia is a fine resource, but it is not considered scholarly.
D—3.	*Counseling Today*
	No
	Counseling Today, ACA's magazine, is not considered scholarly and does not generally include research.
D—4.	National Technology Institute for School Counseling
	Yes
	School counselors can access this resource for research on a variety of school counseling-related topics.
D—5.	Peer-reviewed journals
	Yes
	Peer-reviewed journals are considered the best source for scholarly research.

D—6.	Center for School Counseling Outcome Research Yes School counselors access this resource for school counseling-related research.
D—7.	Webster Dictionary Online No This is a fine resource but does not include scholarly research articles.
D—8.	NBCC Newsletter No The NBCC newsletter provides a wealth of information to members pertaining to the professional of counseling. However, it does not include scholarly research articles.
D—9.	PSC Yes This is ASCA's peer-reviewed journal, which contains the most relevant scholarly research for the profession of school counseling.

Section E: Program Evaluation

The data collected from your social skills group indicated that the group intervention was not effective in meeting the stated objectives. What type of program evaluation would have been useful to determine the program's strengths and weaknesses and provide information that could be used for program improvement?

(Choose ONLY ONE in this section.)

E—1.	Process evaluation Yes Process evaluation provides data about the strengths and weaknesses of a program.
E—2.	Summative evaluation No Summative evaluation, also referred to as outcome evaluation, provides objective data about the effectiveness of the intervention in meeting stated goals and objectives.

E—3.	Outcome evaluation No Provides data related to program effectiveness.
E—4.	Program evaluation No May be process or outcome, and the school counselor is seeking process data.
E—5.	Student evaluation No Identifies who is participating in the evaluation instead of the type of evaluation.

Chapter 5: Guided Reflection

Examine and compare the concepts of research and evaluation. Then, define each in a way that illustrates the differences.

Design a blurb to market the Center for School Counseling Outcome Research and Evaluation.

Design a blurb to market the School Counseling Analysis, Leadership, and Evaluation Research Center.

Define program evaluation, and describe its importance to school counselors and its connections to accountability.

Compare outcome and process evaluations and describe each to include how they are different.

Compare proximal and distal evaluations and describe each to include how they are different.

Examine the construct of methodology, and describe how the construct relates to program evaluation and research.

Discuss the role of data in school counseling.

What are results reports and why are they needed in school counseling?

Identify the essential components of a results report.

Chapter 6

Academic Development

Academic development, one of the three developmental domains of a comprehensive school counseling program, gained considerable ground when it became the focus of new vision school counseling. New vision school counseling shifted the paradigm from individual- and mental health-focused practices to systems- and academic-focused practices. The shift to an academic focus recognizes the school counselor's professional identity of counselor and its importance in maintaining an intact sense of our chief function and specialization: counseling. However, the academic focus of the new vision does call upon our dual role of educator to aid in aligning the school counseling program with the fundamental mission of schools: academic achievement.

Like a well-played game of chess, we are strategically planning our moves and positioning ourselves to check the king and seize academic success for all. Hand in hand with teachers and administrators, school counselors assist in identifying systemic areas of academic deficits and specific low-achieving student populations. Programming is tailored to target those academic needs while simultaneously meeting the personal, social, and career development needs of all students. School counselors deliver services using classroom guidance, small groups, and systems support methods aimed at enhancing knowledge of testing programs, developing test-taking skills, reducing testing anxiety, teaching study methods, and identifying sources for test preparation and tutoring.

ASCA's Position on Test Preparation Programs

Professional school counselors assist students in preparing for standardized tests by promoting opportunities designed to increase knowledge and improve test-taking skills. Professional school counselors help students and their families become aware of test preparation programs and assist them as they decide which programs best meet their needs.

Position statement adopted 1989; revised 1993, 1999, 2001, 2006

School counselors apply their knowledge of human development, behavior and learning theories, and principles of motivation to enhance student academic achievement and attitudes toward school. Believing in the capacity of all students to obtain high levels of academic achievement, school counselors help to prepare students for meaningful futures in a global economy and technologically advanced world. In the words of Journey's timeless, sleep-deprived classic that took the midnight train to the number one digital track of all time—"Don't Stop Believin."

Curriculum Development

Chapters 4 and 5 discussed how school counselors identify stakeholder needs, turn those needs into measurable objectives, and identify methods for evaluating the effectiveness of the program. This chapter focuses on creating research-supported curriculum that directly aligns with the objectives. For example, if the goal is to improve student test scores, a measurable objective supporting this goal is "Students will identify five strategies for overcoming test-taking anxiety." The curriculum will include research-supported content and activities specific to achieving this objective. That is, the content will, in some fashion, introduce five research-supported strategies for reducing test-taking anxiety.

Let us consider the concept of self-esteem. Negative self-esteem has had a long and prosperous career in invading minds, hearts, and souls with self-destructive rubbish, making the self our best friend or our worst enemy. The benefits of positive self-esteem are as widely recognized as the entertaining Geico gecko for offering an insurance policy that kicks in when life serves up spontaneous catastrophe.

SCHOOL CLIMATE

The school counselor, Fernando, is creating a video program to enhance the school's social climate, identified as an area of need on the recently completed needs assessment. One of the program's measurable objectives is "Students will identify and apply three strategies for improving social skills." What would the video program content need to include?

Relying on research, school counselors reveal the link between self-esteem and personal, social, career, and academic development. The school counselor will particularly underscore the relationship between academic success and self-esteem to demonstrate a clear alignment with the academic mission of schools. Once this link is established, research-supported interventions that have been successful in building a positive self-esteem are identified. The following questions help to guide school counselors toward this end:

■ Does a correlation exist between self-esteem and academic performance?
■ What does the research say about the academic proficiency of students who have negative self-esteem versus those who have positive self-esteem?
■ Is poor self-esteem considered a barrier to academic achievement? If so, would it be logical to conclude that programs that enhance self-esteem remove a barrier to academic achievement?
■ Which counseling and instructional interventions have been used in the past with positive outcomes?
■ With what populations were the counseling and instructional interventions successful?

When developing curriculum, school counselors are sensitive to the diverse learning styles of their target population, as discussed in Chapter 1. School counselors are also mindful of the theory of *multiple intelligences* when seeking to create lessons and group sessions that are geared toward holistic student development.

Howard Gardner (1983) proposed the theory of multiple intelligences, contending that human cognition is made up of eight independent, yet interactive, intelligences across a variety of disciplines. Gardner defines intelligence as "biopsychological potential to process information that can be activated in a cultural setting to solve problems or create products that are of value in a culture" (Gardner & Moran, 2006, p. 1). The eight intelligences (i.e., linguistic, logical–mathematical, musical, spatial, bodily kinesthetic, naturalistic, interpersonal, and intrapersonal) along with possible counseling strategies for students with a propensity toward a particular intelligence are summarized in Table 6.1.

The interactive nature of multiple intelligences offers insight into the workings of the human mind. Whether intriguing or deeply disturbing, this information is nothing less than invaluable in developing and delivering curriculum that nurtures the diverse intelligences for optimal cognitive and

Table 6.1 Overview of Gardner's Multiple Intelligences and School Counseling Strategies

Intelligence	Description	Counseling Strategies
Linguistic	Reliance on spoken and written words; individuals generally adept in reading, writing, and speaking.	Narrative counseling, storytelling, journaling, letter writing, sentence completion, bibliotherapy.
Logical–mathematical	Reliance on reasoning, numbers, and logic; individuals generally adept in scientific thinking, investigation, and making complex calculations.	Genograms, games, strategic planning, objectifying, outlining, exploring, topic specific crossword or word search activities.
Musical	Reliance on rhythmic sounds, pitch, and tones; individuals generally adept in singing, playing musical instruments, and composing music.	Creating lyrics to music, moving to music, musical motivation (e.g., during homework, classwork); musical meditation (e.g., meditation that involves soothing tunes).
Spatial	Reliance on the mind's eye; individuals generally adept in design, puzzles, navigation.	Cognitive mapping, visualization/imagery, pretend.
Bodily kinesthetic	Reliance on touch and movement; individuals generally adept in dance and sports.	Role playing, psychodrama, exercise, Yoga, dance, interactive games/play.

Table 6.1 Overview of Gardner's Multiple Intelligences and School Counseling Strategies *(Continued)*

Naturalistic	Reliance on nurturing and that which is associated with nature; individuals generally adept at classifying organisms and understanding of the natural environment.	Outdoor activities, discussions and observations related to natural consequences and human nature.
Interpersonal	Reliance on interactions with others; individuals generally adept at identifying the needs of others and working cooperatively with others.	Role play, group counseling, collaborative work/play.
Intrapersonal	Reliance on introspection, intuition, and self-reflection; individuals generally adept in understanding self and self-control.	Questioning, journaling, studying, meditation, self-play, quiet time.

Source: Adapted from Gardner, H., & Moran, S. (2006). *Educational Psychologist, 41*(4), 227–232.

affective learning experiences. Also noted in Chapter 2, identifying students' propensities toward specific intelligences provides information useful in career decision making.

Response-to-intervention

Response-to-intervention (RTI) is an early intervention process used to help struggling students to improve behavior, achieve academically, and stay in school. RTI is a responsive service driven by data. School counselors can reduce self-punishing data seeking behaviors by making use of the sizeable variety of data sources already available in the schools when seeking to identify populations in need of RTI. Chapter 5 provides a selection of flavors to satisfy your intellectual preference.

The understanding that some students need more intense or individualized instruction in order to be successful learners is the core belief of RTI. Struggling students are identified and screened so that individualized services can be designed to meet their unique, multifaceted, and sometimes complex needs. Interventions are put into place, and students are monitored to ensure progress toward established goals.

ASCA's Position on RTI

Professional school counselors are stakeholders in the development and implementation of the RTI process. Professional school counselors align with the RTI process through the implementation of a comprehensive school counseling program designed to improve student achievement and behavior.

Position statement adopted 2008

Multidisciplinary RTI teams of professional educators are established in each school. The RTI team consists of a special blend of expertise (e.g., school counselor, school psychologist, teacher, school social worker, reading specialist). The union of disciplines allow for a deeper conceptualization of student needs and a holistic and integrated perspective from which to identify promising interventions and tools. RTI services may be delivered by select professionals within and outside of the school based on student needs.

School counselors use a multitier approach to aligning the comprehensive school counseling program with the RTI process. Educational and behavioral data are examined to monitor student progress. Table 6.2 demonstrates this alignment (ASCA Position Statements, RTI, 2008 [ASCA, 2011]).

RTI services are as unique as the students, varying in type, intensity, and duration. RTI services are based on student needs and established educational, career, and personal–social goals. A sampling of services may include

- Dropout prevention
- Decision making
- Behavioral support
- Referral
- Counseling
- Career planning
- Assessment
- Goal setting
- Parenting skills
- Transitioning

Table 6.2   Response-to-Intervention in a Comprehensive School Counseling Program

RTI Tiers and Processes	ASCA National Model Systems and Related Components
Tier one: Universal core instructional interventions: all students, preventative, and proactive	Foundation: Standards and competencies Delivery: Classroom guidance and individual student planning Management: Action plans Accountability: Results reports
Tier two: Supplemental/strategic interventions: students at some risk	Foundation: Standards and competencies Delivery: Responsive services (i.e., individual counseling, individual student planning, small group advising/ counseling and consultation). Management: Closing the achievement gap action plans Accountability: Closing the achievement gap results reports
Tier three: Intensive, individual interventions: students at high risk	Foundation: Standards and competencies Delivery: Responsive services (i.e., individual student counseling, small group counseling, consultation, and referral). Management: Closing the achievement gap action plans Accountability: Closing the achievement gap results reports

Source: Adapted from American School Counselor Association. (2011). *ASCA position statements*. Retrieved June 2, 2011, from www.schoolcounselor.org.

Closing the Achievement Gap

The school counselor's role in academic development includes assisting in meeting the mandates of No Child Left Behind (NCLB) (United States Department of Education, 2001). NCLB is considered by many to be the most significant and controversial of educational reform legislation in our nation's history. The primary goal of NCLB is to ensure that all students obtain proficiency in mathematics and language arts by 2013–2014.

All in all, educators agree with NCLB legislation. However, there are some who view NCLB as an encounter with the Ebola virus and others who would prefer to contract the Ebola virus. Disenchantment with NCLB does not appear to be grounded in its philosophies and goals, but in the

WHITNEY'S BEHAVIOR

A school counselor has been working with Whitney, a middle school student, for several months. Whitney is having many behavioral problems. The school counselor began working with Whitney when she was referred to the school's early intervention team. The intervention plan was not successful in creating behavioral change. The school counselor continued to consult and collaborate with the school psychologist and school social worker but the strategies designed to help Whitney continued to be unsuccessful. The school counselor is now strongly encouraging Whitney's parents to seek outside mental health counseling services and has provided the family with a resource list from which to select an individual and family counselor. When considering ASCA's tiers of the RTI process, which tier represents the current role of the school counseling in helping Whitney?

    a. Tier two
    b. Tier three
    c. Tier one
    d. None of the above

tough realities of its implementation based on limited human and material resources. Driven to do what is best for children, educators are nevertheless giving it their all and hammering out results with minimal provisions.

The TSCI and ASCA support the primary objectives of NCLB. These objectives include closing the achievement gap, demonstrating accountability, and providing students with a safe and positive learning environment. Under NCLB, schools must establish time lines for closing achievement gaps and tracking student progress toward meeting standards, ensuring adequate yearly progress (AYP) toward academic proficiency. Closing achievement, attainment, and opportunity gaps are also considered to be the school counselor's ethical responsibility, as discussed in Chapter 3.

Achievement gaps exist between males and females and between students from underprivileged backgrounds and those from more affluent backgrounds. Achievement gaps have also been identified between students whose native languages differ and between students of differing ability levels. Achievement gaps vary from school to school and state to state. The most consistently documented achievement gap is based on national data.

This data indicates an achievement gap between races, namely Caucasian students and African Americans, Latinos, and Native Americans.

Efforts to close the achievement gap are the impetus behind the call for school counselors to engage in practices that more clearly focus on academic achievement. Historically, school counselors have viewed their function as indirectly increasing academic achievement. School counselors have done this by removing physical, personal, social, emotional, behavioral, and environmental obstacles to learning. School counselors have also contributed to academic achievement by teaching strategies that help students to master the skills needed for academic success and self-directed learning (e.g., testing taking, studying, note taking, time management, goal setting). Communications with school administrators, however, tend to depict the belief that school counselors should take a more direct role in helping students to achieve academically (Shoffner & Williamson, 2000).

Crosswalking Curriculum

ASCA encourages school counselors to develop programs that demonstrate a direct impact on academic achievement and more overt alignment with the mission of schools. Leaders in education and school counseling agree that implementation of standards-based programs that align school counseling programs with academic achievement missions are best practices for professional school counselors. Crosswalking is encouraged by ASCA as an integral and academic-focused component of a comprehensive school counseling program. In case you did not notice, this makes crosswalking our new best friend.

Standards blending is a promising crosswalking approach that demonstrates a more direct alignment and impact on academic achievement. Research on standards blending (Schellenberg, 2007, 2008; Schellenberg & Grothaus, 2009, 2011) has resulted in increased academic achievement in language arts and mathematics as well as achievement in the personal–social and career development domains. Standards blending has also been identified as a culturally sensitive, RTI strategy for closing the achievement gap, discussed later in this chapter.

Crosswalking approaches directly and overtly align school counseling programs with academic achievement missions. School counselors methodically identify and merge specific core academic standards with school counseling standards. This integrated approach aids students in connecting curriculum to real life and across disciplines. School counselors give special consideration to crosswalking the school counseling standards with language arts and mathematics standards to aid schools in meeting the overarching goal of NCLB. Also, reading, writing, and arithmetic are considered the building blocks of a sound educational foundation.

As a primary and anchored appendage to a comprehensive developmental school counseling program, crosswalking strategies help to establish academic-focused practices that make use of school counselors' skills as both educators and counselors. So, pull in those bewildered and unsuspecting jaywalkers who may otherwise collide with the driving force of school administrators who only give way for those who are crosswalking.

NEW VISION SCHOOL COUNSELING

You are the elementary school counselor practicing from the new vision's academic-focused paradigm. You create a small group for fourth-grade African American male students who are having issues related to poor self-esteem. In talking with the teachers of these students, you find that the students are also performing below grade level in mathematics. On the basis of information from teachers and a review of the students standardized test scores, you create a small group that addresses the students personal–social needs (i.e., self-esteem) as well as their academic needs (i.e., mathematics). Your small-group program is an example of:

a. A systems-focused approach
b. A closing the achievement gap strategy
c. A crosswalking approach
d. All of the above

Action Plans/Lesson Plans

School counselors use the term *actions plans* versus *lesson plans* because school counseling activities involve a variety of forums (e.g., group sessions, guidance lessons, workshops, presentations, and programs). Action plans include a minimum of the following components (ASCA, 2005):

■ Data used to measure outcomes
■ Indication of administrative approval

- Identification of the individual responsible for delivery
- Method of evaluation (such as pre–post questionnaire)
- Objectives (expected results in measurable terms)
- School counseling domain, standards, and competencies addressed
- Research-supported curriculum content and activities
- Identification of the participants (subpopulations, number of participants, grade level)
- Timeline

Action plans for closing the achievement gap differ from general action plans in that they include the data sources that identify the academic discrepancies driving the program decision. Figure 6.1 illustrates an action plan using the School Counseling Operational Plan for Effectiveness (SCOPE) (Schellenberg, 2008). SCOPE illustrates needs-based programming with measurable objectives, research-supported curriculum, and a crosswalking approach (e.g., standards blending) that is culturally sensitive, responsive, and aimed at closing the achievement gap (Schellenberg & Grothaus, 2009).

Instructional Strategies and Classroom Management

School counselors draw upon training in counseling, school counseling, and education to create effective instructional and classroom management strategies. There are times when school counselors must make split-second decisions in Chicago winds while holding on to our hats, or royal fascinators for you Kate Middleton fans. Predetermined, reliable classroom management strategies and instructional practices help us to avoid flying by the seat of our pants—or our proper toppers!

School counselors use differentiated instruction and provide teacher support in the use of differentiated instruction to meet the learning needs of diverse students. Differentiated instructional strategies are empirically supported as equitable and effective methods that result in positive student outcomes (Akos, Cockman, & Strickland, 2007). School counselors use differentiated instruction primarily in the delivery of classroom guidance lessons.

CACREP (2009) defines differentiated instruction as "matching curriculum materials, teacher, delivery style, classroom management strategies, and behavioral/learning expectations to the student's motivation and learning needs" (p. 59). The concept of differentiation is grounded in the belief that all students have diverse interests, readiness levels, and *learning profiles*

SCOPE
School Counseling Operational Plan for Effectiveness

School Virginia School **Counselor** Schellenberg **Date** Mar 2007

Needs Assessment, Data Collection and Evaluation
Program Type: ☐ Prevention ☒ Intervention ☒ Closing the Gap Strategy

Evaluation Type: ☒ Outcome ☐ Process ☒ Proximal ☒ Distal

Data Source(s): pre-post measures.

Details: Pre-post for lessons & group. Students selected by parent-teacher: poor self esteem & academic challenge.

Program/Activity Title
The Me I Wanna Be

Goal(s)-Objective(s)
Group Goal: To enhance self-esteem and academic achievement (LA & Mathematics) for all group members.
Session 1 Objectives: Enhance the ability to identify the characteristics of biographies and autobiographies.
　　　　　　　　　Develop an understanding of the importance of positive peer relationships.
Session 2 Objectives: Enhance the ability to gather, evaluate, synthesize data and communicate findings.
　　　　　　　　　Develop an understanding of self in relation to others.
Session 3 Objectives: Develop a greater understanding of mathematical inverse operations.
　　　　　　　　　Gain an understanding of goal setting and attaining.
Session 4 Objectives: Develop a greater understanding of fractions as parts of a whole.
　　　　　　　　　Understand the purpose of and demonstrate the use of positive self-talk.

Target Population
Students in Grade(s): 3　　　　　　Other:

Details: Six African-American males in 3rd grade.

Method of Delivery
☒ Small Group ☐ Classroom Guidance ☐ Presentation/Workshop ☐ Other:

Research-Supported Program Curriculum
Number of lessons/sessions: 4
Program/Lesson Activities and Timeline
Four, 30-minute sessions, once a week for four weeks. Detailed session plans are noted on 2nd page.

National Standards Addressed

Mathematics

☒ Number & Operations NM-NUM.3-5.1.3; NM-NUM.3-5.2.3
☐ Algebra
☐ Geometry
☐ Measurement
☐ Data Analysis & Probability
☒ Problem Solving NM-PROB.PK-12.2
☐ Reasoning and Proof
☐ Communication
☒ Connections NM-PROB.CONN.PK-12.1
☐ Representation

Language Arts

☒ Listen-Speak NLA.4; NLA.12
☒ Read NLA.1
☒ Write NLA.7

School Counseling

☒ Academic A3.2;
☒ Personal/Social A1.1-3,5; A1.9-10; A2.1-8; B1.7,9
☒ Career A1.4, 6, 7; C2.3

Figure 6.1 SCOPE. (From Schellenberg, R., *The new school counselors: Strategies for universal academic achievement*, Lanham, MD: Rowman Littlefield Education, 2006.)

State Standards/Additional Information
School counselors may wish to include standards specific to their state here.
Research-Supported Group Activities:

Session 1 (You and Me):
Literature and research underscores the importance of having a sense of affiliation and friendship during the elementary school years in developing a sense of belonging and positive self-esteem (Dalgas & Pelish, 2006; Leary, Schreindorfer, & Haupt, 1995; Roberts, 2002; Schellenberg, 2000).
Activities: Students are introduced to the counselor, fellow students, topic, and group process. Group rules are discussed. Students pretend to be reporters interviewing an important person--as we all are! In pairs, sudents ask each other three questions that they would like to know about the other. A list of questions are provided for students if desired. Students note the question asked and response received. Characteristics of biographies and autobiographies are described. Individually, students write a biography of the student interviewed. Papers are shared and the importance of friendship and positive relationships with others is discussed.

Session 2 (We are the Same, We are Different):
The self-belief that one does not meet societal norms or have a sense of individual identity contributes to a low sense of competence (Kagan & Snidman, 1991; Schellenberg, 2000). Relationship building activities help students to recognize their own sense of individualism and self in relation to others, fostering an environment of belonging, and creating a feeling of competence, which is linked to academic achievement and self-efficacy (Anderman & Leake, 2005).
Activities: Round-Robin check-in. In pairs, students spend 5-10 minutes talking to each other to gather information about how each are different and alike. Prior to the information gathering, students are given 2 minutes to think about the questions they would like to ask. After the information gathering, individually, students reflect on the information, synthesize it, comparing and contrasting self in relation to the other student, and share their findings. Students are encouraged to think about what they learned from their partner's biography in the previous group session.

Session 3 (Goals are not just for Football):
A sense of mission contributes to motivation and goal attainment (Ross & Broh, 2000; Youngs, 1992), which leads to a sense of competence (Anderman & Leake, 2005). The process of goal achievement requires individuals to identify limitations and problem solve, promoting a sense of autonomy and personal control (Wigfield & Eccles, 2000).
Activities: Round-Robin check-in. Goals (short- and long-term) are defined. Students are asked to select one of the three goals listed on the board to achieve during this session. The goals are: 1) say something nice to a group member, 2) say something nice to the school counselor, 3) ask someone for help during the lesson. A deck of cards, self-created or other, with a goal on one side and the steps to achieve the goal on the other. Students take turns reading the goal and asking fellow group members to identify possible steps to achieve the goal. The cards are manipulated by the school counselor to demonstrate the mathematical concept of inverse operations. Students identify by a show of hands who met their goals. Obstacles encountered? What each might do differently next time?

Session 4 (Thought Power)
Individuals who perceive self as competent and worthy behave in ways that create success and view self as successful (Ellis & Harper, 1997; Ross & Broh, 2000). Self-perception is altered by internal dialogue that creates our thoughts, and, in turn, our feelings and behaviors (Ellis & Harper).
Activities: Self-talk is defined, modeled, and demonstrated by students. The affects of positive vs. negative self-talk are discussed and examples are provided on 20 individual strips of paper (10 positive self-talk statements and 10 negative self-talk statements). The strips of paper are described as a whole and then manipulated to illustrate fractions. Students take turns manipulating the strips. Group closure.

Figure 6.1 *(Continued)*

that when addressed will maximize the student's capacity to learn. School counselors do not attend to every student's unique learning profile but seek to deliver classroom guidance lessons that accommodate various learning profiles by diversifying approaches and offering task and assessment choices (Akos et al., 2007). Indeed, variety is the spice of life—and learning.

Like instructional strategies, classroom management is a skill specialty practiced by school counselors and shared with teachers. While some students stroll through the school years with no greater ambition that to please the teacher, others seem to plow through school with no greater purpose than to make us nuts—just a hare-brained and comforting theory that comes to me periodically as I seek to normalize the phenomena. Of course the other revelatory notion that strikes me is what a brief metamorphosis to nut it would be for some of us. Now, in all fairness to students, it very likely seems the same for them!

Establishing understandable, unbiased, and realistic rules is crucial to effective classroom management. Established rules need to be clearly communicated along with the consequences for breaking the rules. Consequences need a little R-n-R—no, not that R-n-R. Consequences need to be reasonable and respectful. Also, both natural and logical consequences should be explained, that is, "If you grab another student's crayon, they may smack you" (natural consequence) and "If you grab another student's crayon, one minute will be taken off of your recess" (logical consequence). Finally, applying rules and consequences in a consistent manner is critical to continued behavioral management and for reducing behavioral back-sliding. If I can get away with texting even once during your lecture, I will likely try again.

In addition to rules and consequences, it is important to catch students engaging in desired behaviors and reinforce those behaviors. Chapter 1 discusses behavior modification and the use of both extrinsic and intrinsic motivation to shape student behavior.

Classroom management is more than managing student behavior. The arrangement of the classroom is critical to accomplishing targeted instructional goals. For example, some teachers and school counselors may prefer a formal tone to the classroom, and an environment that promotes individual work versus group work. In this case, desks or tables in the classroom might be physically arranged in a U-shape, V-shape, or lecture hall style. School counselors and teachers who desire a more relaxed tone and an environment that promotes cooperative learning may desire a physical arrangement that places the desks or tables in a square, circle, or small groupings.

Well-executed classroom management strategies help students to understand the power of good choices and to understand how our lives are the cumulative consequences of those choices. Additional areas to consider for effective classroom management include

- Noise levels
- Resources
- Volunteers
- Breaks
- Bathroom visits
- Homework and classwork submission
- Procedures for visiting the school nurse or school counselor

Classrooms do not need to resemble holding cells where the sound of the bell is the signal for escape with students firing off vows of freedom while fleeing with inmates. An effective system of classroom management maintains a student-friendly focus and air of nurturing—interrogation is optional and identified as *Socratic dialogue.*

Specialty Programs

Specialty programs have multiple identities such as alternative education programs, special education programs, nontraditional education programs, gifted education, and the list goes on. These programs may entail home schooling, online learning, enrichment courses, and multilingual instruction. Specialty programs are geared toward any number of special needs student populations (e.g., students with IEPs, students with 504 plans, students with limited English proficiency, students who are at risk of dropping out of school, advanced functioning students).

Specialty programs are goal-focused to meet the special needs of a specific student or student population and generally involve more individualized instruction, alternative methods of instruction, smaller class sizes, and/or alternative learning environments. School counselors are diligent in maintaining current information, programs, policies, and legislation as it pertains to specialty programs, approaches, and activities.

Homeschooling

Homeschooling is the education of a student by the parent or a tutor outside of the traditional public or private school setting. Homeschooling has grown in popularity in recent years for a variety of reasons. Some of the most common reasons noted by parents include issues associated with bullying, negative peer pressure, school violence, a desire to provide religious-based education, a lack of confidence in academic instruction, and/or as a matter of convenience.

Parents' homes are sovereign nations where instruction can be customized to the unique learning style and ability level of their child and around the family's schedule. Homeschooling also allows unlimited freedom to provide instruction in a manner that is consistent with family values and religious beliefs. The homeschooling environment is controlled by the parent, who takes on the responsibility for their child's education. The parent, too, provides opportunities for adequate social interaction to promote personal and social development.

Generally, children who are homeschooled tend to spend more time with parents, which can be a double-edged sword. This increased time together can result in a strengthening of family relationships or it can strain the ties that bond. School counselors understand the pros and cons of homeschooling and consider the unique personality and abilities of the child when discussing this as an educational program option. Sharing information and resources and speaking candidly about the realities of homeschooling help parents to make the best decisions for their children and family.

The Virtual Classroom

Virtual classrooms offer online instruction outside of the school building, generally at the high school level. Not all schools offer online instruction; however, the forecast is favorable for continued growth. There are a variety of reasons that a student might wish to take classes in this manner. Some students have an illness that may hinder their ability to participate in daily classes at school, whereas others simply do not like the in-school experience. Still others may wish to take additional courses or advanced courses for college credit supplementing a full daily in-class schedule.

Virtual learning environments require a self-disciplined and self-motivated mind. Online courses are designed to be just as rigorous as those in the traditional school setting, and students will need to be self-motivated time managers. Students also need to possess the skills to manipulate the online environment with basic computer skills (e.g., word processing, e-mail, Internet), or more advanced computer skills, depending upon the educational management system used. While some students flourish in the online learning environment, others learn quickly that it is not the Utopia they had envisioned. Instead, they find themselves mourning the loss of the four classroom walls.

School counselors are becoming increasingly involved in the enrollment and coordination of virtual learning programs. For this reason, school counselors are called upon to understand the nature of online learning in relation to the characteristics of students who would most likely succeed in this unique and challenging environment.

Programs for Students with Disabilities

Students with documented physical, emotional, social, and learning challenges require differentiated instructional strategies, often in a more structured environment with smaller class sizes or placement in *inclusion classrooms*. Special education students who have an IEP and students who have 504 plans are by law entitled to special accommodations to ensure their educational success and well-being (see Chapter 1).

The IEP of special education students experiencing behavior problems will include a *BIP*. The IDEA also requires that the special education student's IEP include a comprehensive transition plan to prepare the student for life after high school. At the present time, transition plans are not required as a component of the 504 plan.

Educators seek to provide special needs students with accommodations that will promote success while doing so in the *least restrictive environment*. Therefore, many special needs students are placed in general education classrooms while also participating in resource classes to provide additional academic support.

IEPs and 504 plans are reviewed upon parent request and updated at least annually to assess progress toward goal attainment and appropriateness of accommodations as the student grows and matures. Accommodations vary by student need and can range from extended time on a test to a personal assistant throughout the school day. School counselors apply their knowledge of child development and learning theories to advocate for balanced accommodations, that is, they identify accommodations that provide the optimal level of assistance: not too little, not too much—just right.

THE INCLUSION CLASSROOM

Genita is an elementary school student who has an IEP. The parent visited the school to discover that Genita was in a regular classroom with about 20 other students. The parent went directly to the school counselor, who had been a part of the IEP meeting, and asked why her daughter was not in a special education classroom. The school counselor said that Genita was performing very well in the inclusion classroom and receiving the IEP accommodations needed to be successful, so there was no need for a more restrictive environment. Is the school counselor correct?

ESL Programs

Students who are limited in their ability to speak English because English is not their native language are referred to as LEP students. ELL has also been used to identify students whose native language is not English. LEP students may qualify for English as a second language (ESL) services/programs. To identify learning needs, LEP students participate in a home language survey. If indicated, students will then be assessed in reading, writing, listening, and speaking to determine their level of English proficiency and thus identify their needs for specialized instruction and accommodation.

Like students with IEPs and 504 plans, LEP students receive special accommodations and services to promote academic success and total student development. The goal of the ESL program is to help LEP students to achieve English proficiency while accommodating their needs to promote academic success until such proficiency is attained. LEP students are monitored and routinely assessed using both formal and informal measures to determine their progress toward achieving English proficiency. Adjustments to instruction and accommodation are made accordingly.

The educational approach selected for assisting LEP students is at the discretion of the school division. Educational approaches are driven by best practices and the number of LEP students in the school as well as the level of English proficiency for the LEP population to be served. Some schools use: (1) immersion in the general classroom with interpreters, (2) ESL courses taught entirely by bilingual instructors, or (3) individual tutoring. Any combination of multiple approaches may be adopted to meet the needs of LEP students.

School counselors are familiar with the process for identifying and meeting the needs of LEP students. School counselors advocate for LEP student participation in all educational programs regardless of their level of English proficiency. School counselors also make every effort to ensure that LEP students receive the accommodations needed in order to participate in the variety of educational programs.

Enrichment Programs

Students with exceptional abilities require differentiated instruction within a more rigorous and engaging curriculum. Enrichment programs often focus on collaboration, communication, and higher-order cognitive skills such as convergent problem solving and divergent problem solving and the application of those skills to real life (Redding, 1990). Meeting the advanced capacities of gifted students is essential to encouraging their full potential.

Enrichment programs begin as early as kindergarten. The names and types of programs offered vary from state to state, school division to school division, and even school to school. Some of the more common programs include the Governor's School for the Arts, Science and Technology Academy and the International Baccalaureate program. Honors and advanced placement courses are also designed to meet the exceptional needs of this special population.

I WANT TO BE A PERFORMANCE ARTIST

Angela is a new professional school counselor at a large suburban high school. Yesterday, Angela met with Tamika, a tenth-grade student who has a GPA of 3.9 and had some questions regarding the PSAT. Tamika came into Angela's office very excited because she just got her first part in the community theatre. Tamika said, "I'm so happy—I want so badly to be a performance artist!" Which of these programs might be the most appropriate to discuss with Tamika at this time?

a. ESL program
b. Homeschooling
c. Virtual classroom
d. Governor's School

Advanced functioning students are sometimes identified as those students in a class that are exhibiting social, emotional, and behavioral problems. With more neurons in the human brain than planets in our Milky Way galaxy, the voltage of billions of transmitting neurons alive in the minds of geniuses at any given time must be astronomical. With this kind of neuroactivity, our most brilliant prodigies could go supernovae. For this simpleton, that kind of inner-galactic energy is mind-boggling.

We can understand, then, why classroom observations often explain the behavioral mishaps of gifted children and adolescents. Advanced functioning students tend to experience boredom with the general education curriculum, viewing it as mundane. Finishing tasks more quickly than peers, gifted students seek ways to occupy an overactive mind until the transition to a new subject. During this time, the gifted child may engage in activities that disrupt class. School counselors collaborate with teachers and students to find creative ways to fill this time with activities that stimulate and challenge the student's intellect and creativity.

The academically high functioning and asynchronous development of gifted students may also manifest itself as affective disturbances such as feelings of loneliness, anxiety, and depression, as well as social isolation and poor relational skills (Peterson, 2006). However, because of their independent and self-sufficient nature, the need to maintain a perfectionist image, and/or the belief that they may disappoint important others, gifted students often do not ask for help. Chapter 3 discusses the personal, social, and emotional issues unique to the advanced cognitive functioning of the gifted child.

GED Programs

Keeping students in school is our goal as educators and as a society. Despite all attempts at intervention, the school setting and structured school day are a struggle for some students. For this reason, school counselors provide students who are at risk of dropping out of school with alternative educational program options. Some programs lead to a high school diploma, while others result in obtaining a GED.

GED-track programs vary in eligibility requirements from state to state but generally require that students are at risk of dropping out of school and are at least 16 years old. Students generally take an official GED practice test with an established minimum score criteria for entrance in to the GED-track program. GED-track programs through the public schools can take weeks to years to complete, although it is generally about 1 month to 12 months depending upon the program. Some programs offer a track to the high school diploma or the GED, such as Job Corps. Job Corps is a nationally recognized, highly structured program directed by the Department of Labor that provides at-risk teens, beginning at age 16, with residential housing, allowances, and vocational training. Completion of the Job Corps program generally takes 8 months to 2 years.

School counselors are resource agents. Knowledge of a single resource can make the difference between a student dropping out of school or gaining an education, securing a satisfying career, and becoming a contributing member of society.

I WANT MY HIGH SCHOOL DIPLOMA

Reginald is a high school junior who has failed 11th grade twice. He told you, his high school counselor, that he hates school and just does not know what to do. He said his mom is about to move in with her mom, and he does not know what is going to happen to him because there is not enough room for him and his sisters and brothers at his grandmother's house. His mother suggested that he get his GED and get a job. Reginald said he thinks he will just quit school but that he really wanted a diploma and a career. Which of the following programs may meet Reginald's needs at this time?

a. Governor's School
b. Virtual classroom
c. Job Corps
d. GED track

Chapter 6: Case Conceptualization Responses

Curriculum Development

School Climate
Fernando's video program content would need to introduce students to at least three strategies for improving social skills and demonstrate the application of those strategies.

Response-to-Intervention

Whitney's Behavior
The correct response is "b." The level at which Whitney's academic and behavioral performance has declined places her at high risk, requiring that the school counselor work at the tier three level to help Whitney to be successful. At the tier three level, students are provided intense individualized attention and referred for additional school or community services. In Whitney's case, in-school supports and referrals have not been successful, calling for more intense support from outside of the school.

Crosswalking Curriculum

New Vision School Counseling
The correct response is "d." The new vision for school counseling is both systems- and academic-focused. Small-group methods for services delivery are systems-focused. And, you are creating and implementing a cross-walking approach because of your integration of both core academic and school counseling standards. Your small group is considered a closing the achievement gap strategy because you have included members of the gap (i.e., African Americans) in your group membership.

Specialty Programs

Programs for Students with Disabilities

The Inclusion Classroom
Yes, the school counselor is advising the parent correctly. By law, special education students are to be in the least restrictive environment with supports as listed in the student's IEP.

Enrichment Programs

I Want to Be a Performance Artist
The correct response is "d." Tamika has the academic performance and a passion for the performing arts that makes her a prime candidate for the Governor's School for the Arts enrichment program.

GED-Track Programs

I Want My High School Diploma
The correct response is "c." The GED track, although an option for Reginald, it is not the best response choice. Reginald has been clear that he really wants his high school diploma. Job Corps offers students the opportunity to earn either a GED or a high school diploma. Reginald also wants a career. Job Corps teaches a variety of occupational skills, and upon earning his high school diploma, Reginald can go to college. Finally, Job Corps can offer Reginald a structured living environment, providing him with a place to live, which is a concern for him at the current time.

Chapter 6: Simulation

Academic Success

Brief Case Description

You are a high school counselor, and a career and technical education teacher requests a classroom guidance lesson on career readiness. Practicing from an academic-focused paradigm, you seek to crosswalk your school counseling curriculum with academic standards.

Section A: Academic Success

What resources/information do you need in order to fully develop your curriculum that will promote universal academic achievement?
   (Select as many as you consider indicated in this section.)

_____A—1.	Percentage of non-Caucasian students in class
_____A—2.	Standardized tests data
_____A—3.	Mathematics standards
_____A—4.	Grade level of students in the class
_____A—5.	Number of special needs students in the class
_____A—6.	Language arts standards
_____A—7.	Special education labels of students in class
_____A—8.	Accommodations for special needs students in the class

Section B: Academic Success

The pre–post lesson evaluation data reveals low scores on both the school counseling and academic domains for five students, who are not special needs students. The teacher shares that there have also been some behavioral issues with these students. Based on the lesson outcome data and the teacher's comments, which of the following would be the best course of action at this time?
   (Choose ONLY ONE in this section.)

_____B—1.	Refer students to peer tutoring
_____B—2.	Design a RTI
_____B—3.	Call a parent conference
_____B—4.	Ask the teacher to provide individual tutoring
_____B—5.	Refer students for child study
_____B—6.	Refer students to a 504 committee

Section C: Academic Success

During a session, one of the students tells you that he is going to drop out of school. The student just turned 17 and is still in the tenth grade. He says that he hates coming to school because his classmates are so immature. He says he hates studying and doing homework. In an effort to prevent this student from dropping out of school, which course of action would be best at this time?

(Select as many as you consider indicated in this section.)

_____C—1.	Refer the student to the peer tutoring program
_____C—2.	Suggest he wait until he is 18 and then he can drop out
_____C—3.	Share information about the GED track
_____C—4.	Encourage the student to talk to his parents about his plan to drop out of school
_____C—5.	Share information about Job Corps
_____C—6.	Give him the official GED practice test during the session

Section D: Academic Success

The student returns to you the next day and says that his parents got so mad because you talked to him about alternative education programs. Tears in his eyes, the student says "I'm already almost 2 years behind, and

I'm failing math and English now … I'm just going to quit school … I don't care what my parents say." What is your best course of action at this time?

(Choose ONLY ONE in this section.)

_____D—1.	Help the student to secure a tutor
_____D—2.	Set up a meeting with the parents and student
_____D—3.	Refer the student for peer tutoring
_____D—4.	Request that the principal contact the student's parents
_____D—5.	Request that the school counseling director contact the student's parents
_____D—6.	Encourage the student to talk to his parents again

Section E: Academic Success

Before the meeting with the student's parents, the student tells you that the only alternative he would consider to dropping out of school is the GED track. He agrees to discuss this openly and calmly with his parents. During a meeting with the student and his parents, the school counselor focuses on the following:

(Choose ONLY ONE in this section.)

_____E—1.	A plan for staying in school
_____E—2.	Pros and cons of the GED track
_____E—3.	Other alternative education programs available
_____E—4.	The parents' unrealistic expectations of their son
_____E—5.	Apologizing for sharing alternative education program information with their son without their knowledge

Chapter 6: Simulation Answers

Academic Success

Brief Case Description

You are a high school counselor, and a career and technical education teacher requests a classroom guidance lesson on career readiness. Practicing from an academic-focused paradigm, you seek to crosswalk your school counseling curriculum with academic standards.

Section A: Academic Success

What resources/information do you need in order to fully develop your curriculum that will promote universal academic achievement?

(Select as many as you consider indicated in this section.)

A—1.	Percentage of non-Caucasian students in class
	No
	This is not needed to develop your academic-focused curriculum.
A—2.	Standardized tests data
	Yes
	Standardized test scores may help you to understand the area of greatest academic need and high school grade levels to customize your curriculum.
A—3.	Mathematics standards
	Yes
	Core academic standards are needed for crosswalking.
A—4.	Grade level of students in the class
	Yes
	Your curriculum needs to be developmentally appropriate.
A—5.	Number of special needs students in the class
	No
	The number of special needs students in the class is not needed to develop your curriculum.

A—6.	Language arts standards
	Yes
	Core academic standards are needed for crosswalking.
A—7.	Special education labels of students in class
	No
	The labels of special needs students in the class is not needed to develop your curriculum.
A—8.	Accommodations for special needs students in the class
	Yes
	Although school counselors often develop curriculum based on grade level and modify the curriculum to the special needs of students during or prior to delivery, it is helpful to know what types of instructional accommodations are needed when developing your curriculum.

Section B: Academic Success

The pre–post lesson evaluation data reveals low scores on both the school counseling and academic domains for five students, who are not special needs students. The teacher shares that there have also been some behavioral issues with these students. Based on the lesson outcome data and the teacher's comments, which of the following would be the best course of action at this time?

(Choose ONLY ONE in this section.)

B—1.	Refer students to peer tutoring
	No
	More needs to be known about these students first, and the only concern is not academic.
B—2.	Design a RTI
	Yes
	RTI is early intervention aimed at exploring the issues related to students' academic and behavioral problems and mediating those issues with individualized strategies designed by a multidisciplinary team.

B—3.	Call a parent conference
	No
	The student needs academic and behavioral intervention; therefore, more than a parent conference is warranted. The parent will be contacted once a plan of action is determined.
B—4.	Ask the teacher to provide individual tutoring
	No
	It is not the teacher's responsibility to provide outside tutoring, and academics are not the only issue.
B—5.	Refer students for child study
	No
	There is not enough information at this time to refer the students to child study.
B—6.	Refer students to a 504 committee
	No
	There is not enough information at this time to refer the students to a 504 team.

Section C: Academic Success

During a session, one of the students tells you that he is going to drop out of school. The student just turned 17 and is still in the tenth grade. He says that he hates coming to school because his classmates are so immature. He says he hates studying and doing homework. In an effort to prevent this student from dropping out of school, which course of action would be best at this time?

(Select as many as you consider indicated in this section.)

C—1.	Refer the student to the peer tutoring program
	No
	Peer tutoring is for additional assistance with specific course material, not an intervention for students who express a desire to drop out of school.
C—2.	Suggest he wait until he is 18 and then he can drop out
	No
	Although students may be eligible to drop out of school as an adult once the student becomes 18, school counselors strive to keep students in school.

C—3.	Share information about the GED track
	Yes
	School counselors have been identified as resource brokers. As such, the school counselor should provide the student with information about alternative education programs that will result in a diploma or GED rather than risk the student dropping out of school.
C—4.	Encourage the student to talk to his parents about his plan to drop out of school
	Yes
	School counselors encourage parent–student communication and empower students to talk to parents about important decisions in their life.
C—5.	Share information about Job Corps
	Yes
	As a resource broker, the school counselor should provide the student with information about Job Corps, an alternative education program that will result in a diploma or GED, rather than risking the student dropping out of school.
C—6.	Give him the official GED practice test during the session
	No
	Unless the student is an emancipated minor, parent permission is required to test the student. Also, parents need to know that their teen is planning to go the GED track versus general education.

Section D: Academic Success

The student returns to you the next day and says that his parents got so mad because you talked to him about alternative education programs. Tears in his eyes, the student says "I'm already almost 2 years behind, and I'm failing math and English now ... I'm just going to quit school ... I don't care what my parents say." What is your best course of action at this time?

(Choose ONLY ONE in this section.)

D—1.	Help the student to secure a tutor
	No
	The student wants to drop out of school; tutoring is not indicated at this time.
D—2.	Set up a meeting with the parents and student
	Yes
	The school counselor is a student and family advocate and collaborator. It is time for the family to come together to discuss all options. Discuss this option with the student.

D—3.	Refer the student for peer tutoring
	No
	Tutoring is not indicated at this time.
D—4.	Request that the principal contact the student's parents
	No
	The principal looks to you, the school counselor, to make parent contacts and apply consultation, collaboration, advocacy, and leadership skills.
D—5.	Request that the school counseling director contact the student's parents
	No
	Parent contact, even in times of adversity, is the function of a professional school counselor.
D—6.	Encourage the student to talk to his parents again
	No
	The student has tried to communicate with his parents. You do not want the student to drop out. Provide the student (and family) with support and discuss with the student a family conference at school.

Section E: Academic Success

Before the meeting with the student's parents, the student tells you that the only alternative he would consider to dropping out of school is the GED track. He agrees to discuss this openly and calmly with his parents. During a meeting with the student and his parents, the school counselor focuses on the following:

(Choose ONLY ONE in this section.)

E—1.	A plan for staying in school
	No
	This is not the purpose of the meeting as agreed upon by you and the student.
E—2.	Pros and cons of the GED track
	Yes
	Helping the family to understand what how the GED track works and what it means to their son's future is crucial.

E—3.	Other alternative education programs available
	No
	This is not the purpose of the meeting as agreed upon by you and the student.
E—4.	The parents' unrealistic expectations of their son
	No
	Unrealistic or not, school counselors respect parents' beliefs and understand that parents want the best for their children.
E—5.	Apologizing for sharing alternative education program information with their son without their knowledge
	No
	The school counselor acted appropriately, providing the student with alternatives to dropping out of high school.

Chapter 6: Guided Reflection

Explain the process of curriculum development, as if your audience knew absolutely nothing about it.

Define RTI, and create one example to illustrate a RTI strategy.

Define achievement gap. Name the populations of students that have been identified as part of the national achievement gap.

Discuss ways that the school counselor can identify achievement gaps in the school.

Design one activity that illustrates the integration (or crosswalking) of mathematics with one of the three school counseling developmental domain standards.

What are action plans and why are they needed in school counseling?

Identify essential components of an action plan.

Define and describe the importance of instructional strategies and classroom management, and when they would most likely be used in school counseling.

Describe and identify key components of the following specialty programs offered in schools:
    Homeschooling

    The virtual classroom

Programs for students with disabilities

ESL programs

Enrichment programs

GED programs

Chapter 7

Collaboration and Consultation

School counselors broaden and strengthen their ability to provide a time-efficient and cost-effective comprehensive school counseling program through collaboration and consultation. School counselors engage in consultation and collaboration on a daily basis involved in activities such as staff development, parenting workshops, parent–teacher conferences, committee membership, and program development.

School counselors provide both direct and indirect services to students through consultation and collaboration. For example, school counselors may collaborate with teachers to develop classroom guidance lessons. School counselors then deliver the classroom guidance lessons directly to students. School counselors may provide indirect services to students by providing direct consulting services to teachers and parents who will in turn deliver this information directly to students.

School counselors may work with the school nurse to develop a school-wide primary prevention program to address teen pregnancy and positive body image. The school counselor might work with school administrators and teachers to create a secondary prevention program to improve school climate and classroom management, respectively. School counselors collaborate and consult with school administrators and teachers to design system-wide programs that may use a combination of primary, secondary, and tertiary prevention interventions to help close the achievement gap, reduce dropout rates, improve attendance, promote positive attitudes toward school, and reinforce instruction using crosswalking strategies as discussed in Chapter 6.

APRIL'S IEP

You are a middle school counselor who just participated in an IEP meeting for April, one of the middle school students at your school. The individuals present at the meeting included the principal, special education teacher, one general education teacher, and the parents. You collaborated with these individuals to identify strategies to include in the student's IEP. Participating in the IEP meeting in this manner is an example of providing what type of services to April?

  a. Direct
  b. Indirect
  c. a and b
  d. None of the above

While delivering consulting and collaborative services, school counselors are mindful of the culturally diverse populations being served. As discussed in Chapter 3, culture impacts our thought processes and the manner in which a given situation or problem is perceived. Thus, cultural sensitivity during the consultation and collaboration process is crucial to establishing shared goals and achieving desired outcomes. The culturally sensitive school counselor is able to identify prejudicial attitudes and stereotyping that permeates and poisons the consultation and collaboration process. School counselors mediate those obstacles to promote effective consultation and collaboration outcomes.

School counselors are aware of the professional hierarchy that exists in the schools, as well as the educational and political forces involved at the school and community levels. This understanding of the unique associations between parents, teachers, school administrators, and important others sets the stage for team decisions and winning results.

Organized forces for engaging consultation and collaboration include the school counseling advisory council and the school leadership team. Professional school counselors establish advisory councils as an important component of a comprehensive school counseling program (discussed in Chapter 8), while school administrators are generally responsible for establishing school leadership teams (Sutton, 2006).

School leadership teams are responsible for analyzing academic data and establishing school-wide goals and objectives. Participation in the school leadership team is invaluable to gaining a greater understanding of the subsystems operating within the school as well as areas of strength and challenge related to the school's unique student population and climate. Membership on the school leadership team also allows school counselors to have a voice on important issues impacting the students and community we serve.

Collaboration

Collaboration involves a partnership between two or more individuals sharing areas of expertise, decision-making power, and responsibility for outcomes (Dougherty, 2009). School counselors generally collaborate with parents, teachers, administrators, and community members, focusing on a unified goal that is grounded in improving student performance and well-being.

Why collaboration? Strange though it may seem, we can look to nature for that answer. I am not saying that we need to be tree-huggers although I find concept appealing. What I am saying is that animals have collaborative instincts that guide their behavior in the most productive ways. Take ants, for example, which our airlines have studied to fashion more effective passenger seating processes. Singularly, ants have little or no ability to make an impact (other than annoying *Homo sapiens*), but altogether ants accomplish amazing feats in the most simplistic of ways with no leadership. Each ant is born with specific traits and applies their expertise as needed to ensure the survival of the species.

Also, consider the flight patterns of geese, which have been adopted by our nation's fighter pilots. By flying in a V-formation, geese conserve energy and maximize coordination and communication while attending to the well-being of each member. Using collaborative efforts, school counselors, like geese, harness the amplified power, energy, intellect, resources, and spirit by engaging the collective. Now, if we only had wings, we could really soar!

Collaboration, a fundamental concept, creates an intense life force through the interdependent nature and the shared resources and expertise of each member. It is this interdependence and sharing of specialties that distinguishes collaborative consultation discussed in the consultation section of this chapter.

Establishing a collaborative cohesive relationship with important individuals in a student's life requires teambuilding. Teambuilding strategies may include (Dougherty, 2009):

- Conflict resolution
- Mediation
- Empowerment
- Cross-cultural training
- Analysis of member interaction
- Facilitation
- Coordination
- Problem solving
- Brainstorming
- Encouragement
- Negotiation

Collaborative partnerships heighten the likelihood of identifying creative solutions to problems or services for the client system that might otherwise go unrecognized by any one individual. Figure 7.1 illustrates the collaboration process. The thick arrows indicate the primary structure of the collaboration process (Dougherty, 2009), while the thin arrows indicate interactions that may take place in collaborative situations in the schools between either the collaborator and the client system at a given time for assessing needs, clarifying information, asking questions.

Partnerships with other professionals in the school allow school counselors to provide optimal services to all students and to better identify and tackle obscured obstacles to student performance. School counselors build collaborative, internal multidisciplinary teams that may include the school

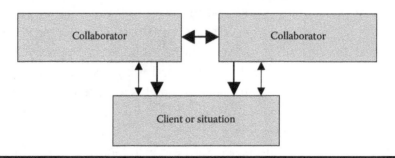

Figure 7.1 The process of collaboration.

nurse, school psychologist, school social worker, *educational diagnostician*, principal, teachers, and other school personnel.

As a member of the collaborative team, a special education teacher may share knowledge and skills related to the developmental needs of students with a variety of disorders and the unique educational approaches and tools available to assist these students. The educational diagnostician may share knowledge of educational assessment and diagnostic approaches to identify students who need more intense services in the school setting. The school nurse is able to provide important medical information regarding specific conditions and treatments.

In-house teams might also include collaboration with students. Peer-helping programs, discussed in Chapter 2, are instrumental in a variety of ways (e.g., mediation, tutoring, speakers, aids, mentors). Student office aids provide helpful services while gaining valuable interpersonal and professional skills. Students also gain a sense of empowerment and confidence by assisting school counselors and other adults in the school. Students, too, are generally more in tune to the needs of other students and the school community, making them an invaluable extension to the comprehensive school counseling program.

School counselors also invest time and energy creating external teams with shared goals, responsibilities, and outcomes. The time is well spent. Partnering with parents and members of the community builds the foundation upon which universal student success can be achieved and systemic change can be realized.

ASCA's Position on School-Family-Community Partnerships

Professional school counselors have an essential and unique role in promoting, facilitating, and advocating for successful collaboration with parents/guardians and community stakeholders. These collaborations are an important aspect of implementing equitable, data-driven, comprehensive school counseling programs that promote the academic success of all students.

Position statement adopted 2010

Collaboration with parents and community members multiplies the players and broadens the playing field. These partnerships may result in more funding and additional materials. Collaboration also helps school counselors to meet demanding student case loads and systemic programming needs.

The school counselor interacts interdependently and collaboratively within the varied systems with which students interact to influence each part in order to bring about systemic change. In this regard, we are systems hackers. The systems perspective acknowledges that important others with whom the student interacts have a tremendous influence on the student's career and academic development and personal, social, physical, and emotional well-being. Understanding the profound impact of the interactions that influence an individual is paramount to understanding the individual. These powerful interactions transcend the family system as the student and family interact with school personnel, all of whom interact with the community.

The importance of collaborative relationships within and outside of the school is most apparent during times of crisis. Collaboration during crisis response and postcrisis response heightens the school counselor's ability to coordinate integrated, multidisciplinary services in an efficient, unified, and timely manner. School counselors are instrumental in serving as community and school liaisons, creating and coordinating effective crisis response plans using the force of the collaborative. Use the force, new vision school counselors.

TEAMBUILDING

You are a school counselor collaborating with parents to establish a parent resource center at your school. Two of the parents are having a significant disagreement, which is interfering with progress. You are engaging your conflict resolution skills by providing mediation services to these parents with the hope that they will be able to negotiate a resolve. Conflict resolution, mediation, and negotiation are teambuilding skills that are helpful during the process of collaboration. Other teambuilding skills identified as helpful in the collaboration process are:

a. Brainstorming
b. Empowerment
c. Cross-cultural training
d. All of the above

Consultation

Collaborative approaches to consultation are the most widely used method of consultation in the schools. The collaborative approach to consultation broadens the traditional process to include the expertise of the consultee. That is, the consultee is recognized for his or her expertise on the clients and the system and shares this expertise in a partnership with the consultant. Together, they define the problem; establish goals; and create, implement, and evaluate a plan of action (Erford, 2011).

Consultation involves three parties: consultant, consultee, and a client or situation to be addressed (Dougherty, 2009). Consultation differs from collaboration in that the consultant (e.g., school counselor) shares a specific area of expertise and directs the consultation process, while responsibility for the outcome rests with the consultee (e.g., teacher, school administrator, or parent). The goal of consultation is to indirectly improve the client or situation by empowering and directly developing the knowledge, skills, and abilities of the consultee.

The triadic (i.e., consultant > consultee > client or situation) nature of the consultation process is illustrated in Figure 7.2. The thick arrows indicate the primary structure of the consulting process (Dougherty, 2009), and the thin arrows indicate interactions that may take place in some consulting situations in the schools between the consultant or the consultee and the client system at a given time for assessing needs, clarifying information, asking questions.

In addition to understanding the structure of consulting relationships, school counselors understand the importance of the consultation process. The consultation process is flexible and generally involves four unique stages that can interact and overlap with consultants often moving backward and forward through stages and phases (Dougherty, 2009).

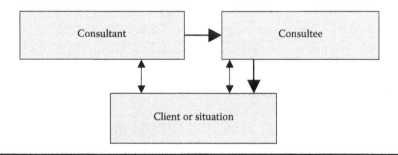

Figure 7.2   The process of consultation.

Stage one is known as the *entry stage*, which involves physically and psychologically entering the system and establishing a rapport with all involved. During the entry stage the school counselor identifies desired outcomes, explores needs, and negotiates a contract. Stage two, the *diagnosis stage*, involves four interconnected phases. During the diagnosis stage the school counselor gathers information and data, analyzes and defines the problem, establishes goals, and identifies possible interventions. Stage three is the *intervention stage*. This stage involves selecting and implementing an intervention and developing, implementing, and evaluating a plan.

Stage four, the *disengagement stage*, is the final stage of consulting. During the disengagement stage, the consultation process is evaluated, the consultant's involvement is reduced, and relationships are terminated while creating a plan for postconsultation (i.e., maintaining achieved goals).

STAGES AND PHASES

You are a school counselor engaging in the consultation process. You have identified and clarified the problem and established goals for consultation. While working on creating a plan, you decide to tweak a couple of your interventions while continuing to move forward with plan development. What stage(s) and phase(s) of consultation are you in?

Providing consultation services to enhance the knowledge and skills of important others in a student's personal and academic life allows the school counselor to make a significant difference in student outcomes. School counselors are in the ideal position to offer consulting services in the schools because of their knowledge of the school's unique culture and student needs.

Parents and teachers are often the first to recognize the needs of students as a result of daily interactions. For this reason, school counselors are often contacted to consult with parents and teachers regarding student cases and to provide parent education. Research has identified parent workshops as highly effective interventions in the schools. Parent education has been linked to heightened involvement in the schools and improved parent–child relations (Wright & Stegelin, 2002).

School administrators, too, refer students who have been brought to their attention because of truancy, suspensions, discipline, and other issues that might otherwise go undetected by the school counselor. Providing consulting services to the school administrator with regard to specific student cases establishes a caring environment that is student-centered and takes into account the circumstances of each individual student.

   School counselors are sensitive to the needs of culturally diverse consultees and client systems when applying models of consultation. Models of consultation are generally ethnocentric; therefore, school counselors adjust consultation models and services to accommodate individual worldviews and bridge cultural differences.

When to Consult and When to Collaborate?

The school counselor's decision to engage in either consultation or collaboration is often a matter of comfort level with a particular approach. Both approaches have resulted in positive outcomes in the school setting with a wide variety of client issues and situations. In addition to preference, the school counselor considers the contextual nature of the issue, desired goals, and the knowledge, skills, and abilities of those who may be involved or who may need to be involved in the helping process.

THE STALEMATE

The school counseling advisory team that you established is holding its third meeting to discuss the progress of the bully prevention program that the team began working on 2 months ago. Two months ago, subteams of individuals were established with specific tasks. You find out that the program has not made much progress because the two advisory team members who were to develop a draft of the program goals and objectives have been unable to reach agreement. One of the team members is an Asian male, who owns a local restaurant and volunteered to be a part of the advisory team to give back to the community and students who support his business. He wants to see a more collaborative program reflected in the goals and objectives. The other member is a Caucasian female who is a stay-at-home parent of one of the students in the elementary school. She said she wants a systems focus, but she believes that the extent of collaboration that the other member is suggesting is not going to be efficient. How would you approach this issue? Are there unique worldviews to consider based on cultural differences? Would collaboration or consultation be the best way to go?

Chapter 7: Case Conceptualization Responses

Collaboration and Consultation

April's IEP
The correct response is "b." You are providing indirect services to April through direct services to those who are working directly with April. As the teachers and parents implement strategies that you helped to put into place for April, you are assisting April, albeit in an indirect manner.

Collaboration

Teambuilding
The correct response is "d." All of the strategies listed have been identified as helpful in the collaboration process.

Consultation

Stages and Phases
You are currently in the implementation stage of the consultation process. Because you are working toward creating the plan while also working on the interventions, you are moving back and forth between phases I and II on the implementation stage.

When to Consult and When to Collaborate?

The Stalemate
A combination of both consultation and collaboration may be the best course of action at this time. Taking into consideration the unique and possibly opposing worldviews of these two members (Eastern and Western cultural philosophies), while listening to and validating their thoughts pertaining to the direction for the program, will promote a trusting and safe climate for sharing ideas. Having these two members begin by sharing their ideas allows the school counselor to observe their interactions and identify commonalities upon which to encourage their positive relations. Also, invite the other team members to engage in positive communications about the program's direction and empower the entire team to begin the program planning process by establishing a primary goal(s) for the program and

knocking around some measurable objectives. This would also be a good time to make use of team building strategies (e.g., mediation, problem solving, and negotiation) and engage in collaborative consultation, that is, offering your ideas based on your training and experience in school counseling programming and student development as well as your knowledge of the school and student population. It is important to revisit the data that is driving the program in order to stay focused on meeting the needs of the students and school community and maintaining the shared focus.

Chapter 7: Simulation

Collaboration

Brief Case Description

The principal of your high school asks you, the school counselor, to develop and deliver an Internet safety and cyberbullying program to the entire student body. Time is critical, and the expertise of others would be helpful in this endeavor. So, you decide to collaborate with others within and outside of the school.

Section A: Collaboration

Which of the following best describes your function in relation to other members of the team during the collaboration process?
   (Choose ONLY ONE in this section.)

_____A−1.	Expert
_____A−2.	Equal
_____A−3.	Advisor
_____A−4.	Educator
_____A−5.	Coordinator

Section B: Collaboration

A teacher hears that you are developing an Internet safety program and comes to you about a student in her class, Kenji, who she believes is a victim of cyberbullying, based on the student's behaviors. She is not sure how to approach the issue or what resources she can provide. When she brings up the subject, the student has little to say. What information should you obtain from the teacher before proceeding?
   (Select as many as you consider indicated in this section.)

_____B−1.	What behaviors indicate that the student is a victim of cyberbullying
_____B−2.	What friends say about the student's situation

_____B—3.	Frequency of behaviors
_____B—4.	Magnitude of behaviors and emotions
_____B—5.	Level of academic functioning
_____B—6.	The duration of specific behaviors
_____B—7.	Extracurricular activity involvement
_____B—8.	What the student has expressed

Section C: Collaboration

The teacher offers some insight into the situation, which depicts Kenji in considerable distress this morning in her class. You believe that giving the teacher resources may not be active enough in this situation. Kenji seems highly and negatively impacted by text messages he is receiving from an unidentified other. Which course of action would be most appropriate at this time?

(Select ONLY ONE in this section.)

_____C—1.	Refer the case to peer mediation
_____C—2.	Involve the assistant principal
_____C—3.	Take away the cell phone
_____C—4.	Recommend an immediate school counseling session with Kenji
_____C—5.	Refer the student to the police
_____C—6.	Talk to the student's friends
_____C—7.	Recommend a school counseling session with Kenji during this teacher's block tomorrow after receiving parent permission

Section D: Collaboration

The teacher insists that you contact the parents because Kenji is Asian, and the parents need to be involved. The teacher says, "It is the Asian way."

The culturally sensitive school counselor might respond in the following manner:

(Select as many as you consider indicated in this section.)

_____D—1.	"You are correct, I will call the parents"
_____D—2.	"Yes, however, I would not want to stereotype Kenji based on his culture"
_____D—3.	"You are quite culturally diverse"
_____D—4.	"I appreciate your sharing; however, the Asian culture is also very respectful of parents, so Kenji may not wish to involve them at this point"
_____D—5.	"Kenji is a typical teen; we get too caught up in cultural differences"
_____D—6.	"Does Kenji have Asian friends we can talk to?"

Section E: Collaboration

After speaking with Kenji, you learn that he is a senior and 18 years old next month. Kenji is not distressed as a result of cyberbullying, but because he and his girlfriend of three years, who is not Asian and who is also a senior, are not accepted by his parents. They have been having some issues related to their families. As a culturally sensitive counselor, how would you help Kenji?

(Select as many as you consider indicated in this section.)

_____E—1.	Advise Kenji to sit down and chat with his family
_____E—2.	Ask Kenji to let his parents know what is going on
_____E—3.	Find quality time to sit down with his girlfriend because texting is not the best way to resolve their issues
_____E—4.	Call in Kenji's girlfriend and talk with both of them at the same time
_____E—5.	Encourage Kenji to understand the importance of family to his culture and take into consideration what his parents are advising
_____E—6.	Express your concern for him and invite him to share the issues and possible solutions he has considered

Chapter 7: Simulation Answers

Collaboration

Brief Case Description

The principal of your high school asks you, the school counselor, to develop and deliver an Internet safety and cyberbullying program to the entire student body. Time is critical, and the expertise of others would be helpful in this endeavor. So, you decide to collaborate with others within and outside of the school.

Section A: Collaboration

Which of the following best describes your function in relation to other members of the team during the collaboration process?
 (Choose ONLY ONE in this section.)

A—1.	Expert
	No
	Generally, this is the function taken on by the school counselor as a consultant.
A—2.	Equal
	Yes
	During the collaboration process, the school counselors works with others within and outside of the school as an equal member of the team, sharing knowledge as well as task and outcome responsibility.
A—3.	Advisor
	No
	Although the school counselor may offer advice during the collaboration process, this is not the distinguishing function of the school counselor during collaboration.
A—4.	Educator
	No
	The school counselor is certainly an educator during the process of collaboration; however, this is not the distinguishing function of the school counselor during collaboration.

A—5.	Coordinator
	No
	The school counselor may coordinate tasks and activities during collaboration; however, this is not the distinguishing function of the school counselor during collaboration.

Section B: Collaboration

A teacher hears that you are developing an Internet safety program and comes to you about a student in her class, Kenji, who she believes is a victim of cyberbullying, based on the student's behaviors. She is not sure how to approach the issue or what resources she can provide. When she brings up the subject, the student has little to say. What information should you obtain from the teacher before proceeding?

(Select as many as you consider indicated in this section.)

B—1.	What behaviors indicate that the student is a victim of cyberbullying
	Yes
	Clarifying "behaviors" that the teacher has specifically observed as "behaviors" is important to understanding Kenji's situation.
B—2.	What friends say about the student's situation
	No
	It is inappropriate for the teacher and school counselor to begin questioning the student's friends about Kenji's situation.
B—3.	Frequency of behaviors
	Yes
	Gaining a greater understanding of how often the observed behaviors occur is critical to behavioral assessment and timely intervention.
B—4.	Magnitude of behaviors and emotions
	Yes
	Gaining a greater understanding of the level of behavioral and emotional disturbances is vital to timely behavioral and emotional assessment and intervention.

B—5.	Level of academic functioning No There is no indication for assessing academic functioning at the present time. The teacher has not indicated concern in this area. Should the issue persist, assessing its impact on academic functioning may be warranted.
B—6.	The duration of specific behaviors Yes Understanding how long behavioral and emotional disturbances have been present is useful in providing timely behavioral and emotional assessment and intervention.
B—7.	Extracurricular activity involvement No There is no indication for assessing extracurricular involvement at the present time. The teacher has not indicated concern in this area. Should the problematic behaviors persist or worsen, it may useful to assess change in this area (e.g., the student's lack of interest in extracurricular activities that the student had considered enjoyable in the past).
B—8.	What the student has expressed Yes Understanding what the student has to say about the situations is critical.

Section C: Collaboration

The teacher offers some insight into the situation, which depicts Kenji in considerable distress this morning in her class. You believe that giving the teacher resources may not be active enough in this situation. Kenji seems highly and negatively impacted by text messages he is receiving from an unidentified other. Which course of action would be most appropriate at this time?

(Select ONLY ONE in this section.)

C—1.	Refer the case to peer mediation No Peer mediation requires two identifiable others. More information is needed before considering mediation.

C—2.	Involve the assistant principal No At some point, this may become necessary, but this is not the best course of action at the present time.
C—3.	Take away the cell phone No Although texting should not be allowed during instructional time, this will not mediate Kenji's distress.
C—4.	Recommend an immediate school counseling session with Kenji Yes This is the best course of action at the present time. The teacher has observed that Kenji is in considerable distress and believes that it is linked to bullying. The school counselor needs to assess Kenji's emotionality and explore the situation. Bullying and cyberbullying has been linked to suicide and homicide. Immediate contact with the student is warranted.
C—5.	Refer the student to the police No This may become necessary. More information is needed.
C—6.	Talk to the student's friends No It is not appropriate to involve Kenji's friends at this point in this situation.
C—7.	Recommend a school counseling session with Kenji during this teacher's block tomorrow, after receiving parent permission. No The teacher has shared that Kenji presents with considerable distress today. The school counselor may be able to mediate Kenji's distress, and acting immediately could save lives.

Section D: Collaboration

The teacher insists that you contact the parents because Kenji is Asian, and the parents need to be involved. The teacher says, "It is the Asian way." The culturally sensitive school counselor might respond in the following manner:

(Select as many as you consider indicated in this section)

D—1.	"You are correct, I will call the parents" No Parent involvement is not indicated at the present time. Hearing what the student has to say first is the appropriate action at this time.
D—2.	"Yes, however, I would not want to stereotype Kenji based on his culture" Yes This statement is indicative of a culturally sensitive school counselor.
D—3.	"You are quite culturally diverse" No The school counselor would be reinforcing the teacher's stereotyping behavior.
D—4.	"I appreciate your sharing; however, the Asian culture is also very respectful of parents, so Kenji may not wish to involve them at this point" Yes This is the response of a culturally sensitive school counselor.
D—5.	"Kenji is a typical teen; we get too caught up in cultural differences" No Sensitivity to cultural, individual, and developmental differences is critical to effective counseling.
D—6.	"Does Kenji have Asian friends we can talk to?" No It is inappropriate to involve Kenji's friends in this situation at this time.

Section E: Collaboration

After speaking with Kenji, you learn that he is a senior and 18 years old next month. Kenji is not distressed as a result of cyberbullying, but because he and his girlfriend of three years, who is not Asian and who is also a senior, are not accepted by his parents. They have been having some issues related to the families. As a culturally sensitive counselor, how would you help Kenji?

(Select ONLY ONE in this section.)

E—1.	Advise Kenji to sit down and chat with his family No Kenji is a young adult capable of making this decision. Exploring the level of family involvement Kenji would like to have and/or exploring possible support systems within and outside of the family is warranted.
E—2.	Ask Kenji to let his parents know what is going on No Kenji is a young adult capable of making this decision. Exploring the level of parent involvement Kenji would like to have and/or exploring possible support systems within and outside of the family is warranted.
E—3.	Find quality time to sit down with his girlfriend because texting is not the best way to resolve their issues No The school counselor does not provide solutions to Kenji's issues but allows Kenji to explore and discover his own solutions.
E—4.	Call in Kenji's girlfriend and talk with both of them at the same time No It is not appropriate in this situation for the school counselor to pull Kenji's girlfriend out of class and away from instructional time to engage in personal counseling related to their relationship.
E—5.	Encourage Kenji to understand the importance of family to his culture and take into consideration what his parents are advising No Counselors do not espouse their own values onto the student, nor do counselors advise students with regard to the student's behavior in relation to the student's culture. Counselors work within the worldview of the student.
E—6.	Express your concern for him and invite him to share the issues and possible solutions he has considered Yes Empathizing and validating Kenji's concerns are warranted. Also, encouraging Kenji to explore the situation and solutions within his own worldview is appropriate.

Chapter 7: Guided Reflection

Compare collaboration and consultation. Then define both in a way that demonstrates the differences, include the nature of relationships.

Describe the difference between direct and indirect service delivery.

Identify at least five teambuilding strategies deemed important in consultation and collaboration.

Describe the process of collaboration, and create two examples that illustrate when it would be appropriate to collaborate as a school counselor.

Explain the stages of consultation, identifying key activities at each stage. Create two examples that illustrate when it would be appropriate to engage in consultation as a school counselor.

Chapter 8

Leadership

The multifaceted nature of the concept of leadership has caused some difficulty in establishing one definition that can be agreed upon by all. But, what is agreed upon is that effective leaders are role models who are able to establish positive environments, lead by example, and inspire. John Quincy Adams said it nicely:

> If your actions inspire others to dream more, learn more, do more, and become more, you are a leader.

The language of leadership varies with one fundamental commonality: a vision—the focus on *what is* and *what could be*. Leaders understand the interdependent flow of organizational systems and subsystems. Producing change on a systems level is not a solo act but requires all members of the cast and crew to unify toward a common vision.

Effective leaders possess basic skill sets such as decision making, problem solving, conflict management, communication, time management, team-building, planning, and assessing. Leadership is also widely recognized as a source of power that to be used effectively, reverently, and judiciously requires a healthy number of attributes such as

- Self-awareness
- Personal and social consciousness
- A sense of social responsibility and social justice
- Cultural sensitivity
- Moral and ethical fortitude
- Discernment

- Positive attitude
- Dependability
- Integrity
- Dedication
- Professionalism

Leadership and Learning

ASCA and CACREP have recognized leadership as essential to the effectiveness of school counseling programs, systemic change, and student learning. Research and literature exploring the effective leadership qualities of a school counselor defines leadership in terms of a collaborative practice grounded in skills, relationships, and processes.

The collaborative concept of leadership is akin to the transformational leadership that positions the leader in an egalitarian role with power shared by other stakeholders. This view of leadership also supports student learning and aligns with the new vision for school counseling and supports a systems-focused comprehensive school counseling program (Mason & McMahon, 2009). Although currently in the throes of leadership identity crises, we are making progress toward clearly establishing a profile for school counselor leadership (Mason & McMahon, 2009). It will not be long now—but, I make no guarantees.

Triumphant school counseling programs, student success, and systemic change have been linked to specific leadership skills and characteristics (Dollarhide, Gibson & Saginak, 2008; Shillingford & Lambie, 2010). These include

- A clear vision (there's that *vision* word again—must be important)
- A realistic, goal-focused plan of action
- Clearly defined school counselor roles
- Ability to build a support system
- Ability to work through and grow from resistance
- A sense of responsibility for program effectiveness
- Ability to encourage, motivate, and empower others
- Actively seeking out supervision
- Willingness to continue to develop leadership skills
- Tackling tasks with determination

STAFF DEVELOPMENT

A high school counselor is planning to implement a teacher workshop during staff development day on the topic of bullying. The principal has announced that the workshop is mandatory, due to the high incidence of bullying in the school. The teachers are complaining that they should not be required to attend a workshop when they are not experiencing any problems with bullying in their classrooms and when it is not related to teaching and learning, but the "job of the school counselor." The school counselor asks the principal if she can speak during the next faculty meeting to let the teachers know a bit more about the bullying workshop that will be presented during staff development. The school counselor shares with the teachers the hidden aspects of victims of bullying, and how it is often the "silent killer" that only teachers can detect given the substantial amount of time they spend with the students in their classes and in light of the special relationship teachers have with their students. The school counselor goes on to say that the workshop will offer some ways to identify and intervene on behalf of these students and involve the school counselor so that teachers can get back to the important task of teaching. Which leadership strategy is the school counselor using with the teachers?

a. Role modeling
b. Overcoming resistance
c. Empowering
d. All of the above

Program Management

What?

A comprehensive school counseling program is built on a strong foundation that clearly defines *what* students will learn as a result of the program (ASCA, 2005, p. 27). School counselors accomplish this by attaching program activities to standards, such as the ASCA National Standards (Campbell & Dahir, 1997) and the state's school counseling and core academic standards. School counselors create a mission statement and beliefs statements that depict a standards-based program that supports the three domains of student development: (1) academic, (2) career, and (3) persona-social (ASCA, 2005).

The philosophical statement is a set of belief statements that serve as guiding principles for the school counseling program in support of student success. Belief statements include what school counselors believe about stakeholders, primarily teachers, administrators, parents, students, families, and the process of teaching and learning. The school counseling program mission statement supports the school's mission statement and links directly to the school counseling beliefs statements. Literary buffs may be tempted to create the next unabridged, complete, deluxe edition of John Dewey's works. I do not mean to blow the mood because hey, I get it. The printed word is my ambrosia. Similar to the stirring that consumes my soul when I walk into a basilica, a euphoric virus invades my mind at the mere scent of books when I walk into a library. Lord knows, I hope Kindle and Nook do not kill the printed text like "video killed the radio star." My true birthplace must have been the self-help or home-and-garden stacks in a *biblioteca pubblica* in south-central Europe.

Okay, if I am not careful, we could be on that subject for the remainder of this chapter. The point is that the school counseling program mission statement briefly (in a few sentences) describes the purpose and vision of the school counseling program with regard to all stakeholders, specifically students. The ASCA National Model offers guidance in writing superb mission and beliefs statements.

BELIEF OR MISSION STATEMENT?

Is the following an example of a belief or mission statement?
"All students have the capacity to learn and be supported academically."

When, Why, Who, and On What Authority

Managing a comprehensive school counseling program requires answering the question "When, why, who, and on what authority" is the school counseling program put into action (ASCA, 2005, p. 45)? There are several components necessary to addressing this important question: management agreements, advisory councils, time, calendars, data, and action plans.

The advisory council and management agreement establish the authority upon which the school counseling program is implemented. The ASCA National Model (ASCA, 2005) provides guidelines for creating viable school counseling advisory councils and management agreements. ASCA recommends establishing an advisory council in which stakeholder membership is representative of the community's diversity. Membership will likely include the principal, general and special education teachers, parents, school psychologist, school nurse, and community members, including representatives from local businesses and organizations.

The primary purpose of the advisory council is to allow all stakeholders to whom the school counseling program belongs to have a rightful voice. Council members assist in (1) creating and implementing needs assessments, (2) providing program recommendations, and (3) assisting in program evaluation and data analysis. Advisory council members also help to identify sources of funding and promote the mission of the school counseling program.

School counselor and school administrator management agreements help school administrators to better understand the goals and activities of the school counseling program. The agreement also provides the school administrator with information that clearly demonstrates how the school counseling program aligns with the academic achievement mission of the school.

At times it may feel as though unearthing support from an administrator is like locating a rental car in Bermuda. Management agreements are mediums by which school counselors can forge important alliances and gain the support of principals to ensure the success of the school counseling program. Recent research reveals the most powerful influences for securing principal support involve demonstrating (1) evidence of systemic impact, (2) leadership abilities, and (3) positive relationships with faculty, staff, students, and the community (Dollarhide, Smith, & Lemberger, 2007). Therefore, school counselor–administrator agreements should reflect these critical influences in order to gain principal support—you may still have to explore Bermuda by horse, taxi, bicycle, or carriage.

If school counselors do not plan their time, others will and historically they have, resulting in inappropriate duties for the school counselor. ASCA provides school counselors with guidance regarding that which constitutes appropriate and inappropriate duties for the school counselor under the ASCA National Model (ASCA, 2005). ASCA also offers recommendations for determining appropriate *time* allocations in each of the four methods of program delivery (see Table 8.1). In order to safeguard and balance the time needed to implement a school counseling program, school counselors create

Table 8.1 Sample Distribution of Total School Counselor Time

Delivery System Component	Elementary School % of Time	Middle School % of Time	High School % of Time
Guidance curriculum	35%–45%	25%–35%	15%–25%
Individual student planning	5%–10%	15%–25%	25%–35%
Responsive services	30%–40%	30%–40%	25%–35%
Systems support	10%–15%	10%–15%	15%–20%

Source: Adapted from American School Counselor Association. (2005). *The ASCA national model: A framework for school counseling programs* (2nd ed.). Alexandria, VA: Author.

weekly, monthly, and yearly calendars. Creating and posting school counseling program calendars also informs stakeholders of scheduled activities.

Action plans also help to establish the *when* of a school counseling program (ASCA, 2005, p. 45). Action plans document planned and purposeful school counseling program activities outlined in the school counseling calendars. Action plans are discussed and illustrated in Chapter 6.

An essential part of program management is data management. School counseling programs are data-driven, that is, school counselors make use of data to identify *why* a particular program, approach, or activity was selected for implementation (ASCA, 2005, p. 45). In addition to identifying stakeholder needs, data is critical to monitoring student performance, closing the achievement gap, and demonstrating program outcomes and accountability. The vital role of data in the school counseling program is discussed in Chapter 5.

DR. NEEDATEEM

Dr. Needateem, a high school counselor, is putting together an advisory council. The following are appropriate potential advisory council members:

a. A cosmetologist in the vocational education center
b. A special education teacher
c. A parent of one of the ninth-grade students
d. All are appropriate

How?

A comprehensive school counseling program describes *how* the program will be implemented (ASCA, 2005, p. 39). School counselors implement the school counseling program using four broad delivery methods: (1) classroom guidance and group work, (2) individual student planning and counseling, (3) responsive services, and (4) systems support (ASCA, 2005). These methods of delivery are discussed in Chapter 2.

Addressing the how of a school counseling program also involves answering the program-sustaining question "How are students different as a result of the school counseling program?" (ASCA, 2005, p. 59). School counselors achieve this by using program evaluation and documenting outcomes using results reports, which are discussed in Chapter 5.

DEMONSTRATING RESULTS

You are a school counselor at Weecanduit High School. Your principal lets you know at the start of the school year that he wants you to be prepared to make a presentation during the spring open house demonstrating how the school counseling program has made a difference in the lives of the students at Weecanduit High School. How will you be able to demonstrate a results-driven program to stakeholders at the open house?

a. Share action plans
b. Highlight program evaluation outcomes
c. Review the management agreement
d. Emphasize the work of the advisory council

School Counselor Use of Technology

The technological literacy of school counselors is becoming increasingly important in order to: (1) meet the demands of the information age, (2) enhance the learning environment, and (3) effectively manage and promote the school counseling program. Recognizing that counselors need to be leaders in use technology, ACES (2007) has identified 12 technology competencies that should be covered during master's level counselor education programs (see Table 8.2).

Table 8.2 ACES Technology Competencies

1. Be able to use productivity software to develop Web pages, word processing documents (letters, reports), basic databases, spreadsheets, and other forms of documentation or materials applicable to practice.
2. Be able to use such audiovisual equipment as video recorders, audio recorders, projection equipment, video conferencing equipment, playback units, and other applications available through education and training experiences.
3. Be able to acquire, use, and develop multimedia software (i.e., PowerPoint/ keynote presentations, animated graphics, digital audio, digital video) applicable to education, training, and practice.
4. Be able to use statistical software to organize and analyze data.
5. Be able to use computerized and/or Internet-based testing, diagnostic, and career decision-making programs with clients.
6. Be able to use e-mail.
7. Be able to help clients search for and evaluate various types of counseling-related information via the Internet, including information about careers, employment opportunities, educational and training opportunities, financial assistance/scholarships, treatment procedures, and social and personal information.
8. Be able to subscribe, participate in, and sign off on counseling-related listservs or other Internet-based professional communication applications.
9. Be able to access and use counseling-related research databases.
10. Be able to use the Internet to locate, evaluate, and use continuing education, professional development, and supervision options in counseling.
11. Be able to perform basic computer operation and maintenance tasks.
12. Be knowledgeable about legal, ethical, and efficacy issues associated with delivery of counseling services via the Internet.

Source: Adapted from Association for Counselor Education and Supervision. (2007). *ACES technology competencies for counselor education students.* Retrieved November 10, 2010 from, http://files.acesonline.net/doc/2007_aces_ technology_competencies.pdf

The use of technology may well be the mechanism that determines the level of success of school counseling programs and student learning outcomes. School counselors use technology to:

■ Deliver education and special education accommodations.
■ Communicate with the masses.

- Share and disseminate information.
- Coordinate activities.
- Consult and collaborate.
- Advocate for students, families, and the profession.
- Broaden service delivery.
- Expedite tasks.
- Simplify data analysis and reporting.
- Fortify accountability efforts.
- Provide supervision and mentoring.
- Engage in video conferencing.
- Conduct research.
- Participate in professional development.

School Counseling Websites

School counselors are encouraged to make use of technology to develop a presence on the Web. Creating a departmental website or a personal website is a cost-effective and efficient way to provide information about the school counseling program to parents, students, and the community as recommended by ASCA. When advertising your website remember your ethical mandate to identify ways that students and parents without Internet access can get this valuable information. Ideally, school counseling department websites communicate

- Information about the comprehensive school counseling program
- Information related to the counseling process, including referral, signed consent, and confidentiality
- Professional school counselor roles and functions
- Links to ASCA's ethical standards and professional competencies
- The professional school counselors' education, training, and credentials
- Information regarding professional associations
- Current trends and developments in the profession (the ASCA National Model, TSCI)
- Mission statements and program goals that clearly connect school counseling to the academic achievement mission of schools
- Program outcome data, including efforts to close the achievement gap
- Parent, student, teacher, and community resources
- Opportunities for school involvement

Information and resources listed on school counseling websites can enhance student development and well-being and help to support healthy schools, homes, and communities. Many adults and students who experience distress are reluctant to ask for help and do not actively seek out support (Auger, 2004). Others simply cannot find the time to make an appointment to meet with the school counselor. It is the professional responsibility of school counselors to be creative in getting meaningful information to stakeholders for sound decision making, problem solving, and family support. Web-based information and resources might include information on

- Crisis response information
- Support programs
- Parenting programs
- Tutoring contacts and test preparation
- Substance use/abuse
- Eating disorders
- Counseling services
- Problem solving, communication, and conflict resolution
- Self-mutilation
- Suicide and homicide ideation
- Financial aid and scholarships
- Summer programs and study abroad
- Special events
- Warning signs of troubled youth

Student Use of Technology

The school counselor's technological literacy and knowledge of human development intersect to provide students with developmentally appropriate technological interventions and training. Students must not leave high school without proficiency in the use of technology, which drives every aspect of our computerized world of work. Section A.10 of the ASCA *Ethical Standards for School Counselors* (ASCA, 2010) calls for school counselors to "promote the benefits of and clarify the limitations of various appropriate technological applications (1) that are appropriate for students' individual needs, (2) that students understand how to use and (3) for which follow-up counseling assistance is provided … school counselors advocate for equal access to technology for all students, especially those historically underserved" (p. 3).

JEREMIAH'S CONCERN

Jeremiah is a high school counselor who is quite versed in Web applications and website development. He created an outstanding website for the school counseling program. The website has all the information deemed important for school counseling websites. His director was pleased since they no longer have to spend time, energy, and any of the budget to maintain the binders that housed summer and special programs, scholarships, study abroad, after school jobs, and more. The director was pleased that now students and parents only need to look at the website. Jeremiah had an ethical concern about his school counseling director's response. What do you think it is?

Some of the more common information and networking technologies may include e-mail, Internet, blogs, electronic bulletin boards, text messaging, video conferencing, chat rooms, gaming devices, graphics software, websites, and SMART technologies. School counselors introduce these and other more sophisticated technologies and related terminology to enhance students' readiness for entry into today's workforce. ASCA provides an e-newsletter, *ASCA Aspects*, to association members in order to stay abreast of current technologies and tools on the Internet. School counselors incorporate information and networking technologies into all methods of service delivery.

Similar to industry certification assessments noted in Chapter 2 by NRF and NOCTI, students can earn industry certifications in specific software packages while attending high school to demonstrate advanced levels of competence in technology. Industry certification assessments such as Brainbench and Microsoft Office Specialist are attached to numerous elective courses in business and technical education. Passing the course and assessment leads to certification in a variety of Adobe and Microsoft software packages. School counselors take the lead in ensuring that students gain information and opportunities to participate in industry certifications of interest.

School counselors provide students, parents, and teachers with information pertaining to the safe use of technology. This is particularly critical in light of the increased prevalence of cyberbullying, seduction by Internet predators, and the misuse of cell phones. Chapter 2 discusses the school counselor's responsibility for providing students with education related to the potential threats posed when using technology.

ASCA's Position on Student Safety and Technology

Professional school counselors encourage students to take advantage of the wealth of opportunities, information, and resources available through the use of technology. However, due to the potential vulnerabilities and risks created by technology, professional school counselors collaborate with students, parents, educators, and law enforcement officials to promote student safety related to the use of the technology.

Position statement adopted 2000; revised 2006

Systemic Change

As systems change agents, school counselors identify groups of students (versus a select few) who are not being successful and intervene to remove obstacles or add supports to ensure success and access to a rigorous curriculum (Perusse & Goodnough, 2004). Toward this end, school counselors engage in leadership, advocacy, collaboration, consultation, coordination, and referral. Serving as an agent for systemic change also necessitates an understanding of strategic planning and the principles of systems theory discussed in Chapter 2.

Schools are both systems and subsystems in a web of interconnectedness that makes virtually everyone a stakeholder and client. Systemic school counseling programs are those that encompass programming that is purposeful in its intentions to provide prevention and intervention to the entire student body and other stakeholders within and outside of the school. The ASCA National Model exemplifies such a systems-focused model. Only through systems-focused practices can the school counselor fully eliminate access, achievement, and attainment gaps.

School, Family, and Community Partnerships

School administrators across the nation have made tremendous progress in promoting community and school relations, particularly through the AASA Stand Up for Public Education call to action. The AASA call to action describes public education as the "heart of our democracy" (Gee, 2005, p. 44). School counselors, too, are called upon to engage in action that removes the barriers that impede cooperative and productive partnerships with a child's most valuable educational resource—the parent.

It is strange to me that parents often remain an untapped resource in schools where human resources are generally limited. School counselors are encouraged to establish or tap into school-based parent–teacher–student resource centers (PTSRCs). PTSRCs provide information and resources that promote student development and family well-being. Who better than parent volunteers to oversee daily PTSRC operations. Parents, familiar with the community, are in an ideal position to coordinate requests for information and maintain the informational flow. Many parents want to get in the game but for a variety of reasons do not step up to the plate. Extend an invitation to parents and be specific about the position for which they are being recruited—with the bases loaded and the batter up, there is sure to be a home run!

In addition to parents, the level of success of the school counseling program is dependent upon the involvement and support of community businesses and agencies. These are your educational soul mates—individuals and agencies impacting or impacted by the schools. Many school systems have institutionalized the soul mate philosophy, adopting Partners-in-Education programs. These programs are often facilitated by the school counselor who links the school to specific local organizations and businesses. The organization unites with the school to support school improvement and student learning by providing invaluable human, financial, and consumable resources. Organizations (e.g., retail stores, banks, hospitals, fire stations, and restaurants) proudly display certificates of appreciation from the schools they support, which helps their business to prosper as parents and members of the community offer patronage in appreciation.

Chapter 8: Case Conceptualization Responses

Leadership

Staff Development

The correct response is "b." The teachers are displaying resistance to the idea of mandatory training on a topic that they perceive as unrelated to teaching. The school counselor in a nonconfrontational manner helps teachers to understand how the topic of bullying is connected to the role of teacher and the importance of that role.

Program Management

What?

Belief or Mission Statement?

"All students have the capacity to learn and be supported academically" is an example of a belief statement. This brief statement clearly articulates a belief about students, versus a more comprehensive purpose and vision for the school counseling program.

When, Why, Who, and On What Authority?

Dr. Needateem

The correct response is "d." ASCA recommends that the advisory council be representative of the community's diversity, which means that all stakeholders are potential advisory council members.

How?

Demonstrating Results

The correct response is "b." Program evaluation provides school counselors with program outcomes that demonstrate *how* the school counseling program is making a positive difference in the lives of students. Action plans and management agreements may depict what the school counselor is planning to implement and how the program or activity is to be evaluated, but these documents do not provide outcome data. Discussing the good work of the council is not the same as providing outcome data assessing program effectiveness.

Student Use of Technology

Jeremiah's Concern

Section A.10, Ethical Standard b, of the ASCA *Ethical Standards for School Counselors* (2010) calls for school counselors to "advocate for equal access to technology for all students, especially those historically underserved" (p. 3). Jeremiah is rightfully concerned that many of the students in his school will not get access to this important information because some do not have home computers and some with home computers do not have Internet access.

Chapter 8: Simulation

Comprehensive School Counseling Program

Brief Case Description

You are a middle school counselor who just came from a national conference where you learned more about establishing an accountable, developmental, comprehensive school counseling program that is data driven, data producing, needs based, and systems focused. You believe the school counseling program in your school is developmental and comprehensive since you fashioned it after the ASCA National Model.

Section A: Comprehensive School Counseling Program

Although the school counseling program at your school is comprehensive, you are considering how you can make the school counseling program more accountable. What strategies might you want to adopt in order to demonstrate outcomes to stakeholders?

(Select as many as you consider indicated in this section.)

_____ A–1.	Student feedback
_____ A–2.	Pre–post program data from a multiple-choice assessment created from program content
_____ A–3.	Mission statement
_____ A–4.	Administrator–school counselor agreement
_____ A–5.	Results reports using quantitative data
_____ A–6.	Teacher feedback
_____ A–7.	Action plans

Section B: Comprehensive School Counseling Program

You understand that action plans are a vital component for accountability. What types of information need to be included in the action plan in order to demonstrate credible program planning?

(Select as many as you consider indicated in this section.)

_____ B—1.	Activity topic
_____ B—2.	Academic standards
_____ B—3.	Data sources for needs identification
_____ B—4.	Number of students receiving intervention
_____ B—5.	Data sources for program evaluation
_____ B—6.	School counseling standards
_____ B—7.	Dates for implementation
_____ B—8.	Principle signature
_____ B—9.	Student names receiving intervention

Section C: Comprehensive School Counseling Program

You want to ensure that your results report clearly demonstrates the outcomes of your program. For this reason, the primary component to include in your results report is:
(Select ONLY ONE in this section.)

_____ C—1.	Data analysis of your quantitative pre–post program measure
_____ C—2.	School administrator data collected during observation of program implementation
_____ C—3.	Data from school counselor self-report of program effectiveness
_____ C—4.	Data form student evaluations of the program
_____ C—5.	Teacher and student program evaluation data

Section D: Comprehensive School Counseling Program

You present your school principal with the administrative agreement for support of school counseling program activities. He notices that you have quite a bit of time set aside for individual student counseling and planning.

He would like you to conduct direct services that are more systems-focused. You revise the plan to include more:
(Select as many as you consider indicated in this section.)

_____ D—1.	Classroom guidance
_____ D—2.	Parent–teacher–student conferences
_____ D—3.	Small groups
_____ D—4.	Parent–teacher workshops
_____ D—5.	Professional development for faculty and staff

Section E: Comprehensive School Counseling Program

During your meeting with the principal about the school administrator and school counselor agreement, your principal expresses that he would like to enhance community awareness of the good work that you are doing and let parents know what the school counseling program is all about. He expresses that budget is a concern, so the cost-effectiveness of promotional efforts must be a consideration. What suggestions do you make?
(Select as many as you consider indicated in this section.)

_____ E—1.	Give each student a flyer to take home
_____ E—2.	Create a website
_____ E—3.	Mail a flyer to each home
_____ E—4.	Speak at PTSAs
_____ E—5.	Send a mass telephone message
_____ E—6.	Invite parents to an evening school counseling information session

Chapter 8: Simulation Answers

Comprehensive School Counseling Program

Brief Case Description

You are a middle school counselor who just came from a national conference where you learned more about establishing an accountable, developmental, comprehensive school counseling program that is data driven, data producing, needs based, and systems focused. You believe the school counseling program in your school is developmental and comprehensive since you fashioned it after the ASCA National Model.

Section A: Comprehensive School Counseling Program

Although the school counseling program at your school is comprehensive, you are considering how you can make the school counseling program more accountable. What strategies might you want to adopt in order to demonstrate outcomes to stakeholders?

(Select as many as you consider indicated in this section.)

A—1.	Student feedback
	No
	Student feedback is valuable in identifying the strengths and weaknesses of the school counseling program, but it does not demonstrate outcomes.
A—2.	Pre–post program data from a multiple choice assessment created from program content
	Yes
	Objective pre–post program measures provide data that demonstrates outcomes.
A—3.	Mission statement
	No
	Mission statements do not demonstrate program outcomes.
A—4.	Administrator–school counselor agreement
	No
	Agreements do not demonstrate program outcomes.

A—5.	Results reports using quantitative data
	Yes
	Results reports that include quantitative data demonstrate outcomes.
A—6.	Teacher feedback
	No
	Teacher feedback is valuable in identifying the strengths and weaknesses of the school counseling program, but it does not demonstrate outcomes.
A—7.	Action plans
	No
	Action plans may indicate how program outcomes will be measured, but they do not demonstrate program outcomes.

Section B: Comprehensive School Counseling Program

You understand that action plans are a vital component for accountability. What types of information need to be included in the action plan in order to demonstrate credible program planning?

(Select as many as you consider indicated in this section.)

B—1.	Activity topic
	Yes
	Stakeholders need to know the topic being covered.
B—2.	Academic standards
	Yes
	Accountable practices include standards-based practices.
B—3.	Data sources for needs identification
	Yes
	Establishing data-driven programming that meets stakeholder needs is essential to accountability.
B—4.	Number of students receiving intervention
	Yes
	It is necessary to identify the number of students receiving the intervention in order to better understand the scope of program outcomes.

B—5.	Data sources for program evaluation
	Yes
	Stakeholders need to understand what was used to measure program effectiveness.
B—6.	School counseling standards
	Yes
	Establishing a standards-based program is essential to accountability.
B—7.	Dates for implementation
	Yes
	Timelines for program implementation aid in establishing accountability.
B—8.	Principal signature
	No
	Principals do not have time to sign every action plan created by the school counselor. Principals have already reviewed management agreements and rely on the school counselor to develop and implement accountable programs. School counselors also provide principals with a copy of the action plan and results report upon program completion.
B—9.	Student names receiving intervention
	No
	The names of students and teachers are not listed in action plans or results reports. Data is collected on the number of classes, students, groups, participants, not names. This is especially important since pre–post program evaluation of school counseling programs ensures participant confidentiality.

Section C: Comprehensive School Counseling Program

You want to ensure that your results report clearly demonstrates the outcomes of your program. For this reason, the primary component to include in your results report is:

(Select ONLY ONE in this section.)

C—1.	Data analysis of your quantitative pre–post program measure
	Yes
	Objective pre–post program data establishes program outcomes.

C—2.	School administrator data collected during observation of program implementation No Observation data is subjective and does not establish program outcomes.
C—3.	Data from school counselor self-report of program effectiveness No Self-report data is subjective and does not establish program outcomes.
C—4.	Data from student evaluations of the program No Student evaluation data is subjective and does not establish program outcomes.
C—5.	Teacher and student program evaluation data No Teacher and student evaluation data is subjective and does not establish program outcomes.

Section D: Comprehensive School Counseling Program

You present your school principal with the administrative agreement for support of school counseling program activities. He notices that you have quite a bit of time set aside for individual student counseling and planning. He would like you to conduct direct services that are more systems-focused. You revise the plan to include more:

(Select as many as you consider indicated in this section.)

D—1.	Classroom guidance Yes Classroom guidance is a direct, systems-focused method of program delivery.
D—2.	Parent–teacher–student conferences No Parent–teacher conferences aid in helping individual students both directly and indirectly.
D—3.	Small groups Yes Small group counseling is a direct, systems-focused method of program delivery.

D—4.	Parent–teacher workshops
	No
	Parent–teacher workshops are systems-focused, but an indirect method for helping students.
D—5.	Professional development for faculty and staff
	No
	Professional development is a systems-focused strategy, but an indirect method for helping students.

Section E: Comprehensive School Counseling Program

During your meeting with the principal about the school administrator and school counselor agreement, your principal expresses that he would like to enhance community awareness of the good work that you are doing and let parents know what the school counseling program is all about. He expresses that budget is a concern, so the cost-effectiveness of promotional efforts must be a consideration. What suggestions do you make?

(Select as many as you consider indicated in this section.)

E—1.	Give each student a flyer to take home
	No
	This is not cost-effective.
E—2.	Create a website
	Yes
	Websites are cost-effective way to advocate for your school counseling program. Websites provide a method for immediate access by stakeholders to school counseling resources, contacts, services, and program outcomes.
E—3.	Mail a flyer to each home
	No
	This is not cost-effective.
E—4.	Speak at PTSAs
	Yes
	Repeated presentations at the PTSA meetings is cost-effective and will promote and advocate for the school counseling program.

E—5.	Send a mass telephone message Yes System and school-wide telephone messages are cost-effective methods for relaying information to stakeholders.
E—6.	Invite parents to an evening school counseling information session Yes Parents appreciate after-school events, and it is a cost-effective way to get information out about the school counseling program and services.

Chapter 8: Guided Reflection

Define leadership and describe its significance in school counseling.

Connect leadership in school counseling and learning.

Examine program management and discuss its importance in helping to establish the school counselor as a leader. Explain what each of the following components of program management entails:
What?

When, why, who, and on what authority?

How?

Summarize how school counselors make use of technology to enhance professional practices and student learning. Create an example of an activity to illustrate (1) a school counselor making use of technology to enhance professional practices, and (2) a school counselor making use of technology to improve student learning.

Identify the importance of professional school counseling websites and identify the recommended information for website inclusion.

Discuss the school counselor's responsibility with regard to the students' use of technology.

Full-Length Practice Exam

Scenario 1: College Readiness

Brief Case Description

You are a high school counselor reviewing student surveys that were collected from 10th- and 11th-grade students, which indicate that 85% of the students in these grades plan to attend a 4-year college. However, an analysis of 10th- and 11th-grade academic performance records reveals that only 35% currently have the academic standing needed to get into college.

Section A: College Readiness

What information would help you to identify that which may be contributing to this gap?

(Select as many as you consider indicated in this section.)

_____A—1.	Access to enrichment activities
_____A—2.	Promotion and retention rates
_____A—3.	Hobbies
_____A—4.	Course enrollment patterns
_____A—5.	Time spent on the computer
_____A—6.	Standardized test scores
_____A—7.	Attendance rates
_____A—8.	College application completion
_____A—9.	Career assessment participation
_____A—10.	FAFSA completion
_____A—11.	Course completion rates
_____A—12.	Parent participation rates

Section B: College Readiness

What types of programming or strategies might you consider to help students to understand the connection between grades and getting into college and to close the gap between college goals and college readiness?

(Select as many as you consider indicated in this section.)

_____B—1.	Classroom guidance lessons on career planning
_____B—2.	Student participation in a small group on study skills
_____B—3.	College visitations/field trips
_____B—4.	Individual academic advising
_____B—5.	SAT and ACT preparation program
_____B—6.	Peer tutoring program
_____B—7.	Development of a career and academic plan
_____B—8.	Encourage participation in SCA
_____B—9.	Parent involvement programs

Section C: College Readiness

During your analysis of the school data, you find that there are high numbers of 10th-grade students failing the same required English class taught by the same teacher for the past 3 years. You pointed this out to your school counseling director, who said she has talked to the teacher several times about this, but the teacher just gets angry. What would be the best course of action at this time?

(Select ONLY ONE in this section.)

_____C—1.	Ask for a meeting with the teacher and principal
_____C—2.	Try to talk with the teacher again
_____C—3.	Bring this data to the attention of the principal
_____C—4.	Ask for a meeting with the teacher and school counseling director
_____C—5.	Do not fight this battle
_____C—6.	Encourage students to take a different English teacher during scheduling

Section D: College Readiness

Further data analysis reveals an alarming number of absences among the 10th- and 11th-grade student population. After talking to these grade level teachers, you find that many students are performing poorly or failing classes due to excessive absences that result in missing homework and failing course tests, although they are passing the standardized tests. The majority of absences do not qualify for extenuating circumstances. What might you want to consider as possible courses of action to address this issue?

(Select as many as you consider indicated in this section.)

_____D—1.	Phone calls to parents from the attendance office after a specified number of days
_____D—2.	Phone calls to parents from the teacher after a specified number of days
_____D—3.	Send letters home after a specified number of days
_____D—4.	Grade level assemblies to stress the importance of attendance to academic success and college entrance
_____D—5.	Administer a needs assessment to the 10th- and 11th-grade students asking them to identify perceived obstacles to school attendance and to provide suggestions to improve attendance
_____D—6.	Develop harsher penalties for unexcused absences
_____D—7.	Strengthen attendance policy with fewer absences allowed each year

Section E: College Readiness

Further analysis revealed a pattern. Hundreds of students identified needs at home as the reason for missing so much school. Most of those reasons included after school jobs to help parent(s) pay bills and staying home to take care of younger siblings while the parent worked. You also find out that these students do not have materials at home to complete homework and study (e.g., calculators, paper, pencils, study space). These students do not have a home computer, printer, or Internet access in order to conduct required research and type papers. It is difficult, if not impossible, for these students to go to the library due to demands at home. Transportation is also an issue if they miss the bus. What can you, the school counselor, do to help these students?

(Select as many as you consider indicated in this section.)

_____E—1.	Reduce homework for these students
_____E—2.	Sponsor school-wide drives for school supplies
_____E—3.	Work with community agencies to identify resources to help parents with child care and financial burdens
_____E—4.	Coordinate partnerships with local businesses to provide supplies
_____E—5.	Provide after school homework assistance for these students
_____E—6.	Work with the principal to develop an academic enrichment class as a resource/elective class
_____E—7.	Give a list of student names needing school supplies to local media to "adopt a student"
_____E—8.	Do not require homework for these special needs students
_____E—9.	Apply for a grant to assist students in your school in "achieving the college dream"

Scenario 2: School Violence

Brief Case Description

A teacher comes to you, the eighth-grade middle school counselor, because she has three male students in her science class who are entirely disengaged, quiet, and only hang out with each other. She saw them at lunch today sitting only with each other and not eating lunch. No other students were anywhere near them. The students dress in black most every day and routinely appear tired and unkempt. A student observed the teacher gazing at the three male students during lunch and said, "I hope someone is finally going to look more closely at those guys—they are so scary and make gestures when anyone gets near them while teachers are not looking."

Section A: School Violence

What information might you want to gather about the students at this point in time?

   (Select as many as you consider indicated in this section.)

_____A—1.	Current and past grades
_____A—2.	Attendance patterns
_____A—3.	Parents' knowledge of student behavior as reported by teachers
_____A—4.	After-school activities
_____A—5.	Information from other students
_____A—6.	Observations of these students by their other teachers
_____A—7.	Educational history from student records
_____A—8.	Time spent on the computer at home and school
_____A—9.	More information from the student who talked to the teacher about the three male students in the lunch room
_____A—10.	Disciplinary infractions
_____A—11.	Relationship with siblings and parents

Section B: School Violence

The information you gathered demonstrates a pattern of increasingly negative behavior by all three of the students despite school and parent intervention. One of the three students was expelled during middle school for threatening to kill a teacher. Based on the information you have gathered, you decide on the following course of action:

(Choose ONLY ONE in this section.)

_____B—1.	Request an intervention by the principal
_____B—2.	Request an intervention by the schools' resource officer
_____B—3.	Meet with the students together
_____B—4.	Meet with the students individually
_____B—5.	Contact the students' parents for an urgent meeting

Section C: School Violence

The art teacher comes to you the next morning with a picture one of the three male students drew during art class. The picture appears to be one of the school cafeteria with all the doors closed. There are people lying face down on the floor and others that appear to be dead with blood on the floors and walls. There are three individuals on three sides of the cafeteria with guns pointed toward other individuals. The art teacher said the student tried to hide the picture and did not want to show it to her, but she demanded to see it. The art teacher had the student walk with her to the school counseling office during which time he continued to reassure her that it was "just a picture and nothing more." Your concern is heightened because you know that this was the student who had threatened to kill his teacher during middle school. What is the best course of action at this time?

(Select ONLY ONE in this section.)

_____C—1.	Involve the resource officer
_____C—2.	Involve the principal
_____C—3.	Talk to the student about the meaning of the picture
_____C—4.	Pull the other two students from class to discuss the picture
_____C—5.	Contact the student's parents
_____C—6.	Contact local police
_____C—7.	Contact Child Protective Services

Section D: School Violence

The following day, you called the home of the student, who had been suspended, to offer the parent counseling resources for her son. In conversation, the parent noted that she could give those to her son, who had just left with his two friends to come to the school to get some books he needed to complete some assignments while on the 3-day suspension. You confirmed the names of his friends and let the parent know that suspended students were not allowed on school property during the suspension period, so you would be letting the principal know. Although the parent appeared unalarmed, you checked attendance on the other two students to find that they had been reported absent by the teachers. What action should you take at this point?

(Select ONLY ONE in this section.)

_____D—1.	No action required
_____D—2.	Call the parents of the other two students to report their absences
_____D—3.	Go directly to the truancy officer
_____D—4.	Notify the resources officer
_____D—5.	Go directly to the school principal to report this information
_____D—6.	Call the local police

Section E: School Violence

The resource officer sees two students letting the suspended student in the hall door that is locked. He recognizes the three students and sees suspiciously bulky zipped jacked. He quickly notifies the principal via the two-way radio, who immediately calls a lockdown. The resource officer yelled to the students while the lockdown was being called, but the students darted down the halls in separate directions. After some gunfire throughout the halls of the schools, the police swarm the school, apprehend the three students, and secure the school. As the school counselor, what intervention would you consider after such an incident has occurred?

(Select ONLY ONE in this section.)

_____E—1.	Begin meeting with small groups of students until you have met with all students school wide
_____E—2.	No action required at this time by the school counselor
_____E—3.	Just have teachers report any behavioral changes in students
_____E—4.	Visit all classes in the building to invite students to see the school counselor to talk about what they experienced
_____E—5.	Encourage students to resume their normal activities so as not to draw attention to the incident

Scenario 3: Esther

Brief Case Description

You are an elementary school counselor. A parent refers her third-grade daughter to you. She said she does not have the money to pay for counseling right now and understands that you meet with students for a limited number of individual sessions. This year, Esther, her daughter, began picking her arms so badly that they bleed. She took her daughter to the family physician, and he said it did not appear to be allergies or a rash but seems to be more emotionally driven. When she asks Esther what is wrong, she says, "I don't know." The parent adds that her grades have continued to be good, and the problem does not seem to be related to friendship issues because Esther has positive relations with peers at home and at school.

Section A: Esther

What information might be useful from the parent at this time?
    (Select as many as you consider indicated in this section.)

_____A—1.	Frequency of behavior
_____A—2.	Student's diet
_____A—3.	Duration of behavior
_____A—4.	Medical history
_____A—5.	Onset of behavior
_____A—6.	Family events
_____A—7.	School events
_____A—8.	Student–family relations
_____A—9.	Mother's relationship with father
_____A—10.	Student's hobbies
_____A—11.	Living arrangements
_____A—12.	Time spent on the computer

Section B: Esther

You meet with Esther and notice that she is a small third grader and very shy. You ask a few open-ended questions related to friends and family, but

Esther just gives a quick response that offers you no substantial insight. What approach might be the best to use with Esther at this time?

(Choose ONLY ONE in this section.)

_____B—1.	Strengths-based counseling
_____B—2.	Cognitive behavioral counseling
_____B—3.	Play therapy
_____B—4.	Gestalt
_____B—5.	REBT

Section C: Esther

During the second session, Esther enters the room and walks over to the toys, and selects a female doll and a plastic shark off your toy shelf. Esther sits on the mat on the floor and proceeds to have the shark eat the head off the female doll. What might be the most appropriate communication by you in order to gather needed information about this behavior?

(Select as many as you consider indicated in this section.)

_____C—1.	Esther, you seem to be angry at that doll.
_____C—2.	Esther, do you like sharks?
_____C—3.	Esther, who is that doll?
_____C—4.	Esther, what is that shark doing?
_____C—5.	Esther, that is a mean shark, why did you choose to play with it?
_____C—6.	Esther, why are you angry?
_____C—7.	Esther, who is that shark?

Section D: Esther

During the third session, Esther expresses her anger toward her mother stating, "Mom doesn't love me, all she cares about is my getting good grades." Which counseling approach might be the most useful at this time to help Esther confront this irrational thought?

(Choose ONLY ONE in this section.)

_____D—1.	Reality
_____D—2.	Solution-focused
_____D—3.	Strength-based
_____D—4.	Behavioral
_____D—5.	REBT
_____D—6.	Person-centered

Section E: Esther

As Esther enters your office for her fourth session, you notice that her arms are really picked and she is picking at her arms as she walks into your office. You ask her if she realizes that she is picking her arms. She says, "Yes." You ask her what she has been thinking about today. She says, "My test." You realize that this morning third-grade students took an important standardized test. You asked, "What are you thinking about the test?" She responds, "I am so scared that I did not make an A, so mom is going to take away my birthday party this summer." You ask, "Have you talked about this with your mother?" Esther says, "No, I'm afraid she will get mad and yell at me." What might be the best course of action at this time?

(Choose ONLY ONE in this section.)

_____E—1.	Friendship group
_____E—2.	Self-esteem building
_____E—3.	Encourage and role play communication with mother
_____E—4.	Strategies for reducing test-taking anxiety
_____E—5.	Study-skills group
_____E—6.	Encourage and role-play communication with teacher

Scenario 4: Early Intervention

Brief Case Description

You are a middle school counselor. Your principal comes to you concerned about the disproportionately high number of students identified as special education and students with a 504 plan as compared to other schools in the district of similar size and population. He asks for suggestions that could reduce the number of students identified as special needs in your school while still providing students with the assistance that is needed to be successful. The principal also expresses his concern with the lack of referrals to the school-wide early intervention team, which you chair.

Section A: Early Intervention

You provide the principal with the following suggestion:
    (Choose ONLY ONE in this section.)

_____A—1.	Require that teachers refer students to the early intervention team prior to referral to the 504 or child study teams, unless a parent objects
_____A—2.	Pay teachers for the time they spend in early intervention team meetings
_____A—3.	Require a minimum number of early intervention team meetings each academic year
_____A—4.	Require teachers and parent to refer students to the early intervention team prior to referral to a 504 or the child study committee
_____A—5.	Require particular grade levels to go through the early intervention team prior to going through child study or the 504 team

Section B: Early Intervention

Joshua, a sixth-grade student, was referred to the early intervention team for academic difficulties. His teacher expressed that he is well liked by other students and he is cooperative and that she has not noticed any other concerns apart from academic performance. What type of information or data would be important to acquire from the teacher and parents during the initial team meeting to assess Joshua's issues?

    (Select as many as you consider indicated in this section.)

_____B—1.	Hobbies and interests
_____B—2.	Past and present social functioning
_____B—3.	Sleeping habits
_____B—4.	Medical information
_____B—5.	Behavioral records
_____B—6.	Family income
_____B—7.	Past and present academic performance
_____B—8.	Subjects with which the student is struggling
_____B—9.	Past and present emotional functioning
_____B—10.	Student's eating habits
_____B—11.	Environmental factors

Section C: Early Intervention

During the team meeting, an individualized intervention plan is established to target Joshua's areas of academic difficulty. After the early intervention team meeting, as the team's chair you would do the following:

(Select ONLY ONE in this section.)

_____C—1.	Distribute a copy of the intervention plan to all the members of the team, the students' teachers, the parents, and to the student's record
_____C—2.	Provide only the intervention team members and parents with a copy of the intervention plan
_____C—3.	Meet with principal regarding the meeting outcome
_____C—4.	Ensure that the intervention plan does not become a part of the student's educational record

Section D: Early Intervention

Two weeks later, the team reconvenes at the request of the teacher who reports that although Joshua's academics have improved slightly, Joshua is displaying behavioral issues such as agitation and bullying of other students, which is out of character for Joshua, according to his teacher. During the meeting, the parent shares that she and her husband are going through a divorce, which began just about the time that Joshua's academic performance declined. Based on this new information, Joshua's intervention plan was modified to include participation in a small group on divorce. The following permissions must be obtained:

(Select ONLY ONE in this section.)

_____D−1.	Informed consent from the parents of all group members
_____D−2.	Because small groups are a primary method of school counseling program delivery, parental consent is assumed
_____D−3.	Informed consent of parents of all group members and participants
_____D−4.	Informed consent only from Joshua's parent because the activity is connected to an intervention plan
_____D−5.	No informed consent is required

Section E: Early Intervention

During your first group session, one of the most important issues you want to discuss with these adolescents relates to

(Select ONLY ONE in this section.)

_____E−1.	Goals
_____E−2.	Topic
_____E−3.	Member rights
_____E−4.	Confidentiality
_____E−5.	Informed consent
_____E−6.	Termination
_____E−7.	Process
_____E−8.	Emergency contact information

Section F: Early Intervention

During the third group session, one of the group members becomes very angry and says, "I never even got to tell the jerk what I thought of him before he left us." Which counseling techniques might be useful at this time to mediate the student's emotional distress and work through the issue presented?

(Select as many as you consider indicated in this section.)

_____F—1.	Clarifying
_____F—2.	Empty chair
_____F—3.	Paraphrasing
_____F—4.	Relaxation techniques
_____F—5.	Guided imagery
_____F—6.	Stress inoculation
_____F—7.	Behavior contract

Scenario 5: Academic Achievement

Brief Case Description

You are a school counselor at a large, pluralistic elementary school. Twenty percent of the student body is special education and ESL students. Nearly half of the student body receives free or reduced lunch. Your school did not make AYP last year, so everyone is academic-focused and implementing programs that will result in the immediate improvement of standardized test scores.

Section A: Academic Achievement

What information do you need in order to begin planning strategies to improve academic achievement?

(Select as many as you consider indicated in this section.)

_____A—1.	Parent support
_____A—2.	Student interests
_____A—3.	Past successes
_____A—4.	School and community resources
_____A—5.	Target populations
_____A—6.	Students' favorite subjects
_____A—7.	Subject areas of weakness
_____A—8.	Subject areas of strength

Section B: Academic Achievement

Which data sources would provide useful information for creating classroom guidance lessons to target specific grade levels and subjects?

(Select as many as you consider indicated in this section.)

_____B—1.	Standardized test score reports
_____B—2.	School report card
_____B—3.	School-wide attendance patterns
_____B—4.	Individual disciplinary records
_____B—5.	Family structure
_____B—6.	Each student's academic record

Section C: Academic Achievement

Data analysis reveals grade 3 math and grade 5 English as areas of specific weakness, particularly among the special education and ESL populations and African American males. Which intervention would be most useful for providing responsive services for these struggling students?

(Select ONLY ONE in this section.)

_____C—1.	Small group on study skills
_____C—2.	Classroom guidance lesson on study skills that crosswalks school counseling standards and core academic standards
_____C—3.	Small group on study skills that crosswalks school counseling standards and math and English standards
_____C—4.	Small group on test taking that crosswalks school counseling standards and core academic standards
_____C—5.	Classroom guidance lesson on test taking skills that crosswalks school counseling standards and core academic standards
_____C—6.	Small group on test taking

Section D: Academic Achievement

While chatting with your school's test coordinator, you discover that many special education students have not been given special accommodations during standardized testing. When you voiced your concern to the test coordinator, she said that as long as examiners and proctors are in short supply and because teachers are not always giving these students the accommodations during the school year, then she is not going to worry about it at testing time. What is the best course of action to take at this time?

(Select ONLY ONE in this section.)

_____D—1.	Let the test coordinator know that you will be making the principal aware of these unlawful instructional and standardized testing practices
_____D—2.	Let the test coordinator know that you will be making the principal aware of these questionable instructional and standardized testing practices
_____D—3.	Let the test coordinator know that if this continues you will need to notify the principal

(Continued)

_____D—4.	Call a meeting of the teachers, test coordinator, and principal about these practices
_____D—5.	Voice your concerns to the test coordinator and trust her to correct the standardized testing practices
_____D—8.	Notify the school division's testing administrator about these questionable standardized testing practices

Section E: Academic Achievement

The actions of the teachers and test coordinator concerned you, so you reviewed some of the special education students' IEPs to find that several students were given special accommodations only on standardized tests, not on classroom tests. When you spoke to one of the teachers of these students, he said that this was an IEP team decision that included the principal and that the decision was based on the lack of manpower during the school day. What is the best course of action to take at this time?

(Select as many as you consider indicated in this section.)

_____E—1.	Talk to the principal about ways that these students can get the accommodations during the school day, not just on standardized testing days
_____E—2.	Contact the school division's test administrator
_____E—3.	Discuss with the principal your concern about setting the students up for failure on standardized testing day if they have not been pulled out of the class the entire year for testing
_____E—4.	Contact the State Department of Education
_____E—5.	Let the principal know that if he does not do something about this then you are going to contact the Department of Education
_____E—6.	Contact your school division's supervisor of instructional practices so that he or she can talk to the principal about these practices
_____E—7.	Request to be a part of the IEP meetings, so that you can have a voice in the creation of students' IEPs

Scenario 6: Assessment

Brief Case Description

You are a high school counselor. Terrance is a junior at the high school whose parent has requested that you pull his record and go over the grades and assessments with her so that she might better understand his academic status and level of functioning. She wants to know if her son, Terrance, has the grades and intelligence to get into a 4-year college and to be successful in college. She said Terrance has identified seven colleges that offer majors in communication, which is his area of interest.

Section A: Assessment

The first assessment you came to was the WAIS-II. You explained that Terrance has a verbal IQ score of 95 and a performance IQ score of 85, giving Terrance a full scale IQ of 90. Terrance's mother responds, "I don't know what that means." What information would you share with the student's mother?

(Select as many as you consider indicated in this section.)

_____A−1.	Most individuals have an IQ score between 85 and 115	
_____A−2.	Because the assessment uses a 95% confidence level, Terrance's score could, at any given time, fall within 5 points in either direction	
_____A−3.	Terrance's IQ score indicates genius	
_____A−4.	Terrance has an average IQ	
_____A−5.	Terrance has a very low IQ	
_____A−6.	Terrance's IQ indicates mild retardation	

Section B: Assessment

Terrance's mother also said that Terrance told her that he got a 34 on his ACT test. She began to cry stating that her son would "never get into college with such low scores on his college entrance exams." You look at Terrance's score report from ACT and see that, indeed, Terrance's score on the ACT was 34. What information would you share with this parent?

(Select as many as you consider indicated in this section.)

_____B—1.	The average score of the ACT is 21
_____B—2.	The average score on the ACT is 71
_____B—3.	Because the high score is 75, Terrance did not do well
_____B—4.	ACT scores range from 1 to 36
_____B—5.	ACT scores range from 25 to 75
_____B—6.	Because the high score is 36, Terrance did very well

Section C: Assessment

As you go through Terrance's record you notice that there are no SAT scores. His mother said that he is not taking the SAT because he took the ACT. What advice would you give to the parent at this point?

(Select ONLY ONE in this section.)

_____C—1.	The ACT is all he needs
_____C—2.	The SAT should be taken and is the most widely used college entrance exam in the country
_____C—3.	The ACT measures the same thing as the SAT
_____C—4.	The SAT is not used very often for college entrance; however, it is a good measure of achievement
_____C—5.	The SAT is the only assessment that should be taken for college entrance

Section D: Assessment

Terrance's mother says that she is still a bit concerned about Terrance's choice of major. She worries that it will not be a good match. She adds that she knows Terrance is interested in communication, but she is not sure about his skills and abilities or that the work environment would fit his personality. The school counselor suggests that the career counselor administer the following career interest inventory:

(Select ONLY ONE in this section.)

_____D—1.	ASVAB
_____D—2.	Kaufman
_____D—3.	SDS

____D—4.	Super's model of career development
____D—5.	WAIS
____D—6.	Vineland

Section E: Assessment

Terrance's mother thanks you for your time and asks, "What do we need to do next because it is the spring of Terrance's junior year?" The following information would be useful for the parent at this time:

(Select as many as you consider indicated in this section.)

____E—1.	FAFSA deadlines
____E—2.	SAT information and deadlines
____E—3.	ACT information and deadlines
____E—4.	PSAT information and deadlines
____E—5.	College fair dates
____E—6.	GED Official Practice Test information and deadlines
____E—7.	Scholarship websites
____E—8.	Financial aid website

Scenario 7: Julianna

Brief Case Description

Julianna is a fifth-grade African American student diagnosed with ADHD, and you are the elementary school counselor at her school. The teacher and parent report that Julianna consistently presents as hyperactive, restless, argumentative, and impulsive. Julianna's mother reports that the medication Julianna is taking does not appear to be working because Julianna continues to experience academic, social, and behavioral issues. Julianna's mother is a single parent and admits that she does not have much time to spend with Julianna and her other two children to help with their studies because she works two jobs. A 504 committee meeting was just held, and Julianna qualified for a 504 plan due to the academic and social impact related to Julianna's ADHD.

Section A: Julianna

During the 504 meeting, you identified the following strategies and approaches to help Julianna and her family:

(Select as many as you consider indicated in this section.)

_____A—1.	Homeschooling
_____A—2.	Social skills development
_____A—3.	Reduced television time
_____A—4.	Parenting skills training
_____A—5.	Family counseling
_____A—6.	Reduced computer time
_____A—7.	Change in diet
_____A—8.	Increased time spent with friends
_____A—9.	Counseling
_____A—10.	Reduced length of academic work
_____A—11.	Increased length of academic work
_____A—12.	Providing choices (academic and home tasks)

Section B: Julianna

Julianna's mother asks about what other things she can do at home to improve Julianna's behavior and increase cooperation. In addition to organization and maintaining a consistent schedule, you name the following:

(Select as many as you consider indicated in this section.)

_____B—1.	Positive reinforcement
_____B—2.	Loss of privileges
_____B—3.	Allow more computer time
_____B—4.	Negotiated rewards
_____B—5.	Contracts
_____B—6.	Resist setting goals
_____B—7.	Mild consequences
_____B—8.	Give specific behavioral feedback

Section C: Julianna

What counseling theory might be most useful when working with Julianna?

(Select ONLY ONE in this section)

_____C—1.	Gestalt counseling
_____C—2.	Behavioral counseling
_____C—3.	Reality counseling
_____C—4.	Person-centered counseling
_____C—5.	Adlerian counseling
_____C—6.	Cognitive behavioral counseling

Section D: Julianna

Several months into the 504 plan, the teacher and parent report that Julianna's behavioral and peer relations problems have increased, and her academic performance has declined. Julianna is now having full-blown temper tantrums at home, at school, and in the community. She is disobedient and blames others for her actions. The school counselor strongly encourages the following actions to help Julianna and her family:

(Select as many as you consider indicated in this section.)

_____D−1.	Referral to child study for possible testing and special education services
_____D−2.	Homeschooling
_____D−3.	Participation in Governor's School
_____D−4.	Medical examination by the child's physician
_____D−5.	Less time with peers
_____D−6.	Appointment with a child psychiatrist
_____D−7.	More time with peers
_____D−8.	Family counseling
_____D−9.	Resources related to helping children with disruptive behavior issues/disorders

Section E: Julianna

Julianna's mother returns to you a few weeks later and says that the psychiatrist has diagnosed Juliann with oppositional defiance disorder and recommended ongoing individual counseling for Julianna and the family. She asks if you would be Julianna's counselor over the next couple of years. Your response is:

(Select ONLY ONE in this section.)

_____E−1.	Of course.
_____E−2.	I would like to, as I have enjoyed working with Julianna very much; however, I just do not have time as the only school counselor in the building.
_____E−3.	Julianna's needs are beyond the scope of school counseling, but I have a list of counseling resources, which may be helpful in identifying a counselor.
_____E−4.	I would not be able to do this during the school day, as it is beyond the scope of school counseling. However, I can provide counseling services to Julianna outside of school hours at your home or mine for a minimal charge.
_____E−5.	Oppositional defiance disorder is not really my area of expertise, but I will work with Julianna because she and I already have a positive relationship.

Practice Exam Answers

Scenario 1 Answers: College Readiness

Brief Case Description

You are a high school counselor reviewing student surveys that were collected from 10th- and 11th-grade students, which indicate that 85% of the students in these grades plan to attend a 4-year college. However, an analysis of 10th- and 11th-grade academic performance records reveals that only 35% currently have the academic standing needed to get into college.

Section A: College Readiness

What information would help you to identify that which may be contributing to this gap?

(Select as many as you consider indicated in this section.)

A—1.	Access to enrichment activities
	Yes
	Struggling students need access to enrichment activities to improve performance.
A—2.	Promotion and retention rates
	Yes
	This information will help school counselors to identify which populations of students are being successful in meeting their college goals and which are not.
A—3.	Hobbies
	No
	Hobbies will not provide useful information for identifying reasons for the gap.

(Continued)

A—4.	Course enrollment patterns Yes This information is helpful in providing insight into low GPAs.
A—5.	Time spent on the computer No This information would not be helpful in identifying that which is contributing to the gap in this scenario.
A—6.	Standardized test scores Yes Scores on these assessments will help to identify areas of struggle for targeted intervention.
A—7.	Attendance rates Yes Poor attendance can be a factor in low GPAs.
A—8.	College application completion No This information will not be helpful in identifying what may be contributing to the gap, which is related to academic performance prior to college application.
A—9.	Career assessment participation Yes Students who connect learning to real life and career aspirations are more likely to achieve at higher levels and experience higher levels of academic motivation.
A—10.	FAFSA completion No This information will not be helpful in identifying what may be contributing to the gap, which is related to academic performance prior to FAFSA and college application completion.
A—11.	Course completion rates Yes If students are not be successful in the courses in which they enroll, this needs to be identified and mediated. This data may also reveal specific classes in which masses of students are not being successful, indicating a problem with the course structure, content, and/or instructor.

A—12.	Parent participation rates
	Yes
	Students whose parents are involved in their education generally experience higher levels of academic achievement.

Section B: College Readiness

What types of programming might you consider to help students to understand the connection between grades and getting into college and to close the gap between college goals and college readiness?

(Select as many as you consider indicated in this section.)

B—1.	Classroom guidance lessons on career planning
	Yes
	Connecting academic performance to college entrance and career goal attainment has been linked to heightened academic achievement.
B—2.	Student participation in a small group on study skills
	Yes
	Study skills have been linked to improved academic achievement.
B—3.	College visitations/field trips
	Yes
	Campus tours help to motivate students toward college attendance and provide students with the opportunity to further understand the importance of high school grades and college admission.
B—4.	Individual academic advising
	Yes
	Individual academic advising is a primary delivery method used by school counselors.
B—5.	SAT and ACT preparation program
	No
	This strategy will not be a helpful strategy for closing the gap that exists between students' school performance and college entrance (e.g., high school GPA and required GPA for college entrance).
B—6.	Peer tutoring program
	Yes
	Peer tutoring may be helpful for some of the population of 10th- and 11th-grade students that are struggling due to a specially challenging subject matter.

(Continued)

B—7.	Development of a career and academic plan
	Yes
	Students benefit from a plan of action that lays out exactly what courses and types of training are needed to meet postsecondary goals.
B—8.	Encourage participation in SCA
	No
	Participation in SCA would not necessarily be helpful in mediating the academic gap indicated in this scenario.
B—9.	Parent involvement programs
	Yes
	Parent involvement has been linked to higher levels of academic achievement.

Section C: College Readiness

During your analysis of the school data, you find that there are high numbers of 10th-grade students failing the same required English class taught by the same teacher for the past 3 years. You pointed this out to your school counseling director, who said she has talked to the teacher several times about this, but the teacher just gets angry. What would be the best course of action at this time?

(Select ONLY ONE in this section.)

C—1.	Ask for a meeting with the teacher and the principal
	No
	This may result in the teacher feeling "cornered."
C—2.	Try to talk with the teacher again
	No
	Because your director already tried on multiple occasions, all indications are that the teacher will not heed your concern either. Meanwhile, more students continue to experience closed college doors.
C—3.	Bring this data to the attention of the principal
	Yes
	The principal will be able to address this with the teacher individually, allowing the teacher a private forum in which to communicate. These actions are indicative of student advocacy—a critical role for school counselors.

C−4.	Ask for a meeting with the teacher and the school counseling director
	No
	The teacher has already dismissed the concerns of your director. A meeting with you and the director may result in the teacher feeling "ganged-up" on.
C−5.	Do not fight this battle
	No
	This is a battle worth fighting. Addressing issues of equity in access, attainment, and achievement for students is a critical aspect of the role of the school counselor in systems support, leadership, and advocacy.
C−6.	Encourage students to take a different English teacher during scheduling
	No
	This will not resolve the issue as some students will still have to take the required course with this teacher once other English classes reach capacity.

Section D: College Readiness

Further data analysis reveals an alarming number of absences among the 10th- and 11th-grade student population. After talking to these grade level teachers, you find that many students are performing poorly or failing classes due to excessive absences that result in missing homework and failing course tests, although they are passing the standardized tests. The majority of absences do not qualify for extenuating circumstances. What might you want to consider as possible courses of action to address this issue?

(Select as many as you consider indicated in this section.)

D−1.	Phone calls to parents from the attendance office after a specified number of days
	Yes
	Tracking student attendance and keeping parents informed is critical to helping to keep students in school.
D−2.	Phone calls to parents from the teacher after a specified number of days
	Yes
	Tracking student attendance and keeping parents informed is critical to helping to keep students in school. This also gives the teacher a chance to share the impact of attendance issues on the students' performance with the parent.

(Continued)

D—3.	Send letters home after a specified number of days
	No
	This is not cost-effective, and there is no way to be sure that parents will receive the letters.
D—4.	Grade level assemblies to stress the importance of attendance to academic success and college entrance
	Yes
	Assemblies offer a systems-focused approach to informing the masses.
D—5.	Administer a needs assessment to the 10th- and 11th-grade students asking them to identify perceived obstacles to school attendance and to provide suggestions to improve attendance
	Yes
	If you want to know why masses of students are not attending school—ask them!
D—6.	Develop harsher penalties for unexcused absences
	No
	The penalty is already harsh—students are not performing academically and not meeting their postsecondary goal to get into college.
D—7.	Strengthen attendance policy by reducing the number of absences allowed each year
	No
	Because students cannot meet the attendance expectations as they are now, this action will likely result in increased numbers of students out of compliance with the attendance policy.

Section E: College Readiness

Further analysis revealed a pattern. Hundreds of students identified needs at home as the reason for missing so much school. Most of those reasons included after school jobs to help parent(s) pay bills and staying home to take care of younger siblings while the parent worked. You also find out that these students do not have materials at home to complete homework and study (e.g., calculators, paper, pencils, study space). These students do not have a home computer, printer, or Internet access in order to conduct required research and type papers. It is difficult, if not impossible, for these students to go to the library due to demands at home. Transportation is also an issue if they miss the bus. What can you, the school counselor, do to help these students?

(Select as many as you consider indicated in this section.)

E—1.	Reduce homework for these students No Rigorous standards still need to be maintained, and without a special need (e.g., ESL, 504, IEP), students do not receive special accommodations.
E—2.	Sponsor school-wide drives for school supplies Yes Collaborating with student groups to donate school supplies is helpful.
E—3.	Work with community agencies to identify resources to help parents with child care and financial burdens Yes Parents appreciate this support and may not have the time or resources to identify the assistance needed.
E—4.	Coordinate partnerships with local businesses to provide supplies Yes Generally, businesses are responsive to the needs of the schools in their communities and understand the interdependent nature of the system.
E—5.	Provide after-school homework assistance for these students No These students have identified transportation and after school jobs and caring for younger siblings as barriers. This might work for some, if transportation was also provided, and you find significant interest. Further information would be needed before implementing this strategy.
E—6.	Work with the principal to develop an academic enrichment class as a resource/elective course or to develop a component to an existing course Yes This course could prove to be more valuable than some elective courses in helping students to prepare for postsecondary opportunities, particularly for this school's student population.
E—7.	Do not require homework for these students No Rigorous standards still need to be maintained, and without a special need (e.g., ESL, 504, IEP), students do not receive special accommodations.
E—8.	Apply for a grant to assist students in your school in "achieving the college dream" Yes There are many education grants available for the asking; you have the data to support your need, and your grant could include many items (e.g., transportation, supplies, equipment, child care).

Scenario 2 Answers: School Violence

Brief Case Description

A teacher comes to you, the eighth-grade middle school counselor, because she has three male students in her science class who are entirely disengaged, quiet, and only hang out with each other. She saw them at lunch today sitting only with each other and not eating lunch. No other students were anywhere near them. The students dress in black most every day and routinely appear tired and unkempt. A student observed the teacher gazing at the three male students during lunch and said, "I hope someone is finally going to look more closely at those guys—they are so scary and make gestures when anyone gets near them while teachers are not looking."

Section A: School Violence

What information might you want to gather about the students at this point in time?

(Select as many as you consider indicated in this section.)

A—1.	Current and past grades
	Yes
	It is important to look for educational impact to understand how students' behavior may be affecting other areas of life or vice versa.
A—2.	Attendance patterns
	Yes
	It is important to look for impact on daily functioning to understand how students' behavior may be affecting other areas of life or vice versa.
A—3.	Parents' knowledge of student behavior as reported by teachers
	Yes
	Understanding how involved parents are in the students' lives and their level of support provides the school counselor with insight, resources, and direction.
A—4.	After-school activities
	No
	Although this may become important at a later time, this information at this time would not be useful.

A—5.	Information from other students No Perhaps in a time of crisis it may become necessary to elicit information about the three students from peers, but it is not warranted or appropriate at this time.
A—6.	Observation of these students by their other teachers Yes It is important for the school counselor to explore how these students interact with other teachers and in diverse classroom settings in order to establish patterns of behaviors and to understand the frequency and magnitude of behaviors.
A—7.	Educational history from student records Yes It is important for the school counselor to explore the students' history of academic performance and behavior in order to establish patterns of behaviors and to understand the frequency, magnitude, and onset of behaviors.
A—8.	Time spent on the computer at home and school No Although time spent on the computer would not be useful at this time, what the students are doing on the home computer (school computers are generally monitored) may be useful (e.g., violent video games, disturbing communications in chat rooms and blogs, disturbing Facebook pages).
A—9.	More information from the student who talked to the teacher about the three male students in the lunchroom No Perhaps in a time of crisis it may become necessary to elicit information about the three students from peers, but it is not warranted or appropriate at this time.
A—10.	Disciplinary infractions Yes A history of disciplinary actions aids the school counselor in identifying patterns, frequency, and magnitude of behaviors in order to adequately assess level, immediacy, and type of intervention needed.
A—11.	Relationship with siblings and parents No This information may be important at a later time, but it is not useful at this particular time.

Section B: School Violence

The information you gathered demonstrates a pattern of increasingly negative behavior by all three of the students despite school and parent intervention. One of the three students was expelled during middle school for threatening to kill a teacher. Based on the information you have gathered you decide on the following course of action:

(Choose ONLY ONE in this section.)

B—1.	Request an intervention by the principal
	No
	The principal understands that some students may have a history of disciplinary infractions by the time they get to high school. The principal looks to the school counselor to mediate behavioral issues with counseling interventions.
B—2.	Request an intervention by the school's resource officer
	No
	The resource officer is a valuable resource; however, there is no action for the officer to take at this time.
B—3.	Meet with the students together
	No
	Together, the students will not likely openly communicate.
B—4.	Meet with the students individually
	Yes
	This is the most appropriate course of action to take at this time. Individually, the students may openly communicate, and you can explore each student's unique situation/issues.
B—5.	Contact the students' parents for an urgent meeting
	No
	At the present time there is no indication of urgency, and the academic history records parental awareness of each disciplinary incident to date.

Section C: School Violence

The art teacher comes to you the next morning with a picture one of the three male students drew during art class. The picture appears to be one of the school cafeteria with all the doors closed. There are people lying face down on the floor and others that appear to be dead with blood on the floors and walls. There are three individuals on three sides of the cafeteria with guns pointed toward other individuals. The art teacher said the student tried to hide the picture and did not want to show it to her, but she demanded to see it. The art teacher had the student walk with her to the school counseling office during which time he continued to reassure her that it was "just a picture and nothing more." Your concern is heightened because you know that this was the student who had threatened to kill his teacher during middle school. What is the best course of action at this time?

(Select ONLY ONE in this section.)

C−1.	Involve the resource officer
	No
	The artwork should be viewed as an illustration of threat to others, particularly when coupled with the student's past disciplinary infractions and present behavioral concerns reported by the teacher. For this reason, the threat must be brought to the attention of the building head.
C−2.	Involve the principal
	Yes
	This student's actions in context with other behavioral issues call for immediate action and must be taken seriously despite his contention that it is "just a picture and nothing more."
C−3.	Talk to the student about the meaning of the picture
	No
	This is a matter of school-wide safety that will likely result in disciplinary actions, which should be handled by the principal/assistant principals.
C−4.	Pull the other two students from class to discuss the picture
	No
	The school counselor cannot assume to know who the other two individuals in the picture are and should not pull additional students out of class to discuss the actions of the other in this case. The principal's investigation may call for this, but it would not be an appropriate responsibility of the school counselor.
C−5.	Contact the student's parents
	No
	The principal will make this determination after talking with the student.

(Continued)

C−6.	Contact local police
	No
	The principal will make this determination after talking with the student.
C−7.	Contact Child Protective Services
	No
	The principal will make this determination after talking with the student. Child Protective Services is generally involved in cases of abuse, neglect, and suicide threat or ideation that implicate the parent or guardian.

Section D: School Violence

The following day, you called the home of the student, who had been suspended, to offer the parent counseling resources for her son. In conversation, the parent noted that she could give those to her son, who had just left with his two friends to come to the school to get some books he needed to complete some assignments while on the 3-day suspension. You confirmed the names of his friends and let the parent know that suspended students were not allowed on school property during the suspension period, so you would be letting the principal know. Although the parent appeared unalarmed, you checked attendance on the other two students to find that they had been reported absent by the teachers. What action should you take at this point?

(Select ONLY ONE in this section.)

D−1.	No action required
	No
	Action on your part is absolutely required because this information indicates a violation of suspension and could indicate a school-wide threat.
D−2.	Call the parents of the other two students to report their absences
	No
	Although this would be appropriate, it is not the most appropriate action at this time.
D−3.	Go directly to the truancy officer
	No
	This would not be the most appropriate action at this time, and generally truancy officers get involved after a specific number of unexcused absences.

D—4.	Notify the resource officer
	No
	This would not be the most appropriate action at this time because the principal/assistant principals determine actions related to suspension and school threat.
D—5.	Go directly to the school principal to report this information
	Yes
	This is the most appropriate action to take at this time. The principal should determine the next course of action.
D—6.	Call the local police
	No
	The principal will make this determination.

Section E: School Violence

The resource officer sees two students letting the suspended student in the hall door that is locked. He recognizes the three students and sees suspiciously bulky zipped jacked. He quickly notifies the principal via the two-way radio, who immediately calls a lockdown. The resource officer yelled to the students while the lockdown was being called, but the students darted down the halls in separate directions. After some gunfire throughout the halls of the schools, the police swarm the school, apprehend the three students, and secure the school. As the school counselor, what intervention would you consider after such an incident has occurred?

(Select ONLY ONE in this section.)

E—1.	Begin meeting with small groups of students until you have met with all students school wide
	No
	There are many students who will not need intervention and would rather not participate in counseling.
E—2.	No action required at this time by the school counselor
	No
	The school counselor needs to be proactive in reaching out to students who may need counseling to process what they experienced.

(Continued)

E—3.	Just have teachers report any behavioral changes in students No Although it is important for teachers to report such changes in behavior to the school counselor as a possible indicator for counseling, this action is not enough because some students may not overtly display stress reactions.
E—4.	Visit all classes in the building to invite students to see the school counselor to talk about what they experienced Yes This would be the most appropriate action at this time. This would allow the school counselor to identify students in need of counseling services based on overt emotional reactions while also encouraging and offering counseling for other experiencing distress.
E—5.	Encourage students to resume their normal activities so as not to draw attention to the incident No Ignoring the emotional reaction will not make it go away and promotes dysfunction. Although resuming daily functioning and activities is the ultimate goal and may be just fine for some students immediately following a stress-inducing incident, it is important to offer the assistance needed and allow students decide when they are ready to resume daily routines.

Scenario 3 Answers: Esther

Brief Case Description

You are an elementary school counselor. A parent refers her third-grade daughter to you. She said she does not have the money to pay for counseling right now and understands that you meet with students for a limited number of individual sessions. This year, Esther, her daughter, began picking her arms so badly that they bleed. She took her daughter to the family physician, and he said it did not appear to be allergies or a rash but seems to be more emotionally driven. When she asks Esther what is wrong, she says, "I don't know." The parent adds that her grades have continued to be good, and the problem does not seem to be related to friendship issues because Esther has positive relations with peers at home and at school.

Section A: Esther

What information might be useful from the parent at this time?
    (Select as many as you consider indicated in this section.)

A—1.	Frequency of behavior
	Yes
	Frequency of behavior is important to assessing the severity of the issue.
A—2.	Student's diet
	No
	This is not indicated at this time because the student has already seen a physician.
A—3.	Duration of behavior
	Yes
	Duration of behavior is important to assessing the severity of the issue.
A—4.	Medical history
	No
	The student has already visited the physician. The school counselor might suggest that the parent consider a second opinion by a medical doctor.

(Continued)

A—5.	Onset of behavior
	Yes
	Onset of the behavior may help to identify precipitating events or triggers that may be causing or contributing to the behavior.
A—6.	Family events
	Yes
	Family events may help to identify life changes or triggers that may be causing or contributing to the behavior.
A—7.	School events
	Yes
	School events may help to identify life changes or triggers that may be causing or contributing to the behavior.
A—8.	Student–family relations
	Yes
	Changes in relationships can have a significant impact on functioning and behavioral patterns.
A—9.	Mother's relationship with father
	Yes
	Changes in marital relationships impact family dynamics, functioning, and behavior.
A—10.	Student's hobbies
	No
	Exploring the student's hobbies is not indicated at the present time. The student's physician would have explored exposure to skin irritants.
A—11.	Living arrangements
	Yes
	It is important to gain an understanding of the student's environment in order to better understand the student.
A—12.	Time spent on the computer
	No
	Time spent on the computer would not offer insight into Esther's behavior at this time.

Section B: Esther

You meet with Esther and notice that she is a small third grader and very shy. You ask a few open-ended questions related to friends and family, but Esther just gives a quick response that offers you no substantial insight. What approach might be the best to use with Esther at this time?

(Choose ONLY ONE in this section.)

B—1.	Strengths-based counseling
	No
	Promoting Esther's strengths is certainly useful; however, it is difficult to identify and access those strengths without counselor–client communication.
B—2.	Cognitive behavioral counseling
	No
	The CBT focus on thought processes could be useful in this case, but the school counselor must first promote counselor–client communication and build trust with this student.
B—3.	Play therapy
	Yes
	Play therapy is an excellent choice at this time for Esther because play often promotes communication and relationship building between the client and counselor. This is also particularly helpful in cases where the child is reluctant to express thoughts and emotions and is in the initial stages of counseling.
B—4.	Gestalt
	No
	Gestalt is certainly a good choice for helping students to resolve current life issues to become more self-aware and offers practical techniques for daily living. However, the school counselor will need to first establish communications with Esther.
B—5.	REBT
	No
	Perhaps Esther's issues are related to faulty thinking or irrational beliefs, but REBT would not be indicated at this time.

Section C: Esther

During the second session, Esther enters the room and walks over to the toys selecting a female doll and a plastic shark off your toy shelf. Esther sits on the mat on the floor and proceeds to have the shark eat the head off the female doll. What might be the most appropriate communication by you in order to gather needed information about this behavior?

(Select as many as you consider indicated in this section.)

C—1.	Esther, you seem to be angry at that doll. No The school counselor does not want to presume this emotion without exploring how the student perceived the action.
C—2.	Esther, do you like sharks? No Focus on the action and what may be implied by the action in the child's world.
C—3.	Esther, who is that doll? Yes This will help the school counselor to understand who the doll represents in the child's world.
C—4.	Esther, what is that shark doing? Yes This is a good choice as it will help the school counselor to interpret the child's thoughts and emotions.
C—5.	Esther, that is a mean shark, why did you choose to play with it? No Focus on the action and what may be implied by the action in the child's world.
C—6.	Esther, why are you angry? No The school counselor does not want to presume this emotion without exploring how the student perceived the action.
C—7.	Esther, who is that shark? Yes This will help the school counselor to understand who or what the shark signifies in the child's world.

Section D: Esther

During the third session, Esther expresses her anger toward her mother stating, "Mom doesn't love me, all she cares about is my getting good grades." Which counseling approach might be the most useful at this time to help Esther confront this irrational thought?
(Choose ONLY ONE in this section.)

D−1.	Reality
	No
	Reality counseling is a great approach for examining how current behaviors are meeting or not meeting client needs, but this may or may not be related to irrational thoughts.
D−2.	Solution-focused
	No
	It is important to focus on solutions to the problem, but at the present time addressing Esther's irrational belief would be appropriate.
D−3.	Strengths-based
	No
	Focusing on Esther's strengths to encourage self-help is important, but she had expressed an irrational thought that the school counselor would be wise to address before moving on.
D−4.	Behavioral
	No
	Behavioral counseling, which focuses on learned behaviors, is not indicated at this time.
D−5.	REBT
	Yes
	REBT will provide the school counselor with the approach needed to debunk Esther's irrational belief.
D−6.	Person-centered
	No
	Although the nurturing and warm approach of person-centered counseling is useful in Esther's case, it is not the best choice for countering irrational beliefs.

Section E: Esther

As Esther enters your office for her fourth session, you notice that her arms are really picked and she is picking at her arms as she walks into your office. You ask her if she realizes that she is picking her arms. She says, "Yes." You ask her what she has been thinking about today. She says, "My test." You realize that this morning third-grade students took an important standardized test. You asked, "What are you thinking about the test?" She responds, "I am so scared that I did not make an A, so mom is going to take away my birthday party this summer." You ask, "Have you talked about this with your mother?" Esther says, "No, I'm afraid she will get mad and yell at me." What might be the best course of action at this time?

(Choose ONLY ONE in this section.)

E—1.	Friendship group
	No
	Peer relationship issues have not been identified.
E—2.	Self-esteem building
	No
	Although Esther is shy, her issues are not presented as related to self-esteem. Esther's issues are more likely related to her lack of candid communication with her parent and her respect for her parent's feelings.
E—3.	Encourage and role play communication with mother
	Yes
	Esther is having difficulty communicating with her mother. Empowering Esther to communicate her thoughts and emotions with her parent is critical to continued family communications. Esther's behavior appears to be related to stress associated with the performance pressure she perceives from her mother.
E—4.	Strategies for reducing test-taking anxiety
	No
	This is not the immediate course of action, but the school counselor may want to consider this intervention after communication between Esther and her mother.
E—5.	Study-skills group
	No
	This is not the immediate course of action, but the school counselor may want to consider this intervention after communication between Esther and her mother.
E—6.	Encourage and role-play communication with teacher
	No
	Esther has not identified communications issues with her teacher.

Scenario 4 Answers: Early Intervention

Brief Case Description

You are a middle school counselor. Your principal comes to you concerned about the disproportionately high number of students identified as special education and students with a 504 plan as compared to other schools in the district of similar size and population. He asks for suggestions that could reduce the number of students identified as special needs in your school while still providing students with the assistance that is needed to be successful. The principal also expresses his concern with the lack of referrals to the school-wide early intervention team, which you chair.

Section A: Early Intervention

You provide the principal with the following suggestion:
   (Choose ONLY ONE in this section.)

A—1.	Require that teachers refer students to the early intervention team prior to referral to the 504 or child study teams, unless a parent objects
	Yes
	This would be the best course of action at this time, allowing for early and least-restrictive intervention that may be all the student needs to be successful.
A—2.	Pay teachers for the time they spend in early intervention team meetings
	No
	Attending school-related meetings to help students to be successful is the responsibility of the educator.
A—3.	Require a minimum number of early intervention team meetings each academic year
	No
	This would create unwarranted team meetings to meet a quota.
A—4.	Require teachers and parents to refer students to the early intervention team prior to referral to a 504 or child study committee
	No
	Parents of children in the public schools have a legal right to make referrals to these committees and at any time.

(Continued)

A—5.	Require particular grade levels to go through the early intervention team prior to going through child study or the 504 team
	No
	This is not equitable access to educational programs.

Section B: Early Intervention

Joshua, a sixth-grade student, was referred to the early intervention team for academic difficulties. His teacher expressed that he is well liked by other students and he is cooperative and that she has not noticed any other concerns apart from academic performance. What type of information or data would be important to acquire from the teacher and parents during the initial team meeting to assess Joshua's issues?

(Select as many as you consider indicated in this section.)

B—1.	Hobbies and interests
	No
	This would not be useful to assess Joshua's issues related to academic difficulties.
B—2.	Past and present social functioning
	Yes
	Interpersonal relations impacts diverse areas of life.
B—3.	Sleeping habits
	Yes
	Sleep impacts daily functioning and performance.
B—4.	Medical information
	Yes
	There may be a medical explanation for Joshua's academic difficulties.
B—5.	Behavioral records
	No
	Behavior is not identified as a concern.
B—6.	Family income
	No
	Family income will not provide insight into the student's academic difficulties.
B—7.	Past and present academic performance
	Yes
	This will help the school counselor to identify the onset of academic difficulties and patterns in academic strengths and weaknesses.

B—8.	Subjects with which the student is struggling
	Yes
	It is important to know the academic areas of difficulty in order to target strategies for remediation.
B—9.	Past and present emotional functioning
	No
	Emotional disturbance is not identified as a concern.
B—10.	Student's eating habits
	No
	Student's eating habits would not offer insight into his academic difficulties at this time.
B—11.	Environmental factors
	Yes
	A change in environment may impact academic functioning.

Section C: Early Intervention

During the team meeting, an individualized intervention plan is established to target Joshua's areas of academic difficulty. After the early intervention team meeting, as the team's chair you would do the following:

(Select ONLY ONE in this section.)

C—1.	Distribute a copy of the intervention plan to all the members of the team, the students' teachers, the parents, and to the student's record
	Yes
	The intervention plan needs to be shared with all those who work with the student, and it becomes a part of the student's permanent school record.
C—2.	Provide only the intervention team members and parents with a copy of the intervention plan
	No
	The plan needs to go to all those who work with the student and become a part of the students academic record.
C—3.	Meet with principal regarding the meeting outcome
	No
	The principal does not have time to meet and discuss the outcome of every education meeting that takes place in their building.

(Continued)

C—4.	Ensure that the intervention plan does not become a part of the student's educational record
	No
	The intervention plan is to become part of the student's educational record.

Section D: Early Intervention

Two weeks later, the team reconvenes at the request of the teacher who reports that although Joshua's academics have improved slightly, Joshua is displaying behavioral issues such as agitation and bullying of other students, which is out of character for Joshua according to his teacher. During the meeting, the parent shares that she and her husband are going through a divorce, which began just about the time that Joshua's academic performance declined. Based on this new information, Joshua's intervention plan was modified to include participation in a small group on divorce. The following permissions must be obtained:

(Select ONLY ONE in this section.)

D—1.	Informed consent from the parents of all group members
	Yes
	Although school counselors are not legally obligated to obtain parental permission prior to counseling, unless there is a federal or state statute to the contrary, considering that most school divisions do require parental permission for ongoing individual and small group counseling and considering the sensitive nature of the topic and age of the student, parental permission should be secured.
D—2.	Because small groups are a primary method of school counseling program delivery, parental consent is assumed
	No
	School counselors do not assume parental consent for student participation in group counseling.
D—3.	Informed consent of parents of all group members and participants
	No
	Students can give verbal consent, while the school counselor seeks written consent from parents.

D—4.	Informed consent only from Joshua's parent because the activity is connected to an intervention plan
	No
	School counselors should secure written consent from parents for student participation in group counseling.
D—5.	No Informed consent is required
	No
	Although school counselors are not legally obligated to obtain parental permission prior to counseling, unless there is a federal or state statute to the contrary, most school divisions require parental permission for ongoing individual and small group counseling and when meeting with students on sensitive topics.

Section E: Early Intervention

During your first group session, one of the most important issues you want to discuss with these adolescents relates to
   (Select ONLY ONE in this section.)

E—1.	Goals
	No
	Not the most important among the choices.
E—2.	Topic
	No
	Not the most important among the choices.
E—3.	Member rights
	No
	Not the most important among the choices.
E—4.	Confidentiality
	Yes
	It is critical to discuss with students the limits of confidentiality in group work during the first group session.
E—5.	Signed consent
	No
	Signed consent should be secured prior to the first session of the group.

(Continued)

E—6.	Termination
	No
	Termination is not generally discussed until the final stages of the group.
E—7.	Process
	No
	Not the most important among the choices.
E—8.	Emergency contact information
	No
	Generally, emergency contact information is on file in the school already.

Section F: Early Intervention

During the third group session, one of the group members becomes very angry and says, "I never even got to tell the jerk what I thought of him before he left us." Which counseling techniques might be useful at this time to mediate the student's emotional distress and work through the issue presented?

(Select as many as you consider indicated in this section.)

F—1.	Clarifying
	No
	This will not help to mediate the student's emotional distress or help the student to work through the distressing experience.
F—2.	Empty chair
	Yes
	This is an excellent gestalt enacting dialogue technique to assist the student in appropriately experiencing the unresolved issues with his father.
F—3.	Paraphrasing
	No
	This will not help to mediate the student's emotional distress or help the student to work through the distressing experience.
F—4.	Relaxation techniques
	Yes
	This will help the student to self-regulate.

F—5.	Guided imagery
	Yes
	An excellent cognitive behavioral technique that will teach the student to use mental pictures to self-regulate.
F—6.	Stress inoculation
	Yes
	An excellent cognitive behavioral technique for teaching skills that head off stress and identify triggers to stress.
F—8.	Behavior contract
	No
	Behavioral interventions are not indicated for this student at this time.

Scenario 5 Answers: Academic Achievement

Brief Case Description

You are a school counselor at a large, pluralistic elementary school. Twenty percent of the student body is special education and ESL students. Nearly half of the student body receives free or reduced lunch. Your school did not make AYP last year, so everyone is academic focused and implementing programs that will result in the immediate improvement of standardized test scores.

Section A: Academic Achievement

What information do you need in order to begin planning strategies to improve academic achievement?

(Select as many as you consider indicated in this section.)

A—1.	Parent support Yes Parents are resourceful and excellent sources of manpower and creativity.
A—2.	Student interests No Knowledge of the students' interests will not aid in planning strategies for academic achievement.
A—3.	Past successes Yes Draw upon what has worked before within the school and with your unique student population.
A—4.	School and community resources Yes Knowing what resources are available to you is helpful in the planning process.
A—5.	Target populations Yes School counselors need to know who is to receive the intervention.

A—6.	Students' favorite subjects No Knowing which subjects students like best will not, generally, be helpful in planning strategies for academic achievement. However, teaching styles and methods of instruction preferred by students could be helpful.
A—7.	Subject areas of weakness Yes School counselors need to know the subjects for which students need intervention.
A—8.	Subject areas of strength No School counselors need to identify subject areas of weakness for intervention planning.

Section B: Academic Achievement

Which data sources would provide useful information for creating classroom guidance lessons to target specific grade levels and subjects?

(Select as many as you consider indicated in this section.)

B—1.	Standardized test score reports Yes Standardized test score reports can identify specific students, groups of students, subject areas, content specific to subject areas, and teachers.
B—2.	School report card Yes Data from school report cards can serve as an indicator of systems-level student needs in specific academic areas.
B—3.	School-wide attendance patterns Yes Schools with poor student attendance will likely experience low academic performance because the two have been found to be correlated.
B—4.	Individual disciplinary records No Behavior can be an obstacle to academic performance; however, it would be time-consuming to review every student's disciplinary record and is not indicated for a systems-focused intervention.

(Continued)

B—5.	Family structure No Knowing students' family structure would not be particularly useful in planning systems-focused strategies for academic achievement.
B—6.	Each student's academic record No This will allow for individualized intervention; however, it can be time-consuming to review every students academic record and is not indicated for systems-focused intervention planning.

Section C: Academic Achievement

Data analysis reveals grade 3 math and grade 5 English as areas of specific weakness, particularly among the special education and ESL populations and African American males. Which intervention would be most useful for providing responsive services for these struggling students?

(Select ONLY ONE in this section.)

C—1.	Small group on study skills No This would be a useful responsive service for these students; however, it is not the best choice among those listed.
C—2.	Classroom guidance lesson on study skills that crosswalks school counseling standards and core academic standards No Study skills would be useful for this population; however, the target subjects are math and English, which may not be the core subjects covered in this classroom guidance lesson.
C—3.	Small group on study skills that crosswalks school counseling standards and math and English standards Yes Small groups would provide a systems-focused responsive service that targets the two specific areas of need for these students.
C—4.	Small group on test taking that crosswalks school counseling standards and core academic standards No Test-taking skills would be useful for this population; however, the target subjects are math and English, which may not be the core subjects covered in this classroom guidance lesson.

C—5.	Classroom guidance lesson on test taking skills that crosswalks school counseling standards and core academic standards
	No
	Test taking skills would be useful for this population; however, the target subjects are math and English, which may not be the core subjects covered in this classroom guidance lesson.
C—6.	Small group on test taking
	No
	This would be a useful responsive service for these students; however, it is not the best choice among those listed.

Section D: Academic Achievement

While chatting with your school's test coordinator, you discover that many special education students have not been given special accommodations during standardized testing. When you voiced your concern to the test coordinator, she said that as long as examiners and proctors are in short supply and because teachers are not always giving these students the accommodations during the school year, then she is not going to worry about it at testing time. What is the best course of action to take at this time?

(Select ONLY ONE in this section.)

D—1.	Let the test coordinator know that you will be making the principal aware of these unlawful instructional and standardized testing practices
	Yes
	The principal needs to be made aware that the special education students are not receiving their accommodations as written on the legally binding IEP.
D—2.	Let the test coordinator know that you will be making the principal aware of these questionable instructional and standardized testing practices
	No
	These practices are not only questionable but unlawful because they clearly deprive special education students of their rights to testing accommodations.
D—3.	Let the test coordinator know that if this continues you will need to notify the principal
	No
	School counselors are student advocates and advocates for social justice. Also, knowing and not doing anything about it can make the school counselor liable as well.

(Continued)

D—4.	Call a meeting of the teachers, test coordinator, and principal about these practices No This is the responsibility of the principal/designated school administrator.
D—5.	Voice your concerns to the test coordinator and trust her to correct the standardized testing practices No This is an unlawful practice that must be brought to the attention of the school administrator for immediate correction and possible exploration into past testing impacts and action.
D—8.	Notify the school division's testing administrator about these questionable standardized testing practices No School counselors should follow the chain of command by reporting this information to the school principal.

Section E: Academic Achievement

The actions of the teachers and test coordinator concerned you, so you reviewed some of the special education students' IEPs to find that several students were given special accommodations only on standardized tests, not on classroom tests. When you spoke to one of the teachers of these students, he said that this was an IEP team decision that included the principal and that the decision was based on the lack of manpower during the school day. What is the best course of action to take at this time?

(Select as many as you consider indicated in this section.)

E—1.	Talk to the principal about ways that these students can get the accommodations during the school day, not just on standardized testing days Yes School counselors use their leadership skills to partner with school administrators.
E—2.	Contact the school division's test administrator No School counselors partner with their building principals to effect change.

E—3.	Discuss with the principal your concern about setting the students up for failure on standardized testing day if they have not been pulled out of the class the entire year for testing Yes Helping the principal to understand the adverse impact that this practice can have on student performance during standardized testing would be beneficial.
E—4.	Contact the State Department of Education No School counselors can best serve students by working within the school's policies, and because this is an IEP team decision, it is not an unlawful or unethical practice that warrants going over the head of the building principal.
E—5.	Let the principal know that if he does not do something about this then you are going to contact the Department of Education No Although the situation may adversely impact student scores, the situation is not unlawful and was based on a team decision, which included the parent.
E—6.	Contact your school division's supervisor of instructional practices so that he or she can talk to the principal about these practices No This action could harm your relationship with your principal, and thus your ability to provide optimal services to students.
E—7.	Request to be a part of the IEP meetings, so that you can have a voice in the creation of students' IEPs Yes School counselors can advocate for students by taking part in child study, IEP, and other academic-related meetings.

Scenario 6 Answers: Assessment

Brief Case Description

You are a high school counselor. Terrance is a junior at the high school whose parent has requested that you pull his record and go over the grades and assessments with her so that she might better understand his academic status and level of functioning. She wants to know if her son, Terrance, has the grades and intelligence to get into a 4-year college and to be successful in college. She said Terrance has identified seven colleges that offer majors in communication, which is his area of interest.

Section A: Assessment

The first assessment you came to was the WAIS-II. You explained that Terrance has a verbal IQ score of 95 and a performance IQ score of 85, giving Terrance a full scale IQ of 90. Terrance's mother responds, "I don't know what that means." What information would you share with the student's mother?

(Select as many as you consider indicated in this section.)

A—1.	Most individuals have an IQ score between 85 and 115 Yes This is accurate and helpful information to give the parent.
A—2.	Because the assessment uses a 95% confidence level, Terrance's score could, at any given time, fall within 5 points in either direction Yes This will help the parent to understand the how the score might be captured on other similar assessments.
A—3.	Terrance's IQ score indicates genius No This is not an accurate interpretation of Terrance's score.
A—4.	Terrance has an average IQ Yes This is an accurate interpretation of Terrance's score.

A—5.	Terrance has a very low IQ
	No
	This is not an accurate interpretation of Terrance's score.
A—6.	Terrance's IQ indicates mild retardation
	No
	This is not an accurate interpretation of Terrance's score.

Section B: Assessment

Terrance's mother also said Terrance told her that he got a 34 on his ACT test. She began to cry stating that her son would "never get into college with such low scores on his college entrance exams." You look at Terrance's score report from ACT and see that, indeed, Terrance's score on the ACT was 34. What information would you share with this parent?

  (Select as many as you consider indicated in this section.)

B—1.	The average score of the ACT is 21
	Yes
	This is accurate information that will help the parent to understand the meaning of her son's score.
B—2.	The average score on the ACT is 71
	No
	This is not accurate; the average score on the ACT is 21.
B—3.	Because the high score is 75, Terrance did not do well
	No
	This is not accurate; the high score on the ACT is 36.
B—4.	ACT scores range from 1 to 36
	Yes
	This is accurate and will help Terrance's mother to understand his score.
B—5.	ACT scores range from 25 to 75
	No
	This is not accurate information; the ACT score range is 1 to 36.
B—6.	Because the high score is 36, Terrance did very well
	Yes
	This is an accurate interpretation of Terrance's ACT score.

Section C: Assessment

As you go through Terrance's record you notice that there are no SAT scores. His mother said he is not taking the SAT because he took the ACT. What advice would you give to the parent at this point?

(Select ONLY ONE in this section.)

C—1.	The ACT is all he needs
	No
	It is best to take the one that the college of your choice requires. Many will take either test, but both are encouraged because each tests you in a different way.
C—2.	The SAT is the most widely used college entrance exam in the country although many college accept either the ACT or SAT
	Yes
	This is accurate information. Students should also be advised to take the test required by the college of their choice.
C—3.	The ACT measures the same thing as the SAT
	No
	This is not accurate information.
C—4.	The SAT is not used very often for college entrance; however, it is a good measure of achievement
	No
	The SAT is the most widely used college entrance exam in the country.
C—5.	The SAT is the only assessment that should be taken for college entrance
	No
	Students who do not wish to take both the ACT and the SAT should take the test required by the college of their choice.

Section D: Assessment

Terrance's mother says that she is still a bit concerned about Terrance's choice of major. She worries that it will not be a good match. She adds that she knows Terrance is interested in communication, but she is not sure about his skills and abilities or that the work environment would fit his personality. The school counselor suggests that the career counselor administer the following career interest inventory:

(Select ONLY ONE in this section.)

D—1.	ASVAB No The ASVAB is an aptitude test.
D—2.	Kaufman No The Kaufman is an assessment of cognitive development and not generally used as a career decision-making tool.
D—3.	SDS Yes The SDS will match Terrance's skills and interests to specific careers.
D—4.	Super's model of career development No This is a career development model not a career assessment.
D—5.	WAIS No This is an intelligence test and not generally used to make career decisions.
D—6.	Vineland No This assessment measures adaptive behavior.

Section E: Assessment

Terrance's mother thanks you for your time and asks, "What do we need to do next because it is already the spring of Terrance's junior year?" The following information would be useful for the parent at this time:

(Select as many as you consider indicated in this section.)

E—1.	FAFSA deadlines Yes This form should be completed in January of the student's senior year.
E—2.	SAT information and deadlines Yes Students are encouraged to take both the SAT and the ACT, unless their school(s) of choice specifies one or the other.

(Continued)

E—3.	ACT information and deadlines No The student already took the ACT and scored well.
E—4.	PSAT information and deadlines Yes Although this test is generally taken in the 9th and 10th grade years, it is sometimes taken in the 11th grade year for scholarship awards and as a practice test for the SAT.
E—5.	College fair dates Yes This would be beneficial to Terrance, who has not identified a specific college.
E—6.	GED Official Practice Test information and deadlines No This is an alternative education route for students who do not desire to graduate from high school or who are at risk of dropping out of high school.
E—7.	Scholarship websites Yes This is useful information for college-bound students.
E—8.	Financial aid website Yes This is useful information for college-bound students.

Scenario 7 Answers: Julianna

Brief Case Description

Julianna is a fifth-grade African American student diagnosed with ADHD, and you are the elementary school counselor at her school. The teacher and parent report that Julianna consistently presents as hyperactive, restless, argumentative, and impulsive. Julianna's mother reports that the medication Julianna is taking does not appear to be working because Julianna continues to experience academic, social, and behavioral issues. Julianna's mother is a single parent and admits that she does not have much time to spend with Julianna and her other two children to help with their studies because she works two jobs. A 504 committee meeting was just held, and Julianna qualified for a 504 plan due to the academic and social impact related to Julianna's ADHD.

Section A: Julianna

During the 504 meeting, you identified the following strategies and approaches to help Julianna and her family:
    (Select as many as you consider indicated in this section.)

A—1.	Homeschooling
	No
	Julianna can benefit from the social interaction and structure of school.
A—2.	Social skills development
	Yes
	Students with ADHD often experience interpersonal relationship issues.
A—3.	Reduced television time
	No
	A reduction in television time is not indicated at this time.
A—4.	Parenting skills training
	Yes
	It is important to help parents to acquire the skills needed to help their children with ADHD.

(Continued)

A—5.	Family counseling
	Yes
	ADHD is a challenge that impacts the entire family.
A—6.	Reduced computer time
	No
	A reduction in computer time is not indicated at this time.
A—7.	Change in diet
	Yes
	There is much research to support the effectiveness of diet in mediating the symptoms of ADHD. This is an option worthy of further investigation.
A—8.	Increased time spent with friends
	No
	An increase in the amount of time spent with friends is not indicated at this time. Additionally, more time with friends does not equal enhanced social skills. It is possible that more time with friends will lead to more rejection until proper social skills are developed.
A—9.	Counseling
	Yes
	A combination of counseling and medication has been found to be effective in mediating the symptoms of ADHD.
A—10.	Reduced length of academic work
	Yes
	This is a 504 plan accommodation that has been found to be helpful for students with ADHD.
A—11.	Increased length of academic work
	No
	Lengthening academic work and the time required to complete such assignments is frustrating for a child with ADHD, who is already having difficulty focusing on the work load assigned.
A—12.	Providing choices (academic and home tasks)
	Yes
	Allowing choices for students with ADHD will help them to select a "means to the end" that is best suited for them and helps them to stay on task.

Section B: *Julianna*

Julianna's mother asks about what other things she can do at home
to improve Julianna's behavior and increase cooperation. In addition
to organization and maintaining a consistent schedule, you name the
following:

   (Select as many as you consider indicated in this section.)

B–1.	Positive reinforcement
	Yes
	Positive reinforcement for following rules at home and school has been used successfully with children and adolescents with ADHD.
B–2.	Loss of privileges
	Yes
	Loss of privileges has been used successfully as a mild consequence to undesired behaviors for children with ADHD.
B–3.	Allow more computer time
	No
	Increasing computer time is not indicated.
B–4.	Negotiated rewards
	Yes
	Allowing choices and negotiating rewards helps children with ADHD to participate in their own behavioral plan.
B–5.	Contracts
	Yes
	Behavior contracts have been found to be useful in mediating the negative behaviors associated with ADHD and provide a clearly defined process of rewards and consequences.
B–6.	Resist setting goals
	No
	Goals are useful for children with ADHD, aiding in directing behavior.
B–7.	Mild consequences
	Yes
	Mild consequences are enough to shape behavior.
B–8.	Give specific behavioral feedback
	Yes
	Specific feedback allows for specific change and clear understanding.

Section C: Julianna

What counseling theory might be most useful when working with Julianna? (Select ONLY ONE in this section.)

C—1.	Gestalt counseling
	No
	This is not the best counseling approach among those listed here for children with ADHD.
C—2.	Behavioral counseling
	Yes
	Behavioral counseling is the approach most widely used with children with ADHD.
C—3.	Reality counseling
	No
	This is not the best counseling approach among those listed here for children with ADHD.
C—4.	Person-centered counseling
	No
	This is not the best counseling approach among those listed here for children with ADHD.
C—5.	Adlerian counseling
	No
	This is not the best counseling approach among those listed here for children with ADHD.
C—6.	Cognitive behavioral counseling
	No
	This is not the best counseling approach among those listed here for children with ADHD.

Section D: Julianna

Several months into the 504 plan, the teacher and parent report that Julianna's behavioral and peer relations problems have increased, and her academic performance has declined. Julianna is now having full-blown temper tantrums at home, at school, and in the community. She is disobedient and blames others for her actions. The school counselor strongly encourages the following actions to help Julianna and her family:

(Select as many as you consider indicated in this section.)

D—1.	Referral to child study for possible testing and special education services
	Yes
	It is a good idea to explore possible coexisting conditions.
D—2.	Homeschooling
	No
	The structure provided by attending school and the social interactions with age-appropriate others is beneficial for children with ADHD.
D—3.	Participation in Governor's School
	No
	Governor's School is for students who have been identified as gifted.
D—4.	Medical examination by the child's physician
	Yes
	It is important to rule out medical conditions that may be a contributing factor.
D—5.	Less time with peers
	No
	Less time with peers is not indicated as this time.
D—6.	Appointment with a child psychiatrist
	Yes
	An appointment with a child psychiatrist is indicated based on presenting behaviors and current diagnosis.
D—7.	More time with peers
	No
	More time with peers is not indicated.
D—8.	Family counseling
	Yes
	The entire family is impacted by the behavioral conditions of a family member.
D—9.	Resources related to helping children with disruptive behavior issues/disorders
	Yes
	School counselors provide parents with information and resources related to behavioral and emotional issues.

Section E: Julianna

Julianna's mother returns to you a few weeks later and says that the psychiatrist has diagnosed Juliann with oppositional defiance disorder and recommended ongoing individual counseling for Julianna and the family. She asks if you would be Julianna's counselor over the next couple of years. Your response is

(Select ONLY ONE in this section.)

E—1.	Of course.
	No
	Julianna's counseling needs are beyond the scope of school counseling.
E—2.	I would like to, as I have enjoyed working with Julianna very much, however, I just do not have time as the only school counselor in the building.
	No
	Time is not the primary issue.
E—3.	Julianna's needs are beyond the scope of school counseling, but I have a list of counseling resources, which may be helpful in identifying a counselor.
	Yes
	School counselors do not provide individuals with ongoing counseling for chronic behavioral, emotional, and mental health issues. This type of long-term counseling is beyond the scope of school counseling.
E—4.	I would not be able to do this during the school day, as it is beyond the scope of school counseling. However, I can provide counseling services to Julianna outside of school hours at your home or mine for a minimal charge.
	No
	This is a dual relationship and an ethical violation.
E—5.	Oppositional defiance disorder is not really my area of expertise, but I will work with Julianna because she and I already have a positive relationship.
	No
	Practicing outside of your areas of expertise is an ethical violation and could become a legal issue as well.

Glossary

Academic development: one of three developmental domains within a comprehensive school counseling program, promoting skills, relating learning to life, and enhancing academic success and a positive attitude toward school and learning.

Accommodation: adjustments made to instruction, homework, testing, and the physical environment in order to promote the success of students with special needs (e.g., special education, 504, and ESL students), as well as students with temporary conditions (e.g., illness, injury).

Accountability: practices that are data-driven, standards-based, research-supported, evaluated for effectiveness and ongoing program improvement, and demonstrate *how* school counselors make a difference in the lives of students.

Achievement gap: the disparity in educational performance that exists between specific populations of students, primarily low-income and minority students when compared to peers on a variety of educational measures, namely standardized tests.

Action plan: written plans that describe specific programming and how programming will achieve stated objectives, including closing the achievement gap activities. SCOPE, the School Counseling Operational Plan for Effectiveness, is an example of an ASCA-recommended action plan.

Action research: research conducted for the purpose of enhancing the effectiveness of one's practices and/or measuring program outcomes.

Active listening: a basic counseling skill and communication skill that attends to the student's verbal and nonverbal behaviors.

Addiction: psychological and/or physiological dependence on a substance or activity.

Advisory council: a committee of stakeholders, established by the school counselor, to direct and assist the school counseling program.

ASCA recommends an advisory committee as part of the school counseling program management system to promote program success.

Advocacy: a function of the school counselor that involves acting and speaking on behalf of others to support equity and access to programming and to promote student, family, school, and community relations and development.

Aggression: verbal, physical, and psychological behaviors intended to cause harm, threat, or pain.

Americans with Disabilities Act (ADA): national legislation that prohibits discrimination against persons with a disability in employment, public institutions, public transportation, and telecommunications. A *qualified individual with a disability* is entitled to reasonable accommodations.

Anorexia: an eating disorder that is characterized primarily by a consistent and extreme restriction of food intake and a refusal to maintain minimum normal body weight for age and height.

Antisocial behavior: behavior, covert and overt, that disregards the rights and privacy of others and the norms, laws, and standards of a society.

Appraisal (also see assessment): approaches and/or measures (standardized and nonstandardized) used to gain a greater understanding of a student's functioning (e.g., intellectual, educational, mental, emotional, social, physical, or occupational).

ASCA National Model: the only national model for the profession of school counseling designed to serve as a framework from which to implement a comprehensive, developmental, and primarily preventative school counseling program.

ASCA National Standards: national standards (a foundational component of the ASCA National Model) that depict what students should know and be able to do as a result of a comprehensive school counseling program in three broad developmental areas: career, academic, and personal–social.

Assessment (also see appraisal): approaches and/or measures (standardized and nonstandardized) used to gain a greater understanding of a student's functioning (e.g., intellectual, educational, mental, emotional, social, physical, or occupational).

Behavior contract: a plan of action used for general education students to reduce or eliminate specific, observable, and measurable undesirable behaviors by applying specific interventions and rewards.

Behavior intervention plan: a plan of action, often part of an IEP for special education students, aimed at reducing or eliminating specific, observable, and measurable undesirable behaviors by applying individualized interventions and rewards.

Behavioral rehearsal: practicing new skills and behaviors for application outside of the counseling environment.

Bibliotherapy: the use of books/literature in counseling toward established counseling goals.

Bulimia: an eating disorder that is characterized primarily by reoccurring episodes of binging and purging (e.g., vomiting, laxatives) and a preoccupation with body weight.

Bullying (also see cyberbullying): any verbal, nonverbal, or physical behavior intended to intimidate, threaten, harm, or cause physical, emotional, and/or psychological pain.

Career awareness: the focus on career development at the elementary level that promotes students' knowledge of the world of work.

Career counseling: counseling aimed at career development at a specific time and across the lifespan.

Career development: one of three developmental domains of a comprehensive school counseling program that promotes students' identification of, and preparation for, desired post–high school occupations, education, and training and relating school and the world of work.

Career development inventories: instruments used to enhance a student's knowledge pertaining to occupational choices, self-knowledge (e.g., interests, values, skills), and education and training related to specific careers.

Career exploration: a focus at the middle school level that enhances students' understanding of career opportunities and the link between school and work, developing an academic plan to meet postsecondary career choices.

Career planning: a focus at the high school level that encourages students to continue to update and follow through on established career and academic plans for career readiness.

Child abuse: harm toward a child caused by neglect or exploitation and/or physical, emotional, psychological, or sexual mistreatment.

Child neglect: failure to provide for the social, psychological, emotional, and biological needs of a child; failure to prevent suffering or to act on behalf of the child that places the child in imminent danger; behaviors that place the child in harm's way.

Child study: a team approach to identifying and understanding the needs of a student who is not achieving academically in comparison to peers or who is demonstrating physical, emotional, verbal, or psychological issues that are interfering with daily functioning.

Closed group: groups that are no longer open to new membership once group facilitation begins.

Collaboration: a function of the school counselor that involves working cooperatively with others toward a common goal.

Computer-assisted career guidance systems: electronic systems designed to promote career readiness.

Conflict resolution: the process by which students resolve conflict peacefully by engaging a variety of skills (e.g., problem solving, empathy, clarification, questioning, communication, and negotiation).

Consultation: a function of the school counselor that involves providing services in their area of expertise to other stakeholders (e.g., teachers, parents, and school administrators).

Crisis: traumatic or extremely stressful situations that require immediate action to secure the safety and well-being of students and others (e.g., suicide or homicide risk, post-student suicide, homicide, accidental death, terrorism, natural disaster, and child abuse/neglect).

Cyberbullying (also see bullying): any electronic (e.g., via texting, Internet, email, chat rooms, or social networks) behavior intended to intimidate, threaten, harm, or cause physical, emotional, and/or psychological pain.

Data analysis: an examination of information that aids school counselors in identifying stakeholder needs, targeting programming, and determining program effectiveness and areas for improvement.

Data-driven: programs, practices, and activities that are created based on an analysis of data.

Diagnostic test: an assessment used to identify areas of academic competencies and areas of deficit.

Disability: a cognitive/psychological, behavioral, and/or physical impairment that limits one or more daily living functions.

Educational diagnostician: an individual employed by school divisions to assess levels of student academic functioning and to suggest interventions to meet individual student needs; often a member of child study teams.

Emancipated minor: a minor who has been granted by the courts the decision-making power of an adult with regard to their own affairs.

Emancipated minors do not need parental consent to engage in counseling services.

Encapsulation: ignorance of one's cultural background and how culture impacts one's total being.

English as a second language: students whose primary or native language is not English.

Equity and access: equal opportunity to rigorous curriculum and school and community programs.

Extrinsic motivation: motivation that is achieved with external rewards (e.g., stickers, certification, treats, or praise).

Family Educational Rights and Privacy Act (FERPA): legislation enacted to protect the privacy of students' academic records and to allow parents and students to inspect academic records and petition for the removal of information perceived as inaccurate. FERPA is also known as the Buckley Amendment.

504 plan: a written document that identifies special accommodations afforded to students with qualifying conditions pursuant to Section 504 of the Rehabilitation Act of 1973.

Free and appropriate public education: legislation that ensures individualized curriculum that meets unique student needs and prepares students for post-high school education, careers, and independent living.

General equivalency diploma (GED): an alternative to a high school diploma and completion of high school, the GED established mastery of high school core course content and may be obtained during the high school years through alternative educational programs or post–high school for those adults who "dropped out" of high school.

Guidance counselor: an outdated title for the counselor in the pre-K–12 school setting, depicting only one component of the many functions of the contemporary school counselor that is associated primarily with more directive approaches and education and career planning.

High stakes testing: standardized testing used to determine passing or failure of select core courses and graduation from high school; it also drives the type of diploma received.

In loco parentis: a common-law doctrine that allows educators to act as parents, protecting students and their rights while under their care at school.

Inclusion classroom: a general education classroom that provides additional supports and accommodations for special education student participation.

Individual-focused: school counseling practices that are more focused on intervention for a select individual than on prevention and intervention services for all students.

Individualized education program: a written document that identifies specific and individualized strategies for the personal–social, academic, and career success of students with a qualifying disability under IDEA as part of special education services.

Individuals with Disabilities Education Act (IDEA): national legislation that ensures that the educational needs of students with disabilities are met.

Intelligence quotient: a score from standardized intelligence tests, which represents one's level of intelligence.

Intelligence test: standardized tests intended to assess an individual's cognitive abilities and yield an intelligence quotient score.

Intervention: activities and strategies applied with the purpose of reducing or eliminating specific thoughts, actions, or situations.

Intrinsic motivation: motivation that is achieved with internal rewards (e.g., specific positive feedback, or earned recognition through accomplishment).

Leadership: the ability to inspire, influence, and persuade others to follow or act.

Learning profile: a comprehensive conceptualization that considers an individual's learning styles, predisposition toward specific intelligences (see **multiple intelligences**), as well as cultural and gender differences.

Least restrictive environment: special education students are to receive educational services that promote success in the least restrictive manner while receiving accommodations and supports as outlined in the student's IEP; the least restrictive environments in the public school setting are the general education classrooms (also see **inclusion classroom**).

Limited English proficient (LEP): individuals whose first language is not English and who are therefore are restricted in their English-speaking ability.

Medical plan: used in schools for students with medical conditions that may warrant special accommodations for a specified amount of time.

Modeling: observing and imitating others.

Motivation: a force, energy, desire, or state of being that directs thoughts and behavior.

Multicultural counseling: counseling that is sensitive to the needs of all people and their unique worldviews grounded in gender, race, ethnicity, culture, social status, economic status, sexual orientation, and religion.

Multiple intelligences: eight independent cognitive and affective intelligences working interactively for a holistic understanding of human intelligence.

Needs assessment: formal and informational measures that result in the identification of stakeholder needs.

Negative reinforcement: removal of a stimulus in an effort to increase a desired behavior or response.

New Vision School Counseling: the current movement to transform school counseling into an academic- and systems-focused paradigm.

No Child Left Behind: legislation that supports standards-based education and the measurement of goals to enhance academic outcomes and to close achievement gaps between specific classes and racial groups of students.

Nontraditional occupation: occupations in which few individuals of a specific gender generally work. For example, occupations historically dominated by females would be nontraditional occupations for males (e.g., nurse), and occupations historically dominated by males would be nontraditional for females (e.g., mechanic).

Occupational Information Network: national database for career information, exploration, assessment, and career decision making.

***Occupational Outlook Handbook*:** nationally recognized source for career information and career decision making.

Open group: groups that allow new membership once group facilitation begins.

Outcome evaluation: program evaluation that determines the effectiveness of a program or intervention in meeting established goals and objectives.

Paraphrasing: a basic counseling technique that involves the school counselor restating what a student has shared to communicate understanding.

Peer helping: programs that involve students helping students (e.g., peer tutoring, peer mentoring, or peer mediation).

Peer mediation: a process by which students help students to resolve conflict peacefully by engaging a variety of skills (e.g., problem solving, empathy, clarification, questioning, communication, and negotiation). Peer mediation involves more than two individuals.

Personal–social development: one of three developmental domains within a comprehensive school counseling program that promotes total student well-being through the application of counseling theory and techniques and teaches skills for living (e.g., safety, problem solving, decision making, conflict resolution, and communication).

Play therapy: the use of directive and nondirective play facilitated by the school counselor as a therapeutic medium for emotional expression and communication.

Positive reinforcement: application of a stimulus in an effort to increase a desired behavior or response.

Prevention: activities and strategies applied with the purpose of averting specific thoughts, actions, or situations.

Primary prevention: programming that focuses on prevention and wellness for a large population (e.g., the entire student body), who may or may not be potentially at risk for a specific targeted behavior or problem.

Process evaluation: program evaluations that assess the program's strengths and weaknesses for program improvement.

Professional associations: school counseling related associations that support the profession with resources, professional development opportunities, unification, and advocacy.

Professional school counselor: the contemporary title for the counselor in the pre-K–12 school setting, depicting a comprehensive counseling specialty that shares the dual roles of educator and counselor and practices using a comprehensive developmental model.

Program evaluation: an ongoing component of accountable school counseling practices that results in data that demonstrates program outcomes and answers the question "How do school counselors make a difference in the lives of students?"; also provides information for program improvement.

Reciprocal determinism: a term coined by Albert Bandura to describe how behavior is determined by the shared relationship (one acting upon the other) between a person and the environment.

Reinforcement/reinforcer (also see positive/negative reinforcement): a concept used in operant conditioning to refer to a stimulus, positive or negative, to increase the likelihood of desired behaviors or reduce or eliminate undesired behaviors.

Research-based: school counseling practices and programming that are supported by research.

Resilience: the capacity of an individual to cope with stress and harsh conditions.

Response to intervention: an intervention process used to help struggling students to improve behavior and achieve academically.

Responsive services: services that meet the immediate needs and distressing issues of students.

Results report: written reports that describe the outcomes of specific programming as outlined in action plans, including closing the achievement gap activities. SCORE, the School Counseling Operational Report of Effectiveness, is an example of an ASCA-recommended results report.

Risk factors: any physical, personal, social, familial, environmental, or economical condition that places students at a disadvantage and serves as an obstacle to well-being, academic achievement, and healthy student development.

School nurse: an individual employed by school divisions to attend to student injury, coordinate medical care with physicians, psychologists, and parents, and administer medications during the school day; often a member of child study teams.

School psychologist: an individual employed by school divisions to assess levels of student psychological functioning and to suggest interventions to meet individual student needs; often a member of child study teams.

School social worker: an individual employed by school divisions to assess levels of student social and family functioning and to suggest interventions to meet individual student needs; often a member of child study teams.

School-to-Work Opportunities Act: legislation that seeks to ensure that students will be well prepared to succeed in our multifaceted and technologically advanced workforce.

Secondary prevention: programming aimed at mediating a specific behavior or problem that has been identified as a potential threat among a particular population or subgroup of students.

Section 504: A part of the ADA, also known as the Rehabilitation Act of 1973, that protects individuals with disabilities from discrimination and allows for equal access to services and the provision of reasonable accommodations related to the disability.

Social responsibility: an ethical ideology that is grounded in the principles of equality, unity, and respect for human rights and acting on behalf of the good of society.

Special needs students: students who are limited English proficient or have a 504 plan or IEP.

Stakeholder: any individual or organization that impacts or is impacted by the school.

Standards: statements that delineate what students should know and be able to do.

Strengths-based counseling: a counseling approach that emphasizes the value of protective factors in combating risk factors and enhancing resilience.

Substance abuse: repeated use of a chemical substance that may or may not include dependence.

Substance use: repeated use of a chemical substance without dependence.

Suicide assessment: screening an individual to determine their risk for suicide.

Suicide ideation: thinking about taking one's own life.

Summarizing: a basic counseling technique whereby the school counselor condenses into a few brief statements that which the student has conveyed over a period of time during the counseling session.

Systems-focused: school counseling practices that are more focused on prevention and intervention services for all students rather than a select few.

Teaming: joining together with other stakeholders to accomplish a common goal.

Tertiary prevention: programming that targets a specific population who are already engaging in the at-risk behavior or experiencing a specific problem in order to reduce or eliminate the problem or behavior and improve quality of life.

Transforming school counseling initiative: the movement to change the paradigm of school counseling to one that is academic- and systems-focused.

Universal Academic Achievement: academic achievement for all students.

Wellness: a sense of personal, social, emotional, physical, and spiritual well-being.

Worldview: how an individual conceptualizes and interprets the world, views their relationship with the world, and interacts with the world that is grounded in presupposition, beliefs, and values.

Zeitgeist: the thought or spirit of the time in a specified time period or generation.

References

Adler, A. (1925). *The practice and theory of individual psychology* (P. Radin, Trans., Rev. ed., 1929). London: Routledge.

Akos, P. (2002). Student perceptions of the transition from elementary to middle school. *Professional School Counseling, 5,* 339–345.

Akos, P., Cockman, C. R., & Strickland, C. A. (2007). Differentiating classroom guidance. *Professional School Counseling, 10,* 455–463.

Amatea, E. S., & West-Olatunji, C. S. (2007). Joining the conversation about educating our poorest children: Emerging leadership roles for school counselors in high-poverty schools. *Professional School Counseling, 11,* 81–89.

Amato, P. R., & Cheadle, J. (2005). The long reach of divorce: Divorce and child well-being across three generations. *Journal of Marriage and Family, 67,* 191–206.

American Counseling Association. (2003). *ACA taskforce on counselor wellness and impairment.* Retrieved October 1, 2010, from www.counseling.org/wellness_taskforce/index.htm.

American Counseling Association. (2005). *Code of ethics and standards of practice.* Alexandria, VA: Author.

American Evaluation Association. (1994). Guiding principles for evaluators. *New Directions for Program Evaluation, 66,* 19–26.

American School Counselor Association. (2004). Effectiveness of school counseling. Alexandria, VA: Author.

American School Counselor Association. (2005). *The ASCA national model: A framework for school counseling programs* (2nd ed.). Alexandria, VA: Author.

American School Counselor Association. (2008). *ASCA school counselor competencies.* Retrieved September 1, 2009, from www.schoolcounselor.org.

American School Counselor Association. (2010). *Ethical standards for school counselors.* Alexandria, VA: Author.

American School Counselor Association. (2011). *ASCA position statements.* Retrieved June 2, 2011, from www.schoolcounselor.org.

Anderman, L. H., & Leake, V. S. (2005). The ABCs of motivation: An alternative framework for teaching preservice teachers about motivation. *The Clearing House, 78,* 192–197.

Anderson, L. W., & Krathwohl, D. R. (Eds.). (2001). *A taxonomy for learning, teaching, and assessing: A revision of Bloom's taxonomy of educational objectives.* New York, NY: Longman.

Association for Assessment in Counseling and Education. (1998). *Competencies in assessment and evaluation for school counselors.* Retrieved September 3, 2009, from http://aace.ncat.edu.

Association for Counselor Education and Supervision. (2007). ACES technology competencies for counselor education students. Retrieved November 10, 2010 from, http://files.acesonline.net/doc/2007_aces_technology_competencies.pdf.

Association of Computer-Based Systems for Career Information. (1999). *Handbook of standards for the operation of computer-based career information systems.* Alexandria, VA: Author.

Astramovich, R. L., Coker, J. K., & Hoskins, W. J. (2005). Training school counselors in program evaluation. *Professional School Counseling, 9,* 49–55.

Auger, R. W. (2004). Responding to terror: The impact of September 11 on K-12 schools and schools' responses. *Professional School Counseling, 7,* 222–231.

Baker, S. B., & Gerler, E. R. (2004). *School counseling for the twenty-first century* (4th ed.). Upper Saddle River, NJ: Pearson.

Bandura, A. (1969). *Principles of behavior modification.* New York, NY: Holt, Rinehard & Winston.

Bandura, A. (1977). *Social learning theory.* Englewood Cliffs, NJ: Prentice Hall.

Bauman, S. (2008). *Essential topics for the helping professional.* Boston, MA: Allyn & Bacon.

Beale, A. V. (1995). Selecting school counselors: The principal's perspective. *The School Counselor, 42,* 211–217.

Beck, A. (1979). *Cognitive therapies and emotional disorders.* New York, NY: International Universities Press.

Bell, S. K., Coleman, J. K., Anderson, A., Whelan, J. P., & Wilder, C. (2000). The effectiveness of peer mediation in a low-SES rural elementary school. *Psychology in the Schools, 37,* 505–516.

Bernard, J. M., & Goodyear, R. K. (2004). *Fundamentals of clinical supervision* (3rd ed.). Boston, MA: Allyn & Bacon.

Berne, E. (1961). Transactional analysis in psychotherapy. New York: Grove Press.

Birkeland, S., Murphy-Graham, E., & Weiss, C. (2005). Good reasons for ignoring good evaluation: The case of the drug abuse resistance education (DARE) program. *Evaluation and Program Planning, 28,* 247–256.

Bloom, B. S. (1953). Thought processes in lectures and discussions. *Journal of General Education, 7,* 160–169.

Breakwell, G. M., Hammond, S., & Fife-Schaw, C. (2001). Research methods in psychology (2nd ed.). Thousand Oaks, CA: Sage.

Brown, D. (2002). The role of work and cultural values in occupational choice, success, and satisfaction. *Journal of Counseling and Development, 80,* 48–56.

Bryan, J., & Henry, L. (2008). Strengths-based partnerships: A school-family-community partnership. *Professional School Counseling, 12,* 149–156.

Campbell, C. A., & Dahir, C. A. (1997). *Sharing the vision: The national standards for school counseling programs*. Alexandria, VA: American School Counselor Association Press.

Cameron, S., & Turtle-Song, I. (2002). Learning to write case notes using the SOAP format. *Journal of Counseling & Development, 80*(3), 286.

Capuzzi, E., & Stauffer, M. D. (2012). *Foundations of addictions counseling* (2nd ed.). Boston, MA: Pearson.

Chibbaro, J. S. (2007). School counselors and the cyberbully: Interventions and implications. *Professional School Counseling, 11*, 65–68.

Child Welfare Information Gateway. (2007). *Recognizing child abuse and neglect: Signs and symptoms*. United States department of health and human resources fact sheets. Retrieved November 10, 2010, from www.childwelfare.gov/pubs/factsheets/signs.cfm.

Child Welfare Information Gateway. (2009). *Definitions of child abuse and neglect: Summary of state laws*. Retrieved August 2, 2010, from www.childwelfare.gov/systemwide/laws_policies/statutes/define.cfm.

Cochran, L. (1997). *Career counseling: A narrative approach*. Newbury Park, CA: Sage.

Corey, G. (2008). *Theory and practice of group counseling*. Belmont, CA: Thomson Brooks/Cole.

Corsini, R., & Wedding, D. (1995). *Current psychotherapies* (5th ed.). Itasca, IL: Peacock.

Council for Accreditation of Counseling and Related Educational Programs. (2009). *CACREP accreditation manual* (1st ed.). Alexandria, VA: Author.

Dalgas-Pelish, P. (2006). Effects of self-esteem intervention program on school-age children. *Pediatric Nursing, 32*, 341–349.

Deci, E. L., Koestner, R., & Ryan, R. M. (2001). Extrinsic rewards and intrinsic motivation in education: Reconsidered once again. *Review of Educational Research, 71*, 1–27.

DeLucia-Waack, J. L., & Gerrity, D. (2001). Effective group work for elementary school-age children whose parents are divorcing. *Family Journal: Counseling and Therapy for Couples and Families, 9*(3), 273–284.

de Shazer, S. (1985). *Keys to solution in brief therapy*. New York, NY: Norton.

Dilley, J., Foster, W., & Bowers, I. (1973). Effectiveness ratings of counselors without teaching experience. *Counselor Education and Supervision, 13*, 24–29.

Dollarhide, C. T., Gibson, D. M., & Saginak, K. A. (2008). New counselors' leadership efforts in school counseling: Themes from a year-long qualitative study. *Professional School Counseling, 11*, 262–271.

Dollarhide, C. T., Smith, A. T., & Lemberger, M. E. (2007). Critical incidents in the development of supportive principals: Facilitating school counselor–principal relationships. *Professional School Counseling, 10*, 360–369.

Donne, J. (n.d.). *Quotes.net*. Retrieved May 12, 2011, from www.quotes.net/quote/3018.

Dougherty, M. (2009). *Psychology consultation and collaboration in school and community settings* (5th ed.). Belmont, CA: Brooks/Cole.

Education Trust, The (1997, February) *The national guidance and counseling reform program*. Washington, DC: Author.

Ellis, A., & Dryden, W. (1997). *The practice of rational emotive behavior therapy*. New York, NY: Springer.

Ellis, A., & Harper, R. A. (1997). *A guide to rational living* (3rd ed.). Hollywood: Wilshire.

Erford, B. T. (2011). *Transforming the school counseling profession* (3rd ed.). Boston, MA: Pearson.

Erikson, E. H. (1950). *Childhood and society*. New York, NY: Norton.

Erikson, E. H. (1959). *Identity and the life cycle*. New York, NY: International Universities Press.

Forester-Miller, H., & Davis, T. E. (1996). *A practitioner's guide to ethical decision making*. Alexandria, VA: American Counseling Association.

Fowler, J. (1981). *Stages of faith: The psychology of human development and the quest for meaning*. New York, NY: Harper Collins.

Gardner, H. (1983) *Frames of Mind: The theory of multiple intelligences*. New York: Basic Books.

Gardner, H., & Moran, S. (2006). The science of multiple intelligences theory: A response to Lynn Waterhouse. *Educational Psychologist, 41*(4), 227–232.

Gee, D. E. (2005). The cornerstone of our freedom. *School Administrator, 62,* 44.

Gerrity, D. A., & DeLucia-Waack, J. L. (2007). Effectiveness of groups in the schools. *Journal for Specialists in Group Work, 32,* 97–106.

Gibbons, M. M., & Studer, J. R. (2008). Suicide awareness training for faculty and staff: A training model for school counselors. *Professional School Counseling, 11,* 272–275.

Gilchrist-Banks, S. (2009). *Choice theory: Using choice theory and reality therapy to enhance student achievement and responsibility*. Alexandria, VA: American School Counselor Association.

Gladding, S. T. (2001). *The counseling dictionary*. Upper Saddle River, NJ: Merrill-Prentice Hall.

Glasser, W. (1998). *Choice theory*. New York, NY: Harper Collins.

Goals 2000: Educate America Act, H.R. 1804. (1994). Retrieved September 8, 2009, from www.ed.gov/legislation/GOALS2000/TheAct/index.html.

Gottfredson, L. S. (1981). Circumscription and compromise: A developmental theory of occupational aspirations. *Journal of Counseling Psychology, 28*(6), 545–579.

Guetzloe, E. (1999). Violence in children and adolescents—a threat to public health and safety: A paradigm of prevention. *Preventing School Failure, 44,* 21.

Gysbers, N. C., & Henderson, P. (2006). *Developing and managing your school guidance program* (4th ed.). Alexandria, VA: American Counseling Association.

Haine, R. A., Sandier, I. N., Wolchik, S. A., Tein, J., & Dawson-McClure, S. R. (2003). Changing the legacy of divorce: Evidence from prevention programs and future directions. *Family Relations, 52,* 397–405.

Havighurst, R. J. (1972). *Developmental tasks and education*. New York, NY: McKay.

Hernandez, D. M., Jozefowicz-Simbeni, D. M. H., & Israel, N. (2006). Services to homeless students and families: The McKinney-Vento Act and its implications for school social work practice. *Children and Schools, 28*, 37–44.

Holcomb-McCoy, C. C. (2004). Assessing the multicultural competence of school counselors: A checklist. *Professional School Counseling, 7*, 178–183.

Holcomb-McCoy, C. C. (2007). School counseling to close the achievement gap: A social justice framework for success. Thousand Oaks, CA: Corwin Press.

Holland, J. L. (1966). *The psychology of vocational choice*. Waltham, MA: Blaisdell.

Holland, J. L. (1974). *Self-directed search*. Palo Alto, CA: Consulting Psychologists Press.

Holland, J. L. (1985). *Making vocational choices: A theory of personalities and work environments* (2nd ed.). Englewood Cliffs, NJ: Prentice Hall.

Houser, R. (1998). *Counseling and educational research*. Thousand Oaks, CA: Sage.

Ingersoll, R. E., & Bauer, A. (2004). An integral approach to spiritual wellness in school counseling. *Professional School Counseling, 7*, 301–308.

Isaacs, M. L. (2003). Data-driven decision making: The engine of accountability. *Professional School Counseling, 6*, 288–295.

Joint Committee on Testing Practices. (2004). *Code of fair testing practices in education*. Washington, DC: Author.

Kagan, J., & Snidman, N. (1991). Temperamental factors in human development. *American Psychologist, 46*, 856–862.

Kerr, M. M. (2009). *School crisis prevention and intervention*. Upper Saddle River, NJ: Merrill.

Kitchener, K. S. (1984). Intuition, critical evaluation, and ethical principles: The foundation for ethical decisions in counseling psychology. *Counseling Psychologist, 12*(3), 43–55.

Kohlberg, L. (1967). Moral and religious education in the public schools: A developmental view. In T. R. Sizer (Ed.), *The roles of religion in public education*, 164–183. Boston, MA: Houghton Mifflin.

Kohlberg, L. (1969). *Stages in the development of moral thought*. New York, NY: Holt, Rinehart & Winston.

Kottman, T. (2003). *Partners in play: An Adlerian approach to play therapy* (2nd ed.). Alexandria, VA: American Counseling Association.

Krumboltz, J. D. (1994). Improving career development theory from a social learning theory perspective. In M. L. Savickas & R. W. Lent (Eds.), *Convergence in career development theory*, 9–32. Palo Alto, CA: CPP Books.

Kubler-Ross, E. (1969). On death and dying. Routledge.

Kuder, G. F. (1964). *Kuder general interest survey: Manual*. Chicago, IL: Science Research Associates.

Lazarus, A. A. (1976). *Multimodal behavior therapy*. New York, NY: Springer.

Leary, M. A., Schreindorfer, L. S., & Haupt, A. L. (1995). The role of self-esteem in emotional and behavioral problems: Why is low self-esteem dysfunctional? *Journal of Social and Clinical Psychology, 14*, 297–314.

Lewis, J., Arnold, M., House, R., & Toporek, R. (2003). *Advocacy competencies*. Retrieved March 7, 2011, from www.counseling.org/resources.

Marzano, R. J. (2004). *Building background knowledge for academic achievement: Research on what works in schools.* Alexandria, VA: Association for Supervision and Curriculum Development.

Maslow, A. H. (1970). *Motivation and personality* (2nd ed.). New York, NY: Harper & Row.

Mason, E. M., & McMahon, H. (2009). Leadership practices of school counselors. *Professional School Counseling, 13*, 107–1150.

Matsumoto, D., & Juang, L. (2008). *Culture and psychology* (4th ed.). Belmont, CA: Thomson/Wadsworth.

McClelland, D. C. (1961). *The achieving society.* Princeton, NJ: Van Nostrand.

McClelland, D. C. (1985). *Human motivation.* Glenview, IL: Scott, Foresman.

McDevitt, T., & Ormond, J. (2002). *Child development and education.* Upper Saddle River, NJ: Merrill Prentice Hall.

McWhirter, J. J., McWhirter, B. T., McWhirter, A. M., & McWhirter, E. H. (2007). *At-risk youth: A comprehensive response* (3rd ed.). Pacific Grove, CA: Brooks/Cole.

Milsom, A., & Akos, P. (2007). National certification: Evidence of a professional school counselor? *Professional School Counseling, 10*, 346–351.

Morrison, J. (2007). *Diagnosis made easier: Principles and techniques for mental health clinicians.* New York, NY: Guilford Press.

Moyer, M., & Nelson, K. W. (2007). Investigating and understanding self-mutilation: The student voice. *Professional School Counseling, 11*, 42–48.

Olson, M. J., & Allen, D. N. (1993). Principals' perceptions of the effectiveness of school counselors with and without teaching experience. *Counselor Education and Supervision, 33*, 10–21.

National Board for Certified Counselors. (2005). *Code of ethics.* Greenboro, NC: Author.

National Board for Professional Teaching Standards. (2002). *School counseling standards.* Retrieved September 4, 2010, from www.nbpts.org.

National Career Development Association. (2009). *Multicultural career counseling minimal competencies.* Retrieved July 1, 2010, from http://associationdatabase.com/aws/NCDA/pt/sp/guidelines.

National Council for Accreditation of Teacher Education (2008). *Knowledge, skills, and professional dispositions.* Retrieved July 1, 2010, from http://ncate.org/Standards/NCATEUnitStandards/UnitStandardsinEffect2008/tabid/476/Default.aspx#stnd1.

National Law Center on Homelessness and Poverty, The. (2007). *The National law center on homelessness and poverty 2007 annual report (2007).* Retrieved October 21, 2009, from www.nlchp.org/content/pubs/2007–Annual_Report2.pdf.

Nye, R. D. (1975). *Three psychologies: Perspectives from Freud, Skinner, and Rogers.* Pacific Grove, CA: Brooks/Cole.

Olweus, D. (1995). Bullying or peer abuse at school: Facts and intervention. *Current Directions in Psychological Science, 4*, 196–200.

Page, B., Pietrzak, D., & Sutton, J. (2001). National survey of school counselor supervision. *Counselor Education and Supervision, 41*, 142–150.

Paisley, P. O., & Milsom, A. (2007). Group work as an essential contribution to transforming school counseling. *Journal for Specialist in Group Work, 32*, 9–17.

Parsons, F. (1909). *Choosing your vocation*. Boston, MA: Houghton Mifflin.

Peris, T. S., & Emery, R. E. (2004). A prospective study of the consequences of marital disruption for adolescents: Predisruption family dynamics and post-disruption adolescent adjustment. *Journal of Clinical Child and Adolescent Psychology, 33*, 694–704.

Perls, F. S. (1969). *Gestalt therapy verbatim*. Moab, UT: Real People Press.

Perusse, R., & Goodnough, G. E. (2004). *Leadership, advocacy, and direct services strategies for professional school counselors*. Pacific Grove, CA: Brooks/Cole.

Peterson, J. S. (2006). Addressing counseling needs of gifted students. *Professional School Counseling, 10*, 43–49.

Phillips, S. D., Christopher-Sisk, E., & Gravino, K. L. (2001). Making career decisions in a relational context. *The Counseling Psychologist, 29*, 193–213.

Piaget, J. (1932). *The moral judgment of the child*. London: Routledge & Kegan Paul.

Piaget, J. (1963). *The origins of intelligence in children*. New York, NY: Norton.

Porfeli, E. J., Hartung, P. J., & Vondracek, F. W. (2008). Children's vocational development: A research rationale. *Career Development Quarterly, 57*, 25–37.

Posavac, E. J., & Carey, R. G. (2003). *Program evaluation: Methods and case studies* (6th ed.). Upper Saddle River, NJ: Prentice Hall.

Poynton, T. A., & Carey, J. C. (2006). An integrative model of data-based decision making for school counseling. *Professional School Counseling, 10*, 121–131.

Rayburn, C. (2004). Assessing students for morality education: A new role for school counselors. *Professional School Counseling, 7*, 356–362.

Redding, R. E. (1990). Learning preferences and skills patterns among underachieving gifted adolescents. *The Gifted Quarterly, 34*, 72–75.

Remley, T., & Herlihy, B. (2010). Ethical, legal, and professional issues in counseling (3rd ed.). Upper Saddle River, NJ: Pearson.

Roberts, R. (2002). *Self-esteem and early learning* (2nd ed.). Thousand Oaks, CA: Sage.

Roe, A. (1957). Early determinants of vocational choice. *Journal of Counseling Psychology, 4*, 212–217.

Rogers, C. (1961). *On becoming a person: A therapist's view of psychotherapy*. New York, NY: Houghton Mifflin.

Rogers, C. (1969). *Freedom to learn*. Columbus, OH: Merrill Publishing.

Ross, C. E., & Broh, B. A. (2000). The roles of self-esteem and the sense of personal control in the academic achievement process. *Sociology of Education, 73*, 270–285.

Rothrauff, T. C., Cooney, T. M., & Shin An, J. (2009). Remembered parenting styles and adjustment in middle and late adulthood. *The Journals of Gerontology, 64b*, 137–147.

Ruschena, E., Prior, M., Sanson, A., & Smart, D. (2005). A longitudinal study of adolescent adjustment following family transition. *Journal of Child Psychology and Psychiatry, 46*, 353–363.

Santrock, J. (2010). Life-span development (13th ed.). New York, NY: McGraw-Hill.

Savickas, M. L. (1997). Constructivist career counseling: Models and methods. *Advances in Personal Construct Psychology, 4*, 149–182.

Savickas, M. L. (2000). Renovating the psychology of careers for the twenty-first century. In A. Collin & R. A. Young (Eds.), *The future of career*, 53–68. New York, NY: Cambridge University Press.

Scheel, M. J., & Gonzalez, J. (2007). An investigation of a model of academic motivation for school counseling. *Professional School Counseling, 11*, 49–56.

Schellenberg, R. (2000). Aggressive personality: When does it develop and why? *Virginia Counselors Journal, 26*, 67–76.

Schellenberg, R. (2007). Standards blending: Aligning school counseling programs with school academic achievement missions. *Virginia Counselors Journal, 29*, 13–20.

Schellenberg, R. (2008). *The new school counselors: Strategies for universal academic achievement.* Lanham, MD: Rowman Littlefield Education.

Schellenberg, R., & Grothaus, T. (2009). Promoting cultural responsiveness and closing the achievement gap with standards blending. *Professional School Counseling, 12*, 440–449.

Schellenberg, R., & Grothaus, T. (2011). Using culturally competent responsive services to improve student achievement and behavior. *Professional School Counseling, 14*, 222–230.

Schellenberg, R., Parks-Savage, A., & Rehfuss, M. (2007). Reducing levels of elementary school violence with peer mediation. *Professional School Counseling, 10*, 475–481.

School-to-Work Opportunities Act, P.L. 103–239. (1994). Retrieved October 1, 2010, from www.fessler.com/SBE/act.htm.

Search Institute. (2007). *Development assets lists.* Retrieved September 12, 2010, from www.search-institute.org/developmental-assets/lists.

Seligman, L. (2004). Diagnosis and treatment planning in counseling. *Professional School Counseling, 2*, 244–247.

Shillingford, M. A., & Lambie, G. W. (2010). Contribution of professional school counselors' values and leadership practices to their programmatic service delivery. *Professional School Counseling, 13*, 208–217.

Shoffner, M. F., & Williamson, R. D. (2000). Engaging preservice school counselors and principals in dialogue and collaboration. *Counselor Education and Supervision, 40*, 128–141.

Skinner, B. F. (1971). *Beyond freedom and dignity.* New York, NY: Vintage Books.

Stone, C. (Speaker). (2001). *Legal and ethical issues in working with minors in schools [Film].* Alexandria, VA: American School Counseling Association.

Stone, C. (2009). *School counseling principles, ethics, and law.* Alexandria, VA: American School Counseling Association.

Strong, E. K., & Campbell, D. P. (1974). *Strong-Campbell interest inventory.* Stanford, CA: Stanford University Press.

Suh, S., & Suh, J. (2007). Risk factors and levels of risk for high school dropouts. *Professional School Counseling, 10,* 297–306.

Super, D. E. (1949). *Appraising vocational fitness.* New York, NY: Harper & Brothers.

Super, D. E. (1970). *Work values inventory.* Boston, MA: Houghton Mifflin.

Super, D. E. (1980). A life-span, life-space approach to career development. *Journal of Vocational Behavior, 16,* 282–298.

Sutton, C. M. (2006). The leader's role in reaching universal success for all. *School Administrator, 63,* 47.

Tiedeman, D. V. (1961). Decision and vocational development: A paradigm and its implications. *The Personnel and Guidance Journal, 40,* 15–21.

Turner, S. L. (2007). Introduction to special issue: Transitional issues for K-16 students. *Professional School Counseling, 10,* 225–226.

United States Department of Education. (2000). *Education for Homeless Children and Youth Program title VII, subtitle B of the McKinney-Vento Homeless Assistance Act: Report to congress, fiscal year 2000.* Retrieved October 1, 2009, from www.ed.gov/programs/homeless/resources.html.

United States Department of Education. (2001). *No Child Left Behind Act of 2001.* Retrieved October 1, 2009, from www.ed.gov/policy/elsec/leg/esea02/index.html.

United States Department of Education. (2009). *Rehabilitation Act of 1973, section 504.* Retrieved October 11, 2010, from www2.ed.gov/about/offices/list/ocr/504faq.html.

United States Department of Education. (2003). *Guidance on constitutionally protected prayer in public elementary and secondary schools.* Retrieved October 11, 2010, from www2.ed.gov/policy/gen/guid/religionandschools/prayer_guidance.html.

United States Department of Education. (2004). *Individuals with Disabilities Act.* Retrieved October 18, 2009, from www.wrightslaw.com/idea/law/idea.regs.subparte.pdf.

United States Department of Education. (2008). *Family Educational Rights and Privacy Act of 1974.* Final Rule. Retrieved May 3, 2009, from www.ed.gov/legislation/FedRegister/finrule/2008-4/120908a.pdf.

United States Census Bureau. (2008). Official statistics. Washington, DC: Author.

Vygotsky, L. S. (1934). *Thought and language.* Cambridge, MA: Massachusetts Institute of Technology Press.

Vygotsky, L. S. (1978). *Mind and society.* Cambridge, MA: Harvard University Press.

Whiston, S. C., Tai, W. L., Rahardja, D., & Eder, K. (2011). School counseling outcome: A meta-analytic examination of interventions. *Journal of Counseling & Development, 89,* 37–55.

Wigfield, A., & Eccles, J. S. (2000). Expectancy-value theory of achievement motivation. *Contemporary Educational Psychology, 25,* 68–81.

Willard, N. E. (2006). *Cyberbullying and cyberthreats: Responding to challenge of online cruelty, threats, and distress* (2nd ed.). Eugene, OR: Center for Safe and Responsible Internet Use.

Wolf, J. T. (2004). Teach, but don't preach: Practical guidelines for addressing spiritual concerns of students. *Professional School Counseling, 7,* 363–366.

Wright, K., & Stegelin, D. A. (2002). *Building school and community partnerships through parent involvement* (2nd ed.). Upper Saddles River, NJ: Merrill/ Prentice Hall.

Appendix I: ASCA Ethical Standards for School Counselors*

Ethical Standards for School Counselors were adopted by the ASCA Delegate Assembly (adopted March 19,1984, revised 1992, 1998, 2004, 2010).

Preamble

The American School Counselor Association (ASCA) is a professional organization whose members are school counselors certified/licensed in school counseling with unique qualifications and skills to address all students' academic, personal/social and career development needs. Members are also school counseling program directors/supervisors and counselor educators. These ethical standards are the ethical responsibility of school counselors. School counseling program directors/supervisors should know them and provide support for practitioners to uphold them. School counselor educators should know them, teach them to their students and provide support for school counseling candidates to uphold them.

Professional school counselors are advocates, leaders, collaborators and consultants who create opportunities for equity in access and success in educational opportunities by connecting their programs to the mission of schools and subscribing to the following tenets of professional responsibility:

■ Each person has the right to be respected, be treated with dignity and have access to a comprehensive school counseling program that advocates for and affirms all students from diverse populations including: ethnic/racial identity, age, economic status, abilities/disabilities, language, immigration status, sexual orientation, gender, gender identity/ expression, family type, religious/spiritual identity and appearance.

■ Each person has the right to receive the information and support needed to move toward self-direction and self-development and affirmation within one's group identities, with special care being given to students who have historically not received adequate educational services, e.g., students of color, students living at a low socio-economic status, students with disabilities and students from non-dominant language backgrounds.

■ Each person has the right to understand the full magnitude and meaning of his/her educational choices and how those choices will affect future opportunities.

■ Each person has the right to privacy and thereby the right to expect the school-counselor/student relationship to comply with all laws, policies and ethical standards pertaining to confidentiality in the school setting.

■ Each person has the right to feel safe in school environments that school counselors help create, free from abuse, bullying, neglect, harassment or other forms of violence.

In this document, ASCA specifies the principles of ethical behavior necessary to maintain the high standards of integrity, leadership and professionalism among its members. The Ethical Standards for School Counselors were developed to clarify the nature of ethical responsibilities held in common by school counselors, supervisors/directors of school counseling programs and school counselor educators. The purposes of this document are to:

■ Serve as a guide for the ethical practices of all professional school counselors, supervisors/directors of school counseling programs and school counselor educators regardless of level, area, population served or membership in this professional association;

■ Provide self-appraisal and peer evaluations regarding school counselors' responsibilities to students, parents/guardians, colleagues and professional associates, schools, communities and the counseling profession; and

■ Inform all stakeholders, including students, parents and guardians, teachers, administrators, community members and courts of justice, of best ethical practices, values and expected behaviors of the school counseling professional.

A.1. Responsibilities to Students

Professional school counselors:

a. Have a primary obligation to the students, who are to be treated with dignity and respect as unique individuals.
b. Are concerned with the educational, academic, career, personal and social needs and encourage the maximum development of every student.
c. Respect students' values, beliefs and cultural background and do not impose the school counselor's personal values on students or their families.
d. Are knowledgeable of laws, regulations and policies relating to students and strive to protect and inform students regarding their rights.
e. Promote the welfare of individual students and collaborate with them to develop an action plan for success.
f. Consider the involvement of support networks valued by the individual students.
g. Understand that professional distance with students is appropriate, and any sexual or romantic relationship with students whether illegal in the state of practice is considered a grievous breach of ethics and is prohibited regardless of a student's age.
h. Consider the potential for harm before entering into a relationship with former students or one of their family members.

A.2. Confidentiality

Professional school counselors:

a. Inform individual students of the purposes, goals, techniques and rules of procedure under which they may receive counseling. Disclosure includes the limits of confidentiality in a developmentally appropriate manner. Informed consent requires competence on the part of students to understand the limits of confidentiality and therefore, can be difficult to obtain from students of a certain developmental level. Professionals are aware that even though every attempt is made to obtain informed consent it is not always possible and when needed will make counseling decisions on students' behalf.

b. Explain the limits of confidentiality in appropriate ways such as classroom guidance lessons, the student handbook, school counseling brochures, school Web site, verbal notice or other methods of student, school and community communication in addition to oral notification to individual students.

c. Recognize the complicated nature of confidentiality in schools and consider each case in context. Keep information confidential unless legal requirements demand that confidential information be revealed or a breach is required to prevent serious and foreseeable harm to the student. Serious and foreseeable harm is different for each minor in schools and is defined by students' developmental and chronological age, the setting, parental rights and the nature of the harm. School counselors consult with appropriate professionals when in doubt as to the validity of an exception.

d. Recognize their primary obligation for confidentiality is to the students but balance that obligation with an understanding of parents'/guardians' legal and inherent rights to be the guiding voice in their children's lives, especially in value-laden issues. Understand the need to balance students' ethical rights to make choices, their capacity to give consent or assent and parental or familial legal rights and responsibilities to protect these students and make decisions on their behalf.

e. Promote the autonomy and independence of students to the extent possible and use the most appropriate and least intrusive method of breach. The developmental age and the circumstances requiring the breach are considered and as appropriate students are engaged in a discussion about the method and timing of the breach.

f. In absence of state legislation expressly forbidding disclosure, consider the ethical responsibility to provide information to an identified third party who, by his/her relationship with the student, is at a high risk of contracting a disease that is commonly known to be communicable and fatal. Disclosure requires satisfaction of all of the following conditions:
 – Student identifies partner or the partner is highly identifiable
 – School counselor recommends the student notify partner and refrain from further high-risk behavior
 – Student refuses
 – School counselor informs the student of the intent to notify the partner

   - School counselor seeks legal consultation from the school district's legal representative in writing as to the legalities of informing the partner

g. Request of the court that disclosure not be required when the release of confidential information may potentially harm a student or the counseling relationship.

h. Protect the confidentiality of students' records and release personal data in accordance with prescribed federal and state laws and school policies including the laws within the Family Education Rights and Privacy Act (FERPA). Student information stored and transmitted electronically is treated with the same care as traditional student records. Recognize the vulnerability of confidentiality in electronic communications and only transmit sensitive information electronically in a way that is untraceable to students' identity. Critical information such as a student who has a history of suicidal ideation must be conveyed to the receiving school in a personal contact such as a phone call.

A.3. Academic, Career/College/Post-Secondary Access and Personal/Social Counseling Plans

Professional school counselors:

a. Provide students with a comprehensive school counseling program that parallels the ASCA National Model with emphasis on working jointly with all students to develop personal/social, academic and career goals.

b. Ensure equitable academic, career, post-secondary access and personal/social opportunities for all students through the use of data to help close achievement gaps and opportunity gaps.

c. Provide and advocate for individual students' career awareness, exploration and post-secondary plans supporting the students' right to choose from the wide array of options when they leave secondary education.

A.4. Dual Relationships

Professional school counselors:

a. Avoid dual relationships that might impair their objectivity and increase the risk of harm to students (e.g., counseling one's family members or the children of close friends or associates). If a dual relationship is unavoidable, the school counselor is responsible for taking action to eliminate or reduce the potential for harm to the student through use of safeguards, which might include informed consent, consultation, supervision and documentation.

b. Maintain appropriate professional distance with students at all times.

c. Avoid dual relationships with students through communication mediums such as social networking sites.

d. Avoid dual relationships with school personnel that might infringe on the integrity of the school counselor/student relationship.

A.5. Appropriate Referrals

Professional school counselors:

a. Make referrals when necessary or appropriate to outside resources for student and/or family support. Appropriate referrals may necessitate informing both parents/guardians and students of applicable resources and making proper plans for transitions with minimal interruption of services. Students retain the right to discontinue the counseling relationship at any time.

b. Help educate about and prevent personal and social concerns for all students within the school counselor's scope of education and competence and make necessary referrals when the counseling needs are beyond the individual school counselor's education and training. Every attempt is made to find appropriate specialized resources for clinical therapeutic topics that are difficult or inappropriate to address in a school setting such as eating disorders, sexual trauma, chemical dependency and other addictions needing sustained clinical duration or assistance.

c. Request a release of information signed by the student and/or parents/ guardians when attempting to develop a collaborative relationship with other service providers assigned to the student.

d. Develop a reasonable method of termination of counseling when it becomes apparent that counseling assistance is no longer needed or a referral is necessary to better meet the student's needs.

A.6. Group Work

Professional school counselors:

a. Screen prospective group members and maintain an awareness of participants' needs, appropriate fit and personal goals in relation to the group's intention and focus. The school counselor takes reasonable precautions to protect members from physical and psychological harm resulting from interaction within the group.
b. Recognize that best practice is to notify the parents/guardians of children participating in small groups.
c. Establish clear expectations in the group setting, and clearly state that confidentiality in group counseling cannot be guaranteed. Given the developmental and chronological ages of minors in schools, recognize the tenuous nature of confidentiality for minors renders some topics inappropriate for group work in a school setting.
d. Provide necessary follow up with group members, and document proceedings as appropriate.
e. Develop professional competencies, and maintain appropriate education, training and supervision in group facilitation and any topics specific to the group.
f. Facilitate group work that is brief and solution-focused, working with a variety of academic, career, college and personal/social issues.

A.7. Danger to Self or Others

Professional school counselors:

a. Inform parents/guardians and/or appropriate authorities when a student poses a danger to self or others. This is to be done after careful deliberation and consultation with other counseling professionals.
b. Report risk assessments to parents when they underscore the need to act on behalf of a child at risk; never negate a risk of harm as students sometimes deceive in order to avoid further scrutiny and/or parental notification.
c. Understand the legal and ethical liability for releasing a student who is in danger to self or others without proper and necessary support for that student.

A.8. Student Records

Professional school counselors:

a. Maintain and secure records necessary for rendering professional services to the student as required by laws, regulations, institutional procedures and confidentiality guidelines.

b. Keep sole-possession records or individual student case notes separate from students' educational records in keeping with state laws.

c. Recognize the limits of sole-possession records and understand these records are a memory aid for the creator and in absence of privileged communication may be subpoenaed and may become educational records when they are shared or are accessible to others in either verbal or written form or when they include information other than professional opinion or personal observations.

d. Establish a reasonable timeline for purging sole-possession records or case notes. Suggested guidelines include shredding sole possession records when the student transitions to the next level, transfers to another school or graduates. Apply careful discretion and deliberation before destroying sole-possession records that may be needed by a court of law such as notes on child abuse, suicide, sexual harassment or violence.

e. Understand and abide by the Family Education Rights and Privacy Act (FERPA, 1974), which safeguards student's records and allows parents to have a voice in what and how information is shared with others regarding their child's educational records.

A.9. Evaluation, Assessment and Interpretation

Professional school counselors:

a. Adhere to all professional standards regarding selecting, administering and interpreting assessment measures and only utilize assessment measures that are within the scope of practice for school counselors and for which they are trained and competent.

b. Consider confidentiality issues when utilizing evaluative or assessment instruments and electronically based programs.

c. Consider the developmental age, language skills and level of competence of the student taking the assessments before assessments are given.

d. Provide interpretation of the nature, purposes, results and potential impact of assessment/evaluation measures in language the students can understand.

e. Monitor the use of assessment results and interpretations, and take reasonable steps to prevent others from misusing the information.

f. Use caution when utilizing assessment techniques, making evaluations and interpreting the performance of populations not represented in the norm group on which an instrument is standardized.

g. Assess the effectiveness of their program in having an impact on students' academic, career and personal/social development through accountability measures especially examining efforts to close achievement, opportunity and attainment gaps.

A.10. Technology

Professional school counselors:

a. Promote the benefits of and clarify the limitations of various appropriate technological applications. Professional school counselors promote technological applications (1) that are appropriate for students' individual needs, (2) that students understand how to use and (3) for which follow-up counseling assistance is provided.

b. Advocate for equal access to technology for all students, especially those historically underserved.

c. Take appropriate and reasonable measures for maintaining confidentiality of student information and educational records stored or transmitted through the use of computers, facsimile machines, telephones, voicemail, answering machines and other electronic or computer technology.

d. Understand the intent of FERPA and its impact on sharing electronic student records.

e. Consider the extent to which cyberbullying is interfering with students' educational process and base guidance curriculum and intervention programming for this pervasive and potentially dangerous problem on research-based and best practices.

A.11. Student Peer Support Program

Professional school counselors:

   a. Have unique responsibilities when working with peer-helper or student-assistance programs and safeguard the welfare of students participating in peer-to-peer programs under their direction.
   b. Are ultimately responsible for appropriate training and supervision for students serving as peer-support individuals in their school counseling programs.

B. RESPONSIBILITIES TO PARENTS/GUARDIANS

B.1. Parent Rights and Responsibilities

Professional school counselors:

   a. Respect the rights and responsibilities of parents/guardians for their children and endeavor to establish, as appropriate, a collaborative relationship with parents/guardians to facilitate students' maximum development.
   b. Adhere to laws, local guidelines and ethical standards of practice when assisting parents/guardians experiencing family difficulties interfering with the student's effectiveness and welfare.
   c. Are sensitive to diversity among families and recognize that all parents/guardians, custodial and noncustodial, are vested with certain rights and responsibilities for their children's welfare by virtue of their role and according to law.
   d. Inform parents of the nature of counseling services provided in the school setting.
   e. Adhere to the FERPA act regarding disclosure of student information.
   f. Work to establish, as appropriate, collaborative relationships with parents/guardians to best serve student.

B.2. Parents/Guardians and Confidentiality

Professional school counselors:

   a. Inform parents/guardians of the school counselor's role to include the confidential nature of the counseling relationship between the counselor and student.

b. Recognize that working with minors in a school setting requires school counselors to collaborate with students' parents/guardians to the extent possible.

c. Respect the confidentiality of parents/guardians to the extent that is reasonable to protect the best interest of the student being counseled.

d. Provide parents/guardians with accurate, comprehensive and relevant information in an objective and caring manner, as is appropriate and consistent with ethical responsibilities to the student.

e. Make reasonable efforts to honor the wishes of parents/guardians concerning information regarding the student unless a court order expressly forbids the involvement of a parent(s). In cases of divorce or separation, school counselors exercise a good-faith effort to keep both parents informed, maintaining focus on the student and avoiding supporting one parent over another in divorce proceedings.

C. RESPONSIBILITIES TO COLLEAGUES AND PROFESSIONAL ASSOCIATES

C.1. Professional Relationships

Professional school counselors, the school counseling program director/site supervisor and the school counselor educator:

a. Establish and maintain professional relationships with faculty, staff and administration to facilitate an optimum counseling program.

b. Treat colleagues with professional respect, courtesy and fairness.

c. Recognize that teachers, staff and administrators who are high functioning in the personal and social development skills can be powerful allies in supporting student success. School counselors work to develop relationships with all faculty and staff in order to advantage students.

d. Are aware of and utilize related professionals, organizations and other resources to whom the student may be referred.

C.2. Sharing Information with Other Professionals

Professional school counselors:

a. Promote awareness and adherence to appropriate guidelines regarding confidentiality, the distinction between public and private information and staff consultation.

b. Provide professional personnel with accurate, objective, concise and meaningful data necessary to adequately evaluate, counsel and assist the student.

c. Secure parental consent and develop clear agreements with other mental health professionals when a student is receiving services from another counselor or other mental health professional in order to avoid confusion and conflict for the student and parents/guardians.

d. Understand about the "release of information" process and parental rights in sharing information and attempt to establish a cooperative and collaborative relationship with other professionals to benefit students.

e. Recognize the powerful role of ally that faculty and administration who function high in personal/social development skills can play in supporting students in stress, and carefully filter confidential information to give these allies what they "need to know" in order to advantage the student. Consultation with other members of the school counseling profession is helpful in determining need-to-know information. The primary focus and obligation is always on the student when it comes to sharing confidential information.

f. Keep appropriate records regarding individual students, and develop a plan for transferring those records to another professional school counselor should the need occur. This documentation transfer will protect the confidentiality and benefit the needs of the student for whom the records are written.

C.3. Collaborating and Educating Around the Role of the School Counselor

The school counselor, school counseling program supervisor/ director and school counselor educator:

a. Share the role of the school counseling program in ensuring data-driven academic, career/college and personal/social success competencies for every student, resulting in specific outcomes/indicators with all stakeholders.

b. Broker services internal and external to the schools to help ensure every student receives the benefits of a school counseling program and specific academic, career/college and personal/social competencies.

D. RESPONSIBILITIES TO SCHOOL, COMMUNITIES AND FAMILIES

D.1. Responsibilities to the School

Professional school counselors:

a. Support and protect students' best interest against any infringement of their educational program.
b. Inform appropriate officials, in accordance with school policy, of conditions that may be potentially disruptive or damaging to the school's mission, personnel and property while honoring the confidentiality between the student and the school counselor.
c. Are knowledgeable and supportive of their school's mission, and connect their program to the school's mission.
d. Delineate and promote the school counselor's role, and function as a student advocate in meeting the needs of those served. School counselors will notify appropriate officials of systemic conditions that may limit or curtail their effectiveness in providing programs and services.
e. Accept employment only for positions for which they are qualified by education, training, supervised experience, state and national professional credentials and appropriate professional experience.
f. Advocate that administrators hire only qualified, appropriately trained and competent individuals for professional school counseling positions.
g. Assist in developing: (1) curricular and environmental conditions appropriate for the school and community; (2) educational procedures and programs to meet students' developmental needs; (3) a systematic evaluation process for comprehensive, developmental, standards-based school counseling programs, services and personnel; and (4) a data-driven evaluation process guiding the comprehensive, developmental school counseling program and service delivery.

D.2. Responsibility to the Community

Professional school counselors:

a. Collaborate with community agencies, organizations and individuals in students' best interest and without regard to personal reward or remuneration.

b. Extend their influence and opportunity to deliver a comprehensive school counseling program to all students by collaborating with community resources for student success.

c. Promote equity for all students through community resources.

d. Are careful not to use their professional role as a school counselor to benefit any type of private therapeutic or consultative practice in which they might be involved outside of the school setting.

E. RESPONSIBILITIES TO SELF

E.1. Professional Competence

Professional school counselors:

a. Function within the boundaries of individual professional competence and accept responsibility for the consequences of their actions.

b. Monitor emotional and physical health and practice wellness to ensure optimal effectiveness. Seek physical or mental health referrals when needed to ensure competence at all times.

c. Monitor personal responsibility and recognize the high standard of care a professional in this critical position of trust must maintain on and off the job and are cognizant of and refrain from activity that may lead to inadequate professional services or diminish their effectiveness with school community members Professional and personal growth are ongoing throughout the counselor's career.

d. Strive through personal initiative to stay abreast of current research and to maintain professional competence in advocacy, teaming and collaboration, culturally competent counseling and school counseling program coordination, knowledge and use of technology, leadership, and equity assessment using data.

e. Ensure a variety of regular opportunities for participating in and facilitating professional development for self and other educators and school counselors through continuing education opportunities annually including: attendance at professional school counseling conferences; reading *Professional School Counseling* journal articles; facilitating workshops for education staff on issues school counselors are uniquely positioned to provide.

f. Enhance personal self-awareness, professional effectiveness and ethical practice by regularly attending presentations on ethical decision-making.

Effective school counselors will seek supervision when ethical or professional questions arise in their practice.

g. Maintain current membership in professional associations to ensure ethical and best practices.

E.2. Multicultural and Social Justice Advocacy and Leadership

Professional school counselors:

a. Monitor and expand personal multicultural and social justice advocacy awareness, knowledge and skills. School counselors strive for exemplary cultural competence by ensuring personal beliefs or values are not imposed on students or other stakeholders.

b. Develop competencies in how prejudice, power and various forms of oppression, such as ableism, ageism, classism, familyism, genderism, heterosexism, immigrationism, linguicism, racism, religionism and sexism, affect self, students and all stakeholders.

c. Acquire educational, consultation and training experiences to improve awareness, knowledge, skills and effectiveness in working with diverse populations: ethnic/racial status, age, economic status, special needs, ESL or ELL, immigration status, sexual orientation, gender, gender identity/expression, family type, religious/spiritual identity and appearance.

d. Affirm the multiple cultural and linguistic identities of every student and all stakeholders. Advocate for equitable school and school counseling program policies and practices for every student and all stakeholders including use of translators and bilingual/multilingual school counseling program materials that represent all languages used by families in the school community, and advocate for appropriate accommodations and accessibility for students with disabilities.

e. Use inclusive and culturally responsible language in all forms of communication.

f. Provide regular workshops and written/digital information to families to increase understanding, collaborative two-way communication and a welcoming school climate between families and the school to promote increased student achievement.

g. Work as advocates and leaders in the school to create equity-based school counseling programs that help close any achievement, opportunity and attainment gaps that deny all students the chance to pursue their educational goals.

F. RESPONSIBILITIES TO THE PROFESSION

F.1. Professionalism

Professional school counselors:

a. Accept the policies and procedures for handling ethical violations as a result of maintaining membership in the American School Counselor Association.
b. Conduct themselves in such a manner as to advance individual ethical practice and the profession.
c. Conduct appropriate research, and report findings in a manner consistent with acceptable educational and psychological research practices. School counselors advocate for the protection of individual students' identities when using data for research or program planning.
d. Seek institutional and parent/guardian consent before administering any research, and maintain security of research records.
e. Adhere to ethical standards of the profession, other official policy statements, such as ASCA's position statements, role statement and the ASCA National Model and relevant statutes established by federal, state and local governments, and when these are in conflict work responsibly for change.
f. Clearly distinguish between statements and actions made as a private individual and those made as a representative of the school counseling profession.
g. Do not use their professional position to recruit or gain clients, consultees for their private practice or to seek and receive unjustified personal gains, unfair advantage, inappropriate relationships or unearned goods or services.

F.2. Contribution to the Profession

Professional school counselors:

a. Actively participate in professional associations and share results and best practices in assessing, implementing and annually evaluating the outcomes of data-driven school counseling programs with measurable academic, career/college and personal/social competencies for every student.

b. Provide support, consultation and mentoring to novice professionals.

c. Have a responsibility to read and abide by the ASCA Ethical Standards and adhere to the applicable laws and regulations.

F.3. Supervision of School Counselor Candidates Pursuing Practicum and Internship Experiences:

Professional school counselors:

a. Provide support for appropriate experiences in academic, career, college access and personal/social counseling for school counseling interns.

b. Ensure school counselor candidates have experience in developing, implementing and evaluating a data-driven school counseling program model, such as the ASCA National Model.

c. Ensure the school counseling practicum and internship have specific, measurable service delivery, foundation, management and accountability systems.

d. Ensure school counselor candidates maintain appropriate liability insurance for the duration of the school counseling practicum and internship experiences.

e. Ensure a site visit is completed by a school counselor education faculty member for each practicum or internship student, preferably when both the school counselor trainee and site supervisor are present.

F.4 Collaboration and Education about School Counselors and School Counseling Programs with other Professionals

School counselors and school counseling program directors/supervisors collaborate with special educators, school nurses, school social workers, school psychologists, college counselors/admissions officers, physical therapists, occupational therapists and speech pathologists to advocate for optimal services for students and all other stakeholders.

G. MAINTENANCE OF STANDARDS

Professional school counselors are expected to maintain ethical behavior at all times.

G.1. When there exists serious doubt as to the ethical behavior of a colleague(s) the following procedure may serve as a guide:

1. The school counselor should consult confidentially with a professional colleague to discuss the nature of a complaint to see if the professional colleague views the situation as an ethical violation.
2. When feasible, the school counselor should directly approach the colleague whose behavior is in question to discuss the complaint and seek resolution.
3. The school counselor should keep documentation of all the steps taken.
4. If resolution is not forthcoming at the personal level, the school counselor shall utilize the channels established within the school, school district, the state school counseling association and ASCA's Ethics Committee.
5. If the matter still remains unresolved, referral for review and appropriate action should be made to the Ethics Committees in the following sequence:
   - State school counselor association
   - American School Counselor Association
6. The ASCA Ethics Committee is responsible for:
   - Educating and consulting with the membership regarding ethical standards
   - Periodically reviewing and recommending changes in code
   - Receiving and processing questions to clarify the application of such standards. Questions must be submitted in writing to the ASCA Ethics Committee chair.
   - Handling complaints of alleged violations of the ASCA Ethical Standards for School Counselors. At the national level, complaints should be submitted in writing to the ASCA Ethics Committee, c/o the Executive Director, American School Counselor Association, 1101 King St., Suite 625, Alexandria, VA 22314.

G.2. **When school counselors are forced to work in situations or abide by policies that do not reflect the ethics of the profession, the school counselor works responsibly through the correct channels to try and remedy the condition.**

G.3. **When faced with any ethical dilemma school counselors, school counseling program directors/ supervisors and school counselor educators use an ethical decision-making model such as Solutions to Ethical Problems in Schools (STEPS) (Stone, 2001):**

1. Define the problem emotionally and intellectually

2. Apply the ASCA Ethical Standards and the law

3. Consider the students' chronological and developmental levels

4. Consider the setting, parental rights and minors' rights

5. Apply the moral principles

6. Determine Your potential courses of action and their consequences

7. Evaluate the selected action

8. Consult

9. Implement the course of action

Appendix II: ASCA National Standards for School Counseling Programs*

Academic Development

ASCA National Standards for academic development guide school counseling programs to implement strategies and activities to support and maximize each student's ability to learn.

Standard A: Students will acquire the attitudes, knowledge and skills that contribute to effective learning in school and across the life span.

A:A1 Improve Academic Self-concept

A:A1.1 Articulate feelings of competence and confidence as learners
A:A1.2 Display a positive interest in learning
A:A1.3 Take pride in work and achievement
A:A1.4 Accept mistakes as essential to the learning process
A:A1.5 Identify attitudes and behaviors that lead to successful learning

A:A2 Acquire Skills for Improving Learning

A:A2.1 Apply time-management and task-management skills

A:A2.2 Demonstrate how effort and persistence positively affect learning

A:A2.3 Use communications skills to know when and how to ask for help when needed

A:A2.4 Apply knowledge and learning styles to positively influence school performance

A:A3 Achieve School Success

A:A3.1 Take responsibility for their actions

A:A3.2 Demonstrate the ability to work independently, as well as the ability to work cooperatively with other students

A:A3.3 Develop a broad range of interests and abilities

A:A3.4 Demonstrate dependability, productivity and initiative

A:A3.5 Share knowledge

Standard B: Students will complete school with the academic preparation essential to choose from a wide range of substantial post-secondary options, including college.

A:B1 Improve Learning

A:B1.1 Demonstrate the motivation to achieve individual potential

A:B1.2 Learn and apply critical-thinking skills

A:B1.3 Apply the study skills necessary for academic success at each level

A:B1.4 Seek information and support from faculty, staff, family and peers

A:B1.5 Organize and apply academic information from a variety of sources

A:B1.6 Use knowledge of learning styles to positively influence school performance

A:B1.7 Become a self-directed and independent learner

A:B2 Plan to Achieve Goals

A:B2.1 Establish challenging academic goals in elementary, middle/jr. high and high school

A:B2.2 Use assessment results in educational planning

A:B2.3 Develop and implement annual plan of study to maximize academic ability and achievement

A:B2.4 Apply knowledge of aptitudes and interests to goal setting

A:B2.5 Use problem-solving and decision-making skills to assess progress toward educational goals

A:B2.6 Understand the relationship between classroom performance and success in school

A:B2.7 Identify post-secondary options consistent with interests, achievement, aptitude and abilities

Standard C: Students will understand the relationship of academics to the world of work and to life at home and in the community.

A:C1 Relate School to Life Experiences

A:C1.1 Demonstrate the ability to balance school, studies, extracurricular activities, leisure time and family life

A:C1.2 Seek co-curricular and community experiences to enhance the school experience

A:C1.3 Understand the relationship between learning and work

A:C1.4 Demonstrate an understanding of the value of lifelong learning as essential to seeking, obtaining and maintaining life goals

A:C1.5 Understand that school success is the preparation to make the transition from student to community member

A:C1.6 Understand how school success and academic achievement enhance future career and vocational opportunities

Career Development

ASCA National Standards for career development guide school counseling programs to provide the foundation for the acquisition of skills, attitudes and knowledge that enable students to make a successful transition from school to the world of work, and from job to job across the life span.

Standard A: Students will acquire the skills to investigate the world of work in relation to knowledge of self and to make informed career decisions.

C:A1 Develop Career Awareness

C:A1.1   Develop skills to locate, evaluate and interpret career information
C:A1.2   Learn about the variety of traditional and nontraditional occupations
C:A1.3. Develop an awareness of personal abilities, skills, interests and motivations
C:A1.4   Learn how to interact and work cooperatively in teams
C:A1.5   Learn to make decisions
C:A1.6   Learn how to set goals
C:A1.7   Understand the importance of planning
C:A1.8   Pursue and develop competency in areas of interest
C:A1.9   Develop hobbies and vocational interests
C:A1.10 Balance between work and leisure time

C:A2 Develop Employment Readiness

C:A2.1 Acquire employability skills such as working on a team, problem-solving and organizational skills
C:A2.2 Apply job readiness skills to seek employment opportunities
C:A2.3 Demonstrate knowledge about the changing workplace
C:A2.4 Learn about the rights and responsibilities of employers and employees
C:A2.5 Learn to respect individual uniqueness in the workplace
C:A2.6 Learn how to write a résumé
C:A2.7 Develop a positive attitude toward work and learning
C:A2.8 Understand the importance of responsibility, dependability, punctuality, integrity and effort in the workplace
C:A2.9 Utilize time- and task-management skills

Standard B: Students will employ strategies to achieve future career goals with success and satisfaction.

C:B1 Acquire Career Information

C:B1.1 Apply decision-making skills to career planning, course selection and career transition
C:B1.2 Identify personal skills, interests and abilities and relate them to current career choice
C:B1.3 Demonstrate knowledge of the career-planning process

C:B1.4 Know the various ways in which occupations can be classified

C:B1.5 Use research and information resources to obtain career information

C:B1.6 Learn to use the Internet to access career-planning information

C:B1.7 Describe traditional and nontraditional career choices and how they relate to career choice

C:B1.8 Understand how changing economic and societal needs influence employment trends and future training

C:B2 Identify Career Goals

C:B2.1 Demonstrate awareness of the education and training needed to achieve career goals

C:B2.2 Assess and modify their educational plan to support career

C:B2.3 Use employability and job readiness skills in internship, mentoring, shadowing and/or other work experience

C:B2.4 Select course work that is related to career interests

C:B2.5 Maintain a career-planning portfolio

Standard C: Students will understand the relationship between personal qualities, education, training and the world of work.

C:C1 Acquire Knowledge to Achieve Career Goals

C:C1.1 Understand the relationship between educational achievement and career success

C:C1.2 Explain how work can help to achieve personal success and satisfaction

C:C1.3 Identify personal preferences and interests influencing career choice and success

C:C1.4 Understand that the changing workplace requires lifelong learning and acquiring new skills

C:C1.5 Describe the effect of work on lifestyle

C:C1.6 Understand the importance of equity and access in career choice

C:C1.7 Understand that work is an important and satisfying means of personal expression

C:C2 Apply Skills to Achieve Career Goals

C:C2.1 Demonstrate how interests, abilities and achievement relate to achieving personal, social, educational and career goals

C:C2.2 Learn how to use conflict management skills with peers and adults

C:C2.3 Learn to work cooperatively with others as a team member

C:C2.4 Apply academic and employment readiness skills in work-based learning situations such as internships, shadowing and/or mentoring experiences

Personal/Social Development

ASCA National Standards for personal/social development guide school counseling programs to provide the foundation for personal and social growth as students progress through school and into adulthood.

Standard A: Students will acquire the knowledge, attitudes and interpersonal skills to help them understand and respect self and others.

PS:A1 Acquire Self-knowledge

PS:A1.1   Develop positive attitudes toward self as a unique and worthy person

PS:A1.2   Identify values, attitudes and beliefs

PS:A1.3   Learn the goal-setting process

PS:A1.4   Understand change is a part of growth

PS:A1.5   Identify and express feelings

PS:A1.6   Distinguish between appropriate and inappropriate behavior

PS:A1.7   Recognize personal boundaries, rights and privacy needs

PS:A1.8   Understand the need for self-control and how to practice it

PS:A1.9   Demonstrate cooperative behavior in groups

PS:A1.10 Identify personal strengths and assets

PS:A1.11 Identify and discuss changing personal and social roles

PS:A1.12 Identify and recognize changing family roles

PS:A2 Acquire Interpersonal Skills

PS:A2.1 Recognize that everyone has rights and responsibilities

PS:A2.2 Respect alternative points of view

PS:A2.3 Recognize, accept, respect and appreciate individual differences

PS:A2.4 Recognize, accept and appreciate ethnic and cultural diversity

PS:A2.5 Recognize and respect differences in various family configurations

PS:A2.6 Use effective communications skills

PS:A2.7 Know that communication involves speaking, listening and nonverbal behavior

PS:A2.8 Learn how to make and keep friends

Standard B: Students will make decisions, set goals and take necessary action to achieve goals.

PS:B1 Self-knowledge Application

PS:B1.1 Use a decision-making and problem-solving model

PS:B1.2 Understand consequences of decisions and choices

PS:B1.3 Identify alternative solutions to a problem

PS:B1.4 Develop effective coping skills for dealing with problems

PS:B1.5 Demonstrate when, where and how to seek help for solving problems and making decisions

PS:B1.6 Know how to apply conflict resolution skills

PS:B1.7 Demonstrate a respect and appreciation for individual and cultural differences

PS:B1.8 Know when peer pressure is influencing a decision

PS:B1.9 Identify long- and short-term goals

PS:B1.10 Identify alternative ways of achieving goals

PS:B1.11 Use persistence and perseverance in acquiring knowledge and skills

PS:B1.12 Develop an action plan to set and achieve realistic goals

Standard C: Students will understand safety and survival skills.

PS:C1 Acquire Personal Safety Skills

PS:C1.1 Demonstrate knowledge of personal information (i.e., telephone number, home address, emergency contact)

PS:C1.2 Learn about the relationship between rules, laws, safety and the protection of rights of the individual

PS:C1.3 Learn about the differences between appropriate and inappropriate physical contact

PS:C1.4 Demonstrate the ability to set boundaries, rights and personal privacy

PS:C1.5 Differentiate between situations requiring peer support and situations requiring adult professional help

PS:C1.6 Identify resource people in the school and community, and know how to seek their help

PS:C1.7 Apply effective problem-solving and decision-making skills to make safe and healthy choices

PS:C1.8 Learn about the emotional and physical dangers of substance use and abuse

PS:C1.9 Learn how to cope with peer pressure

PS:C1.10 Learn techniques for managing stress and conflict

PS:C1.11 Learn coping skills for managing life events

Appendix III: ASCA School Counselor Competencies*

History and Purpose

The American School Counselor Association (ASCA) supports school counselors' efforts to help students focus on academic, personal/social and career development so they achieve success in school and are prepared to lead fulfilling lives as responsible members of society. In recent years, the ASCA leadership has recognized the need for a more unified vision of the school counseling profession. "The ASCA National Model: A Framework for School Counseling Programs" was a landmark document that provided a mechanism with which school counselors and school counseling teams could design, coordinate, implement, manage and enhance their programs for students' success. The ASCA National Model® provides a framework for the program components, the school counselor's role in implementation and the underlying philosophies of leadership, advocacy, collaboration and systemic change.

The School Counselor Competencies continue the effort for a unified vision by outlining the knowledge, attitudes and skills that ensure school counselors are equipped to meet the rigorous demands of our profession and the needs of our Pre-K-12 students. These competencies are necessary to better ensure that our future school counselor workforce will be able to continue to make a positive difference in the lives of students.

Development of the Competencies

The development of the School Counselor Competencies document was a highly collaborative effort among many members of the school counseling profession.

A group of school counseling professionals that included practicing school counselors, district school counseling supervisors and counselor educators from across the country met in January 2007 to discuss ways to ensure that school counselor education programs adequately train and prepare future school counselors to design and implement comprehensive school counseling programs. The group agreed that the logical first task should be the development of a set of competencies necessary and sufficient to be an effective professional school counselor.

The group created a general outline of competencies and asked ASCA to form a task force to develop draft school counselor competencies supporting the ASCA National Model. The task force used sample competencies from states, universities and other organizations to develop a first draft, which was presented to the whole group for feedback. After comments and revisions were incorporated, the revised draft was released for public review and comment. Revisions through the public comment were incorporated to develop the final version. The school counselor competencies document is unique in several ways. First, this set of competencies is organized around and consistent with the ASCA National Model. Second, the competencies are comprehensive in that they include skills, knowledge and attitudes necessary for meritoriously performing the range of school counselor responsibilities (e.g., counseling, coordinating, consulting, etc.) in all four components of comprehensive school counseling programs: foundation, management, delivery and accountability. These competencies have been identified as those that will equip new and experienced school counselors with the skills to establish, maintain and enhance a comprehensive, developmental, results-based school counseling program addressing academic achievement, personal and social development and career planning.

Applications

ASCA views these competencies as being applicable along a continuum of areas. For instance, school counselor education programs may use the competencies as benchmarks for ensuring students graduate with the knowledge, skills and dispositions needed for developing comprehensive school counseling programs. Professional school counselors could use the School Counselor Competencies as a checklist to self-evaluate their own competencies and, as a result, formulate an appropriate professional development plan. School administrators may find these competencies useful as a guide for seeking and hiring highly competent school counselors and for developing meaningful school counselor performance evaluations. Also, the School Counselor Competencies include the necessary technological competencies needed for performing effectively and efficiently in the 21st century.

I. School Counseling Programs

School counselors should possess the knowledge, abilities, skills and attitudes necessary to plan, organize, implement and evaluate a comprehensive, developmental, results-based school counseling program that aligns with the ASCA National Model.

I-A: KNOWLEDGE

ASCA's position statement, The Professional School Counselor and School Counseling Preparation Programs, states that school counselors should articulate and demonstrate an understanding of:

I-A-1. The organizational structure and governance of the American educational system as well as cultural, political and social influences on current educational practices

I-A-2. The organizational structure and qualities of an effective school counseling program that aligns with the ASCA National Model

I-A-3. Impediments to student learning and use of advocacy and data-driven school counseling practices to act effectively in closing the achievement/opportunity gap

I-A-4. Leadership principles and theories

I-A-5. Individual counseling, group counseling and classroom guidance programs ensuring equitable access to resources that promote academic achievement; personal, social and emotional development; and career development including the identification of appropriate post-secondary education for every student

I-A-6. Collaborations with stakeholders such as parents and guardians, teachers, administrators and community leaders to create learning environments that promote educational equity and success for every student

I-A-7. Legal, ethical and professional issues in pre-K-12 schools

I-A-8. Developmental theory, learning theories, social justice theory, multiculturalism, counseling theories and career counseling theories

I-A-9. The continuum of mental health services, including prevention and intervention strategies to enhance student success

I-B: ABILITIES AND SKILLS

An effective school counselor is able to accomplish measurable objectives demonstrating the following abilities and skills.

I-B-1. Plans, organizes, implements and evaluates a school counseling program aligning with the ASCA National Model

I-B-1a. Creates a vision statement examining the professional and personal competencies and qualities a school counselor should possess

I-B-1b. Describes the rationale for a comprehensive school counseling program

I-B-1c. Articulates the school counseling themes of advocacy, leadership, collaboration and systemic change, which are critical to a successful school counseling program.

I-B-1d. Describes, defines and identifies the qualities of an effective school counseling program

I-B-1e. Describes the benefits of a comprehensive school counseling program for all stakeholders, including students, parents, teachers, administrators, school boards, department of education, school counselors, counselor educators, community stakeholders and business leaders

I-B-1f. Describes the history of school counseling to create a context for the current state of the profession and comprehensive school counseling programs

I-B-1g. Uses technology effectively and efficiently to plan, organize, implement and evaluate the comprehensive school counseling program

I-B-1h. Demonstrates multicultural, ethical and professional competencies in planning, organizing, implementing and evaluating the comprehensive school counseling program

I-B-2. Serves as a leader in the school and community to promote and support student success

I-B-2a. Understands and defines leadership and its role in comprehensive school counseling programs

I-B-2b. Identifies and applies a model of leadership to a comprehensive school counseling program

I-B-2c. Identifies and demonstrates professional and personal qualities and skills of effective leaders

I-B-2d. Identifies and applies components of the ASCA National Model requiring leadership, such as an advisory council, management system and accountability

I-B-2e. Creates a plan to challenge the non-counseling tasks that are assigned to school counselors

I-B-3. Advocates for student success

I-B-3a. Understands and defines advocacy and its role in comprehensive school counseling programs

I-B-3b. Identifies and demonstrates benefits of advocacy with school and community stakeholders

I-B-3c. Describes school counselor advocacy competencies, which include dispositions, knowledge and skills

I-B-3d. Reviews advocacy models and develops a personal advocacy plan

I-B-3e. Understands the process for development of policy and procedures at the building, district, state and national levels

I-B-4. Collaborates with parents, teachers, administrators, community leaders and other stakeholders to promote and support student success

I-B-4a. Defines collaboration and its role in comprehensive school counseling programs

I-B-4b. Identifies and applies models of collaboration for effective use in a school counseling program and understands the similarities and differences between consultation, collaboration and counseling and coordination strategies.

I-B-4c. Creates statements or other documents delineating the various roles of student service providers, such as school social worker, school psychologist, school nurse, and identifies best practices for collaborating to affect student success

I-B-4d. Understands and knows how to apply a consensus-building process to foster agreement in a group

I-B-4e. Understands how to facilitate group meetings to effectively and efficiently meet group goals

I-B-5. Acts as a systems change agent to create an environment promoting and supporting student success

    I-B-5a. Defines and understands system change and its role in comprehensive school counseling programs

    I-B-5b. Develops a plan to deal with personal (emotional and cognitive) and institutional resistance impeding the change process

    I-B-5c. Understands the impact of school, district and state educational policies, procedures and practices supporting and/or impeding student success

I-C: ATTITUDES

School counselors believe:

I-C-1. Every student can learn, and every student can succeed

I-C-2. Every student should have access to and opportunity for a high-quality education

1-C-3. Every student should graduate from high school and be prepared for employment or college and other postsecondary education

I-C-4. Every student should have access to a school counseling program

I-C-5. Effective school counseling is a collaborative process involving school counselors, students, parents, teachers, administrators, community leaders and other stakeholders

I-C-6. School counselors can and should be leaders in the school and district

I-C-7. The effectiveness of school counseling programs should be measurable using process, perception and results data

II: Foundations

School counselors should possess the knowledge, abilities, skills and attitudes necessary to establish the foundations of a school counseling program aligning with the ASCA National Model.

II-A: KNOWLEDGE

School counselors should articulate and demonstrate an understanding of:

II-A-1. Beliefs and philosophy of the school counseling program that align with current school improvement and student success initiatives at the school, district and state level

II-A-2. Educational systems, philosophies and theories and current trends in education, including federal and state legislation

II-A-3. Learning theories

II-A-4. History and purpose of school counseling, including traditional and transformed roles of school counselors

II-A-5. Human development theories and developmental issues affecting student success

II-A-6. District, state and national student standards and competencies, including ASCA Student Competencies

II-A-7. Legal and ethical standards and principles of the school counseling profession and educational systems, including district and building policies

II-A-8. Three domains of academic achievement, career planning, and personal and social development

II-B: ABILITIES AND SKILLS

An effective school counselor is able to accomplish measurable objectives demonstrating the following abilities and skills.

II-B-1. Develops the beliefs and philosophy of the school counseling program that aligns with current school improvement and student success initiatives at the school, district and state level

II-B-1a. Examines personal, district and state beliefs, assumptions and philosophies about student success, specifically what they should know and be able to do

II-B-1b. Demonstrates knowledge of a school's particular educational philosophy and mission

II-B-1c. Conceptualizes and writes a personal philosophy about students, families, teachers, school counseling programs and the educational process consistent with the school's educational philosophy and mission

II-B-2. Develops a school counseling mission statement aligning with the school, district and state mission.

II-B-2a. Critiques a school district mission statement and identifies or writes a mission statement aligning with beliefs

II-B-2b. Writes a school counseling mission statement that is specific, concise, clear and comprehensive, describing a school counseling program's purpose and a vision of the program's benefits every student

II-B-2c. Communicates the philosophy and mission of the school counseling program to all appropriate stakeholders

II-B-3. Uses student standards, such as ASCA Student Competencies, and district or state standards, to drive the implementation of a comprehensive school counseling program

II-B-3a. Crosswalks the ASCA Student Competencies with other appropriate standards

II-B-3b. Prioritizes student standards that align with the school's goals

II-B-4. Applies the ethical standards and principles of the school counseling profession and adheres to the legal aspects of the role of the school counselor

II-B-4a. Practices ethical principles of the school counseling profession in accordance with the ASCA Ethical Standards for School Counselors

II-B-4b. Understands the legal and ethical nature of working in a pluralistic, multicultural, and technological society.

II-B-4c. Understands and practices in accordance with school district policy and local, state and federal statutory requirements.

II-B-4d. Understands the unique legal and ethical nature of working with minor students in a school setting.

II-B-4e. Advocates responsibly for school board policy, local, state and federal statutory requirements that are in the best interests of students

II-B-4f. Resolves ethical dilemmas by employing an ethical decision-making model appropriate to work in schools.

II-B-4g. Models ethical behavior

II-B-4h. Continuously engages in professional development and uses resources to inform and guide ethical and legal work

II-B-4i. Practices within the ethical and statutory limits of confidentiality

II-B-4j. Continually seeks consultation and supervision to guide legal and ethical decision making and to recognize and resolve ethical dilemmas

II-B-4k. Understands and applies an ethical and legal obligation not only to students but to parents, administration and teachers

II-C: ATTITUDES

School counselors believe:

II-C-1. School counseling is an organized program for every student and not a series of services provided only to students in need

II-C-2. School counseling programs should be an integral component of student success and the overall mission of schools and school districts

II-C-3. School counseling programs promote and support academic achievement, personal and social development and career planning for every student

II-C-4. School counselors operate within a framework of school and district policies, state laws and regulations and professional ethics standards

III: Delivery

School counselors should possess the knowledge, abilities, skills and attitudes necessary to deliver a school counseling program aligning with the ASCA National Model.

III-A: KNOWLEDGE

School counselors should articulate and demonstrate an understanding of:

III-A-1. The concept of a guidance curriculum

III-A-2. Counseling theories and techniques that work in school, such as solution-focused brief counseling, reality therapy, cognitive-behavioral therapy

III-A-3. Counseling theories and techniques in different settings, such as individual planning, group counseling and classroom guidance

III-A-4. Classroom management

III-A-5. Principles of career planning and college admissions, including financial aid and athletic eligibility

III-A-6. Principles of working with various student populations based on ethnic and racial background, English language proficiency, special needs, religion, gender and income

III-A-7. Responsive services

III-A-8. Crisis counseling, including grief and bereavement

III-B: ABILITIES AND SKILLS

An effective school counselor is able to accomplish measurable objectives demonstrating the following abilities and skills.

III-B-1. Implements the school guidance curriculum
    III-B-1a. Crosswalks ASCA Student Competencies with appropriate guidance curriculum
    III-B-1b. Develops and presents a developmental guidance curriculum addressing all students' needs, including closing-the-gap activities
    III-B-1c. Demonstrates classroom management and instructional skills
    III-B-1d. Develops materials and instructional strategies to meet student needs and school goals
    III-B-1e. Encourages staff involvement to ensure the effective implementation of the school guidance curriculum
    III-B-1f. Knows, understands and uses a variety of technology in the delivery of guidance curriculum activities
    III-B-1g. Understands multicultural and pluralistic trends when developing and choosing guidance curriculum
    III-B-1h. Understands the resources available for students with special needs
III-B-2. Facilitates individual student planning
    III-B-2a. Understands individual student planning as a component of a comprehensive program.
    III-B-2b. Develops strategies to implement individual student planning, such as strategies for appraisal, advisement, goal-setting, decision-making, social skills, transition or postsecondary planning
    III-B-2c. Helps students establish goals, and develops and uses planning skills in collaboration with parents or guardians and school personnel
    III-B-2d. Understands career opportunities, labor market trends, and global economics, and uses various career assessment techniques to assist students in understanding their abilities and career interests
    III-B-2e. Helps students learn the importance of college and other post-secondary education and helps students navigate the college admissions process

III-B-2f. Understands the relationship of academic performance to the world of work, family life and community service

III-B-2g. Understands methods for helping students monitor and direct their own learning and personal/social and career development

III-B-3. Provides responsive services

III-B-3a. Understands how to make referrals to appropriate professionals when necessary

III-B-3b. Lists and describes interventions used in responsive services, such as consultation, individual and small-group counseling, crisis counseling, referrals and peer facilitation

III-B-3c. Compiles resources to utilize with students, staff and families to effectively address issues through responsive services

III-B-3d. Understands appropriate individual and small-group counseling theories and techniques such as rational emotive behavior therapy, reality therapy, cognitive-behavioral therapy, Adlerian, solution-focused brief counseling, person-centered counseling and family systems

III-B-3e. Demonstrates an ability to provide counseling for students during times of transition, separation, heightened stress and critical change

III-B-3f. Understands what defines a crisis, the appropriate response and a variety of intervention strategies to meet the needs of the individual, group, or school community before, during and after crisis response

III-B-3g. Provides team leadership to the school and community in a crisis

III-B-3h. Involves appropriate school and community professionals as well as the family in a crisis situation

III-B-3i. Develops a database of community agencies and service providers for student referrals

III-B-3j. Applies appropriate counseling approaches to promoting change among consultees within a consultation approach

III-B-3k. Understands and is able to build effective and high-quality peer helper programs

III-B-3l. Understands the nature of academic, career and personal/social counseling in schools and the similarities and differences among school counseling and other types of counseling, such as mental health, marriage and family, and substance abuse counseling, within a continuum of care

III-B-3m. Understands the role of the school counselor and the school counseling program in the school crisis plan

III-B-4. Implements system support activities for the comprehensive school counseling program

    III-B-4a. Creates a system support planning document addressing school counselor's responsibilities for professional development, consultation and collaboration and program management

    III-B-4b. Coordinates activities that establish, maintain and enhance the school counseling program as well as other educational programs

    III-B-4c. Conducts in-service training for other stakeholders to share school counseling expertise

    III-B-4d. Understands and knows how to provide supervision for school counseling interns consistent with the principles of the ASCA National Model

III-C: ATTITUDES

School counselors believe:

III-C-1. School counseling is one component in the continuum of care that should be available to all students

III-C-2. School counselors coordinate and facilitate counseling and other services to ensure all students receive the care they need, even though school counselors may not personally provide the care themselves

III-C-3. School counselors engage in developmental counseling and short-term responsive counseling

III-C-4. School counselors should refer students to district or community resources to meet more extensive needs such as long-term therapy or diagnoses of disorders

IV: Management

School counselors should possess the knowledge, abilities, skills and attitudes necessary to manage a school counseling program aligning with the ASCA National Model.

IV-A: KNOWLEDGE

School counselors should articulate and demonstrate an understanding of:

IV-A-1. Leadership principles, including sources of power and authority, and formal and informal leadership

IV-A-2. Organization theory to facilitate advocacy, collaboration and systemic change

IV-A-3. Presentation skills for programs such as teacher in-services and results reports to school boards

IV-A-4. Time management, including long- and short-term management using tools such as schedules and calendars

IV-A-5. Data-driven decision making

IV-A-6. Current and emerging technologies such as use of the Internet, Web-based resources and management information systems

IV-B: ABILITIES AND SKILLS

An effective school counselor is able to accomplish measurable objectives demonstrating the following abilities and skills.

IV-B-1. Negotiates with the administrator to define the management system for the comprehensive school counseling program

    IV-B-1a. Discusses and develops the components of the school counselor management system with the other members of the counseling staff

    IV-B-1b. Presents the school counseling management system to the principal, and finalizes an annual school counseling management agreement

    IV-B-1c. Discusses the anticipated program results when implementing the action plans for the school year

    IV-B-1d. Participates in professional organizations

    IV-B-1e. Develops a yearly professional development plan demonstrating how the school counselor advances relevant knowledge, skills and dispositions

    IV-B-1f. Communicates effective goals and benchmarks for meeting and exceeding expectations consistent with the administrator-counselor agreement and district performance appraisals

IV-B-1g. Uses personal reflection, consultation and supervision to promote professional growth and development

IV-B-2. Establishes and convenes an advisory council for the comprehensive school counseling program

　　　IV-B-2a. Uses leadership skills to facilitate vision and positive change for the comprehensive school counseling program

　　　IV-B-2b. Determines appropriate education stakeholders who should be represented on the advisory council

　　　IV-B-2c. Develops meeting agendas

　　　IV-B-2d. Reviews school data, school counseling program audit and school counseling program goals with the council

　　　IV-B-2e. Records meeting notes and distributes as appropriate

　　　IV-B-2f. Analyzes and incorporates feedback from advisory council related to school counseling program goals as appropriate

IV-B-3. Collects, analyzes and interprets relevant data, including process, perception and results data, to monitor and improve student behavior and achievement

　　　IV-B-3a. Analyzes, synthesizes and disaggregates data to examine student outcomes and to identify and implement interventions as needed

　　　IV-B-3b. Uses data to identify policies, practices and procedures leading to successes, systemic barriers and areas of weakness

　　　IV-B-3c. Uses student data to demonstrate a need for systemic change in areas such as course enrollment patterns; equity and access; and the achievement, opportunity and information gap

　　　IV-B-3d. Understands and uses data to establish goals and activities to close the achievement, opportunity and information gap

　　　IV-B-3e. Knows how to use and analyze data to evaluate the school counseling program, research activity outcomes and identify gaps between and among different groups of students

　　　IV-B-3f. Uses school data to identify and assist individual students who do not perform at grade level and do not have opportunities and resources to be successful in school

　　　IV-B-3g. Knows and understands theoretical and historical bases for assessment techniques

IV-B-4. Organizes and manages time to implement an effective school counseling program

IV-B-4a. Identifies appropriate distribution of school counselor's time based on delivery system and school's data

IV-B-4b. Creates a rationale for school counselor's time to focus on the goals of the comprehensive school counseling program

IV-B-4c. Identifies and evaluates fair-share responsibilities, which articulate appropriate and inappropriate counseling and non-counseling activities

IV-B-4d. Creates a rationale for the school counselor's total time spent in each component of the school counseling program

IV-B-5. Develops calendars to ensure the effective implementation of the school counseling program

IV-B-5a. Creates annual, monthly and weekly calendars to plan activities to reflect school goals

IV-B-5b. Demonstrates time management skills including scheduling, publicizing and prioritizing time and task

IV-B-6. Designs and implements action plans aligning with school and school counseling program goals

IV-B-6a. Uses appropriate academic and behavioral data to develop guidance curriculum and closing-the-gap action plan and determines appropriate students for the target group or interventions

IV-B-6b. Identifies ASCA domains, standards and competencies being addressed by the plan

IV-B-6c. Determines the intended impact on academics and behavior

IV-B-6d. Identifies appropriate activities to accomplish objectives

IV-B-6e. Identifies appropriate resources needed

IV-B-6f. Identifies data-collection strategies to gather process, perception and results data

IV-B-6g. Shares results of action plans with staff, parents and community.

IV-C: ATTITUDES

School counselors believe:

IV-C-1. A school counseling program and guidance department must be managed like other programs and departments in a school

IV-C-2. One of the critical responsibilities of a school counselor is to plan, organize, implement and evaluate a school counseling program

IV-C-3. Management of a school counseling program must be done in collaboration with administrators.

V: Accountability

School counselors should possess the knowledge, abilities, skills and attitudes necessary to monitor and evaluate the processes and results of a school counseling program aligning with the ASCA National Model.

V-A: KNOWLEDGE

School counselors should articulate and demonstrate an understanding of:

V-A-1. Basic concept of results-based school counseling and accountability issues

V-A-2. Basic research and statistical concepts to read and conduct research

V-A-3. Use of data to evaluate program effectiveness and to determine program needs

V-A-4. Program audits and results reports

V-B: ABILITIES AND SKILLS

An effective school counselor is able to accomplish measurable objectives demonstrating the following abilities and skills.

V-B-1. Uses data from results reports to evaluate program effectiveness and to determine program needs

    V-B-1a. Uses formal and informal methods of program evaluation to design and modify comprehensive school counseling programs

    V-B-1b. Uses student data to support decision making in designing effective school counseling programs and interventions

    V-B-1c. Measures results attained from school guidance curriculum and closing-the-gap activities

    V-B-1d. Works with members of the school counseling team and with the administration to decide how school counseling programs are evaluated and how results are shared

V-B-1e. Collects process, perception and results data
V-B-1f. Uses technology in conducting research and program evaluation
V-B-1g. Reports program results to professional school counseling community
V-B-1h. Uses data to demonstrate the value the school counseling program adds to student achievement
V-B-1i. Uses results obtained for program improvement
V-B-2. Understands and advocates for appropriate school counselor performance appraisal process based on school counselors competencies and completion of the guidance curriculum and agreed-upon action plans
V-B-2a. Conducts self-appraisal related to school counseling skills and performance
V-B-2b. Identifies how school counseling activities fit within categories of performance appraisal instrument
V-B-2c. Encourages administrators to use performance appraisal instrument reflecting appropriate responsibilities for school counselors
V-B-3. Conducts a program audit
V-B-3a. Completes a program audit to compare current school counseling program implementation with the ASCA National Model
V-B-3b. Shares the results of the program audit with administrators, the advisory council and other appropriate stakeholders
V-B-3c. Identifies areas for improvement for the school counseling program

V-C: ATTITUDES

School counselors believe:

V-C-1. School counseling programs should achieve demonstrable results
V-C-2. School counselors should be accountable for the results of the school counseling program
V-C-3. School counselors should use quantitative and qualitative data to evaluate their school counseling program and to demonstrate program results
V-C-4. The results of the school counseling program should be analyzed and presented in the context of the overall school and district performance

Appendix IV: CACREP 2009 Standards*

INTRODUCTION

When a program applies for CACREP accreditation, it is evidence of an attitude and philosophy that program excellence is a fundamental goal. Accreditation entails assessing a program's quality and its continual enhancement through compliance with the CACREP standards. The accreditation process uses both self-assessment and peer assessment to determine how well professional standards are being met. Accredited status indicates to the public at large that a program has accepted and is fulfilling its commitment to educational quality.

The CACREP Standards are written to ensure that students develop a professional counselor identity and master the knowledge and skills to practice effectively. Graduates of CACREP-accredited programs are prepared for careers in mental health and human service agencies; educational institutions; private practice; and government, business, and industrial settings.

The CACREP Standards are not intended to discourage program innovation. Programs that wish to institute variations in how these standards are met may submit statements of rationale as part of their self-studies. CACREP will determine whether these variations accomplish the outcomes the standards are designed to ensure.

Note: Glossary definitions are integral to understanding and implementing the standards. These definitions will be used by the CACREP Board in making accreditation decisions.

SECTION I   THE LEARNING ENVIRONMENT: STRUCTURE AND EVALUATION

THE INSTITUTION

A. The institutional media accurately describe the academic unit and each program offered, including admissions criteria, accreditation status, delivery systems used for instruction, minimum program requirements, matriculation requirements (e.g., examinations, academic-standing policies), and financial aid information.

B. The academic unit is clearly identified as part of the institution's graduate degree offerings and has primary responsibility for the preparation of students in the program. If more than one academic unit has responsibility for the preparation of students in the program, the respective areas of responsibility and the relationships among and between them must be clearly documented.

C. The institution is committed to providing the program with sufficient financial support to ensure continuity, quality, and effectiveness in all of the program's learning environments.

D. The institution provides encouragement and support for program faculty to participate in professional organizations and activities (e.g., professional travel, research, and leadership positions).

E. Access to learning resources is appropriate for scholarly inquiry, study, and research by program faculty and students.

F. The institution provides technical support to program faculty and students to ensure access to information systems for learning, teaching, and research.

G. The institution provides information to students in the program about personal counseling services provided by professionals other than program faculty and students.

H. A counseling instruction environment (on or off campus) is conducive to modeling, demonstration, supervision, and training, and is available and used by the program. Administrative control of the counseling instruction environment ensures adequate and appropriate access by faculty and students. The counseling instruction environment includes all of the following:

1. Settings for individual counseling, with assured privacy and sufficient space for appropriate equipment.
2. Settings for small-group work, with assured privacy and sufficient space for appropriate equipment.
3. Necessary and appropriate technologies and other observational capabilities that assist learning.
4. Procedures that ensure that the client's confidentiality and legal rights are protected.

THE ACADEMIC UNIT

I. Entry-level degree programs in Career Counseling, School Counseling, and Student Affairs and College Counseling are comprised of approved graduate-level study with a minimum of 48 semester credit hours or 72 quarter credit hours required of all students. Entry-level degree programs in Addiction Counseling and in Marriage, Couple, and Family Counseling are comprised of approved graduate-level study with a minimum of 60 semester credit hours or 90 quarter credit hours required of all students.

Beginning July 1, 2009, all applicant programs in Clinical Mental Health Counseling must require a minimum of 54 semester credit hours or 81 quarter credit hours for all students. As of July 1, 2013, all applicant programs in Clinical Mental Health Counseling must require a minimum of 60 semester credit hours or 90 quarter credit hours for all students.

J. The counselor education academic unit has made systematic efforts to attract, enroll, and retain a diverse group of students and to create and support an inclusive learning community.

K. Admission decision recommendations are made by the academic unit's selection committee and include consideration of the following:

1. Each applicant's potential success in forming effective and culturally relevant interpersonal relationships in individual and small-group contexts.
2. Each applicant's aptitude for graduate-level study.
3. Each applicant's career goals and their relevance to the program.

L. Before or at the beginning of the first term of enrollment in the academic unit, the following should occur for all new students:
  1. A new student orientation is conducted.
  2. A student handbook is disseminated that includes the following:
     a. mission statement of the academic unit and program objectives;
     b. information about appropriate professional organizations, opportunities for professional involvement, and activities potentially appropriate for students;
     c. written endorsement policy explaining the procedures for recommending students for credentialing and employment;
     d. student retention policy explaining procedures for student remediation and/or dismissal from the program; and
     e. academic appeal policy.
M. For any calendar year, the number of credit hours delivered by noncore faculty must not exceed the number of credit hours delivered by core faculty.
N. Institutional data reflect that the ratio of full-time equivalent (FTE) students to FTE faculty should not exceed 10:1.
O. Students have an assigned faculty advisor at all times during enrollment in the program. Students, with their faculty advisor, develop a planned program of study within the first 12 months of graduate study.
P. The program faculty conducts a systematic developmental assessment of each student's progress throughout the program, including consideration of the student's academic performance, professional development, and personal development. Consistent with established institutional due process policy and the American Counseling Association's (ACA) code of ethics and other relevant codes of ethics and standards of practice, if evaluations indicate that a student is not appropriate for the program, faculty members help facilitate the student's transition out of the program and, if possible, into a more appropriate area of study.
Q. The practicum and internship experiences are tutorial forms of instruction; therefore, when individual and/or triadic supervision is provided by program faculty, the ratio of six students to one faculty member is considered equivalent to the teaching of one 3-semester-hour course. Such a ratio is considered maximum per course.
R. Group supervision for practicum and internship should not exceed 12 students.

S. Programs provide evidence that students are covered by professional liability insurance while enrolled or participating in practicum, internship, or other field experiences.

T. Opportunities for graduate assistantships for program students are commensurate with graduate assistantship opportunities in other clinical training programs in the institution.

FACULTY AND STAFF

U. The academic unit has made systematic efforts to recruit, employ, and retain a diverse faculty.

V. The teaching loads of program faculty members are consistent with those of the institution's other graduate level units that require intensive supervision as an integral part of professional preparation, and incorporate time for supervising student research using formulae consistent with institutional policies and practices.

W. The academic unit has faculty resources of appropriate quality and sufficiency to achieve its mission and objectives. The academic unit has an identifiable core faculty who meet the following requirements:
   1. Number at least three persons whose full-time academic appointments are in counselor education.
   2. Have earned doctoral degrees in counselor education and supervision, preferably from a CACREP-accredited program, or have been employed as full-time faculty members in a counselor education program for a minimum of one full academic year before July 1, 2013.
   3. Have relevant preparation and experience in the assigned program area.
   4. Identify with the counseling profession through memberships in professional organizations (i.e., ACA and/or its divisions), and through appropriate certifications and/or licenses pertinent to the profession.
   5. Engage in activities of the counseling profession and its professional organizations, including all of the following:
      a. development/renewal (e.g., appropriate professional meetings, conventions, workshops, seminars);
      b. research and scholarly activity; and
      c. service and advocacy (e.g., program presentations, workshops, consultations, speeches, direct service).
   6. Have the authority to determine program curricula within the structure of the institution's policies and to establish the operational policies and procedures of the program.

X. The academic unit has clearly defined administrative and curricular leadership that is sufficient for its effective operation. A faculty member may hold more than one of the following positions:

1. A faculty member is clearly designated as the academic unit leader for counselor education who
   a. is responsible for the coordination of the counseling program(s);
   b. receives inquiries regarding the overall academic unit;
   c. makes recommendations regarding the development of and expenditures from the budget;
   d. provides or delegates year-round leadership to the operation of the program(s); and
   e. has release time from faculty member responsibilities to administer the academic unit.

2. A faculty member or administrator is identified as the practicum and internship coordinator for the academic unit and/or program who
   a. is responsible for the coordination of all practicum and internship experiences in each counselor education program for which accreditation is sought;
   b. is the person to whom inquiries regarding practicum and internship experiences are referred; and
   c. has clearly defined responsibilities.

Y. The academic unit may employ noncore faculty (e.g., adjunct, affiliate, clinical) who support the mission, goals, and curriculum of the program and meet the following requirements:

1. Hold graduate degrees, preferably in counselor education from a CACREP-accredited program.
2. Have relevant preparation and experience in the assigned area of teaching.
3. Identify with the counseling profession through memberships in professional organizations, appropriate certifications, and/or licenses pertinent to the profession.

Z. Clerical assistance is available to support faculty/program activities and is commensurate with that provided for similar graduate programs.

EVALUATION

AA. Program faculty members engage in continuous systematic program evaluation indicating how the mission, objectives, and student learning outcomes are measured and met. The plan includes the following:

1. A review by program faculty of programs, curricular offerings, and characteristics of program applicants.
2. Formal follow-up studies of program graduates to assess graduate perceptions and evaluations of major aspects of the program.
3. Formal studies of site supervisors and program graduate employers that assess their perceptions and evaluations of major aspects of the program.
4. Assessment of student learning and performance on professional identity, professional practice, and program area standards.
5. Evidence of the use of findings to inform program modifications.
6. Distribution of an official report that documents outcomes of the systematic program evaluation, with descriptions of any program modifications, to students currently in the program, program faculty, institutional administrators, personnel in cooperating agencies (e.g., employers, site supervisors), and the public.

BB. Students have regular and systematic opportunities to formally evaluate faculty who provide curricular experiences and supervisors of clinical experiences.

CC. Annual results of student course evaluations are provided to faculty.

DD. Written faculty evaluation procedures are presented to program faculty and supervisors at the beginning of each evaluation period and whenever changes are made in the procedures.

SECTION II   PROFESSIONAL IDENTITY

FOUNDATION

A. A comprehensive mission statement has been developed that brings the counseling program into focus and concisely describes the program's intent and purpose. The mission statement is publicly available and systematically reviewed.

B. The program area objectives meet the following requirements:

1. Reflect current knowledge and projected needs concerning counseling practice in a multicultural and pluralistic society.
2. Reflect input from all persons involved in the conduct of the program, including program faculty, current and former students, and personnel in cooperating agencies.

3. Are directly related to program activities.
4. Are written so they can be evaluated.

C. Students actively identify with the counseling profession by participating in professional organizations and by participating in seminars, workshops, or other activities that contribute to personal and professional growth.

KNOWLEDGE

D. Syllabi are distributed at the beginning of each curricular experience, are available for review by all enrolled or prospective students, and include all of the following:
   1. Content areas.
   2. Knowledge and skill outcomes.
   3. Methods of instruction.
   4. Required text(s) and/or reading(s).
   5. Student performance evaluation criteria and procedures.

E. Evidence exists of the use and infusion of current counseling-related research in teaching practice among program faculty and students.

F. Evidence exists of the use and infusion of technology in program delivery and technology's impact on the counseling profession.

G. Common core curricular experiences and demonstrated knowledge in each of the eight common core curricular areas are required of all students in the program.
   1. PROFESSIONAL ORIENTATION AND ETHICAL PRACTICE—studies that provide an understanding of all of the following aspects of professional functioning:
      a. history and philosophy of the counseling profession;
      b. professional roles, functions, and relationships with other human service providers, including strategies for interagency/interorganization collaboration and communications;
      c. counselors' roles and responsibilities as members of an interdisciplinary emergency management response team during a local, regional, or national crisis, disaster or other trauma-causing event;
      d. self-care strategies appropriate to the counselor role;
      e. counseling supervision models, practices, and processes;
      f. professional organizations, including membership benefits, activities, services to members, and current issues;

g. professional credentialing, including certification, licensure, and accreditation practices and standards, and the effects of public policy on these issues;

h. the role and process of the professional counselor advocating on behalf of the profession;

i. advocacy processes needed to address institutional and social barriers that impede access, equity, and success for clients; and

j. ethical standards of professional organizations and credentialing bodies, and applications of ethical and legal considerations in professional counseling.

2. SOCIAL AND CULTURAL DIVERSITY—studies that provide an understanding of the cultural context of relationships, issues, and trends in a multicultural society, including all of the following:

a. multicultural and pluralistic trends, including characteristics and concerns within and among diverse groups nationally and internationally;

b. attitudes, beliefs, understandings, and acculturative experiences, including specific experiential learning activities designed to foster students' understanding of self and culturally diverse clients;

c. theories of multicultural counseling, identity development, and social justice;

d. individual, couple, family, group, and community strategies for working with and advocating for diverse populations, including multicultural competencies;

e. counselors' roles in developing cultural self-awareness, promoting cultural social justice, advocacy and conflict resolution, and other culturally supported behaviors that promote optimal wellness and growth of the human spirit, mind, or body; and

f. counselors' roles in eliminating biases, prejudices, and processes of intentional and unintentional oppression and discrimination.

3. HUMAN GROWTH AND DEVELOPMENT—studies that provide an understanding of the nature and needs of persons at all developmental levels and in multicultural contexts, including all of the following:

a. theories of individual and family development and transitions across the life span;

b. theories of learning and personality development, including current understandings about neurobiological behavior;

    c. effects of crises, disasters, and other trauma-causing events on persons of all ages;

    d. theories and models of individual, cultural, couple, family, and community resilience;

    e. a general framework for understanding exceptional abilities and strategies for differentiated interventions;

    f. human behavior, including an understanding of developmental crises, disability, psychopathology, and situational and environmental factors that affect both normal and abnormal behavior;

    g. theories and etiology of addictions and addictive behaviors, including strategies for prevention, intervention, and treatment; and

    h. theories for facilitating optimal development and wellness over the life span.

4. CAREER DEVELOPMENT—studies that provide an understanding of career development and related life factors, including all of the following:

    a. career development theories and decision-making models;

    b. career, avocational, educational, occupational and labor market information resources, and career information systems;

    c. career development program planning, organization, implementation, administration, and evaluation;

    d. interrelationships among and between work, family, and other life roles and factors, including the role of multicultural issues in career development;

    e. career and educational planning, placement, follow-up, and evaluation;

    f. assessment instruments and techniques relevant to career planning and decision making; and

    g. career counseling processes, techniques, and resources, including those applicable to specific populations in a global economy.

5. HELPING RELATIONSHIPS—studies that provide an understanding of the counseling process in a multicultural society, including all of the following:

    a. an orientation to wellness and prevention as desired counseling goals;

    b. counselor characteristics and behaviors that influence helping processes;

    c. essential interviewing and counseling skills;

    d. counseling theories that provide the student with models to conceptualize client presentation and that help the student select appropriate counseling interventions. Students will be exposed to models of counseling that are consistent with current professional research and practice in the field so they begin to develop a personal model of counseling;

    e. a systems perspective that provides an understanding of family and other systems theories and major models of family and related interventions;

    f. a general framework for understanding and practicing consultation; and

    g. crisis intervention and suicide prevention models, including the use of psychological first aid strategies.

6. GROUP WORK—studies that provide both theoretical and experiential understandings of group purpose, development, dynamics, theories, methods, skills, and other group approaches in a multicultural society, including all of the following:

    a. principles of group dynamics, including group process components, developmental stage theories, group members' roles and behaviors, and therapeutic factors of group work;

    b. group leadership or facilitation styles and approaches, including characteristics of various types of group leaders and leadership styles;

    c. theories of group counseling, including commonalities, distinguishing characteristics, and pertinent research and literature;

    d. group counseling methods, including group counselor orientations and behaviors, appropriate selection criteria and methods, and methods of evaluation of effectiveness; and

    e. direct experiences in which students participate as group members in a small group activity, approved by the program, for a minimum of 10 clock hours over the course of one academic term.

7. ASSESSMENT—studies that provide an understanding of individual and group approaches to assessment and evaluation in a multicultural society, including all of the following:

    a. historical perspectives concerning the nature and meaning of assessment;

    b. basic concepts of standardized and nonstandardized testing and other assessment techniques, including norm-referenced and criterion-referenced assessment, environmental assessment, performance assessment, individual and group test and inventory methods, psychological testing, and behavioral observations;

c. statistical concepts, including scales of measurement, measures of central tendency, indices of variability, shapes and types of distributions, and correlations;

d. reliability (i.e., theory of measurement error, models of reliability, and the use of reliability information);

e. validity (i.e., evidence of validity, types of validity, and the relationship between reliability and validity);

f. social and cultural factors related to the assessment and evaluation of individuals, groups, and specific populations; and

g. ethical strategies for selecting, administering, and interpreting assessment and evaluation instruments and techniques in counseling.

8. RESEARCH AND PROGRAM EVALUATION—studies that provide an understanding of research methods, statistical analysis, needs assessment, and program evaluation, including all of the following:

a. the importance of research in advancing the counseling profession;

b. research methods such as qualitative, quantitative, single-case designs, action research, and outcome-based research;

c. statistical methods used in conducting research and program evaluation;

d. principles, models, and applications of needs assessment, program evaluation, and the use of findings to effect program modifications;

e. the use of research to inform evidence-based practice; and

f. ethical and culturally relevant strategies for interpreting and reporting the results of research and/or program evaluation studies.

SECTION III   PROFESSIONAL PRACTICE

Professional practice, which includes practicum and internship, provides for the application of theory and the development of counseling skills under supervision. These experiences will provide opportunities for students to counsel clients who represent the ethnic and demographic diversity of their community.

SUPERVISOR QUALIFICATIONS AND SUPPORT

A. Program faculty members serving as individual or group practicum/internship supervisors must have the following:
   1. A doctoral degree and/or appropriate counseling preparation, preferably from a CACREP-accredited counselor education program.
   2. Relevant experience and appropriate credentials/licensure and/or demonstrated competence in counseling.
   3. Relevant supervision training and experience.
B. Students serving as individual or group practicum student supervisors must meet the following requirements:
   1. Have completed a master's degree, as well as counseling practicum and internship experiences equivalent to those in a CACREP-accredited entry-level program.
   2. Have completed or are receiving preparation in counseling supervision.
   3. Be supervised by program faculty, with a faculty-student ratio that does not exceed 1:6.
C. Site supervisors must have the following qualifications:
   1. A minimum of a master's degree in counseling or a related profession with equivalent qualifications, including appropriate certifications and/or licenses.
   2. A minimum of two years of pertinent professional experience in the program area in which the student is enrolled.
   3. Knowledge of the program's expectations, requirements, and evaluation procedures for students.
   4. Relevant training in counseling supervision.
D. Orientation, assistance, consultation, and professional development opportunities are provided by counseling program faculty to site supervisors.
E. Supervision contracts for each student are developed to define the roles and responsibilities of the faculty supervisor, site supervisor, and student during practicum and internship.

PRACTICUM

F. Students must complete supervised practicum experiences that total a minimum of 100 clock hours over a minimum 10-week academic term. Each student's practicum includes all of the following:
   1. At least 40 clock hours of direct service with actual clients that contributes to the development of counseling skills.

2. Weekly interaction that averages one hour per week of individual and/or triadic supervision throughout the practicum by a program faculty member, a student supervisor, or a site supervisor who is working in biweekly consultation with a program faculty member in accordance with the supervision contract.
3. An average of 1 1/2 hours per week of group supervision that is provided on a regular schedule throughout the practicum by a program faculty member or a student supervisor.
4. The development of program-appropriate audio/video recordings for use in supervision or live supervision of the student's interactions with clients.
5. Evaluation of the student's counseling performance throughout the practicum, including documentation of a formal evaluation after the student completes the practicum.

INTERNSHIP

G. The program requires completion of a supervised internship in the student's designated program area of 600 clock hours, begun after successful completion of the practicum. The internship is intended to reflect the comprehensive work experience of a professional counselor appropriate to the designated program area. Each student's internship includes all of the following:
   1. At least 240 clock hours of direct service, including experience leading groups.
   2. Weekly interaction that averages one hour per week of individual and/or triadic supervision throughout the internship, usually performed by the onsite supervisor.
   3. An average of 1 1/2 hours per week of group supervision provided on a regular schedule throughout the internship and performed by a program faculty member.
   4. The opportunity for the student to become familiar with a variety of professional activities and resources in addition to direct service (e.g., record keeping, assessment instruments, supervision, information and referral, in-service and staff meetings).
   5. The opportunity for the student to develop program-appropriate audio/video recordings for use in supervision or to receive live supervision of his or her interactions with clients.

6. Evaluation of the student's counseling performance throughout the internship, including documentation of a formal evaluation after the student completes the internship by a program faculty member in consultation with the site supervisor.

SCHOOL COUNSELING

Students who are preparing to work as school counselors will demonstrate the professional knowledge, skills, and practices necessary to promote the academic, career, and personal/social development of all K–12 students. In addition to the common core curricular experiences outlined in Section II.F, programs must provide evidence that student learning has occurred in the following domains.

FOUNDATIONS

A. Knowledge
   1. Knows history, philosophy, and trends in school counseling and educational systems.
   2. Understands ethical and legal considerations specifically related to the practice of school counseling.
   3. Knows roles, functions, settings, and professional identity of the school counselor in relation to the roles of other professional and support personnel in the school.
   4. Knows professional organizations, preparation standards, and credentials that are relevant to the practice of school counseling.
   5. Understands current models of school counseling programs (e.g., American School Counselor Association [ASCA] National Model) and their integral relationship to the total educational program.
   6. Understands the effects of (a) atypical growth and development, (b) health and wellness, (c) language, (d) ability level, (e) multicultural issues, and (f) factors of resiliency on student learning and development.
   7. Understands the operation of the school emergency management plan and the roles and responsibilities of the school counselor during crises, disasters, and other trauma-causing events.

B. Skills and Practices
   1. Demonstrates the ability to apply and adhere to ethical and legal standards in school counseling.
   2. Demonstrates the ability to articulate, model, and advocate for an appropriate school counselor identity and program.

COUNSELING, PREVENTION, AND INTERVENTION

C. Knowledge
   1. Knows the theories and processes of effective counseling and wellness programs for individual students and groups of students.
   2. Knows how to design, implement, manage, and evaluate programs to enhance the academic, career, and personal/social development of students.
   3. Knows strategies for helping students identify strengths and cope with environmental and developmental problems.
   4. Knows how to design, implement, manage, and evaluate transition programs, including school-to-work, postsecondary planning, and college admissions counseling.
   5. Understands group dynamics—including counseling, psycho-educational, task, and peer helping groups—and the facilitation of teams to enable students to overcome barriers and impediments to learning.
   6. Understands the potential impact of crises, emergencies, and disasters on students, educators, and schools, and knows the skills needed for crisis intervention.

D. Skills and Practices
   1. Demonstrates self-awareness, sensitivity to others, and the skills needed to relate to diverse individuals, groups, and classrooms.
   2. Provides individual and group counseling and classroom guidance to promote the academic, career, and personal/social development of students.
   3. Designs and implements prevention and intervention plans related to the effects of (a) atypical growth and development, (b) health and wellness, (c) language, (d) ability level, (e) multicultural issues, and (f) factors of resiliency on student learning and development.
   4. Demonstrates the ability to use procedures for assessing and managing suicide risk.
   5. Demonstrates the ability to recognize his or her limitations as a school counselor and to seek supervision or refer clients when appropriate.

DIVERSITY AND ADVOCACY

E. Knowledge
1. Understands the cultural, ethical, economic, legal, and political issues surrounding diversity, equity, and excellence in terms of student learning.
2. Identifies community, environmental, and institutional opportunities that enhance—as well as barriers that impede—the academic, career, and personal/social development of students.
3. Understands the ways in which educational policies, programs, and practices can be developed, adapted, and modified to be culturally congruent with the needs of students and their families.
4. Understands multicultural counseling issues, as well as the impact of ability levels, stereotyping, family, socioeconomic status, gender, and sexual identity, and their effects on student achievement.

F. Skills and Practices
1. Demonstrates multicultural competencies in relation to diversity, equity, and opportunity in student learning and development.
2. Advocates for the learning and academic experiences necessary to promote the academic, career, and personal/social development of students.
3. Advocates for school policies, programs, and services that enhance a positive school climate and are equitable and responsive to multicultural student populations.
4. Engages parents, guardians, and families to promote the academic, career, and personal/social development of students.

ASSESSMENT

G. Knowledge
1. Understands the influence of multiple factors (e.g., abuse, violence, eating disorders, attention deficit hyperactivity disorder, childhood depression) that may affect the personal, social, and academic functioning of students.
2. Knows the signs and symptoms of substance abuse in children and adolescents, as well as the signs and symptoms of living in a home where substance abuse occurs.
3. Identifies various forms of needs assessments for academic, career, and personal/social development.

H. Skills and Practices
   1. Assesses and interprets students' strengths and needs, recognizing uniqueness in cultures, languages, values, backgrounds, and abilities.
   2. Selects appropriate assessment strategies that can be used to evaluate a student's academic, career, and personal/social development.
   3. Analyzes assessment information in a manner that produces valid inferences when evaluating the needs of individual students and assessing the effectiveness of educational programs.
   4. Makes appropriate referrals to school and/or community resources.
   5. Assesses barriers that impede students' academic, career, and personal/social development.

RESEARCH AND EVALUATION

I. Knowledge
   1. Understands how to critically evaluate research relevant to the practice of school counseling.
   2. Knows models of program evaluation for school counseling programs.
   3. Knows basic strategies for evaluating counseling outcomes in school counseling (e.g., behavioral observation, program evaluation).
   4. Knows current methods of using data to inform decision making and accountability (e.g., school improvement plan, school report card).
   5. Understands the outcome research data and best practices identified in the school counseling research literature.
J. Skills and Practices
   1. Applies relevant research findings to inform the practice of school counseling.
   2. Develops measurable outcomes for school counseling programs, activities, interventions, and experiences.
   3. Analyzes and uses data to enhance school counseling programs.

ACADEMIC DEVELOPMENT

K. Knowledge
   1. Understands the relationship of the school counseling program to the academic mission of the school.
   2. Understands the concepts, principles, strategies, programs, and practices designed to close the achievement gap, promote student academic success, and prevent students from dropping out of school.

3. Understands curriculum design, lesson plan development, classroom management strategies, and differentiated instructional strategies for teaching counseling- and guidance-related material.

L. Skills and Practices

1. Conducts programs designed to enhance student academic development.
2. Implements strategies and activities to prepare students for a full range of postsecondary options and opportunities.
3. Implements differentiated instructional strategies that draw on subject matter and pedagogical content knowledge and skills to promote student achievement.

COLLABORATION AND CONSULTATION

M. Knowledge

1. Understands the ways in which student development, well-being, and learning are enhanced by family-school-community collaboration.
2. Knows strategies to promote, develop, and enhance effective teamwork within the school and the larger community.
3. Knows how to build effective working teams of school staff, parents, and community members to promote the academic, career, and personal/social development of students.
4. Understands systems theories, models, and processes of consultation in school system settings.
5. Knows strategies and methods for working with parents, guardians, families, and communities to empower them to act on behalf of their children.
6. Understands the various peer programming interventions (e.g., peer meditation, peer mentoring, peer tutoring) and how to coordinate them.
7. Knows school and community collaboration models for crisis/disaster preparedness and response.

N. Skills and Practices

1. Works with parents, guardians, and families to act on behalf of their children to address problems that affect student success in school.
2. Locates resources in the community that can be used in the school to improve student achievement and success.
3. Consults with teachers, staff, and community-based organizations to promote student academic, career, and personal/social development.

4. Uses peer helping strategies in the school counseling program.
5. Uses referral procedures with helping agents in the community (e.g., mental health centers, businesses, service groups) to secure assistance for students and their families.

LEADERSHIP

O. Knowledge
1. Knows the qualities, principles, skills, and styles of effective leadership.
2. Knows strategies of leadership designed to enhance the learning environment of schools.
3. Knows how to design, implement, manage, and evaluate a comprehensive school counseling program.
4. Understands the important role of the school counselor as a system change agent.
5. Understands the school counselor's role in student assistance programs, school leadership, curriculum, and advisory meetings.

P. Skills and Practices
1. Participates in the design, implementation, management, and evaluation of a comprehensive developmental school counseling program.
2. Plans and presents school-counseling-related educational programs for use with parents and teachers (e.g., parent education programs, materials used in classroom guidance and advisor/advisee programs for teachers).

Appendix V: NBCC
Code of Ethics*

PREAMBLE

The National Board for Certified Counselors (NBCC) is a professional certification board which certifies counselors as having met standards for the general and specialty practice of professional counseling established by the Board. The counselors certified by NBCC may identify with different professional associations and are often licensed by jurisdictions which promulgate codes of ethics. The NBCC code of ethics provides a minimal ethical standard for the professional behavior of all NBCC certificants. This code provides an expectation of and assurance for the ethical practice for all who use the professional services of an NBCC certificant. In addition, it serves the purpose of having an enforceable standard for all NBCC certificants and assures those served of some resource in case of a perceived ethical violation. This code is applicable to National Certified Counselors and those who are seeking certification from NBCC. The NBCC Ethical Code applies to all those certified by NBCC regardless of any other professional affiliation. Persons who receive professional services from certified counselors may elect to use other ethical codes which apply to their counselor. Although NBCC cooperates with professional associations and credentialing organizations, it can bring actions to discipline or sanction NBCC certificants only if the provisions of the NBCC Code are found to have been violated.

---

* Reprinted with the permission of the National Board for Certified Counselors (NBCC®), Inc. and Affiliates; 3 Terrace Way, Greensboro, NC 27403-3660. Further reproduction is prohibited without the written permission of NBCC®.

The National Board for Certified Counselors, Inc. (NBCC) promotes counseling through certification. In pursuit of this mission, the NBCC:

■ Promotes quality assurance in counseling practice
■ Promotes the value of counseling
■ Promotes public awareness of quality counseling practice
■ Promotes professionalism in counseling
■ Promotes leadership in credentialing

Section A: General

1. Certified counselors engage in continuous efforts to improve professional practices, services, and research. Certified counselors are guided in their work by evidence of the best professional practices.
2. Certified counselors have a responsibility to the clients they serve and to the institutions within which the services are performed. Certified counselors also strive to assist the respective agency, organization, or institution in providing competent and ethical professional services. The acceptance of employment in an institution implies that the certified counselor is in agreement with the general policies and principles of the institution. Therefore, the professional activities of the certified counselor are in accord with the objectives of the institution. If the certified counselor and the employer do not agree and cannot reach agreement on policies that are consistent with appropriate counselor ethical practice that is conducive to client growth and development, the employment should be terminated. If the situation warrants further action, the certified counselor should work through professional organizations to have the unethical practice changed.
3. Ethical behavior among professional associates (i.e., both certified and non-certified counselors) must be expected at all times. When a certified counselor has doubts as to the ethical behavior of professional colleagues, the certified counselor must take action to attempt to rectify this condition. Such action uses the respective institution's channels first TM and then uses procedures established by the NBCC or the perceived violator's profession.
4. Certified counselors must refuse remuneration for consultation or counseling with persons who are entitled to these services through the certified counselor's employing institution or agency. Certified counselors

must not divert to their private practices, without the mutual consent of the institution and the client, legitimate clients in their primary agencies or the institutions with which they are affiliated.

5. In establishing fees for professional counseling services, certified counselors must consider the financial status of clients. In the event that the established fee status is inappropriate for a client, assistance must be provided in finding comparable services at acceptable cost.

6. Certified counselors offer only professional services for which they are trained or have supervised experience. No diagnosis, assessment, or treatment should be performed without prior training or supervision. Certified counselors are responsible for correcting any misrepresentations of their qualifications by others.

7. Certified counselors recognize their limitations and provide services or use techniques for which they are qualified by training and/or supervision. Certified counselors recognize the need for and seek continuing education to assure competent services.

8. Certified counselors are aware of the intimacy in the counseling relationship and maintain respect for the client. Counselors must not engage in activities that seek to meet their personal or professional needs at the expense of the client.

9. Certified counselors must insure that they do not engage in personal, social, organizational, financial, or political activities which might lead to a misuse of their influence.

10. Sexual intimacy with clients is unethical. Certified counselors will not be sexually, physically, or romantically intimate with clients, and they will not engage in sexual, physical, or romantic intimacy with clients within a minimum of two years after terminating the counseling relationship.

11. Certified counselors do not condone or engage in sexual harassment, which is defined as unwelcome comments, gestures, or physical contact of a sexual nature.

12. Through an awareness of the impact of stereotyping and unwarranted discrimination (e.g., biases based on age, disability, ethnicity, gender, race, religion, or sexual orientation), certified counselors guard the individual rights and personal dignity of the client in the counseling relationship.

13. Certified counselors are accountable at all times for their behavior. They must be aware that all actions and behaviors of the counselor reflect on professional integrity and, when inappropriate, can damage the public

trust in the counseling profession. To protect public confidence in the counseling profession, certified counselors avoid behavior that is clearly in violation of accepted moral and legal standards.

14. Products or services provided by certified counselors by means of classroom instruction, public lectures, demonstrations, written articles, radio or television programs or other types of media must meet the criteria cited in this code.

15. Certified counselors have an obligation to withdraw from the practice of counseling if they violate the Code of Ethics, or if the mental or physical condition of the certified counselor renders it unlikely that a professional relationship will be maintained.

16. Certified counselors must comply with all NBCC policies, procedures and agreements, including all information disclosure requirements.

Section B: Counseling Relationship

1. The primary obligation of certified counselors is to respect the integrity and promote the welfare of clients, whether they are assisted individually, in family units, or in group counseling. In a group setting, the certified counselor is also responsible for taking reasonable precautions to protect individuals from physical and/or psychological trauma resulting from interaction within the group.

2. Certified counselors know and take into account the traditions and practices of other professional disciplines with whom they work and cooperate fully with such. If a person is receiving similar services from another professional, certified counselors do not offer their own services directly to such a person. If a certified counselor is contacted by a person who is already receiving similar services from another professional, the certified counselor carefully considers that professional relationship as well as the client's welfare and proceeds with caution and sensitivity to the therapeutic issues. When certified counselors learn that their clients are in a professional relationship with another counselor or mental health professional, they request release from the clients to inform the other counselor or mental health professional of their relationship with the client and strive to establish positive and collaborative professional relationships that are in the best interest of the client. Certified counselors discuss these issues with clients and the counselor or professional so as to minimize the risk of confusion and conflict and

encourage clients to inform other professionals of the new professional relationship.

3. Certified counselors may choose to consult with any other profession-ally competent person about a client and must notify clients of this right. Certified counselors avoid placing a consultant in a conflict-of-interest situation that would preclude the consultant serving as a proper party to the efforts of the certified counselor to help the client.

4. When a client's condition indicates that there is a clear and imminent danger to the client or others, the certified counselor must take rea-sonable action to inform potential victims and/or inform responsible authorities. Consultation with other professionals must be used when possible. The assumption of responsibility for the client's behavior must be taken only after careful deliberation, and the client must be involved in the resumption of responsibility as quickly as possible.

5. Records of the counseling relationship, including interview notes, test data, correspondence, audio or visual tape recordings, electronic data storage, and other documents are to be considered professional infor-mation for use in counseling. Records should contain accurate factual data. The physical records are property of the certified counselors or their employers. The information contained in the records belongs to the client and therefore may not be released to others without the consent of the client or when the counselor has exhausted challenges to a court order. The certified counselors are responsible to insure that their employees handle confidential information appropriately. Confidentiality must be maintained during the storage and disposition of records. Records should be maintained for a period of at least five (5) years after the last counselor/client contact, including cases in which the client is deceased. All records must be released to the client upon request.

6. Certified counselors must ensure that data maintained in electronic stor-age are secure. By using the best computer security methods available, the data must be limited to information that is appropriate and neces-sary for the services being provided and accessible only to appropriate staff members involved in the provision of services. Certified counselors must also ensure that the electronically stored data are destroyed when the information is no longer of value in providing services or required as part of clients' records.

7. Any data derived from a client relationship and used in training or research shall be so disguised that the informed client's identity is fully

protected. Any data which cannot be so disguised may be used only as expressly authorized by the client's informed and uncoerced consent.

8. When counseling is initiated, and throughout the counseling process as necessary, counselors inform clients of the purposes, goals, techniques, procedures, limitations, potential risks and benefits of services to be performed, and clearly indicate limitations that may affect the relationship as well as any other pertinent information. Counselors take reasonable steps to ensure that clients understand the implications of any diagnosis, the intended use of tests and reports, methods of treatment and safety precautions that must be taken in their use, fees, and billing arrangements.

9. Certified counselors who have an administrative, supervisory and/or evaluative relationship with individuals seeking counseling services must not serve as the counselor and should refer the individuals to other professionals. Exceptions are made only in instances where an individual's situation warrants counseling intervention and another alternative is unavailable. Dual relationships that might impair the certified counselor's objectivity and professional judgment must be avoided and/or the counseling relationship terminated through referral to a competent professional.

10. When certified counselors determine an inability to be of professional assistance to a immediately terminate the relationship. In either event, the certified counselor must suggest appropriate alternatives. Certified counselors must be knowledgeable about referral resources so that a satisfactory referral can be initiated. In the event that the client declines a suggested referral, the certified counselor is not obligated to continue the relationship.

11. When certified counselors are engaged in intensive, short-term counseling, they must ensure hat professional assistance is available at normal costs to clients during and following the short-term counseling.

12. Counselors using electronic means in which counselor and client are not in immediate proximity must present clients with local sources of care before establishing a continued short or long-term relationship. Counselors who communicate with clients via Internet are governed by NBCC standards for Web Counseling.

13. Counselors must document permission to practice counseling by electronic means in all governmental jurisdictions where such counseling takes place.

14. When electronic data and systems are used as a component of counseling services, certified counselors must ensure that the computer application, and any information it contains, is appropriate for the respective needs of clients and is non-discriminatory. Certified counselors must ensure that they themselves have acquired a facilitation level of knowledge with any system they use including hands-on application, and understanding of the uses of all aspects of the computer-based system. In selecting and/or maintaining computer-based systems that contain career information, counselors must ensure that the system provides current, accurate, and locally relevant information. Certified counselors must also ensure that clients are intellectually, emotionally, and physically compatible with computer applications and understand their purpose and operation. Client use of a computer application must be evaluated to correct possible problems and assess needs.

15. Certified counselors who develop self-help/stand-alone computer software for use by the general public, must first ensure that it is designed to function in a stand-alone manner that is appropriate and safe for all clients for which it is intended. A manual is required. The manual must provide the user with intended outcomes, suggestions for using the software, descriptions of inappropriately used applications, and descriptions of when and how other forms of counseling services might be beneficial. Finally, the manual must include the qualifications of the developer, the development process, validation date, and operating procedures.

16. The counseling relationship and information resulting from it remains confidential, consistent with the legal and ethical obligations of certified counselors. In group counseling, counselors clearly define confidentiality and the parameters for the specific group being entered, explain the importance of confidentiality, and discuss the difficulties related to confidentiality involved in group work. The fact that confidentiality cannot be guaranteed is clearly communicated to group members. However, counselors should give assurance about their professional responsibility to keep all group communications confidential.

17. Certified counselors must screen prospective group counseling participants to ensure compatibility with group objectives. This is especially important when the emphasis is on self-understanding and growth through self-disclosure. Certified counselors must maintain an awareness of the welfare of each participant throughout the group process.

Section C: Counselor Supervision

NCCs who offer and/or provide supervision must:

a. Ensure that they have the proper training and supervised experience through contemporary continuing education and/or graduate training
b. Ensure that supervisees are informed of the supervisor's credentials and professional status as well as all conditions of supervision as defined/outlined by the supervisor's practice, agency, group, or organization
c. Ensure that supervisees are aware of the current ethical standards related to their professional practice
d. Ensure that supervisees are informed about the process of supervision, including supervision goals, paradigms of supervision and the supervisor's preferred research-based supervision paradigm(s)
e. Provide supervisees with agreed upon scheduled feedback as part of an established evaluation plan (e.g., one (1) hour per week)
f. Ensure that supervisees inform their clients of their professional status (i.e., trainee, intern, licensed, non-licensed, etc.)
g. Establish procedures with their supervisees for handling crisis situations
h. Render timely assistance to supervisees who are or may be unable to provide competent counseling services to clients and
i. Intervene in any situation where the supervisee is impaired and the client is at risk

In addition, because supervision may result in a dual relationship between the supervisor and the supervisee, the supervisor is responsible for ensuring that any dual relationship is properly managed.

Section D: Measurement and Evaluation

1. Because many types of assessment techniques exist, certified counselors must recognize the limits of their competence and perform only those assessment functions for which they have received appropriate training or supervision.
2. Certified counselors who utilize assessment instruments to assist them with diagnoses must have appropriate training and skills in educational

and psychological measurement, validation criteria, test research, and guidelines for test development and use.

3. Certified counselors must provide instrument specific orientation or information to an examinee prior to and following the administration of assessment instruments or techniques so that the results may be placed in proper perspective with other relevant factors. The purpose of testing and the explicit use of the results must be made known to an examinee prior to testing.

4. In selecting assessment instruments or techniques for use in a given situation or with a particular client, certified counselors must carefully evaluate the specific theoretical bases and characteristics, validity, reliability and appropriateness of the instrument.

5. When making statements to the public about assessment instruments or techniques, certified counselors must provide accurate information and avoid false claims or misconceptions concerning the meaning of the instrument's reliability and validity terms.

6. Counselors must follow all directions and researched procedures for selection, administration and interpretation of all evaluation instruments and use them only within proper contexts.

7. Certified counselors must be cautious when interpreting the results of instruments that possess insufficient technical data, and must explicitly state to examinees the specific limitations and purposes for the use of such instruments.

8. Certified counselors must proceed with caution when attempting to evaluate and interpret performances of any person who cannot be appropriately compared to the norms for the instrument.

9. Because prior coaching or dissemination of test materials can invalidate test results, certified counselors are professionally obligated to maintain test security.

10. Certified counselors must consider psychometric limitations when selecting and using an instrument, and must be cognizant of the limitations when interpreting the results. When tests are used to classify clients, certified counselors must ensure that periodic review and/or retesting are made to prevent client stereotyping.

11. An examinee's welfare, explicit prior understanding, and consent are the factors used when determining who receives the test results. Certified counselors must see that appropriate interpretation accompanies any release of individual or group test data (e.g., limitations of instrument and norms).

12. Certified counselors must ensure that computer-generated test administration and scoring programs function properly thereby providing clients with accurate test results.

13. Certified counselors who develop computer-based test interpretations to support the assessment process must ensure that the validity of the interpretations is established prior to the commercial distribution of the computer application.

14. Certified counselors recognize that test results may become obsolete, and avoid the misuse of obsolete data.

15. Certified counselors must not appropriate, reproduce, or modify published tests or parts thereof without acknowledgment and permission from the publisher, except as permitted by the fair educational use provisions of the U.S. copyright law.

Section E: Research and Publication

1. Certified counselors will adhere to applicable legal and professional guidelines on research with human subjects.

2. In planning research activities involving human subjects, certified counselors must be aware of and responsive to all pertinent ethical principles and ensure that the research problem, design, and execution are in full compliance with any pertinent institutional or governmental regulations.

3. The ultimate responsibility for ethical research lies with the principal researcher, although others involved in the research activities are ethically obligated and responsible for their own actions.

4. Certified counselors who conduct research with human subjects are responsible for the welfare of the subjects throughout the experiment and must take all reasonable precautions to avoid causing injurious psychological, physical, or social effects on their subjects.

5. Certified counselors who conduct research must abide by the basic elements of informed consent:
   a. fair explanation of the procedures to be followed, including an identification of those which are experimental
   b. description of the attendant discomforts and risks
   c. description of the benefits to be expected
   d. disclosure of appropriate alternative procedures that would be advantageous for subjects with an offer to answer any inquiries concerning the procedures

    e. an instruction that subjects are free to withdraw their consent and to discontinue participation in the project or activity at any time

6. When reporting research results, explicit mention must be made of all the variables and conditions known to the investigator that may have affected the outcome of the study or the interpretation of the data.

7. Certified counselors who conduct and report research investigations must do so in a manner that minimizes the possibility that the results will be misleading.

8. Certified counselors are obligated to make available sufficient original research data to qualified others who may wish to replicate the study.

9. Certified counselors who supply data, aid in the research of another person, report research results, or make original data available, must take due care to disguise the identity of respective subjects in the absence of specific authorization from the subjects to do otherwise.

10. When conducting and reporting research, certified counselors must be familiar with and give recognition to previous work on the topic, must observe all copyright laws, and must follow the principles of giving full credit to those to whom credit is due.

11. Certified counselors must give due credit through joint authorship, acknowledgment, footnote statements, or other appropriate means to those who have contributed to the research and/or publication, in accordance with such contributions.

12. Certified counselors should communicate to other counselors the results of any research judged to be of professional value. Results that reflect unfavorably on institutions, programs, services, or vested interests must not be withheld.

13. Certified counselors who agree to cooperate with another individual in research and/or publication incur an obligation to cooperate as promised in terms of punctuality of performance and with full regard to the completeness and accuracy of the information required.

14. Certified counselors must not submit the same manuscript, or one essentially similar in content, for simultaneous publication consideration by two or more journals. In addition, manuscripts that have been published in whole or substantial part should not be submitted for additional publication without acknowledgment and permission from any previous publisher.

Section F: Consulting

Consultation refers to a voluntary relationship between a professional helper and a help-needing individual, group, or social unit in which the consultant is providing help to the client(s) in defining and solving a work-related problem or potential work-related problem with a client or client system.

1. Certified counselors, acting as consultants, must have a high degree of self awareness of their own values, knowledge, skills, limitations, and needs in entering a helping relationship that involves human and/ or organizational change. The focus of the consulting relationship must be on the issues to be resolved and not on the person(s) presenting the problem.
2. In the consulting relationship, the certified counselor and client must understand and agree upon the problem definition, subsequent goals, and predicted consequences of interventions selected.
3. Certified counselors acting as consultants must be reasonably certain that they, or the organization represented, have the necessary competencies and resources for giving the kind of help that is needed or that may develop later, and that appropriate referral resources are available.
4. Certified counselors in a consulting relationship must encourage and cultivate client adaptability and growth toward self-direction. Certified counselors must maintain this role consistently and not become a decision maker for clients or create a future dependency on the consultant.

Section G: Private Practice

1. In advertising services as a private practitioner, certified counselors must advertise in a manner that accurately informs the public of the professional services, expertise, and techniques of counseling available.
2. Certified counselors who assume an executive leadership role in a private practice organization do not permit their names to be used in professional notices during periods of time when they are not actively engaged in the private practice of counseling unless their executive roles are clearly stated.
3. Certified counselors must make available their highest degree (described by discipline), type and level of certification and/or license, address, telephone number, office hours, type and/or description of services, and

other relevant information. Listed information must not contain false, inaccurate, misleading, partial, out-of-context, or otherwise deceptive material or statements.

4. Certified counselors who are involved in a partnership/corporation with other certified counselors and/or other professionals, must clearly specify all relevant specialties of each member of the partnership or corporation.

Appendix: Certification Examination

Applicants for the NBCC Certification Examinations must have fulfilled all current eligibility requirements, and are responsible for the accuracy and validity of all information and/or materials provided by themselves or by others for fulfillment of eligibility criteria.

Approved on July 1, 1982 Amended on February 21, 1987, January 6, 1989, October 31, 1997, June 21, 2002, February 4, 2005 and October 8, 2005.

Acknowledgment

Reference documents, statements, and sources for development of the NBCC Code of Ethics were as follows:

The Ethical Standards of the American Counseling Association, Responsible Uses for Standardized Testing (AAC), codes of ethics of the American Psychological Association and the National Career Development Association, Handbook of Standards for Computer-Based Career Information Systems (ACSCI) and Guidelines for the Use of Computer Based Information and Guidance Systems (ACSCI).

Index

Directory information, 32–33
Disabled students, programs for, 271, 276
Diversity, 159, 163
    equity and access, 163, 166, 174
    gap identification, 162
    guided reflection, 186–187
    multicultural counseling, 168–171, 174
    resolving inequities, 164
    spirituality, 171–173, 175
Divorce, 20, 100–101
    parents be informed, 437
Dropping out of school, 93; *see also* GED
        programs
    prevention, 229, 241
    risk factors for, 93, 269
Drug Abuse Resistance Education (DARE),
        98–99
Dual relationships, 37

E

Early intervention, simulation, 64–75
Elementary and Secondary Education Act
        (ESEA), 173
Ellis, Albert, 131, 132
English as a second language (ESL), 272
English language learners (ELL) students,
        see Limited English proficient (LEP)
        students
Enrichment programs, 272–274, 277
Erikson, Erik, 40, 41
    stages of psychosocial development, 42
ESEA, *see* Elementary and Secondary
        Education Act
ESL, *see* English as a second language
Ethical decision-making model, 14–15
Ethical standards for school counselors,
        14, 16; *see also* Confidentiality
    assessment and interpretation, 434–435
    collaboration and education, 438, 443
    confidentiality, 436–437, 429–431
    contribution to profession, 442–443
    dual relationships, 431–432
    ethical violation guidelines, 444, 445
    group work, 433
    information sharing, 437–438
    informing danger, 433

multicultural and social justice advocacy
        and leadership, 441–442
    parent rights and responsibilities, 436
    professional competence, 440–441, 442
    professional relationships, 437
    promoting technological applications, 435
    providing counseling plan, 431
    purposes of, 428–429
    referrals, 432
    research in schools, 36–37
    responsibilities, 427–428, 429, 439–440
    STEPS, 445
    student peer support program, 436
    student records, 434
    supervising internship candidates, 443
Expressive toys, 124–125
Extrinsic motivation, 55

F

Faith development, 47, 48
Family Education Rights and Privacy Act
        (FERPA), 32, 431, 434; *see also*
        Confidentiality; HIPAA
    student information, 33, 436
FAPE, *see* Free appropriate public education
        (FAPE)
FERPA, *see* Family Education Rights and
        Privacy Act
Fidelity, 14
Foundation building, 7
Fowler, James, 41
    faith development, 47, 48
Free appropriate public education (FAPE), 164
Freud, Sigmund, 41
    personality development, 43
    psychosexual development stages, 45

G

General Aptitude Test Battery (GATB),
        195, 220, 222
General equivalency diploma (GED)
        programs, 274–275, 277
Gestalt counseling, 130–131
Glasser, William, 133
Gottfredson, Linda, 105, 107

GPA, *see* Grade point average
Grade point average (GPA), 119
Group counseling, 115; *see also* Classroom
    guidance
  ASCA's position on, 116
  for children of divorce, 101
  confidentiality, 19, 117, 499
  parental consent, 28, 29
  process of, 118

H

Havighurst, Robert, 41, 43
  stages of personality development, 44
Health Insurance Portability and
    Accountability Act (HIPAA);
    see also Family Education Rights
    and Privacy Act
  confidentiality and security of health
    records, 30
High stakes testing, *see* Achievement—tests
Holland, John, 105, 106
Homelessness, 35–36
Homeschooling, 269–270
Human development, 39; *see also* Cognitive
    development; Moral development;
    Psychosocial development; Spiritual
    development
  cognitive development and learning
    theories, 49–54
  moral development, 46–49
  psychosocial development, 40–46
  spiritual development, 46–49, 172

I

Identity crisis, 40
IEP, *see* Individualized education
    program/plan
Inclusion classroom, 271, 276
Individualized education program/
    plan (IEP), 34
  accommodations, 165
  students with, 271
Individual student counseling, 119–120
Individuals with Disabilities Education Act
    (IDEA), 34–35, 61

Informal assessments, 197–199, 211
Information sharing, 20
Informed consent, 28–30, 60–61
In-home drug testing, 99
Instructional strategies, 53–54
Intelligence, 258
Intelligence quotient (IQ), 195
Intrinsic motivation, 55, 56, 62
IQ, *see* Intelligence quotient

J

Journal of School Counseling (JSC), 228
JSC, *see* Journal of School Counseling
Justice, 14

K

Kaufman Assessment Battery for Children,
    193, 195
Key assessments used in schools, 193
Kohlberg, Lawrence, 41
  stages of moral reasoning, 47, 48
Krumboltz, John, 105, 109
Kuder Occupational Interest Survey (KOIS)
    career inventory, 112, 113, 193

L

Leadership, 313–314
  ACES technology competencies, 320
  guided reflection, 337–338
  and learning, 314
  mission and beliefs statements,
    315–316, 326
  program management, 315–319
  staff development, 315, 326
Learning theories, 49–54
Life-saving assessment, 199
Limited English proficient (LEP) students, 272

M

Management system, 8
Marzano, Robert, 49, 52
  instructional strategies, 53–54
Maslow's theory of motivation, 56–57